Essays on Jewish Chronology and Chronography

By

Ben Zion Wacholder

KTAV PUBLISHING HOUSE, INC.
NEW YORK
1976

Library of Congress Cataloging in Publication Data

Wacholder, Ben Zion.
    Essays on Jewish chronology and chronography.

    Includes bibliographical references.
    CONTENTS: The calendar of sabbatical cycles during
the Second Temple and the early rabbinic period.--How long
did Abram stay in Egypt? A study in hellenistic, Qumran,
and rabbinic chronography.--With Weisberg, D. B. Visibility
of the New Moon in cuneiform and rabbinic sources. [etc.]
    1. Bible. O. T.--Chronology--Addresses, essays,
lectures. 2. Chronology, Jewish--Addresses, essays,
lectures. 3. Abraham, the patriarch. 4. Bible. O. T.
Pentateuch--Liturgical use. 5. Jews. Liturgy and rutual.
Haftaroth. 6. Mekilta. I. Title.
BS637.2.W3   296   75-45443
ISBN 0-87068-260-1

*296
WII*

CONTENTS

INTRODUCTION

An attempt to shed new light on problems relating to Jewish chronology and chronography forms the central theme that binds together the diverse topics of the articles in this volume. Some essays treat calendral matters, such as the origin of the rabbinic nineteen year cycle of the Jewish lunisolar reckoning, the cycle of sabbatical years during the Second Temple, the triennial cycle of Scripture in the synagogue, and the development of eras used by Jews in various historical periods. Other essays endeavor to date obscure figures or rabbinic treatises whose history of composition remains unknown. The articles on Pseudo-Eupolemus and on the Mechilta of Rabbi Ishmael belong to this category. Still other essays attempt to reconstruct the chronographic work of early Jewish writers. Semi-Hellenized Jews, members of the still semi-enigmatic Qumran community, and sages of the Mishnah and Talmud shared a profound interest in the dating of Abraham and Moses. This volume will be of interest to students of Hellenism, Qumran, New Testament, and rabbinic Judaism.

Jewish chronology and chronography once formed part of the main stream of Judaic studies. Witness the work of Leopold Zunz and Solomon Rapoport (Shir). With notable exceptions, articles or books relating to Jewish chronology have vanished from Jewish scholarship. It is as if the myriad problems of dating pivotal personalities and classical works have been satisfactorily solved, or that nothing new can be added to the numerous chronological questions. Hopefully this volume will stimulate a rebirth of interest in an area that urgently needs curious students who are ready to work in the vineyard of the Lord.

I take this opportunity to express my deep gratitude to the editors and publishers of the journals in whose pages these essays originally appeared. Their share in this volume, even if invisible, is significant. Permit me also to express my appreciation for the permission to republish the material.

Ben Zion Wacholder

JEWISH ERAS

1. Exodus from Egypt (ליציאת מצרים)

"In order that you 'record'*(TIZKOR)* the time of your going out from Egypt" (Deut. 16:3) vaguely suggests a Scriptural command to employ the era of the Exodus from Egypt(לצאת בני ישראל מארץ מצרים) It is the only era recorded in the Torah; the Decalogue (Exod. 19:1), the Israelite wanderings in the desert (Num. 33:38), the settlement in Canaan (Josh. 5:6), and God's covenant with Abraham (Gen. 15:13) are dated by it.

The time of the Exodus probably was already lost in biblical times. In 1 Kings 6:1, the Hebrew text dates the Exodus 480 (LXX: 430) years before the building of Solomon's Temple. The Rabbinic calendar assumes that the Exodus occurred 2,448 years after Creation, 1,000 years before the era of the Cessation of Prophecy (the Seleucid era). Although the Israelites left Egypt on the fifteenth of Nisan, the computational year of Exodus commences on Nisan 1 (Exod. 12:2).

2. Regnal Years (למלכים)

The most common form of dating until the Talmudic period was by regnal years. In the historical books of the Bible the kings of Judah are dated by the regnal years of the kings of Israel and vice versa. But we do not know whether the beginning of the regnal year coincided with the dynastic year or, as is assumed in the Talmud, on Nisan 1 preceding the ruler's accession.

3. The Exile

The Book of Ezekiel is the chief source for the era of Exile (לגלותנו) from Judah to Babylon, but other biblical books and the Dead Sea

Scrolls also allude to this era. Ezekiel 1:2 defines the epoch of Exile as beginning with the deportation of King Jehoiachin to Babylon, ten years prior to the fall of Jerusalem (Ezek. 40:1) in 587 B.C.E. Although scholarly opinion differs, it is likely this era commenced on Nisan 10 of 597 B.C.E., the deportation date recorded in the cuneiform tablets and apparently harmonizing with the tenth of the month in the new year (Ezek. 40:1).

4. Rebuilding of the Temple (לבנין הבית)

By Jewish tradition, the era of the Exile ended in year 70, and was followed by the era of the Rebuilding of the Temple (לבנין הבית). There is hardly any evidence of its use in the biblical books, but the era of 'the Rebuilding of the Temple is mentioned in the Mishnah (Gittin 8:5) and Talmud (B. Av.Z. 9a), and was still recorded in the eleventh century C.E. The *Seder Olam* (30) grotesquely dates the era of the Rebuilding 34 years before the Seleucid era, discussed in §6.

5. Sabbaths and Jubilees

Leviticus 25:1−13 ordains the counting of Sabbatical years *(Shemittot)*, seven of which make up a Jubilee cycle. Rabbinic tradition maintains that these cycles were introduced first in the fifty-fifth year after the Exodus and were observed until the destruction of the First Temple, by which time 16 Jubilees and 2 Sabbath cycles (or 814 years) had elapsed. There is, however, no direct evidence how, or whether, these cycles were computed in pre-exilic times. The sages of the Talmud, like modern scholars, differed as to whether a Jubilee cycle consisted of 49 or 50 years.

But considerable evidence remains with respect to the calendar of the *Shemittah* cycles during the Second Temple. The number 70 years, given as the length of the Babylonian exile, presumes the use of a Sabbatical era (Jer. 29:10); (Daniel 9:24−27) made it the basis of his mysterious computations; and the Sabbatical cycles played a prominent role in the calendar of the Qumran sects. The author of Jubilees

(50:4) dated the entrance of the Israelites into Canaan at the end of the fiftieth Jubilee cycle (50 × 49 = 2,450).

Enough proof has been assembled to construct a calendar of *Shemittah* cycles for the period of the Second Temple. But scholars diverge on the question whether the attested Sabbatical years were (as in the current calendar) 164/63 . . . B.C.E.; . . . 68/69 C.E. or (as is more likely) 163/62 . . . B.C.E.; 69/70 C.E. After the destruction of the Second Temple it became customary in Palestine and elsewhere to record the *Shemittah* cycle on monuments and in legal documents, a custom still maintained in part by Rabbinic scholars until the fifteenth century (commentaries on B. Av.Z. 9). A practical hint: given any date of current version of the era of Creation (§11) it is possible to determine the year of the *Shemittah* cycle by dividing any Creation date by 7, the remainder of which represents the order of the *Shemittah* cycle; if the remainder is zero, the year is a Sabbath. For the period of the Second Temple and the Talmudic times, one year must be added to the date of creation before making the computation (Av.Z. 9b). The beginning of the year in the *Shemittah* calendar always commenced on Tishri 1.

6. Seleucus (A.S.)

The Jews knew the Seleucid era by various names: Cessation of Prophecy (להפסקת הנבואה), Reign of the Greeks (למלכות יונים), Documents (לשטרות) or Alexander (לאלכסנדרוס). First introduced in Palestine about 200 B.C.E. its use was banned by Simon the Hasmonean in 142 B.C.E. But the Seleucid era remained popular among some Jews for almost two millennia. It gradually began to lose ground to the era of Creation only after 1000 C.E., but it retained the loyalty of the Yemenite Jews until recent times.

This era commemorated Seleucus' reentry into Babylon in August of 312 B.C.E., but customs in Near Eastern cities varied as to its precise timing. In Jewish sources, however, two versions of A.S. are attested: AS1 = Tishri 1, 312/Elul 29, 311 B.C.E.; and AS2 = Nisan 1,311/Adar 29, 310 B.C.E. In general (although scholars differ), the Jews of Babylonia used AS1; those of Jerusalem, AS2, precisely the converse of what was customary among native Babylonians (who used AS2) and among Tyrians (AS1). Examples: 1 Maccabees 1:10 records the

accession of Antiochus IV in 137 A.S., which must be according to
AS2 (Antiochus became king in Kislev of 175 B.C.E.); for if it were
AS1, the correct date would have been 138 A.S. A synchronistic inscription of Dura-Europos attests to the use of AS1: year 2 of
Emperor Philip (February 245/February 246 C.E.) = 556 A.S. A
problem that has not found a solution is whether during the Second
Temple the Jews who used the pagan Babylonian reckoning of A.S.
from Nisan 311 also followed the Babylonian calendar as a whole,
which has now been reconstructed with remarkable precision on the
basis of cuneiform tablets.

In the Talmudic tradition, the difference between R. Eliezer and
R. Joshua as to whether the world was created in Tishri or in Nisan
(B. R.H. 10b) may in fact reflect the difference between AS1 and AS2.
In Palestine the use of either version of the A.S. remained halakhically
unofficial (M. Gittin 8:5). But *Seder Olam* (30) affirms: "In the
Diaspora [Babylonia] they date documents by the reckoning of the
Greeks," which according to B. Av., Z. 10a, as stated above, com-
menced on Tishri 1. For the relation between A.S. and the Creation
era, see §11.

7. Simon the Great High Priest

In 170 A.S., according to 1 Maccabees 13:41–42, "the yoke of the
Gentiles was removed from Israel, and the people began to write in
their documents and contracts, 'In the first year of Simon the great
high priest and commander and leader of the Jews.'" In other words:
year 1 Simon = 170 A.S. = Nisan 142/Adar 141 B.C.E. = year 1
Simon, marked the abrogation of the Seleucid era. *Megillat Ta'anit*
(Tishri 3) records a similar reckoning by John Hyrcanus, but goes on
to say that the sages abolished the era, not to profane God's name in
the use for business.

Scholars differ on whether Simon (or John) instituted an era of
freedom named after himself or whether he merely brought back the
ancient custom of regnal dating (§2). That the former had been intended may be gauged from the fact that eras of independence had
then become popular in cities which had loosened their ties with the
Seleucid empire. Although Simon's decree was not honored by subse-

quent Judaean rulers, it apparently did result in bringing back the dating by regnal years. In other words, although the attempt to institute a Hasmonean era failed, it did succeed in banning the use of the SA from Judea.

8. Adam

Jewish chroniclers, whether Hellenistic, Qumran, or early Rabbinic, consistently dated events "from Adam" (ἀπὸ Ἀδάμ). Demetrius (221−204 B.C.E.) placed Adam 2,264 years before the flood and 3,569 years before the Exodus. Eapolemus (an adviser of Judah Maccabee), however, dated Adam 3,569 years before the Exodus and 5306 B.C.E. Adam as used by Graeco-Jewish writers was based on the genealogy of the Greek Bible. Josephus' reckoning also follows a similar tradition, but because of his use of diverse chronological schemes, it is difficult to guess the timing of his Adamite epoch. Although there is no evidence that the Adamite era was ever used by Jews for dating documents, it formed the basis of the common Byzantine era of Creation (used until the fourteenth century), timed on March 21 of 5508 B.C.E. and (after the seventh century) on September 1 of 5509 B.C.E.

9. Redemption (Freedom) of Israel I and II

The leaders of the First Revolt against the Romans (66−73 C.E.) ordered a new mode of reckoning, making it the era of Redemption (גאולת) or Freedom (חרות ישראל) of Israel, name(s) also given to the Second Revolt (132−35 C.E.). Coins from the First Revolt contain dates of year 1 to year 5, the last of which were minted in Jerasalem after Nisan but before Av of 70 C.E., when the city fell to the Romans. In the outlying regions, such as Masada, however, the era of Redemption (I) remained in use probably to year 8. although only year 6 is so far attested. From the Second Revolt coins dated years 1 and 2 have been found; undated mints, which mention "the Freedom of Jerusalem," were presumably cast in year 3; papyri dated year 3 and year 4 also remain. The eras of both the First and Second Revolts began the year, as Kanael has shown, on Nisan 1.

10. Ḥurban

The Romans burned the Second Temple, according to Josephus, on the eighth of Loos (about August 26); according to the Rabbinic tradition on the ninth of Av, 70 C.E., the year from which the era of *Ḥurban* (Destruction) began. Although M. Gittin (8:5) regards this reckoning as unauthoritative, the *Seder Olam* (30), after dating the burning of the Temple, adds: "From then onward reckon by *Ḥurban* of the Temple." Medieval scribes copying this Talmudic passage (B.Av.Z. 9a) customarily inserted into their manuscripts at this point the current date of the *Ḥurban*. Widespread use of the *Ḥurban* era is attested on fourth- and fifth-century tombstones in Palestine, and on ninth-century tombstones in Italy. In literary sources the dating by *Ḥurban* became rare after the thirteenth century.

A number of puzzling problems remain in regard to the use of this era. Three epitaphs found in Zoar (Sodom) synchronize the dates of the *Ḥurban* with the Sabbatical cycle, but their synchronisms are inconsistent. There is a difference of one year between the eras of *Ḥurban* and Creation on the tombstones found in Venosa (Italy). Bornstein and Cassuto explain this difference by assuming the new year of the *Ḥurban* era commenced (not on Nisan 1 or Tishri 1) on the ninth of Av. The Jews of Yemen have retained Tish'ah b'Av as the new year of *Ḥurban*; the Karaites date it on the tenth of Av. (cf. Ezek. 40:1). On the chronology of the *Ḥurban* era, see §11.

11. Creation of the World (A.M.)

Although possibly an offspring of the reckoning from Adam, out of which also developed the Byzantine Creation era (§8), the Jewish era of the Creation of the World (בריאה, בריאת העולם, יצירה) reflects an independent chronology and development. This era appeared relatively late in Jewish history. Neither the Mishnah nor the *Seder Olam,* which both allude to other eras, mentions Creation. The two oldest extant allusions by sages who flourished about 300 C.E. use this era to presage the time of the Messiah's coming, either after 4231 A.M. (Old; 469/70 C.E.; Av.Z. 9b); or after 4291 A.M. (Old; 529/30 C.E.; Sanh. 97b). What promised to be the oldest attested use of the Creation era on a monument, contains only a fragment of an inscription with the date 4000 A.M., the remainder destroyed. It may not be supposed to antedate the fifth century C.E., but may in fact be a century or two later *Qadmoniot,* 5 [1972], 47–52). Present evidence suggests that the era of Creation originated in Palestine about 4000 A.M. (240 C.E.), but did not become popular until centuries later. The oldest epitaphs with Anno Mundi outside Palestine appear on the ninth-century tombstones of Venosa (Italy). After 1000 C.E. the use of the Creation era spread to the West, gradually replacing all other forms of Jewish dating. Maimonides' Code still sanctioned the use of either the Seleucid or the Creation era (Gerushin 1:27), but the *Tur Even Ha'ezer* (127) restricted the dating of divorce decrees to Creation.

Although the name of the chronologist who invented the Creation reckoning is not known, his computational assumptions are clear. Using the chronology found in the *Seder Olam,* and combining it with significant Jewish eras, he arrived at the following totals:

From Creation to (but not including the year of) Exodus
2,448 years

From Exodus to (but not including the year of) A.S. 1,000 years
From A.S. to (but not including the year of) *Ḥurban* 380 years
From Creation to (but not including the year of)
Ḥurban 3,828 years

Reckoning the year 3,829 as year 1 of *Ḥurban,* the chronographer added the current number of the *Ḥurban* to 3,828 years, the total of which he named the era of Creation.

Using his new invention, the chronologist could have dated any known event by his Creation reckoning. He did not, apparently because the new era was intended for future use, especially for the timing of Messiah, not for historiographic purposes. Later historians, however, who used the Creation era for dating the past, were not always aware either of the exact basis for this era or of some of the pitfalls resulting from seemingly simple though occasionally deceptive formulas of conversion from one era into another.

The inventor had reckoned *Ḥurban* 1 = 381 A.S. = 3829 A.M. But some medieval and modern scholars have erroneously dated *Ḥurban* 1 = 3828. As to Julian equivalents for the era of Creation, the confusion is almost universal. For dates after 1000 C.E. or so it is quite accurate to add or subtract 3,761/60 years in conversions from C.E. into A.M.

dates or vice versa, respectively. For dates before 1000 C.E., however, as pointed out by Saadia, the Jews of Babylonia assumed the equivalent of 3760/59 B.C.E. = year 1 Creation; Jews of the West, 3761/60 B.C.E. = year 1 of Creation.

To explain this divergence, medieval and modern scholars have proposed complex hypotheses. In fact, its origin is simple. As has been stated above, in almost all Jewish eras (cf. Exod. 12:2) the year began on Nisan 1 and ended on the last day of Adar, but AS1 (§6), in contrast to the native custom, had a new year of Tishri 1. Because of its Palestinian origin, the Old Creation reckoning, too, used a new year of Nisan 1. However, at some unknown date, between 500 and 750–800 C.E., the Jews of Palestine changed from the old new year of Nisan 1 to the new year of Tishri 1, thus adopting the calendar of AS1 (§6), practiced by the Jews of Babylonia. This changeover presented the Palestinian Jews with the dilemma of how to account for the remainder of six months. They chose to "borrow" six months and to add one year to the customary era of Creation. This changeover resulted:

   Old Era of Creation: year 1 *Ḥurban* = 381 A.S. = 3829 A.M.
   New Era of Creation: year 1 *Ḥurban* = 381 A.S. = 3830 A.M.

RaZah (Hamaor, Av.Z. 9a), a twelfth-century talmudist, has given a different explanation for the divergent reckonings of the Creation tion era. The additional year in the Western Creation era presumes that the five days of the world before Adam (created on Friday) count as year 1, the so-called year Chaos תהו. Although often repeated by modern scholars, this theory need not be taken seriously. For a full view of the difference between the old and new eras of Creation, see the acrompanying table.

The computational gain of one (in fact only a half) year in the New Creation reckoning had other calendrical consequences. There occurred a translation backward by one year in the cycles of *Shemittah* (5). The calendar of the Western Jews lacked the confidence of the Babylonian Jewish calendar. The controversy between Saadia Gaon and Ben Meir in the tenth century, and the difference between the Triennial and Annual cycles of Torah readings are other calendrical differences between the Babylonian and Palestinian Jews.

A number of problems in the development of the Jewish eras remain. A detailed mapping of the various uses of the Seleucid and

Creation eras would be a contribution not only to Jewish chronography, but also to significant cultural trends among various segments of Jewry. The date and circumstances of the changeover from the Nisan to the Tishri new year in Palestine await a solution. The immense Talmudic lore relating to this subject ne ds exploring in the light of what is known about the evolution of Jewish eras.

12. The State of Israel

The State of Israel was proclaimed on the fifth of Iyar (May 14, 1948) of 5708. But the official date of the era of the State of Israel begins on Tishri 1 of the year 5708 (September 15, 1947).

Bibliography

ח. י. בורנשטיין, "תאריכי ישראל" התקופה ח (תר"פ) 331־281; ט (תרפ"א) 264־202.

צ. ה. יפה, קורות הלוח העברי. ירושלים תרצ"א.

א. א. עקביא, סדרי זמנים בדברי ימי ישראל. תל אביב תש"ג.

א. א. עקביא, הלוח ושימושו בכרונולוגיה. ירושלים תשי"ג.

J. Finegan. *Handbook of Biblical Chronology.* Princeton, N.J., 1964.
E. Bickerman. *Chronology of the Ancient World.* Ithaca, N.Y., 1968.
B. Z. Wacholder. "Chronomessianism: The Messianic Movements and the Calendar of Sabbatical Cycles," HUCA, 46 (1975).

OLD (TALMUDIC) AND NEW (CURRENT) CREATION (A.M.) RECKONINGS AND SELECTIVE JEWISH ERAS IN JULIAN DATES

YEAR 1	A.M. (Old)	B.C.E.	A.M. (New)	B.C.E.
A.M. (Old)	Nisan/Adar of year 1	3760/59	Nisan of year 1/Adar of year 2	3761/60
A.M. (New)			Tishri/Elul of year 1	3761/60
Exodus	Nisan/Adar 2449	1311/10	Tishri/Elul 2450	1312/11
A.S. (AS1)	Tishri 3449/Elul 3450	312/11	Tishri/Elul 3450	312/11
A.S. (AS2)	Nisan/Adar 3449	311/10	Nisan 3450/Elul 3451	311/10
B.C.E.	3758/59		3759/60	
C.E.	3759/60	C.E.	3760/61	C.E.
Hurban[a]	Nisan/Adar 3829	70/71	Tishri/Elul 3830	69/70
State of Israel	Nisan/Adar 5707	1948/49	Tishri/Elul 5708	1947/48

[a] In some traditions, apparently the new year of the Hurban era is the ninth (the Karaites: tenth) of Av.

THE CALENDAR OF SABBATICAL CYCLES DURING
THE SECOND TEMPLE AND THE EARLY RABBINIC PERIOD

Introduction
The Evidence
1. The Pledge to Keep Shemitah
2. Alexander Exempts the Jews from Taxation during Shemitah
3. Judah Maccabee's Defeat at Beth-Zur Ascribed to Shemitah
4. The Murder of Simon the Hasmonean in 177 A.S.
5. Herod's Conquest of Jerusalem
6. King Agrippa I Recites Deut. 7:15 in a Post-Sabbatical Year
7. A Note of Indebtedness on a Papyrus of Wadi Murabb'at 18
8. Was the Second Temple Destroyed During a Sabbatical or Post-Sabbatical Year?
9. Renting Land from Bar Kosba
10. Three fourth and fifth Century Tombstone Inscriptions in Sodom
Appendix:
   A Calendar of Sabbatical Cycles from 519/18 B.C.E. to 440/41 C.E.

INTRODUCTION

THE observance of the Sabbatical year (also known as Release, Shemitah or Shevi'it), when agricultural activity ceased and debts were cancelled, remained a living institution from post-exilic times to about the fifth century after the Christian era. Of the actual status of Shemitah during the pre-exilic times little is known; some scholars deny its historicity altogether while others compare the antiquity of the Sabbatical year to that of the weekly Sabbath.[1] But from the time of the building of the Second Temple until the period of the Amoraim our knowledge of the institution is not only extensive, but sufficiently precise to enable us to construct a calendar of the cycles of Shemitot.

Three items need to be pointed out. First, the closely related institution of Jubilees is of no importance for the calendar of Shemitot during

---

1 Exod. 23:10–11; Lev. 25:1–7, 19–22; Deut. 15:1–11. For the scholarship. see *Encyclopaedia Judaica* (Jerusalem: Keter, 1971), XIV, cols. 585 f.

153

the post-exilic times. For although Lev. 25:8–28 ordains in addition to the Sabbatical year also a Jubilee year, when bonded men and land were to be restored to tribal ownership, we have no record of the Jubilee's observance during post-exilic times.[2] Furthermore, the exact meaning of the "Sabbath of Sabbaths," or the fiftieth year, as the Jubilee is called, is obscure. Even the rabbinic authorities could not agree whether the Jubilee constituted a separate year from the septennial Shemitah cycle and equaled the fiftieth year or whether there was only a forty-nine year cycle and the Jubilee was considered part of the first Shemitah cycle.[3] But most, if not all, Talmudic authorities grant, what we know to be a fact, that the Jubilee was not observed in the post-exilic Jewish calendar.[4] To be sure, the sectarian literature, found recently in the Judaean desert, and in works such as the Book of Jubilees,[5] frequently alludes to an era of "the Sabbath of Sabbaths," but it is of little significance for this study since it had no effect upon the Judaean calendar during the period under consideration. Modern scholarship is equally divided as to the method by which the year of the Jubilee was computed; but it is agreed that the institution of the Jubilee did not function during the Second Temple.[6]

Second, the Sabbatical year began on the first day of Tishri and

2 See also Lev. 27:17–24; Num. 36:4; Ez. 46:16–18.

3 Bab. Tal. Nedarim 61a; Rosh Hashanah 9a; Arakhin 12b; 24b; 33a. The majority of talmudic sages counted the Jubilee on the 50th year; Rabbi Judah, however, subsumed the Jubilee as part of the new Sabbatical cycle; cf. Sifra, *Emor* 12, 8 (101a); *Behar* I, 6 (105c); Philo, *De sp. leg.*, II, 110; Jos. *A.J.* III, 282. S. Zeitlin offers a modern version of Judah's view, cited by Sidney B. Hoenig, "The Sabbatical Years and the Year of the Jubilee," *JQR*, 49 (1969), 222–36, who defends Zeitlin against the critics.

4 According to Yer. Shevi'it X, 3, 39c; (Sifra, *Behar*, 2,3 [107a]; B. Arakhin, 32b), the Jubilee was abolished after the fall of Samaria (722 B.C.E.), since Lev. 25:10 prescribes this institution only when "all the inhabitants" of Israel live in the Holy Land. Furthermore, since Lev. 25 ordained the Jubilee and Shemitah as a unit, it follows, the Rabbis say, that Shemitah without the observance of Jubilee falls under "rabbinic" rather than "biblical" ordinances. See Bab. Tal. Gittin 36a-b; Yer., IV, 3, 45d. But Sifra, *Behar*, II, 2 (106d); Arakhin, 32b, cites views which maintain that Jubilee and Shemitah are independent of each other. Cf., however, Tosafot on 'Arakhin 32b, s.v. *manu.*

5 The Book of Jubilees' calendar (A. Jaubert, "Le calendrier des Jubilés et de la secte de Qumrân. Ses origines bibliques," *V.T.* 3 (1953), 350–64), assumes a 49-year Jubilee, which accords with Rabbi Judah's position (note 3). See also CD. XVI, 4; 1 QM, VII, 14; cf. B. Noack, "Qumrân and the Book of Jubilees," *Svensk Exegetisk Årsbok* (Lund), 27/28 (1957/58), 191–207; J. Morgenstern, "The Calendar of the Book of Jubilees, its Origin and Character," *V.T.* 5 (1955), 34–76.

6 See Maimonides, Hilkhot Shemitah Veyovel, X, 5–6. Cf. D.E. Eisenstein, in *J.E.* X, 606a; S. Loewenstamm, in *Encyclopaedia Biblica*, II (Jerusalem: Institute Bialik, 1958), 580 f.

ended on the last day of Elul.[7] Thus the Shemitah year differed basically from the civil and religious calendar which in preexilic as well as in postexilic times commenced on the first day of Nisan.[8] Even during the Judaean revolts of 66–70 and 132–35 when the era of "the Redemption of Israel" was proclaimed, the year began in the spring.[9] But such was the influence of the institution of Shemitah that it played a major role in the gradual shifting of the Near Year from Nisan to Tishri, which has been formalized into our Rosh Hashanah. The fact that the Sabbatical year did not coincide during the period of the Second Temple with the civil and religious year probably explains why the Shemitah cycle was rarely employed, except in sectarian circles, for reckoning time.

Third, a study such as this is now possible for the period of the Second Temple, but not, in the present state of knowledge, for the biblical times. It is not only that, as has been mentioned, we do not know the workings of institutions of Shemitah and Jubilee during the days of David and the monarchy, but we are also ignorant of the basic chronology of the period.[10] Midrashic chronography, as advocated in the talmudic treatise Seder Olam, is of no help. Tannaitic chronography assumed an interval of 480 years from the exodus to the building of the Solomonic Temple (I Kings 6:1) and 410 years from its construction to the final destruction by Nebuchadnezzar, for a total of 890 years. Deducting 40 years for the wanderings in the desert and 14 for the conquest of Canaan, or a total of 54 years, whereupon the Sabbatical and Jubilee cycles went

7 M. Rosh Hashanah I, 1; cf. Lev. 25:9.

8 Except for agricultural activities, biblical chronology (Neh. 1:1; 2:1 which is probably corrupt) uniformly assumes that the year begins in the first month of spring, which in post-exilic times is called Nisan. See also Philo, De Sp. leg. I, 180; Josephus, A.J. I, 80–82; M. Rosh Hashanah, I, 1, and talmudic commentaries thereon. Morgenstern, "The Three Calendars of Ancient Israel," HUCA I (1924), 13–78, "Supplementary Studies in the Calendars of Ancient Israel," X (1935), 1–148; S. Zeitlin, Megilat Taanit as a Source for Jewish Chronology and History in the Hellenistic and Roman Periods (Philadelphia: The Dropsie College for Hebrew and Cognate Learning, 1922); E. A. Mahler, Handbuch für jüdischen Chronologie (Frankfurt am-Main, 1916, reprinted in Hildesheim: Georg Olms, 1971), among others, have been misled by a misinterpretation of M. Rosh Hashanah, I, 1, that Tishri, not Nisan, was the first month of the year during the Second Temple. More recent books, such as E. Frank Talmudic and Rabbinical Chronology (New York: P. Feldheim, 1956), 18; J. Finegan, Handbook of Biblical Chronology (Princeton, N.J.: Princeton University Press), 89–92, are also not reliable.

9 See now B. Kanael, "Notes on the Dates Used During the Bar Kokhba Revolt," Israel Exploration Journal, 21 (1971), 39–46. For the evidence from talmudic literature, see Ch. Albeck, Shishah Sidre Mishnah (Jerusalem: Mosad Bialik, 1956), II, 306.

10 See Ch. Tadmor, "Khronologyah," Encyclopaedia Biblica (Jerusalem: Mosad Bialik, 1962), IV, 245–310.

into effect, the Rabbis computed that during the remaining 836 years (890 — [40 + 14] = 836), there were altogether 16 Jubilees (836:50 = 16 + 36) and that the destruction of the Solomonic First Temple occurred during a post-Sabbatical year (36:7 = 5 + 1).[11] Obviously, midrashic chronography is of no help for the student of Shemitah; but neither is modern scholarship dealing with the chronology of the biblical period. For the postexilic period, however, the papyri recently discovered in the Judaean Desert help to solve the problem.

Of the vast literature that deals with our subject, a little known monograph by Benedict Zuckermann deserves special mention. In 1856 Zuckermann published a study of the Jubilee and Sabbatical years to which he appended a table of Shemitot from 535/34 B.C.E. to 2238/39 C.E.[12] Such was Zuckermann's technical competence that, directly or indirectly, his datings of the Shemitot have, often in a modified form, elicited the approval of scholars, including such authorities as Emil Schürer, F. M. Ginzel, Solomon Zeitlin, and T. S. Milik.[13] But a handful of dissenting voices, Heinrich Graetz, Friedrich Unger, and Ralph Marcus, among others, have noted that this accepted chronology of Shemitot was ahead of some recorded dates by one year.[14] Of course, such a difference between the two views may seem insignificant, but let us not forget that a calendar that misses by a year is always wrong. In fact, the dating of

---

11   Seder Olam 11 (ed. B. Ratner, Wilno, 1897) pp. 48–50; Bab. Tal. Arakhin 12b–13a. Actually, it occurred 17 jubilees (850 years) from the entry into Canaan. This calendar, which is contrary to Rabbi Judah's view (cited in note 3; cf. note 4), is based on Ez. 40:1, which synchronizes the 25th of our exile, Rosh Hashanah, 10th of the [7th] month, with 14 years after the fall of the city. Seder Olam interprets the New Year of the 10th day of the month to refer to a Jubilee year, which fell 14 years after Ḥurban, 25 years after the exile of Jechoniah, hence the Ḥurban occurred in the 36th of Jubilee cycle. Cf. also Maimonides, note 6 and Teshuvot Harambam (Jerusalem: Mekize Nirdamim, 1934), No. 234, pp. 221–23.

12   Benedict Zuckermann, "Ueber Sabbatjahrcyclus und Jobelperiode," Jahresbericht des jüdisch-theologischen Seminars "Fraenckelscher Stiftung" (Breslau, 1857). Pages 2–3 list the literature to his day; 43–45, a table of Sabbatical years.

13   Emil Schürer, Geschichte des jüdischen Volkes (Leipzig, 1901), I⁴, 35–37, who updated the literature (p. 37); F. K. Ginzel, Handbuch der mathematischen und technischen Chronologie (Leipzig, 1911), II, 52–54; S. Zeitlin (note 8); The I Book of Maccabees (New York: Harper & Brothers, 1950), 254–57; for T. S. Milik, see below sections 7 and 9. See also Ḥ. J. Bornstein, "Ḥeshbon Shemitim Veyovelot," Hatekufah, 11 (1921), 230–60; Mahler, Handbuch (note 8), 115; Frank (note 8), 74–76.

14   H. Graetz, Geschichte der Juden (Leipzig, 1906), III⁵, 2, 654–57; F. Unger, Sitzungsberichte der Münchener Akademie (philos. philol. und historische Classe [1895]), 208–81; R. Marcus, in notes to A.J. XII, 378; XIII, 234; XIV, 475 (Loeb Classical Library).

events such as John Hyrcanus' accession to the high priesthood and the beginning of the Bar Kosba revolt depend on the chronology of Sabbatical years. This study reviews the entire evidence showing that Zuckermann's calendar of Shemitot is no longer acceptable in light of the recently discovered epigraphical and papyrological documents. Unlike Zuckermann's study, however, which deals with Shemitot from the days of Moses to modern times, this essay is limited to the period of the Second Temple and the Tannaim and Amoraim.

THE EVIDENCE

1. THE PLEDGE TO KEEP SHEMITAH

The memoirs of Ezra, as preserved in Neh. 8–10, record the first allusion to the observance of the Sabbatical year after 587 B.C.E. Chapter 8 reports that, led by Ezra, the Judaeans assembled on the first of Tishri (the year is not given) to hear Ezra and his associates recite from the Mosaic Torah; Chapters 9–10 transcribe the events of the meeting of the assembly on the twenty-fourth of the same month, when the Israelites, fasting and wearing sacks, confessed to their past sins and solemnly swore to observe the Law, specifying significant commandments, such as the prohibition of intermarriage, the observance of the Sabbath, and the routine of the Temple. After mentioning the pledge not to trade with the foreign people on Sabbaths and Holy Days, Neh. 10:32(31) concludes: "We will forego the crops of the seventh year and the exaction of every debt."

Does the pledge to observe the Shemitah suggest that this institution referred to had been only recently inaugurated? If the answer is yes, this passage, assuming it could be dated, would yield the time when the calendar of Shemitah, which apparently continued without interruption to the fifth century of the post-Christian era, was introduced.[15] It is more likely, however, that the pledge to observe the Shemitah referred not to a new but to a well-known but neglected institution. The brevity and technical nature of Neh. 10:32(31)c suggests that the concept of Shemitah was then quite established. In fact, the pledge ונטש את השנה השביעית ומשא כל יד indicates that this wording telescoped Exod. 23: 10–11: ושש שנים תזרע את ארצך ואספת את תבואתה והשביעית תשמטנה וזה דבר השמטה שמוט כל בעל משה ידו... with Deut. 15:2: ונטשתה

---

15 Cf. J. Wellhausen, *Prolegomena to the History of Ancient Israel* (New York: Meridian Library, 1957), 116–20, Hildegard and Julius Lewy, "The Origin of the Week and the Oldest West Asiatic Calendar," *HUCA*, 17 (1942/43), 97, note 391. Wellhausen regarded the institutions of Jubilee and Shemitah as Priestly, hence post-exilic; the Lewy's found their traces in Assyrian records.

with the spaced words directly borrowed from these passages.[16] The Sabbatical year, like the weekly Sabbath, which is also mentioned in the first half of Neh. 10:32(31), apparently had been an ancient norm, certainly going back to pre-exilic times, and possibly to the time of the very inauguration of the Sabbath.

It cannot be denied, however, that Neh. 10:32(31) suggests a situation reflecting greater neglect of the laws of Shemitah than those of the weekly Sabbath. With regard to the latter, our passage alludes to the laxness of trading with foreigners, mentioned again in Neh. 13:14–22; as to the former, the pledge refers to the basic legislation of Shemitah. The evidence is not decisive, however, whether the computation of Shemitot began at the time of this pledge or had then been established. My own inclination is for the latter alternative. If so, the appended calendar of Sabbatical years (Appendix) begins with the period of Zerubabel circa 519–18 B.C.E.

As to the date in Neh. 10, this chapter is part of frequently debated but unresolved issues of post-exilic chronology, into which we cannot enter here.[17] Briefly, the main problem is whether to assign Neh. 10 to Ezra's memoirs though it appears to be a part of Neh. 8–10; or, on the other hand, to assign chapter 10 to Nehemiah alone, since his name heads the list of men who signed the pledge (Neh. 10:2).[18] If our passage belongs to Ezra, then the crucial date is the 7th year of Artaxerxes (Ezra 7:1), either 458 B.C.E. (if Artaxerxes I) or 397 if Artaxerxes II). But if our passage belongs to the days of Nehemiah, as many scholars maintain, the likely date of our passage is sometime after the 20th year of Artaxerxes II (allusions in the Elephantine papyri exclude Artaxerxes I), i.e., 445 B.C.E. (Neh. 1:1).[19]

Briefly, we regard Neh. 10:32(31)c as a reasonably datable allusion to the observance of Shemitah during the post-exilic period, but because of the many doubts involved, forego its precise dating.

2. ALEXANDER EXEMPTS THE JEWS FROM TAXATION

DURING SHEMITAH

A lost semi-fictional semi-historical treatise, partly preserved by Josephus in his *Jewish Antiquities,* XI, 313–47, contains the second post-exilic

16   Cf. Rashi on Neh. 10:32; W. Rudolph, *Ezra und Nehemia.* Handbuch zum Alten Testament (Tübingen: Mohr, 1949), 177.

17   H. H. Rowley, "The Chronological Order of Ezra and Nehemiah," in *The Servant of the Lord*[2] (Oxford: Blackwell, 1965).

18   Cf. Rudolph, *Ezra und Nehemia,* 169; 173.

19   See now Emil G. Kraeling, *The Brooklyn Museum Aramaic Papyri* (New Haven; Yale University Press, 1953), 106–9; Peter Ackroyd, *Israel Under*

allusion to the observance of the Shemitah.[20] In fact, the author of this treatise makes Shemitah the focal point of his argument showing how Alexander favored the Jews, but disliked the allegedly two-faced Samaritans. After his conquest of Gaza the Macedonian king marched against the Judaeans, who had remained faithful to Darius.[21] But upon reaching Jerusalem and seeing the face of the high priest, Alexander recalled that it was the same face of a person he had seen in a dream, and who promised him the conquest of the Persian empire. After sacrificing at the Temple, the conqueror asked what gifts the Jews would like to receive. The high priest then requested that the Jews be permitted "to observe their ancestral laws and that each septenniel year they be exempt from tribute;" all of which Alexander gladly granted.[22] The Samaritans, to whom Alexander had formerly given permission to build a sanctuary on Mount Gerizim, thereupon begged that the same exemption from tribute on the Shemitah be also granted to them. Alexander asked them whether they considered themselves Jews; the Samaritans replied that they were not Jews but Hebrews, known as Sidonians of Shechem. Alexander rejected the Samaritans' request, for the remission of tribute on account of Shemitah was granted only to the Jews.[23]

Since the story of Alexander's visit to Jerusalem is fictional and since this "treatise" is marked by a strong anti-Samaritan bias, Alexander's involvement in the Shemitah may not be historical. It is a fact, however, that the Macedonian rulers, like the Persians who preceded them, and the Romans who followed them, remitted the taxes of the Sabbatical years. It does not matter whether Alexander himself, as our treatise claims, or one of his subordinates, as seems more probable, remitted the taxes. It is likely that the privileges bestowed on the Jews to follow their ancestral laws, including the keeping of Shemitah, were granted sometime after Alexander's conquest of Tyre and Gaza.[24] The only remaining question is the likely date of these privileges.

Babylon and Persia (London: Oxford University Press, 1970), 191–96.

20 Cf. Megillat Ta'anit (*HUCA*, 8–9, (1931/32), 339–40; Yoma 69a; See also Pseudo-Callisthenes, II, 24 (ed. C. Mueller, Paris, 1877); R. Marcus, "Appendix C," in Loeb edition of Josephus, VI, pp. 512–32. But Marcus' doubts concerning the historicity of Alexander's privileges (pp. 530–31) are not justified. See now A. Schalit, in *Encyclopaedia Judaica*, II, 577–79.

21 *A.J.* XI, 317 f.

22 *A.J.* XI, 338: τοῦ δ'ἀρχιερέως αἰτησαμένου χρῆσθαι τοῖς πατρίοις νόμοις καὶ τὸ ἕβδομον ἔτος ἀνείσφορον εἶναι, συνεχώρησε πάντα. See also below, note 25, for a similar privilege by Caesar. The Jews also requested that their coreligionists of Media and Babylonia be permitted to follow their ancestral laws, allowing any Jew to join Alexander's army, while adhering to the customs of his people.

23 *A.J.* XI, 340–45.

24 See note 22. Some scholars, Mahaffy, for example, speculate that Alex-

Alexander's movements during his conquest of the Near East are more or less known. After a six-month siege, Alexander seized Tyre in August of 332 B.C.E.; Gaza's resistance lasted till November, by the end of which month he reached Egypt; and evidently in January of 331 he laid the foundation of Alexandria; in the spring Alexander was back in Tyre, appointing a satrap for Coele-Syria; and in summer he reached Mesopotamia on his way to Babylon and the Far East, never to return to the West. According to Zuckermann's calendar of Sabbatical years, the beginning of the Shemitah of Tishri 332/Elul 331 coincided roughly with Alexander's investment of Gaza. However, according to my reckoning, the Shemitah season occurred a year later, in 331/30 B.C.E. The commencement of the Sabbatical year coincided roughly with the battle of Gaugamela, on Ocober 1, 331. This is the case because although either chronology of Shemitot could be made to fit into the historical events, it would seem that the latter dating is preferable, for it is unlikely that Alexander settled minor problems of governing Judaea at a time when his energies were engaged in conquering the eastern Mediterranean coast. It appears more probable that Alexander or his satrap granted the privileges to the Jews, chief of which was tax exemption during a Shemitah year, in the spring or summer of 331, with the beginning of the Sabbatical year due in the fall of the same year.[25]

3. JUDAH MACCABEE'S DEFEAT AT BETH-ZUR ASCRIBED TO SHEMITAH

The First and Second Books of Maccabees report that Antiochus V Eupator (Dec. 164–Oct. 162 B.C.E.) and his general Lysias, in their attempt to crush the Judaean rebellion, besieged Beth-Zur, a fortified town south of Jerusalem.[26] I Macc. 6:49 attributes the fall of Beth-Zur to the town's "having no food to withstand a siege as it was a Sabbath in the land."[27] Antiochus' forces, after taking this fortress, invested the area of the Temple. The resistance was feeble, according to I Macc.

ander deliberately pursued a pro-Jewish policy, since there were many Jews in Babylonia.

25 Alexander's remission of taxes during Shemitah should be compared to the grant of Julius Caesar: "Gaius Caesar, Imperator (and Dictator: *Lat.*) for the second time, has ruled that they shall pay a tax for the city of Jerusalem, Joppa excluded, every year except in the seventh year, which they call the Sabbatical year, because in this time they neither take fruit from the trees nor do they sow . . ." (Marcus' translation in Loeb's *A.J.* XIV, 202). If the Latin reading "dictator for the second time" is correct (so Niese, in apparatus) which is by no means certain, the decree was issued early 44. Tishri 44/Elul 45 was a Shemitah.

26 I Macc. 6:20–54; II Macc. 13:1–26.

27 καὶ ἐποίησεν εἰρήνην μετὰ τῶν ἐκ Βαιθσουρων, καὶ ἐξῆλθον ἐκ τῆς πόλεως, ὅτι οὐκ ἦν αὐτοῖς ἐκεῖ διατροφὴ τοῦ συγκεκλεῖσθαι ἐν αὐτῇ, ὅτι σάββατον ἦν τῇ γῇ.

6:53 since "there was no food in the storerooms because it was the seventh year."[28] Josephus amplifies this account of First Maccabees with details which apparently reflected the observance of Shemitah in his own day: "This [the Jews'] supply of food, however, had begun to give out, for the present crop had been consumed, and the ground had not been tilled, but had remained unsown because it was the seventh year, during which our laws oblige us to let it lie uncultivated. Many of the besieged, therefore, ran away because of the lack of necessities, so that only a few were left in the temple."[29]

First and Second Maccabees differ, however, as to the date of Antiochus V's march into Judaea. II Macc. 13:1 dates the march in the 149th year of the Seleucid era, I Macc. 6:20, repeated by Josephus, in the 150th year. Presumably (though this remains a question) the capture of Beth-Zur as well as the siege of the Temple during Shemitah, which are described in I Macc. 6:48–53, occurred within the same calendar year as recorded either in II Macc. 13:1 or in I Macc. 6:20, i.e. in the 149th or 150th year of the Seleucid era.

A number of complex technical questions need to be considered before we can confidently give the Julian date of the Shemitah mentioned in First Maccabees.

1. Does the different dating of Antiochus' campaign in First and Second Maccabees reflect a real difference or is the difference only apparent and due merely to a difference in their calendars?

2. The Seleucid era, employed by First and Second Maccabees, commemorates Seleucus' entry into Babylon in October of 312 B.C.E. But the occasion for the beginning of the Seleucid era varied from city to city. In Antioch the year began on the first of the Macedonian month Dios, i.e,, October; in Babylon, on the first of Nisannu.[30] What calendar(s) was (were) used by the authors of the Maccabean Books?[31]

3. Many details of the Judaean calendar during this period remain unknown. A number of scholars have maintained that the festival now known as Rosh Hashanah, which falls on the first of Tishri (September–October) was regarded then as the beginning of the year. But the Mac-

28 βρώματα δὲ οὐκ ἦν ἐν τοῖς ἀγγείοις διὰ τὸ ἕβδομον ἔτος εἶναι.
29 A.J. XII 378 (Marcus' translation, in Loeb).
30 See Elias Bickerman, *Chronology of the Ancient World* (Ithaca, N.Y.: Cornell University Press, 1968), 71.
31 Walther Kolbe, *Beiträge zur syrischen und jüdischen Geschichte* (Beiträge zur Wissenschaft von Alten Testament, Heft 10; Stuttgart, 1926), 19–58, offers a fair summary of the controversy. But his work has become somewhat obsolete since the publication of *Babylonian Chronology* by R. Parker and W. Dubberstein (Providence, R.I.: Brown University Press, 1956). See also Klaus-Dietrich Schunck, *Die Quellen des I. und II. Makkabäerbuches* (Halle: Max Niemeyer, 1954), 16–31.

cabean books, like all other biblical sources, without exception, take it for granted that Nisan was the first month.[32] There is no doubt, however, that the season of Shemitah commenced on the first of Tishri and ended on the last day of Elul.[33]

4. Several scholars have added to these complexities of the problem by suggesting not only that First and Second Maccabees use diverging calendars, but that First Maccabees itself reflects two calendars, depending whether the date used was taken from a Seleucid or from a Jewish source. To this must be added a third variable, when one does not know, which is the case in most instances, whether the source happens to be Seleucid or Jewish.[34]

This is not the place to discuss the pros and cons of the calendrical controversies except as they relate to the Sabbatical year mentioned in I. Macc. 6:49–53. Table One offers five proposed synchronisms, by no means exhaustive, of the Julian dates and the Sabbatical year under discussion.

TABLE ONE

	Source	Anno Sel.	B.C.E.	Shemitah
A.	II Macc. 13:1	149	Tishri 164/Elul 163	Tishri 164/Elul 163
	I Macc. 6:20	150	Tishri 163/Elul 162	Tishri 164/Elul 163
B.	II Macc. 13:1	149	Oct. 164/Sept. 163	Tishri 164/Elul 163
	I Macc. 6:20	150	Nisan 163/Adar 162	Tishri 164/Elul 163
C.	II Macc. 13:1	149	Oct. 164/Sept. 163	Tishri 164/Elul 163
	I Macc. 6:20	150	Nisan 163/Elul 162	Tishri 164/Elul 163
D.	II Macc. 13:1	149	Nisan 163/Adar 162	Tishri 163/Elul 162
	I Macc. 6:20	150	Nisan 162/Adar 161	Tishri 163/Elul 162
E.	II Macc. 13:1	149	Oct. 163/Sept. 162	Tishri 163/Elul 162
	I Macc. 6:20	150	Nisan 162/Adar 161	Tishri 163/Elul 162

Table 1 shows some of the divergent datings of Antiochus V's entry into Judaea during a Sabbatical year. A, B and C follow Zuckermann's table of Sabbatical years; D and E are in accord with the calendar prepared in this paper. A presumes that either the dating of I Macc. 6:20 is in error or that the reference in I Macc. 6:49, 53 to a Shemitah in fact means to say a post-Shemitah year. B assumes that since Antiochus' campaign started in the summer of 163, there is no divergence between

32 See above, note 8.
33 Cf. Lev. 25:9; M. Rosh Hashanah. I.1.
34 See J. C. Dancy. *A Commentary on I Maccabees* (Oxford: Blackwell, 1954), 50 f.

Zuckermann's table of Shemitot and the Maccabean differing datings; this difference resulted from the fact that the First Book of Maccabees follows the Jewish practice of beginning the year in Nisan; Second Maccabees follows the Seleucid calendar of starting the year in October. C accepts B's reasoning, but, because of other alleged divergences between the chronological schemes of the two Maccabean books, assumes that I Macc. posits a Seleucid era which started in Nisan 311; II Macc., in October 312 B.C.E.

D differs from E in that it presumes an error in First Maccabees; while E grants that I Maccabees began the Seleucid era in October 312 and II Maccabees, in Nisan 311; both sources agree that Antiochus V's campaign occurred in the spring or summer of 162.[35]

This somewhat technical discussion suggests that although I Macc. 6:20–53 assures us that a Shemitah occurred in either 164/63 or 163/62 B.C.E., the evidence from here alone is not conclusive.

4, THE MURDER OF SIMON THE HASMONEAN IN 177 A.S.

The next dated Shemitah occurred during the year of the murder of Simon the Hasmonean and the accession of John Hyrcanus. I Macc. 16:14–21 reports that Simon and his two sons, Mattathias and Judas, while visting Simon's son-in-law, Ptolemy, in Dok, near Jericho, were treacherously murdered by Ptolemy, "in the eleventh month, which is called Sabat (Shevat), of the 177th year."[36] The account goes on to relate that Simon's third son, John, escaped the assassin's hands, an episode with which the First Book of Maccabees ends.[37]

Josephus, who here used a source other than that of First Maccabees, does not mention the date of Simon's assassination, but he does say in the *Antiquities* that Simon ruled eight years.[38] Furthermore, Josephus adds in both the *Bellum* and *Antiquities* that John Hyrcanus' efforts to avenge the heinous crime were futile,[39] for while John besieged Ptolemy's fortress, which Josephus calls Dagon, "there came round the year in which the Jews are wont to remain inactive, for they observe the custom every seventh year, just as on the seventh day. And Ptolemy, being relieved

---

35   See note 31. Cf. E. Bickerman, "Mackabäerbücher," *R.E.* 27 (Stuttgart, 1928), 779–97; Schürer, *Gesch. d. jüd. Volkes*, I⁴, 35–37; Zeitlin, *The I Book of Macc.*, 254–61; Starcky, in *Les livres des Maccabées* (La Sainte Bible, Paris: les Éditions du Cerf, 1961), 47; 136, note d.; F. Kugler, *Von Moses bis Paulus* (Münster, 1922), 5; J. Jeremias, *Jerusalem in the Time of Jesus* (Philadelphia: Fortress Press, 1969), 140–44.

36   I Macc. 16:14.
37   I Macc. 16:21–22 (John's escape), 23–24 (book ends).
38   *A.J.* XIII, 228.
39   *B.J.* I, 54–60; *A.J.* XIII, 228–35.

from the war for this reason, killed the brothers and the mother of Hyrcanus (the mother is not mentioned in I Maccabees), and after doing so fled to Zenon, surnamed Cotylas, who was the ruler of the city of Philadelphia." [40]

One might suggest, perhaps gratuitously, as did Walter Otto, that the Shemitah was a historian's invention in order to excuse John Hyrcanus for letting Polemy escape unpunished.[41] But this is highly unlikely, for the 177th A.S. necessarily must have been a Shemitah if the 149th or 150th A.S., mentioned in section three, was one; this excludes the possibility that chroniclers simply manufactured Sabbatical years haphazardly. By juxtaposing the 149 and 177 and Shemitot we can conclude that the calendar of Sabbatical years was required rather than arbitrary, politically motivated, or an invention of apologists.

As to the Julian year of the Shemitah under discussion, Table Two shows three divergent schemes as proposed, among others, by Schür(er),[42] Zuck(ermann),[43] and Wach(older), preceded by the suggested dates of the Shemitah treated in the previous section:

TABLE TWO

A.S.	B.C.E.	Shemitah (Schür)	Shemitah (Zuck)	Shemitah (Wach)
148	Nisan 165/Adar 164	Tishri 164/Elul 163		
149	Tishri 164/Elul 163		Tishri 164/Elul 163	
149	Nisan 163/Adar 162			Tishri 163/Elul 16
		TWENTY-EIGHT YEARS LATER		
176	Nisan 137/Adar 136	Tishri 136/Elul 135		
177	Tishri 136/Elul 135		Tishri 136/Elul 135	
177	Nisan 135/Adar 134			Tishri 135/Elul 13

Granting that Josephus' dating of Simon's assassination in Shebat 177 A.S. presupposes a Julian date of Shemitah in 135/34 B.C.E., Schürer suspects not only the date but also the reliability of the tradition. Josephus' statement that, like the weekly Sabbath, the Sabbath of years was a period of inactivity, according to Schürer, was not factual and

40 A.J. XIII, 234 f.; B.J. I, 60: τριβομένης δὲ διὰ ταῦτα τῆς πολιορκίας ἐπέστη τὸ ἀργὸν ἔτος, ὅ κατὰ ἑπτατείαν ἀργεῖται παρὰ Ἰουδαίοις ὁμοίως τοῖς ἑβδομάσιν ἡμεραῖς...
41 Walter Otto, "Herodes," No. 14, R.E., Suppl. II (1913), 31 note (34); separately printed (Stuttgart, 1913), 33 note (36).
42 Schürer, Gesch. d. jüd. Volkes, I⁴, 36; 259.
43 Zuckermann, "Ueber Sabbatjahrcyclus," 33.

was based on an unreliable pagan source.[44] For the true reason of Hyrcanus' lifting of the siege was not the inactivity of the alleged Shemitah of 135/34, but the hunger of the historical Shemitah of 136/35. Schürer's dating of Simon's death in February of 135, however, results in a chronology of Hasmonean high priests that is inconsistent with Josephus' traditions in general. Josephus says that Simon held the high priestly office eight years (meaning no doubt from 170 to 177 A.S.), but Schürer attributes to Simon only seven years, from 142 to February 135;[45] Josephus gives John Hyrcanus a reign of thirty-one years, Schürer has thirty-two, from February 135 to 104 B.C.E.[46] Some scholars rightly reject Schürer's Hasmonean chronology, but inconsistently follow Schürer's table of Sabbatical years.[47]

Josephus' dating of Simon's death during the Shemitah of 177 A.S., which is equivalent to 135/34 B.C.E., offers unambiguous testimony for the calendar of Sabbatical cycles appended to this study.

5. HEROD'S CONQUEST OF JERUSALEM

In his detailed account of Herod, Josephus speaks of a Sabbatical year in connection with the protracted siege of Jerusalem which was led by the Rome-appointed Jewish king and the Roman general Sossius.[48] The siege evidently began in the spring of 37 B.C.E. and lasted, according to *B.J.*, 5:398, six months; according to *B.J.* 1:351; until the fifth month; but according to *A.J.* 14:487, in the third month. *A.J.* 14:476, says, however, that the taking of the first wall lasted forty days, the second wall fifteen days, making a total of fifty-five days of siege. Some scholars favor the version of minimal length; others, the full five months.[49]

---

44 Schürer, *Gesch. d. jüd. Volkes*, I[4], 36. Schürer's construction of ἀργέω uncultivated or inactive, employed by Josephus, probably means only that it is related to the rest of the Sabbath, not that types of rest of the two were alike. Schürer's understanding of Shemitah as described by Tacitus (*Hist.*, V, 4), that it required total rest, is probably too literal.

45 *A.J.* XIII, 228; Schürer, ibid., I[4], 241, n. 1.

46 *A.J.* XIII, 299; XX, 240; *B.J.*, I, 68 has 33 years. Schürer ibid., I[4], 256.

47 Cf. Kolbe, *Beiträge*, 26–28; Jean Starcky, *in Les livres des Macc.*, 49; Jeremias, *Jerusalem in the Time of Jesus*, 140–44; 377. See also E. Meyer, *Ursprüng und Anfänge des Christentums* (Stuttgart and Berlin, 1921). II. 232. n. 1, who is consistent in coordinating Zuckermann's calendar of Shemitot with Hasmonean chronology; Ralph Marcus, in his notes to *A.J.* XII, 378; XIII, 234, differs with Schürer on the table of Shemitot. but follows Schürer in the dating of the Hasmonean princes.

48 *B.J.* I, 343–57; *A.J.*, XIV, 465–91. Otto, *R.E.*, Suppl. II, 30–34; Reprint, 32–37; see now Abraham Schalit, *König Herodes: Der Mann und sein Werk* (Berlin: Walter de Gruyter & Co.. 1969), 95–97; 764-68.

49 Otto. *R.E.* Suppl. II. 30 f.. Reprint, 36 f. argues that the siege lasted

The latter cite as evidence *A.J.* 14:487, that the city fell "on the day of fast" *(τῇ ἑορτῇ νηστείας)*, which, taken to mean the Day of Atonement, implies that Jerusalem was conquered in October. The scholars who argue that Herod's siege lasted only fifty-five days or so, until June or July, explain that ἑορτῇ here means not the Day of Atonement but (erroneously, they say) the Sabbath, the fast of Tammuz; or, if it does mean Yom Kippur, this was an invention of an anti-Herodian chronicler, which Josephus thoughtlessly copied.[50] But, except for the last explanation, which is conceivable, it seems rather unbelievable that Josephus (or his source) would have either confused the Sabbath with the Yom Kippur or that the fast of Tammuz could have been called *the* fast day, to commemorate a date when Jerusalem was twice conquered, first, by Pompey (63 B.C.E.) and twenty-seven (twenty-six?) years later, in 37 B.C.E.

Josephus gives another datum by referring to a Sabbatical year. Describing Jerusalem's famine during the siege, *A.J.* 14:475 adds that it was aggravated "for a Sabbatical year happened to fall at that time."[51] Since the defense of the Holy City against Herod took place in the spring and summer of 37 B.C.E., as expressly dated by Josephus, the Sabbatical year must have begun in Tishri 1 of 38 B.C.E. If so, it follows that the two Sabbatical years discussed in the previous two sections, sixteen (section 3) and twelve Shemitot (section 4) earlier, must be dated respectively in 164/63 and 135/34 B.C.E. Zuckermann and the scholars who have accepted his calendar of Sabbatical years, cite the Shemitah during Herod's siege of Jerusalem as the basis for their version of the calendar of Shemitot.[52]

But the evidence here from Josephus is not quite as clear-cut as it would seem. For Josephus, in *A.J.* 15:6–7, after describing the terrible sufferings which Herod inflicted upon Jerusalem's population, adds: "And there was no end to their troubles, for on the one hand their greedy master, who was in need [of money], was plundering them, and on the other hand the seventh year, which came round this time, forced them to leave the land unworked, since we are forbidden to sow

---

3 months; J. Klausner, *Historiah shel Habayyit Hasheni*[2] (Jerusalem: Aḥiasaf, 1950), III, 269 f., favors the account of a long siege; Schürer, *Gesch. d. jüd Volkes*, I[4], 358, note 11, cites the literature and the diverse opinions. See also Schalit, *König Herodes*, 464–66.

50 Herzfeld, *MGWJ*, 5 (1855), 109–15, and Graetz, Gesch., III[5] (1905), 161, note 1, maintain that the city fell on a Sabbath day; Schalit (following Otto) rejects the tradition—a fastday—altogether (see note 49).

51 *A.J.* XIV, 475: τὸν γὰρ ἑβδοματικὸν ἐνιαυτὸν συνέβη κατὰ ταῦτ' εἶναι.

52 In a note *A.J.* XIV, 475, Marcus argues that Josephus either erred here in dating Herod's capture of Jerusalem in the summer of 36 B.C.E. (see XIV, 488), rather than in 37, or that he alluded to the forthcoming Sabbatical year of 37–36.

the earth at that time."[53] The phrase ἐνειστήκει γὰρ τότε which Marcus has rendered "which came round at that time," seems to suggest that the Shemitah fell not during the siege but after it had ended, i.e., while Herod was master of Jerusalem. If the city fell on Yom Kippur, as Josephus says it did, *A.J.* 15:7 would seem to refer to the Shemitah of 37/36 B.C.E. But even if the city fell in Tammuz, as some scholars argue, it is quite likely that Josephus here alludes to the first year of Herod's reign, virtually all of which fell during the Sabbatical year of Tishri 37/Elul 36.[54] But however one dates the fall of Jerusalem to Herod, there is no escaping the fact that Josephus' evidence here for the calendar of Sabbatical years appears to be contradictory: *A.J.* 14:475 suggests that the Shemitah fell during the Julian years 38/37; *A.J.* 15:7, 37/36 B.C.E. Both cannot be right.

6. KING AGRIPPA 1 RECITES DEUT. 7:15 IN A POST-SABBATICAL YEAR

Referring to Deut. 31:10–13; which ordains the public recitation of the Law "at the end of every seven years, at the set time of the year of release, at the feast of booths," Mishnah Sotah 7:8 says: "The section of the king, how [is it recited]? On the day following the first day of the Festival (Sukkot), on the eighth year, during a post-Shemitah, they make for him [the king] a platform of wood in the Temple Court on which he sits as it is written: 'At the end . . .' (Deut. 31:10). The *hazzan* of the synagogue takes the scroll of the Torah and hands it to the head of the synagogue, the head of the synagogue hands it to the sagan (assistant of the high priest), the sagan to the high priest, the high priest hands it to the king, the king receives it standing and reads it sitting. But King Agrippa received it standing and read it standing, and the sages praised him. And when he [Agrippa] reached (Deut. 17:15): 'You many not put a foreigner over you who is not your brother,' his eyes flowed with tears. They [the sages] said to him: 'Fear not, Agrippa, you are our brother! you are our brother! you are our brother!' "[55]

---

53 πέρας τε κακῶν οὐδὲν ἦν. τὰ μὲν γὰρ ἡ πλεονεξία τοῦ κρατοῦντος ἐν χρείᾳ γεγενημένον διέφθορει, τὴν δὲ χώραν μένειν ἀγεώργητον τὸ ἑβδοματικὸν ἠνάγκαζεν ἔτος. ἐνειστήκει γὰρ τότε, καὶ σπείρειν ἐν ἐκείνῳ τὴν γῆν ἀπηγορευμένον ἐστιν ἡμῖν.

54 See note 52. The Marcus-Wikgren note to *A.J.*, XV, 7 (Loeb) is worth repeating: "The Sabbatical year extended from Oct. 37 to Oct. 36 B.C., although Josephus may have placed it a year earlier; see the notes to *Ant.* XII. 387, and XIV. 475."

55 פרשת המלך כיצד ? מוצאי יום טוב של חג, בשמיני במוצאי שביעית, עושין לו בימה של עץ בעזרה, והוא יושב עליה, שנאמר: 'מקץ שבע שנים במועד' וגו', חזן הכנסת נוטל ספר תורה ונותנה לראש הכנסת, וראש הכנסת נותנה לסגן, והסגן נותנה לכהן גדול, וכהן גדול נותנה למלך, והמלך עומד ומקבל וקורא יושב. אגריפס המלך עמד וקבל וקרא עומד,

Beginning with Wieseler,[56] the dating of this story has often been debated. Since King Agrippa II (28–92 or 93 C.E.) had no control of Jerusalem and probably could not or would not read Hebrew, scholars generally have assumed that Mishnah Sotah 7:8 referred to King Agrippa I (10 B.C.E.–44 C.E.).[57] A man with a checkered career, he was imprisoned by Tiberius; in 37 C.E. Caligula appointed him king of Herod Phillipus' tetrarchy of Gaulanitis and Trachonitis; in 39, he was awarded Herod Antipas' realm of Galilee and Peraea; in 41 Claudius added Judaea and Samaria to his kingdom. Agrippa died in 44.[58]

What is the date of Agrippa I's reading of Scripture? It is generally assumed that this occurred during the post-Sabbatical Sukkot of 41 C.E., for following Zuckermann's chronology, Tishri 40/Elul 41, was a Shemitah, the only one to fall during Agrippa I's reign of Judaea (41–44) and indeed of his entire realm (37–44).

An incidental remark in Josephus shows, however, that 40/41 could not have been a Shemitah. Describing in great detail the rebellious mood in Judaea which followed Caligula's order to place his statue in the Temple, *A.J.* 18:271–72 speaks of the Jewish petitioners at Tiberias, who said that they were ready to die rather than to violate their ancestral laws: "And falling on their faces and baring their throats, they declared that they were ready to be slain. They continued to make these supplications for forty days (fifty: *B.J.* 2:200). Furthermore, they neglected their fields, and that, too, though it was time to sow the seed."[59] Philo Alexandrinus, referring to the same incident records: "For the wheat crop was just ripe and so were the other cereals."[60] We know that the turmoil in Judaea described by both Josephus and Philo took place during the final months of the reign of Caligula, who was assassinated on the twenty-fourth of January of 41 C.E. Since these Jews were ready to die for the Law, they presumably were observing the laws of Shemitah which, according to Zuckermann, were then in force.

ושבחוהו חכמים. וכשהגיע ל'לא תוכל לתת עליך איש נכרי' זלגו עיניו דמעות. אמרו לו:
.אל תתירא, אגריפס, אחינו אתה, אחינו אתה, אחינו אתה!

56 Wieseler. *Stud. und Krit.* (1879). 529 f.

57 On the other hand. J. Derenbourg. *Essai sur l'histoire et la géographie de la Palestine* I (Paris. 1867). 217: A. Büchler, *Die Priester und der Cultus im letzten Jahrzehnt des jerusalemischen Tempels* (Vienna, 1895). 10–12; and Zeitlin, *JQR*, 9 (1918/19). 99. n. 70, among others, maintain that M. Sotah VII, 8, refers to Agrippa II.

58 On Agrippa I. see N. H. Feldman's general index to the Loeb edition of Josephus. IX (1965). 595.

59 *B.J.* II. 199–200. Schürer: *Gesch. d. jud. Volkes,* 1⁴, 36. grants that this passage suggests a different table of Sabbatical years, but rejects the evidence as indirect and as not sufficient to refute the positive evidence from the other datings of Shemitah.

60 Philo, *De leg.* 249.

16

In fact, however, by our reckoning, Tishri 40/Elul 41 was only the sixth year of the Shemitah cycle. This dating, moreover, adds new dimension to the accounts of Philo and Josephus of the self-sacrificing piety of the petitioners; for though unable to tend the fields the next year on account of Shemitah they nevertheless disdained to work the field in the permitted year, so as to protest Caligula's outrageous orders. It follows that Agrippa I's recitation from the Book of Deuteronomy, if historical, took place on the second day of Sukkot of 42 C.E.

I feel, however, a modicum of uncertainty concerning the historicity of the tale recorded in Mishnah Sotah 7:8. To be sure, there is intrinsically nothing in the anecdote that would contradict Agrippa I's character, as known to us from Josephus' accounts. Shrewd and subtle, pious where piety was called for, the king was quite capable of shedding tears to elicit a reply that would ease the un-Jewish reputation of the Herodian princes.[61] But talmudic literature recounts a handful of anecdotes to illustrate the Jewish king's piety, or even his superpiety in halakhic matters. The Babylonian Talmud, for example, tells that the king's train once encountered a bridal procession. According to halakhah, the bridal procession was supposed to let the king pass by. Agrippa, however, so the tale goes, chivalrously removed himself from the bridal path, saying, according to Semahot 11, "I wear a crown every day, she only once." These anecdotes, like the one we are discussing here, are probably fictional tales that grew around the remarkable personality of Agrippa I.[62] But if Agrippa I did in fact recite Scripture in connection with the septennial celebrations, the incident of Mishnah Sotah 7:8 occurred during the first year of the Sabbatical cycle, on Sukkot of 42 C.E.

7. A NOTE OF INDEBTEDNESS ON A PAPYRUS OF WADI MURABBA'AT 18

Thus far all the passages cited come from literary texts; this section introduces a document recently found in the Judaean desert in the caves of Wadi Murabba'at near Bethlehem. Zachariah bar Yehohanan signed a deed for Abshalom bar Hanin, promising the repayment of twenty (and ?) denars which he had borrowed during a Sabbatical year. We reproduce here the Aramaic text as published by Milik in the *Discoveries in the Judaean Desert*,[63] with corrections and an English translation:

1. [   ] [   ] שנ[ת תרתין לנרון קסר   ]
2. בצויה איתודי אבשלום בר חנין מן צויה
3. בנפי מניה עמי אנה זכריה בר יהוחנן בר ה [   ]

---

61 Cf. the derisive comments of Tos. Sotah VII, 16; Yer. Sotah VII, 7, 22a.
62 See also M. Bikkurim, III, 4; Tos. Pesaḥim, IV, 3: B. ibid. 107b.
63 P. Benoit, J. T. Milik, and R. de Vaux, *Discoveries in the Judaean Desert*,

4. יתב בכסלון כסף זוזין עס[רי]ן [ ] מש[ ] [
5. אנה [ ] ז[ ] [ ] [ ] לא די זבינת עד זמ[נא]
6. דנה אפרוענך בחמש ואפשר בתמ[ימותא]
7. ושנת שמטה דה והן כן לא אעבד תשלומ[תא]
8. לך מנכסי ודי אקנה לקובליך
9. [זכ]ריה בר יהוח[נן ע]ל[ל נפשה
10. [כת]ב יהוסף ב[ר] מאמרה
11. יהונתן בר יהוחנא שהד
12. יהוסף ב[ר י]הודן עד

Recto

1. [of yea]r two of Nero Caesar [   ]
2. in *Swya*; declared by Abshalom bar Ḥanin, of *Swyah*.
3. in his presence, of my own accord,[64] that I Zachariah bar Yehohanan bar Ḥ[   ]
4. dwelling in Keslon, silver denars twen[t]y
5. I [   ] not sell until the ti[me]
6. of this, I will pay you in five and possibly in its enti[rety];
7. in this year of Release; and if not so, I will make a paym[ent]
8. to you from my properties, even those that I will buy later, will be pledged to you as mortgage.

Verso

9. [Zacha]riah bar Yeho[ḥanan, i]n person
10. [writt]en (for) Yehosef ba[r   ], by dictation
11. Yehonatan bar Yehoḥanna, witness
12. Yehosef ba[r Ye]hudan, witness

This document has many ramifications and is of immense interest, but here we must restrict the discussion to lines one and seven. "In the second year of Nero Caesar" (line 1) equals, according to Milik October 13, 55/October 12, 56 C.E.;[65] according to Lehmann and Koffmahnn, 54/55.[66] Milik translates the first three words of line 7: "même si c'est une année sabbatique,"[67] and notes: "ושנת שמטה דה: la phrase subordi-

II, No. 18, 100–04 (Oxford: Clarendon Press, 1961). Republished with a German translation and commentary by E. Koffmahnn, *Die Doppelturkunden aus der Wüste Juda* (Leiden: Brill, 1968), 80–89.
64 Translation doubtful.
65 Milik, in *Discoveries*, II, 100 and 103.
66 Manfred R. Lehmann, "Studies in the Murabba'at and Naḥal Ḥever Documents," *Revue de Qumrân* IV, 13 (1963), 53–81, esp. 56 f.; Koffmahnn, *Doppelturkunden*, 41 f.
67 Milik, in *Discoveries*, II, 102.

née, nominale (דה pour שנתה דה), qui supprime le privilège de l'année sabbatique; c'est la fameuse loi du prosbol, attribuée à Hillel (cf. Sebi'it X 4 où on cite une formule différente et la formule בלא שמטתא des contrats traditionnels)."[68] Koffmahnn, however, translates: "in diesen Erlassjahr."[69]

There is no doubt that, contrary to Lehmann and Koffmahnn, Milik's dating of the second year of Nero in 55/56 C.E. is right, but that Milik's rendition of line seven as a conditional phrase, the legal equivalent of the Hillelite *prozbol,* is wrong.[70] Lehmann-Koffmahnn's "in·this year of Shemitah," however, is a simple and correct rendition.

It seems that Milik chose a complicated rendition of the phrase ושנת שמיטה דה because, according to the standard table of Sabbatical years, the year 54/55, not 55/56, the date of our note, was a Shemitah.[71] But Lehmann, followed ·by Koffmahnn, regards our document a *get mekushar,* ("folded" note), which according Bab. Tal. Baba Batra 164a-b, was to be antedated by a year.[72] If antedated by a year, as Lehmann and Koffmahnn maintain, the document was written in 54/55, a Shemitah in Zuckermann's calendar of Sabbatical years.

There is no reason, however, to assume that our document was in fact antedated. The second year of Nero refers, as Milik says, to Tishri 55/Elul 56 C.E., which was contrary to the general opinion, in fact a Sabbatical year, as attested by the phrase "in this year of Shemitah." Indeed, Murabba'at 18 presents convincing evidence that the calendar of Sabbatical years appended to this study is right.

8. WAS THE SECOND TEMPLE DESTROYED DURING A SABBATICAL OR POST-SABBATICAL YEAR?

Thus far all the passages discussed allude to Shemitah incidentally. In this section, however, the Sabbatical year becomes a crucial symbol of the schematic cycle of Jewish history. The Seder Olam reads:

היה רבי יוסי אומר : מגלגלין זכות ליום זכות וחובה ליום חייב ; נמצאת אומר, כשחרב הבית בראשונה, אותו היום מוצאי שבת היה, ומוצאי שביעית היתה, ומשמרתו של "הויריב היתה, ותשעה באב היתה. וכן שניה. ובזה ובזה הלוים עומדים על דוכנם ואומרים שירה. ומה שירה אומרים ? 'וישב להם את אונם' וכו'.

68 Ibid., II, 103.

69 *Doppelturkunden,* 81; Lehmann, *RQ,* IV, 56 "and the Shemittah year."

70 It should be noted that although the Murabba'at documents allude to Shemitah (see below, section 9), there seems to be no indication of the existence of the Hillelite *prozbol.*

71 See below, section 9, note 85.

72 The talmudic tradition, also attested from other ancient sources (Kraeling, *The Brooklyn Museum Aramaic Papyri,* 50), mentions two types of notes:

Rabbi Jose says: 'Favorable judgment forbode favorable days and guilty judgments guilty days. You find it said: When the Temple was destroyed for the first time, that happened on a day after the Sabbath (Sunday), during a post-Sabbatical year, and during the Watch of Jehoiarib, and on the ninth of Ab; and so also when the Second (Temple was destroyed). And at the point of the destruction of both Temples the Levites were standing at their posts reciting the (same) psalm. And what was the psalm? 'He will bring back on them their iniquity and wipe them out for their wickedness; the Lord our God will wipe them out' (Ps. 94:23).[73]

This passage appears to support Zuckerman unambiguously and to contradict my calendar of Shemitot. For we know that the Second Temple was destroyed in the month of Ab of the year 70, which our passage dates as a post-Sabbatical year. It follows that the preceding year 68/69 was a Shemitah. Counting backwards we get:

TABLE THREE

Section	Shemitah(s)	Julian Date	A.S.
8		68/69 C.E.	379/80
7	2	54/55 ”	365/66
6	4	40/41 ”	351/52
5	15	38/37 B.C.E.	274/73
4	27	136/35 ”	176/75
3	37	164/63 ”	148/49
2	57	332/31 ”	
1	?	?	

גט פשוט a "simple" note and גט מקושר, a "folded" note, with three witnesses not two as in simple notes. The document was folded and the witnesses' signatures appeared on the back of the note. Bab Tal. Baba Bathra, 164a–b, quotes Rabbi (Judah Hanasi) as challenging the view of Rabbi Ḥanina ben Gamaliel, that "folded" notes were customarily antedated. But the reference, if not a misinterpretation of Tos. Baba Bathra, X, 1, must allude to exceptional cases. No other talmudic tradition knows of such antedating; certainly not the Tosephta, as claimed by Lehmann (R.Q., IV, 57). In fact, Mur 22 (Discoveries, II, 118–22; Koffmahnn, Doppelturkunden, 158, apparently a "folded" note, bears the date of the first year of the Redemption of Israel which, according to Lehmann's view of antedating, should be inconceivable.
73. Seder Olam Rabbah, 30, 74a–75a (ed. Ratner); Tos. Ta'anit, III, 9, p. 340 (Lieberman ed.) Yer. Ta'anit, IV, 5, 68d; B. Ta'anit, 29a; Arakhin, 11b.

Indeed, this famous passage, repeated in the Palestinian and Babylonian Talmuds, seems to have been decisive in persuading scholars to adopt Zuckermann's table of Shemitot despite the problematical aspects which such a calendar involves.[74] For surely, could it be seriously argued that Rabbi Jose ben Ḥalafta, a tanna who flourished less than a century after the Second Temple's destruction, a chronographer (the treatise Seder Olam is attributed to him), who wrote at a time when the institution of Shemitah had been part of a millenium-long tradition, might be mistaken as to the Sabbatical date of the Ḥurban?[75]

But the statement attributed to Rabbi Jose is problematical, being based, not on factual information, but on midrashic chronography. Rabbi Jose, no doubt, alludes to another of his exegetical datings. Chapter 28 of Seder Olam reads: רבי יוסי אומר: 'שבעים שבעים' משחרב בית ראשון ועד שחרב בית אחרון, שבעים לחרבנו, וארבע מאות (ועשרה) [ועשרים] לבנינו. ומה תלמוד לומר 'שבעים שבעים' ? אלא שהיתה גזירה גזורה קודם לשבעים שנה.

"Rabbi Jose says: 'Seventy weeks' (Dan. 9:24): From the time of the destruction of the First Temple to the destruction of the Second Temple. The Temple was rebuilt 70 years after its destruction and was destroyed 420 years after its rebuilding (70 + 420) = (7 × 70). Why does Scripture then say 'seventy weeks' (i.e., it would have been more accurate for Daniel 9:24 to say: 10 weeks + 60 weeks)? But because the decree (for the destruction and the rebuilding) had been issued prior to the (beginning of the) seventy years."[76] Rabbi Jose, it would seem, uses chronology to expound upon a difficult prophecy of Daniel, a book which is full of enigmatic statements.[77] But this midrashic exegesis forms the foundation of Talmudic chronology likewise attributed to Rabbi Jose, that a) the Solomonic Temple was destroyed 490 years before the Herodian Sanctuary (actually 587 or 586 B.C.E. + 70 C.E. = 657 or 656); b) both were destroyed in a post-Sabbatical year; c) both were burned on the ninth day of Ab (which is contrary to II Kings 2:8 and to Jer. 52:6 as far as the Solomonic Temple was concerned, and may be contrary to Josephus as to the Herodian

74 Almost all scholars who have dealt with the Sabbatical chronology cite our passage (see notes 12–13), beginning with the sixteenth century Azariah de Rosi, *Meẓaref Lakesef* (Wilno, 1864), 114.

75 On authorship and date of Seder Olam, see Zunz-Albeck, *Die Gottesdienstlichen Vorträge der Juden historisch entwickelt* (Hebrew ed., Jerusalem: Mosad Bialik, 1947), 43; 267 f., and Ratner's *Mavo Lehaseder Olam Rabbah* (Wilno, 1894),

76 Seder Olam Rabbah 28, p. 130 (ed. Ratner). Cf. Tos. Zebaḥim, XIII, 6; Bab. Tal. Yoma 9a; Arakhin, 12a–13a.

77 Jose's exegesis of Dan 9:24 appears to be linked with the rabbinic chronology of the Jubilees during the first Temple. See above, notes 3–5.

Temple), and d) both Temples were destroyed on a Sunday; and e) the Levites happened to chant the same song.[78]

Few students are likely to defend the historicity of any part of Jose's statement, execept for b), a passage that seems to have proved decisive in determining the calendar of Shemitah. In fact only a segment of b), as few students would grant, although quite possible, that the year 587 or 586 B.C.E., the date of Nebuchadnezzar's burning of the First Temple was a Shemitah. Only the author of Seder Olam who, as was pointed out above, maintained that from the time when the laws of Shemitah and Jubilee became effective in the 15th year of Joshua's conquest, until the Ḥurban, there elapsed 836 years, of which sixteen jubilees of fifty years each make a total of 800 years, with a remainder of thirty-six years, or five Shemitot plus one year of the next Sabbatical cycle. To be sure, the fact that other parts of Rabbi Jose's statement reflect midrashic chronography does not exclude the possibility that his dating of the Shemitah nearest to the destruction of the Herodian Temple in 68/68 is necessarily inaccurate. It may just be the historical grain upon which Rabbi Jose built the rest of his hermeneutics of Daniel 9:24. But, regardless of the other evidence, the statement cannot be made the foundation upon which to construct a reliable calendar of the Sabbatical cycles.

Three more points need to be remembered, however. First, technically Rabbi Jose's synchronism of the destruction of the second Temple with the first year of a Sabbatical cycle is not inaccurate. For although Tishri 69/Elul 70, not 68/69, was a Shemitah, it is nevertheless quite true that more than a half of the year of the Ḥurban fell during a post-Sabbatical period. For the Jewish year, as stated in Mishnah Rosh Hashanah 1:1, formally commenced on the first of Nisan and ended on the last day of Adar. When Rabbi Jose says that the year of the Ḥurban was a post-Sabbatical he may be referring to the second part, i.e., between Tishri and Adar.[79]

---

78 On the song of the day, see now 11QPs^a DavComp. in *Discoveries* IV (1965), 48; 92. M. Tamid, VII, 4, knows only of songs varied every day of the week; Seder Olam 28 seems to be alluding to unique songs for every day of the year.

79 Maimonides, moreover, *Hilkhot Shemitah Veyobel*, X, 4, alluding to our passage, says: נמצאת למד שהשנה שחרב בה הבית באחרונה, שתחלתה מתשרי שאחר החורבן כשני חדשים, שהרי מתשרי הוא המנין לשמיטים וליובלות, אותה השנה מוצאי שביעית היתה.

"You must say that the year when the Second Temple was last destroyed, whose beginning commenced in Tishri, about two months after the destruction (since the computation of Shemitot and Jubilees begins in Tishri), that year was a Shemitah." Maimonides thus expressly says that the Ḥurban actually occurred during a Shemitah, but that the post-Sabbatical commenced, according to him, during Tishri of the New Year.

Second, scholars may be misrepresenting the talmudic tradition when they ascribe to it a solid synchronism of the Ḥurban and the first year of the Shemitah cycle. Arakhin 12a–13b, after quoting Rabbi Jose's statement concerning the remarkable coincidences of the two Temples in its entirety, attempts to disprove only the part referring to the Sabbatical synchronism. Quite clearly, the Amoraic sages were quite aware that it did not conform to the facts as they knew them.

Third, a chronological passage, seemingly merely expanding upon Rabbi Jose's dictum, cited in Abodah Zarah 9b, maintains that the Ḥurban of the Second Temple actually occurred during a Shemitah:

אמר רב הונא בריה דרב יהושע: האי מאן דלא ידע כמה שני בשבוע הוא עומד: ניטפי חד שתא ונחשוב כללי ביובלי ופרטי בשבועי, ונשקל ממאה תרי ונשרי אפרטי ונחשובינהו לפרטי בשבועי; וידע כמה שני בשבוע. וסימנך: 'כי זה שנתים הרעב בקרב ׳;ארץ.

> Said Rabbi Huna, the son of Rabbi Joshua: If one does not know the current year of a Sabbatical cycle, let him add one year (to the era of the Hurban). He may then compute jubilees by dividing the date into large numbers (50 years), and Shemitot into small numbers of 7; for each 100 years, let him deduct 2, adding these 2's, and then divide them by 7. Thus, he will know the year of the Sabbatical cycle. And your mnemonic is: 'For there have been two years of hunger in the land ' (Gen. 45:6).[80]

In this passage Rabbi Huna, the son of Rabbi Joshua, a head of the Academy of Naresh, who evidently died in 411, offers a formula to find the year of any Sabbatical cycle if one knows the date of the era of Ḥurban. Simply stated, the formula is: (date of ḥurban + 1): 7. The remainder of the division yields the year of the Sabbatical cycle; if 0, a Sabbatical year. The deduction of 2 from each 100 results from dividing 100 by 7 ($12 \times 7 + 2 = 100$) which has a remainder of 2; which if added and divided by 7, again yields the year of Shemitah cycle.

As Huna's formula, according to our talmudic tradition, calls for adding one year to the era of the Ḥurban, it necessarily assumes a synchronism of the year of the Ḥurban (69/70) with Shemitah, rather than a 68/69 Shemitah. There is simply no need to add one year to an era that begins in the first year of the Sabbatical cycle. Since Huna's formula appears to follow Jose's midrashic exegesis, it follows that Huna interpreted Rabbi Jose to mean that as stated by Maimonides the Ḥurban took place during, not after, a Sabbatical year. Hence, the formula calls for the addition of one year to the date of Ḥurban to make the

---

80 I have reproduced the passage as found in our editions and the Mss. of Abodah Zarah 9b. But a long string of geonic and rabbinic authorities has

division by seven correspond with cycles of Shemitah. Certainly, our reading of Abodah Zarah 9b suggests that 69/70 was a Shemitah.[81]

Finally, a passage in Josephus implies that the year 68/69 was not Sabbatical. According to *B.J.* 4:529–37, "Simon the son of Gioras, the leader of the Zealots, invaded Idumaea in the winter of 68/69 and gained abundant booty and laid hands on vast supplies of corn."[82] This clearly indicates that it was not a part of a Sabbatical season, for surely the Idumeans by now appear to have been following the traditions of Jewish law.[83]

9. RENTING LAND FROM BAR KOSBA

Among the remnants of Simon bar Kosba's (or Kochba's, as he is known from Greek sources) archives found recently at Murabba'at (see Section 7 above) are fragments of a dozen rental contracts which subordinates of the Jewish Prince executed at Herodium.[84] Judging from the remnants, the legal wording of these contracts, aside from the names of the renters, differed slightly, but the state of preservation of Mur 24 A–L (as numbered by Milik) ranges from only traces of scattered letters to nearly approaching the original form. Since each of the twelve contracts, written in Hebrew, apparently contained both the same date of issuance and the clause relating to the Sabbatical year, they

divergent readings, some of them questioned the authenticity of the underlined words ונ'טפי חד שתא "let him add one year." See, for example, *Teshuvot Hageonim*, ed. A. Harkavy (Berlin, 1887), No. 45, 20–22; Razah, *Hama'or Hagadol*, on Alfasi Avodah Zarah, 96; Rabbenu Hananel ad locum; Tosafot Avodah Zarah. 9b, s.v. *hay*. It would seem that because of calendar changes many medieval savants emended the reading of our passage, to make it conform with their own datings; it appears, however, to be authentic as it is in the printed editions.

81 See below, note 109.

82 *B.J.* IV, 537.

83 Edom, judaized by John Hyrcanus (*A.J.*, XIII, 257) was considered part of the Holy Land, unlike Ammon and Moab, over which the Rabbis differed whether or not their territory fell under the laws of Shemitah (see M. Yadayyim, IV, 3; Tos. ibid., II, 15–17). During the war against the Romans, the Idumaeans were associated with the Zealots, suggesting strict observance. Zeitlin, *JQR* 9 (1918–19), however, argues that the date of the march in winter of 68, commonly accepted, must be erroneous; on p. 101 he maintains that "the laws of the sabbatical year affected only the lands of Palestine, and had no application in Edom or in any other country that was annexed to Palestine," citing M. Shevi'it, I, 1, as reference. By Maimonides' definition (Hilkhot Shemitah, IV, 28), however, Edom would be included. See also Yer. Shevi'it, VI., 36; Tosafot, Hagigah, 3b, s.v. *Ammon*.

84 According to Milik, *Discoveries*, II, 125 ff., Herodium served as the Bar Kosba's headquarters. Yadin (*IEJ*, 11 [1961] 51), however, punctuates the documents (see below, line 3) so that Herodium refers to the location of a sub-camp.

are crucial for this sudy. We reproduce here Mur 24 E, partly but plausibly restored on the basis of the parallel fragments of papyri, as transcribed by Milik in the *Diseoveries in the Judaean Desert*, II, p. 131:

1. [On the twentieth of She]vat of the year tw[o] of the Redemp- tion of	1. [בעשרין לש]בט שנת שת[ים לגאלת
2. [I]srael by Shimeon ben K[os] ba, the prince of	2. [י]שראל על יד שמעון בן כ[וס]בא נסיא
3. [Is]rael. In the camp which is located in Herodium,	3. [יש]ראל במחנה שיושב בהרודיס
4. [Ye]hudah ben Raba' said to Hillel ben *Grys*:	4. [י]הודה בן רבא אמר להלל בן גריס
5. "I of my free will have [re]nted from you today the	5. אני מרצוני [ח]כרת המך היום את
6. land which is my re[n]tal in 'Ir	6. העפר שהוא שלי בח>כ<רתי בעיר
7. Naḥash which I hold as a tenant from Shimeon, the Prince of Israel,	7. נחש שחכרת משמעון נסיא ישראל
8. This land I have rented from you from today	8. [א]ת עפר הלז חכרתי המך מן היום
9. until the end of the eve of She- mitah,[85] which are years	9. עד סוף ערב השמטה שהם שנים
10. full, [fi]scal years, five, of tenancy;	10. שלמות שני [מ]כסה חמש תחכיר
11. [that I wi]ll deliver to you in [Her]odium: wheat,	11. [שאה]א מודד לך ב[הר]ודיס חנטין
12. [of good and pure quality,] th[ree *kor*]s and a *lethekh*,	12. [יפות ונקיות] שלו [שת כור]ין ולתך
13. [of which a tenth part of the tithe] of these	13. [מעשרת מעשרת] ת אלה
14. [you will deliver to the silo of the treasury.] And [I am obli] gated	14. [שתהא שוקל על גג האוצר] ו[ק]ים
15. [in regard of this matter thus- ly]	15. [עלי לעמת ככה [
16. [Yehudah ben Raba', in per- son]	16. [יהודה בן רבא על נפשה]
17. [Shim'on ben Kosba', by dic- tation.]	17. [שמעון בן כוסבא מן מאמרה]

85 *Discoveries* II, 122–34. The Shemitah clause, missing in the defective parts of Mur 24 A, is preserved in 24 B, line 14; C, 12; D, 14–15; E, 9; but lost in the fragments of 24 F-L.

BEN ZION WACHOLDER

As pointed out by Milik: "Mur 24 fournit un synchronisme pré-
cieux entre le comput fondé sur les cycles sabbatiques et celui de l'ère
de la Liberté."[86] The date of the contracts (as clearly attested in *Mur*
24 B, line 1; D 1) is certain: the 20th of Shevat of year 2 of the Redemption of Israel. Lines 8–10 of Mur 24 E offer the Sabbatical relationship: "From today," i.e., the 20th of Shebat of year 2, "until the
end of the eve of Shemitah, which are five full years, fiscal years, of
tenancy."[87] Citing Schürer (*Gesch, d. jüd. Volkes,* I[4], 36) and North
(*Biblica,* 34 (1953), 501–15), Milik attributes to Josephus and the
Rabbis the dating of 68/69 C,E. as a Shemitah.[88] It follows, Milik says,
that the Shemitah year nearest to Bar Kosba's revolt was 130/31, since
Roman sources unambiguously date the rebellion's conclusion in 135.[89]
This could only mean, according to Milik, that the date of the rental
contracts was the second year of the Sabbatical cycle, ending in 137/38,
and equalled 132/33 (137/38 — 5 = 132/33). Now since the second
year of the Shemitah cycle was also the second year the Redemption
of Israel (lines 1–2), it necessarily follows, according to Milik, that the
revolt commenced in 131/32, contrary to the accepted view which dates
the beginning of the Bar Kosba rebellion in the spring of 132.[90]

Milik's chronology is mistaken on several levels. First, Josephus
nowhere mentions that 68/69 was a Shemitah year; Schürer (I[4],35)
and others deduce it from the dating of Herod's conquest; mistakenly,
I believe (see above, section 5). Second, assuming the year 68/69 as a
Shemitah, the Sabbatical year nearest Bar Kosba's rebellion was not
130/31, as maintained by Milik, but 131/32 (68/69 + (9×7) = 131/32).[91]
Third, the beginning of the year of Redemption of the Bar Kosba
era commenced not on the first of Tishri of 131, as stated by Milik,

86 *Discoveries,* II, 125.
87 Milik, ibid. (II, 131) translates: "dès aujourd'hui jusqu'à la fin de la
veille de la Rémission, ce qui fait (un nombre d') années complètes, années fis-
cales, (de) cinq."
88 See above, section 8, esp. note 74, for rabbinic citations: since Josephus
nowhere says that 68/69 was a Sabbatical year, Milik probably alludes to the
passages cited above in section 5.
89 "L'année sabbatique la plus proche de la fin de la Révolte, 135 ap.
J.-C. (date assurée par les sources romaines), est donc 130/1 et la deuxième année du cycle suivant correspond à 132/3. Mur 24 a donc été écrit au début de
février 133, qui tombait 'l'an deux de la Libération d'Israël.' Le début de l'ère
de la Liberté se place au premier Tišri 131" (ibid. II, 125). On p. 67, however,
Milik adds: that the New Year of Tishri was valid only for the dating of contracts: for coins, though, the first of Nisan was more likely to have been the
New Year. Cf. Kanael, *IEJ,* 21, (1971), 41 n. 16.
90 Milik, in ibid. II, 125; cf, Sh. Yeivin, *Milḥemet Bar Kokhba* (Jerusalem,
1952), 197–99.
91 This has been also noted by Lehmann. *RQ,* IV (1963), 56.

26

but on the first of Nissan of 132.[92] Fourth, the last Shemitah prior to Mur 24 A-L took place not in 131/32, as Zuckermann says, but in 132/33. Therefore the next Shemitah that is mentioned in line 9 of Mur 24 E refers to Tishri 139/Elul 140.

The contracts of Mur 24 provided, however, that the lease would expire on the last day of Elul of 139: "until the end of the pre-Sabbatical year." The rebellion commenced, according to conventional dating, and now attested by numismatic evidence, in the spring of 132.[93] The first year of the Redemption of Israel equals Nissan 1 of 132/Adar 29 of 133. It follows that the 20th of Shevat of year 2 of the Redemption of Israel corresponds roughly to February of 134; the time of the contract ("five full years") in fact meant five years, six months and ten days; until the last day of Elul (roughly September) of 139. Milik's statement (citing Mur 24 E, 9–10) that the contract provided for "une durée de cinq ans, précise"[94] is not quite exact.

Although his chronology is erroneous, Milik rightly felt that Mur 24's synchronism of the Sabbatical year with the year of Redemption of Israel would yield a more precise chronology of the Bar Kosba's rebellion. The rebellion lasted, according to the chronography of Seder Olam, "three and a half years" (the reading "two and a half" is erroneous).[95] Since the uprising started in the spring or possibly in the summer of 132, it lasted as attested by Eusebius to the fall or early winter of 135. In terms of Jewish dating, the rebellion commenced in the spring of a pre-Sabbatical year and lasted to the beginning of the fourth year of the next Shemitah cycle, the fourth year of the Redemption of Israel by the Prince of Israel, Shim'on bar Kosba.[96]

---

92 See Kanael (note 89). The earliest dated document of the Bar Kosba period appears to be the one found in Naḥal Ḥever 42, published by Yadin, *IEJ* 12 (1962), 248: "On the first of Iyar of year two of the Redemption of Israel...."; Mur 22 (*Discoveries*, II, 118 ff.), dated in 14th of Marḥeshwan of the first year, was written 6½ months later. If this is correct, the revolt started in the spring of 132. Kanael's explanation (*IEJ* 21, [1971], 41, note 15), that the scribe erred is not convincing.

93 See preceding note.

94 Milik, in *Discoveries*, II, 123.

95 See Seder Olam, 30, p. 146 (Ratner), note 82, who cites the Ms reading; Neubauer, *Medieval Jewish Chronicles* (Oxford, 1887), I, 198; II, (1895), 66, note 23.

96 Mur 30 (*Discoveries*, II, 30, pp. 144–46; Koffmahnn, *Doppelturkunden*, 182–85), dates the 21st of Tishri of the 4th year of the Redemption of Israel, in Jerusalem, which suggests that, contrary to general assumptions, the Holy City was still in Bar Kosba's hands in October of 135 (cf. Milik, *Discoveries*, II, 205). But the proof is not conclusive, for Mur 30 may have been composed in a provincial town, whose scribe continued to date according the era of "the Redemption of Israel in Jerusalem" even after the fall of the Holy City.

10. THREE FOURTH AND FIFTH CENTURY TOMBSTONE
INSCRIPTIONS IN SODOM

All three tombstone inscriptions to be discussed in this section have a number of common features, the most important of which for us is the fact that they contain the contemporary date of the Sabbatical cycle. The first inscription was discovered by John Philby in 1924 and published by A. Cowley in 1925; in 1943 E. Sukenik found two more inscriptions which he printed in 1945, together with a reprint of Cowley's find and chronological commentaries by A.H. Frenkel, U. Cassuto, and A. Akavia.[97] All three tombstones were found in or near Zoar, the biblical Sodom, where a Jewish community flourished apparently since Herodian times, if not earlier. The three tombstones contain a synchronism of the Shemitah cycle with the year of the Ḥurban era. We reproduce a Hebrew transcription of Cowley and Sukenik, plus an English translation:

Inscription A (Cowley)

1. May the soul rest,	תתניח [98] נפשה 1
2. of Sha'ul bar[ ]lat	דשאול בר [ ]לת 2
3. who died on the first of the month of	דמית בריש ירח 3
4. Marḥeshwan, of the year	מרחשון משתה 4
5. first of Shemitah;	קדמיתה דשמטתה 5
6. the year of three hundred and sixty	שנת תלת מא ושתין 6
7. and four years after the Ḥurban	וארבע שנין לחרבן 7
8. of the House of the Temple. Peace!	בית מקדשה שלם 8

97 A. Cowley, in *Palestine Exploration Fund* (1925) 207–10; S. Daiches, ibid., (1926), 31 f.; L. H. Vincent, *Revue biblique,* 36 (1927), 404–07; Th. Reinach, *REJ,* 85 (1928), 1–6; A. Marmorstein, in *Yerushalayim* (Lunch Memorial Volume, in Hebrew [1928]), 41 ff.; *Sefer Hayishuv* I (ed. S. Klein; Jerusalem, 1939), 126; J. B. Frey, *Corpus Inscriptionum Iudaicarum* (Vatican City: Pontifico Instituto di Archeologia Cristiana, 1952), 243; E. I. Sukenik, *Kedem,* II (1945), 83–88; A. Frenkel, ibid., 89; M.D. (U.) Cassuto, ibid., 90 f.; A. Akavia, ibid, 92–98. See also Cassuto, ibid., 99–120, who republished the Hebrew 9th century inscriptions of Venosa, dated by the era of the Ḥurban, first edited by G. I. Ascoli, *Inscrizioni inedite or mal note greche, latine, ebraiche di antichi sepolcri guidaici del Napolitano* (Torino and Rome, 1880), 66–79; Frey, *CII,* I, Nos. 469–619. See also S. Baron, *Social and Religious History of the Jews* (Philadelphia: Jewish Publication Society, 1952), 116; 376 n. 33; M. Kasher *Torah Shelemah* (New York: American Biblical Encyclopedia Society, 1949), XIII, 176–79.

98 I follow the reading of Cowley and Sukenik (see previous note), rather than that of Daiches, et al. For the meaning of *nefesh,* see Sukenik (previous note). 84 f., who, however, in line 1 of Inscription B, renders *nefesh* as *ẓiyyun* (monument), but "soul" seems perhaps preferable.

Inscription B (Sukenik)

1. Here (rests) the soul	הדה נפשה	1
2. of Esther the daughter	דאסתר ברתה	2
3. of Edyo, who died	דעדיו דמיתת	3
4. in the month of Shevat	בירח שבט	4
5. of the year "3 of Shemitah"	שנת ג דשמטת[ה]	5
6. the year of three hundred [and 3]	שנת תלת מא [ותלת] [99]	6
7. of the years of the Ḥurban	מן שנין לחרבן	7
8. of the House of the Temple	בית מקדשה	8
9. Peace! Peace!	שלום שלום	9
10. A burnt-offering! (?)	עלת [100]	10

Inscription C (Sukenik)

1. May the soul rest of Ḥalifo	תתניח נפשה דחלפו	1
2. the daughter [of ...] who died	ברתה / / / דמיתת	2
3. on Tuesday, the eleventh	ביום תלתה בחדעשר	3
4. day of the month of Elul, "the year [2]	יומין בירח אלול	4
	בשת [ב] [101]	
5. of Shemitah," which is the year	דשמטתה דהיא שנת	5
6. four hundred and thirty	ארבע מאה ותלתין	6
7. and five years after the Ḥurban	וחמש שנין לחרבן	7
8. of the House of the Temple, Peace	בית מקדשה שלום	8
9. to Israel. Peace!	על ישראל שלום.	9

The readings of the three inscriptions, if not emended, present inconsistent synchronisms of the Ḥurban era and Shemitah:

A	Marḥeshwan	364 of Ḥurban	1 of Shemitah cycle
B	Shevat	300 of Ḥurban	3 of Shemitah cycle
C	Elul	435 of Ḥurban	7 of Shemitah cycle

For if the year 300 of the Ḥurban, as B apparently reads, was the year 3 of the Shemitah, then 364 should have been year 4 $(7 \times 9 + 1 = 64)$, and 435 the year 5 of the Sabbatical cycle. If, however, with Inscrip-

99 See below, p. 182.
100 Sukenik (note 97), 86, leaves the meaning of עלת open. See Targum (Onk, and Ps.-Jon.) on Num. 29:23, though the form usually appears only in the construct עלתא possibly suggests that she died on the Rosh Ḥodesh, when a special burnt offering was sacrificed (Numb. 28–23), the day of the month having been inadvertently omitted (for other omissions see below). Possibly, however, the death of Esther the daughter of Edio resulted from some kind of execution by enemies of the Jews.
101 See below, p. 182.

tion A we assume that 364 was year 1 of Shemitah, then 300 should have been the year 7 and 435 the year 2 of the septennial cycle. Should we take C as the basis, i.e., that 435 was a Sabbatical year, then 300 should have been the year 5, and 364 the year 6 of the Shemitah cycle. To synchronize the dates of the tombstones, Umberto Cassuto proposed to emend line 7 of inscription A: רבע (four) to חמש (five); line 7 of B instead of מן (since) to [ו]מו[ן] ([and] 46), and to assume that the beginning of the year of the Ḥurban era of C began not in Tishri, but on the ninth of Ab.[102] Akavia thought that קדמיתה "of the first year of Shemitah," may perhaps be more properly rendered here as the year preceding (i.e., the year 6) of the Shemitah; in B instead of "the year 3," read "5," but in a note to his own article he conceded that no plausible solution for the reconciliation of the Sabbatical chronology of the three inscriptions is possible.[103] None of the tombstones' dates of Shemitah, if not radically emended, corresponds to Zuckermann's table of Sabbatical years, which Cassuto and Akavia take for granted.

But the calendar appended to this study requires the Julian year of 434/35, which equals 364 of Ḥurban to be the first year of a Sabbatical cycle, in consonance with Inscription A. The synchronisms of B and C remain problematical, however. The solution would seem to lie, as assumed in the transcription above, in the negligence of the engravers of tombstones B and C. On line 6 of B, if not destroyed by age, the engraver forgot to inscribe the last word ותלת or וג "and 3" (three); at the end of line 5 of C, the missing word is ב "of 2."[104] Although with these proposed readings we have a consistent chronology of Shemitah for all three tombstones, we exclude Inscriptions B and C from our discussion since their dates are only conjectural.

If the preceding is correct, Inscription A yields the date of the Ḥurban according to the Jewish era (known as ליצירה or לבריאת העולם) a problem that aroused much controversy among Rashi, Rashbam, Jacob Tam, and Maimonides, and in modern times, between Shir (Shelomoh Yehudah Leib Rapoport) and Ch. J. Bornstein.[105] One reason for the doubt stems from the fact that the era of Yezirah or Beri'at Ha'olam came into vogue some centuries after the Ḥurban, having been superimposed

---

102 Cassuto, *Kedem,* II, (1945), 90 f.

103 Akavia, *Kedem,* II, (1945), 92–98, esp. 94, note 3.

104 For another such negligence by the engraver of B, see his omission of the day of Shevat. It should also be noted that the construction of בשת דשמטתה, in lines 4–5 of C, implies a missing date of the Sabbatical cycle. If the intended meaning were "in the year of Shemitah," it would have said either בשמטתה or בשת שמטתה without the ד.

105 See above notes 74; 79–80. See also Bornstein, *Hatekufah,* 8 (1921), 321–31.

upon the Seleucid era, in which the Babylonian minhag and that of Eretz Israel diverged.[106] Another reason was that in our rabbinic permanent calendar the year follows the Babylonian custom of beginning the year in Tishri in contrast to the Palestinian tradition which commenced the year in Nisan.[107]

Now let us see which of the Jewish dates of the era of the Ḥurban proposed by the rabbinic savants—3828, 3829, or 3830—conforms to our inscription:[108]

1) $3828 + 364 = 4192$ 2) $4192 : 7 = 598 + 6$
    $3829 + 364 = 4193$ $4193 : 7 = 599 + 0$
    $3830 + 364 = 4194$ $4194 : 7 = 599 + 1$

Since Inscription A synchronizes 364 of the era of the Ḥurban with the first year of the Shemitah cycle and since 364 is divisible by 7, it follows that the first year of the Ḥurban era (not the date of the destruction) was also the first year of a Shemitah cycle. It further follows that 3830 equals the first year of the Ḥurban, which is to say that 3829, the date of the Second Temple's actual destruction, and 4193 of Yeẓirah or 363 of Ḥurban were Sabbatical years. Hence, the formula for finding the year of the Shemitah cycle for any given date is either the era of Yeẓirah or Ḥurban or (date + 1): 7.[109] It follows that the inscription's 364 of Ḥurban era equaled our 4194 of Yeẓirah.

The reader should remember, however, that for reasons alluded to above, the era of Yeẓirah discussed here is not identical with the one

106 The oldest reference to this divergence is that of Saadia Gaon, as cited by Abraham bar Hiyya, *Sefer Ha'ibur* (London, 1851), 96 f.: 1238 A.S. (936/7 C.E.) corresponded to the Jewish year of 4686; not 4687, which Saadia says is erroneous. In some computations, however, there is a divergence of two years. See also Bornstein, *Hatekufah,* 9 (1921), 224–30.

107 As explained by Razah (note 80), the difference has its origin in the dispute whether the first lunation (*molad*) of Tishri begins as in the Western Jewish Calendar with בהר"ד (Monday, 5th hour, 204/1080), or, as in the East, one year later, with וי"ד (Friday, 14th hour). See now A. Akavia, *The Calendar and its Use for Chronological Purposes* (Jerusalem: the Magnes Press, 1953), 64–66; Frank, *Talmudic and Rabbinical Chronology,* passim, esp. 13 ff. The divergence between the two eras of Yeẓirah, however, is probably older than the setting of the first *molad*.

108 The reader should keep in mind that the date of the actual destruction of the Temple and the era of the Ḥurban are not necessarily identical. There is no doubt that the Second Temple was burned sometime in Ab (August–September) of the year 70. The first year of the Ḥurban either begins with Nisan 70/Adar 71 or with Tishri 70/Elul 71. The controversy hinges, however, on whether the first year of Ḥurban equaled the 3828, 3829, or 3830 of Yeẓirah. In other words, those who say that 3828 would also say that the current year of 5733 is in fact 5731. See above, note 106.

109 As Reinach noted (*REJ* 85 [1928], 4 f.), the dating of Inscription A conforms to that of Huna in Avodah Zarah, 9a (section 8).

currently in practice. The current Jewish dating has one year more than the old era of Yeẓirah. The Julian date for the latter is October 3760 B.C.E.; for the former October 3761 B.C.E.[110] Table Four lists the Julian, Seleucid, Ḥurban, and Jewish (old and new styles) years of the ten historical Shemitot discussed in this paper.

TABLE FOUR

Source	Section	Julian Year	Anno Sel.	Yeẓirah Old	Yeẓirah New	Ḥurban
Neh. 10:32(31)	1	?		?	?	
A.J. 11:347	2	331/30 B.C.E.		3430	3431	
I Macc. 6:49,53	3	163/62 B.C.E.	149/50	3598	3599	
A.J. 13:234	4	135/34 B.C.E.	177/78	3626	3627	
A.J. 14:475	5	37/36 B.C.E.	275/76	3724	3725	
M. Sotah 7:8	6	41/42 C.E.	352/53	3801	3802	
Mur 18	7	55/56 C.E.	366/67	3815	3816	
Seder Olam 30	8	69/70 C.E.	380/81	3829	3830	
Mur 24	9	132/33 C.E.	443/44	3892	3893	62
Kedem II, 84	10	433/34 C.E.	744/45	4193	4194	363
		440/41 C.E.	751/52	4200	4201	370

110 The third formula, which diverges from the current era of Yeẓirah by two years, is ignored here (see notes 102, 106).

APPENDIX

A CALENDAR OF SABBATICAL CYCLES
FROM 519/18 BEFORE THE CHRISTIAN, ERA TO 440/41 OF
THE CHRISTIAN ERA

Ruler	B.C.E.	Ruler	B.C.E.	Ruler	B.C.E.	Ruler	B.C.E.
Darius I	1. 519/18		1. 477/76		1. 435/34		1. 393/92
	2. 518/17		2. 476/75		2. 434/33		2. 392/91
	3. 517/16		3. 475/74		3. 433/32		3. 391/90
	4. 516/15		4. 474/73		4. 432/31		4. 390/89
	5. 515/14		5. 473/72		5. 431/30		5. 389/88
	6. 514/13		6. 472/71		6. 430/29		6. 388/87
	S. 513/12		S. 471/70		S. 429/28		S. 387/86
	1. 512/11		1. 470/69		1. 428/27		1. 386/85
	2. 511/10		2. 469/68		2. 427/26		2. 385/84
	3. 510/09		3. 468/67		3. 426/25		3. 384/83
	4. 509/08		4. 467/66		4. 425/24		4. 383/82
	5. 508/07		5. 466/65		5. 424/23		5. 382/81
	6. 507/06		6. 465/64	Darius II	6. 423/22		6. 381/80
	S. 506/05	Artaxerxes I	S. 464/63		S. 422/21		S. 380/79
	1. 505/04		1. 463/62		1. 421/20		1. 379/78
	2. 504/03		2. 462/61		2. 420/19		2. 378/77
	3. 503/02		3. 461/60		3. 419/18		3. 377/76
	4. 502/01		4. 460/59		4. 418/17		4. 376/75
	5. 501/00		5. 459/58		5. 417/16		5. 375/74
	6. 500/499		6. 458/57		6. 416/15		6. 374/73
	S. 499/98		S. 457/56		S. 415/14		S. 373/72
	1. 498/97		1. 456/55		1. 414/13		1. 372/71
	2. 497/96		2. 455/54		2. 413/12		2. 371/70
	3. 496/95		3. 454/53		3. 412/11		3. 370/69
	4. 495/94		4. 453/52		4. 411/10		4. 369/68
	5. 494/93		5. 452/51		5. 410/09		5. 368/67
	6. 493/92		6. 451/50		6. 409/08		6. 367/66
	S. 492/91		S. 450/49		S. 408/07		S. 366/65
	1. 491/90		1. 449/48		1. 407/06		1. 365/64
	2. 490/89		2. 448/47		2. 406/05		2. 364/63
	3. 489/88		3. 447/46	Artaxerxes II	3. 405/04		3. 363/62
Xerxes	4. 488/87		4. 446/45		4. 404/03		4. 362/61
	5. 487/86		5. 445/44		5. 403/02		5. 361/60
	6. 486/85		6. 444/43		6. 402/01		6. 360/59
	S. 485/84		S. 443/42		S. 401/00	Artaxerxes III	S. 359/58
	1. 484/83		1. 442/41		1. 400/399		1. 358/57
	2. 483/82		2. 441/40		2. 399/98		2. 357/56
	3. 482/81		3. 440/39		3. 398/97		3. 356/55
	4. 481/80		4. 439/38		4. 397/96		4. 355/54
	5. 480/79		5, 438/37		5. 396/95		5. 354/53
	6. 479/78		6. 437/36		6. 395/94		6. 353/52
	S. 478/77		S. 436/35		S. 394/93		S. 352/51

Ruler	B.C.E.	Ruler	S.E.	B.C.E.	Ruler	S.E.	B.C.E.
	1. 351/50		3	1. 309/08		38	1. 274/73
	2. 350/49		4	2. 308/07		39	2. 273/72
	3. 349/48		5	3. 307/06		40	3. 272/71
	4. 348/47		6	4. 306/05		41	4. 271/70
	5. 347/46	Ptolemy I	7	5. 305/04		42	5. 270/69
	6. 346/45		8	6. 304/03		43	6. 269/68
	S. 345/44		9	S. 303/02		44	S. 268/67
	1. 344/43		10	1. 302/01		45	1. 267/66
	2. 343/42		11	2. 301/00		46	2. 266/65
	3. 342/41		12	3. 300/299		47	3. 265/64
	4. 341/40		13	4. 299/98		48	4. 264/63
	5. 340/39		14	5. 298/97		49	5. 263/62
	6. 339/38		15	6. 297/96		50	6. 262/61
Arses	S. 338/37		16	S. 296/95	Antiochus II	51	S. 261/60
	1. 337/36		17	1. 295/94		52	1. 260/59
Darius III	2. 336/35		18	2. 294/93		53	2. 259/58
	3. 335/34		19	3. 293/92		54	3. 258/57
	4. 334/33		20	4. 292/91		55	4. 257/56
Alexander III	5. 333/32		21	5. 291/90		56	5. 256/55
	6. 332/31		22	6. 290/89		57	6. 255/54
	S. 331/30		23	S. 289/88		58	S. 254/53
	1. 330/29		24	1. 288/87		59	1. 253/52
	2. 329/28		25	2. 287/86		60	2. 252/51
	3. 328/27		26	3. 286/85		61	3. 251/50
	4. 327/26		27	4. 285/84		62	4. 250/49
	5. 326/25		28	5. 284/83		63	5. 249/48
	6. 325/24		29	6. 283/82		64	6. 248/47
	S. 324/23	Ptolemy II	30	S. 282/81		65	S. 247/46
Philip	1. 323/22	Antiochus I	31	1. 281/80	Ptolemy III	66	1. 246/45
	2. 322/21		32	2. 280/79		67	2. 245/44
	3. 321/20		33	3. 279/78		68	3. 244/43
	4. 320/19		34	4. 278/77		69	4. 243/42
	5. 319/18		35	5. 277/76		70	5. 242/41
	6. 318/17		36	6. 276/75		71	6. 241/40
	S. 317/16		37	S. 275/74		72	S. 240/39
Alexander IV	1. 316/15						
	2. 315/14						
	3. 314/13						
	4. 314/12						
	5. 312/11						

S.E.

Ruler	S.E.	B.C.E.
Seleucus I	1	6. 311/10
	2	S. 310/09

Ruler	S.E.	B.C.E.	Ruler	S.E.	B.C.E.
	73	1. 239/38		115	1. 197/96
	74	2. 238/37		116	2. 196/95
	75	3. 237/36		117	3. 195/94
	76	4. 236/35		118	4. 194/93
	77	5. 235/34		119	5. 193/92
	78	6. 234/33		120	6. 192/91
	79	S. 233/32		121	S. 191/90
	80	1. 232/31		122	1. 190/89
	81	2. 231/30		123	2. 189/88
	82	3. 230/29		124	3. 188/87
	83	4. 229/28	Seleucus IV	125	4. 187/86
	84	5. 228/27		126	5. 186/85
	85	6. 227/26		127	6. 185/84
	86	S. 226/25		128	S. 184/83
Seleucus III	87	1. 225/24		129	1. 183/82
	88	2. 224/23		130	2. 182/81
Antiochus III	89	3. 223/22		131	3. 181/80
	90	4. 222/21		132	4. 180/79
	91	5. 221/20		133	5. 179/78
	92	6. 220/19		134	6. 178/77
	93	S. 219/18		135	S. 177/76
	94	1. 218/17		136	1. 176/75
	95	2. 217/16	Antiochus IV	137	2. 175/74
	96	3. 216/15		138	3. 174/73
	97	4. 215/14		139	4. 173/72
	98	5. 214/13		140	5. 172/71
	99	6. 213/12		141	6. 171/70
	100	S. 212/11		142	S. 170/69
	101	1. 211/10		143	1. 169/68
	102	2. 210/09		144	2. 168/67
	103	3. 209/08		145	3. 167/66
	104	4. 208/07		146	4. 166/65
	105	5. 207/06		147	5. 165/64
	106	6. 206/05	Antiochus V	148	6. 164/63
Ptolemy IV	107	S. 205/04		149	S. 163/62
	108	1. 204/03		150	1. 162/61
	109	2. 203/02	Demetrius I	151	2. 161/60
	110	3. 202/01		152	3. 160/59
	111	4. 201/200		153	4. 159/58
	112	5. 200/199		154	5. 158/57
	113	6. 199/198		155	6. 157/56
	114	S. 198/197		156	S. 156/55

Ruler	S.E.	B.C.E.	Ruler	S.E.	B.C.E.
	157	1. 155/54		185	1. 127/26
	158	2. 154/53		186	2. 126/25
	159	3. 153/52		187	3. 125/24
	160	4. 152/51		188	4. 124/23
	161	5. 151/50		189	5. 123/22
Alexander I	162	6. 150/49		190	6. 122/21
	163	S. 149/48		191	S. 121/20
	164	1. 148/47		192	1. 120/19
	165	2. 147/46		193	2. 119/18
	166	3. 146/45		194	3. 118/17
Demetrius II	167	4. 145/44		195	4. 117/16
	168	5. 144/43		196	5. 116/15
Antiochus VI	169	6. 143/42		197	6. 115/14
Simon	170	S. 142/41		198	S. 114/13
	171	1. 141/40		199	1. 113/12
	172	2. 140/39		200	2. 112/11
Antiochus VII	173	3. 139/38		201	3. 111/10
	174	4. 138/37		202	4. 110/09
	175	5. 137/36		203	5. 109/08
	176	6. 136/35		204	6. 108/07
John Hycranus	177	S. 135/34		205	S. 107/06
	178	1. 134/33		206	1. 106/05
	179	2. 133/32		207	2. 105/04
	180	3. 132/31	Aristobulus I	208	3. 104/03
	181	4. 131/30	Alexander Janneus	209	4. 103/02
	182	5. 130/29		210	5. 102/01
	183	6. 129/28		211	6. 101/00
	184	S. 128/27		212	S. 100/99

Ruler	S.E.	B.C.E.		Ruler	S.E.	B.C.E.	
	213	1.	99/98	Pompey	248	1.	64/63
	214	2.	98/97	(Hyrcanus II)	249	2.	63/62
	215	3.	97/96		250	3.	62/61
	216	4.	96/95		251	4.	61/60
	217	5.	95/94		252	5.	60/59
	218	6.	94/93		253	6.	59/58
	219	S.	93/92		254	S.	58/57
	220	1.	92/91		255	1.	57/56
	221	2.	91/90		256	2.	56/55
	222	3.	90/89		257	3.	55/54
	223	4.	89/88		258	4.	54/53
	224	5.	88/87		259	5.	53/52
	225	6.	87/86		260	6.	52/51
	226	S.	86/85		261	S.	51/50
	227	1.	85/84		262	1.	50/49
	228	2.	84/83	Julius Caesar	263	2.	49/48
	229	3.	83/82		264	3.	48/47
	230	4.	82/81		265	4.	47/46
	231	5.	81/80		266	5.	46/45
	232	6.	80/79		267	6.	45/44
	233	S.	79/78	Triumvirate	268	S.	44/43
	234	1.	78/77		269	1.	43/42
	235	2.	77/76		270	2.	42/41
Alexandra	236	3.	76/75		271	3.	41/40
	237	4.	75/74		272	4.	40/39
	238	5.	74/73		273	5.	39/38
	239	6.	73/72		274	6.	38/37
	240	S.	72/71	(Herod)	275	S.	37/36
	241	1.	71/70		276	1.	36/35
	242	2.	70/69		277	2.	35/34
	243	3.	69/68		278	3.	34/33
Aristobulus II	244	4.	68/67		279	4.	33/32
	245	5.	67/66		280	5.	32/31
	246	6.	66/65	Augustus	281	6.	31/30
	247	S.	65/64		282	S.	30/29

Ruler	S.E.	B.C.E.	Ruler	S.E.	C.E.
	283	1. 29/28		318	1. 7/8
	284	2. 28/27		319	2. 8/9
	285	3. 27/26		320	3. 9/10
	286	4. 26/25		321	4. 10/11
	287	5. 25/24		322	5. 11/12
	288	6. 24/23		323	6. 12/13
	289	S. 23/22	Tiberius	324	S. 13/14
	290	1. 22/21		425	1. 14/15
	291	2. 21/20		326	2. 15/16
	292	3. 20/19		327	3. 16/17
	293	4. 19/18		328	4. 17/18
	294	5. 18/17		329	5. 18/19
	295	6. 17/16		330	6. 19/20
	296	S. 16/15		331	S. 20/21
	297	1. 15/14		332	1. 21/22
	298	2. 14/13		333	2. 22/23
	299	3. 13/12		334	3. 23/24
	300	4. 12/11		335	4. 24/25
	301	5. 11/10		336	5. 25/26
	302	6. 10/9		337	6. 26/27
	303	S. 9/8		338	S. 27/28
	304	1. 8/7		339	1. 28/29
	305	2. 7/6		340	2. 29/30
	306	3. 6/5		341	3. 30/31
	307	4. 5/4		342	4. 31/32
(Archelaus)	308	5. 4/3		343	5. 32/33
	309	6. 3/2		344	6. 33/34
	310	S. 2/1		345	S. 34/35
	311	1. 1 B.C.E./1 C.E.		346	1. 35/36
	312	2. 1/2	Caligula	347	2. 36/37
	313	3. 2/3		348	3. 37/38
	314	4. 3/4		349	4. 38/39
	315	5. 4/5		350	5. 39/40
	316	6. 5/6	Claudius	351	6. 40/41
(Procurators)	317	S. 6/7	(Agrippa II)	352	S. 41/42

Ruler	S.E.	C.E.	Ruler	S.E.	S.E.
	353	1. 42/43		388	1. 77/78
	354	2. 43/44	Titus	389	2. 78/79
	355	3. 44/45		390	3. 79/80
	356	4. 45/46		391	4. 80/81
	357	5. 46/47	Domitian	392	5. 81/82
	358	6. 47/48		393	6. 82/83
	359	S. 48/49		394	S. 83/84
	360	1. 49/50		395	1. 84/85
	361	2. 50/51		396	2. 85/86
	362	3. 51/52		397	3. 86/87
	363	4. 52/53		398	4. 87/88
Nero	364	5. 53/54		399	5. 88/89
	365	6. 54/55		400	6. 89/90
	366	S. 55/56		401	S. 90/91
	367	1. 56/57		402	1. 91/92
	368	2. 57/58		403	2. 92/93
	369	3. 58/59		404	3. 93/94
	370	4. 59/60		405	4. 94/95
	371	5. 60/61	Nerva	406	5. 95/96
	372	6. 61/62		407	6. 96/97
	373	S. 62/63	Trajan	408	S. 97/98
	374	1. 63/64		409	1. 98/99
	375	2. 64/65		410	2. 99/100
	376	3. 65/66		411	3. 100/01
	377	4. 66/67		412	4. 101/02
Galba	378	5. 67/68		413	5. 102/03
Otho	379	6. 68/69		414	6. 103/04
Vespasian	380	S. 69/70		415	S. 104/05
	381	1. 70/71		416	1. 105/06
	382	2. 71/72		417	2. 106/07
	383	3. 72/73		418	3. 107/08
	384	4. 73/74		419	4. 108/09
	385	5. 74/75		420	5. 109/110
	386	6. 75/76		421	6. 110/111
	387	S. 76/77		422	S. 111/112

Ruler	S.E.	C.E.	Ruler	S.E.	C.E.
	423	1. 112/13		458	1. 147/48
	424	2. 113/14		459	2. 148/49
	425	3. 114/15		460	3. 149/50
	426	4. 115/16		461	4. 150/51
Hadrian	427	5. 116/17		462	5. 151/52
	428	6. 117/18		463	6. 152/53
	429	S. 118/19		464	S. 153/54
	430	1. 119/20		465	1. 154/55
	431	2. 120/21		466	2. 155/56
	432	3. 121/22		467	3. 156/57
	433	4. 122/23		468	4. 157/58
	434	5. 123/24		469	5. 158/59
	435	6. 124/25		470	6. 159/60
	436	S. 125/26	Marcus Aurelius	471	S. 160/61
	437	1. 126/27		472	1. 161/62
	438	2. 127/28		473	2. 162/63
	439	3. 128/29		474	3. 163/64
	440	3. 129/30		475	4. 164/65
	441	5. 130/31		476	5. 165/66
	442	6. 131/32		477	6. 166/67
	443	S. 132/33		478	S. 167/68
	444	1. 133/34		479	1. 168/69
	445	2. 134/35		480	2. 169/70
	446	3. 135/36		481	3. 170/71
	447	4. 136/37		482	4. 171/72
Antoninus Pius	448	5. 137/38		483	5. 172/73
	449	6. 138/39		484	6. 173/74
	450	S. 139/40		485	S. 174/75
	451	1. 140/41		486	1. 175/76
	452	2. 141/42	Commodus	487	2. 176/77
	453	3. 142/43		488	3. 177/78
	454	4. 143/44		489	4. 178/79
	455	5. 144/45		490	5. 179/80
	456	6. 145/46		491	6. 180/81
	457	S. 146/47		492	S. 181/82

Ruler	S.E.	C.E.	Ruler	S.E.	C.E.
	493	1. 182/83	Elagabalus	528	1. 217/18
	494	2. 183/84		529	2. 218/19
	495	3. 184/85		530	3. 219/20
	496	4. 185/86		531	4. 220/21
	497	5. 186/87		532	5. 221/22
	498	6. 187/88	Severus Alexander	533	6. 222/23
	499	S. 188/89		534	S. 223/24
	500	1. 189/90		535	1. 224/25
	501	2. 190/91		536	2. 225/26
	502	3. 191/92		537	3. 226/27
Pertinax: Julianus	503	4. 192/93		538	4. 227/28
Septimus Severus	504	5. 193/94		539	5. 228/29
	505	6. 194/95		540	6. 229/30
	506	S. 195/96		541	S. 230/31
	507	1. 196/97		542	1. 231/32
	508	2. 197/98		543	2. 232/33
	509	3. 198/99		544	3. 233/34
	510	4. 199/200		545	4. 234/35
	511	5. 200/01	Maximinus Thrax	546	5. 235/36
	512	6. 201/02		547	6. 236/37
	513	S. 202/03	Gordian I	548	S. 237/38
	514	1. 203/04	Gordian III	549	1. 238/39
	515	2. 204/05		550	2. 239/40
	516	3. 205/06		551	3. 240/41
	517	4. 206/07		552	4. 241/42
	518	5. 207/08		553	5. 242/43
	519	6. 208/09	Philip	554	6. 243/44
	520	S. 209/10		555	S. 244/45
	521	1. 210/11		556	1. 245/46
Caracalla	522	2. 211/12		557	2. 246/47
	523	3. 212/13		558	3. 247/48
	524	4. 213/14	Decius	559	4. 248/49
	525	5. 214/15		560	5. 249/50
	526	6. 215/16		561	6. 250/51
Macrinus	527	S. 216/17	Gallus	562	S. 251/52

Ruler	S.E.	C.E.	Ruler	S.E.	C.E.
Aemilianus	563	1. 252/53		598	1. 287/88
Gallienus II	564	2. 253/54		599	2. 288/89
	565	3. 254/55		600	3. 289/90
	566	4. 255/56		601	4. 290/91
	567	5. 256/57		602	5. 291/92
	568	6. 257/58		603	6. 292/93
Gallienus III	569	S. 258/59	Constantius I	604	S. 293/94
	570	1. 259/60		605	1. 294/95
	571	2. 260/61		606	2. 295/96
	572	3. 261/62		607	3. 296/97
	573	4. 262/63		608	4. 297/98
	574	5. 263/64		609	5. 298/99
	575	6. 264/65		610	6. 299/300
	576	S. 265/66		611	S. 300/01
	577	1. 266/67		612	1. 301/02
Claudius II	578	2. 267/68		613	2. 302/03
	579	3. 268/69		614	3. 303/04
Quintillus	580	4. 269/70		615	4. 304/05
Aurelian	581	5. 270/71	Constantine I	616	5. 305/06
	582	6. 271/72		617	6. 306/07
	583	S. 272/73		618	S. 307/08
	584	1. 273/74		619	1. 308/09
Tacitus	585	2. 274/75		620	2. 309/10
Florianus	586	3. 275/76		621	3. 310/11
Probus	587	4. 276/77		622	4. 311/12
	588	5. 277/78		623	5. 312/13
	589	6. 278/79		624	6. 313/14
	590	S. 279/80		625	S. 314/15
	591	1. 280/81		626	1. 315/16
Carus	592	2. 281/82		627	2. 316/17
Carimus	593	3. 282/83		628	3. 317/18
Diocletian	594	4. 283/84		629	4. 318/19
	595	5. 284/85		630	5. 319/20
	596	6. 285/86		631	6. 320/21
	597	S. 286/87		632	S. 321/22

Ruler	S.E.	C.E.	Ruler	S.E.	C.E.
	633	1. 322/23		668	1. 357/58
	634	2. 323/24		669	2. 358/59
	635	3. 324/25		670	3. 359/60
	636	4. 325/26	Julian the Apostate	671	4. 360/61
	637	5. 326/27		672	5. 361/62
	638	6. 327/28		673	6. 362/63
	639	S. 328/29	Jovian	674	S. 363/64
	640	1. 329/30	Valens	675	1. 364/65
	641	2. 330/31		676	2. 365/66
	642	3. 331/32		677	3. 366/67
	643	4. 332/33		678	4. 367/68
	644	5. 333/34		679	5. 368/69
	645	6. 334/35		680	6. 369/70
	646	S. 335/36		681	S. 370/71
Constantius II	647	1. 336/37		682	1. 371/72
	648	2. 337/38		683	2. 372/73
	649	3. 338/39		684	3. 373/74
	650	4. 339/40		685	4. 374/75
	651	5. 340/41		686	5. 375/76
	652	6. 341/42		687	6. 376/77
	653	S. 342/43		688	S. 377/78
	654	1. 343/44	Theodosius I	689	1. 378/79
	655	2. 344/45		690	2. 379/80
	656	3. 345/46		691	3. 380/81
	657	4. 346/47		692	4. 381/82
	658	5. 347/48		693	5. 382/83
	659	6. 348/49	Arcadius	694	6. 383/84
	660	S. 349/50		695	S. 384/85
	661	1. 350/51		696	1. 385/86
	662	2. 351/52		697	2. 386/87
	663	3. 352/53		698	3. 387/88
	664	4. 353/54		699	4. 388/89
	665	5. 354/55		700	5. 389/90
	666	6. 355/56		701	6. 390/91
	667	S. 356/57		702	S. 391/92

Ruler	S.E.	Ruler	Ruler	S.E.	C.E.
	703	1. 392/93		731	1. 420/21
	704	2. 393/94		732	2. 421/22
	705	3. 394/95		733	3. 422/23
	706	4. 395/96		734	4. 423/24
	707	5. 396/97		735	5. 424/25
	708	6. 397/98		736	6. 425/26
	709	S. 398/99		737	S. 426/27
	710	1. 399/400		738	1. 427/28
	711	2. 400/01		739	2. 428/29
	712	3. 401/02		740	3. 429/30
	713	4. 402/03		741	4. 430/31
	714	5. 403/04		742	5. 431/32
	715	6. 404/05		743	6. 432/33
	716	S. 405/06		744	S. 433/34
	717	1. 406/07		745	1. 434/35
	718	2. 407/08		746	2. 435/36
Theodosius II	719	3. 408/09		747	3. 436/37
	720	4. 409/10		748	4. 437/38
	721	5. 410/11		749	5. 438/39
	722	6. 411/12		750	6. 439/40
	723	S. 412/13		751	S. 440/41
	724	1. 413/14			
	725	2. 414/15			
	726	3. 415/16			
	727	4. 416/17			
	728	5. 417/18			
	729	6. 418/19			
	730	S. 419/20			

HOW LONG DID ABRAM STAY IN EGYPT?

A STUDY IN HELLENISTIC, QUMRAN, AND RABBINIC CHRONOGRAPHY

IN GEN. 12:11–20 Sarai's seizure by Pharaoh is related. To the modern reader this episode may appear as minor and not especially edifying. To the ancients, however, the encounter between Pharaoh and the traveler from Ur of the Chaldees seemed as a crucial event in the history of mankind. This was necessarily true during the Hellenistic period when Egypt was a major power and Alexandria the leading metropolis of the world. During the Roman period, to judge from the rabbinic sources, Abram's journey into Egypt is relatively ignored, compared to great wealth of patriarchal lore recorded.[1] The Hellenistic Jewish writers, however, made it appear that the meeting between Abram and Pharaoh was significant for the Jewish people and mankind. This remains evident from the few fragments of the Hellenistic Jewish writers even though the literature is lost.[2] The extent to which some ancients treated the patriarch's journey into Egypt can be seen in the recently deciphered Genesis Apocryphon.[3] This Aramaic scroll devotes more space to the patriarch's adventures

---

[1] See for example Gen. Rabbah, 38–40, pp. 361–90 (Theodor-Albeck), where the patriarch's encounter with Nimrod is retold at length, but knows nothing of Abram's activities in Egypt, though Sarai's miraculous delivery is stressed.

[2] Preserved mainly by Euseb., *Praep. Ev.*, IX, 17 ff. = F. Jacoby, *Die Fragmente der griechischen Historiker*, IIIC, Pt. 2 (Leiden, 1957), Nos. 722–37. Hereafter cited as "*FGrH.*" J. Freudenthal, *Alexander Polyhistor und die von ihm erhaltenen Reste jüdäischer und samaritanischer Geschichtswerke* (Breslau, 1875); Stearns, *Fragments from Graeco-Jewish Writers* (Chicago, 1908).

[3] N. Avigad and Y. Yadin (eds.), *A Genesis Apocryphon* (Jerusalem, 1956). For the secondary literature, see J. A. Fitzmyer, "Some Observations on the *Genesis Apocryphon*," *Catholic Biblical Quarterly*, 22 (1960), 277, n. 6. To which add: E. Osswald, "Beobachtungen zur Erzählung von Abrahams Aufenthalt in Ägypten in 'Genesis Apocryphon,'" *ZAW*, 72 (1960), 7–25; J. Finkel, "The Author of Genesis Apocryphon Knew the Book of Esther," [in Hebrew] *Meḥqarim bamegilloth hagenuzoth* (Jerusalem, 1961), 163–82; H. H. Rowley, "Notes on the Aramaic of Genesis Apocryphon," *Hebrew and Semitic Studies Presented to G. R. Driver* (Oxford, 1963), 116–29.

43

in Egypt than to any other theme.[4] There is, then, no reason to doubt that the ancients, having converted a minor episode into a major theme, infused into it great significance.

Among the questions the ancient authors considered were: What was the real purpose of the patriarch's journey to Egypt? How long did he stay there? The Graeco-Jewish writers, some of whom must have lived in Egypt, were deeply interested in these problems too. Unhappily, the chronology of the professional biblical chronographer, Demetrius (221–204 B. C.) for the Abrahamic period is lost.[5] Artapanus, a biblical romancer (before 80 B. C.), claimed that Abram stayed in Egypt twenty years.[6] Other Hellenistic Jewish writers, such as Pseudo-Eupolemus (a Samaritan, *circa* 200 B. C.), did not give an exact date.[7] But the general point of view of these writers was that the patriarch introduced the sciences including astrology to Egypt. According to Pseudo-Eupolemus, Abram lived in Heliopolis where he instructed the Egyptians in the discoveries made by Enoch and by himself.[8] These claims, repeated in one way or another by Josephus and other Graeco-Jewish writers, as well as in the literature dependent on them, assumed that the patriarch lived in Egypt long enough to have been able to carry out his educational mission.[9]

In contrast to Artapanus' fantastic claim of a twenty-year stay, the author of the Book of Jubilees offers a detailed chronology, adding a scriptural citation, presumably to prove his dating: "And Abram went into Egypt in the third year of the week (1956 A. M.) and he dwelt in Egypt five years before his wife was torn away from him. Now Tanais in Egypt was at that time built — seven years after Hebron."[10] Omitting the patriarch's deception of Pharaoh, Jubilees repeats the account given in Gen. 12:14–17 concerning Sarai's seizure by the king, the plagues that followed, the numerous gifts Abram received upon her release, but intentionally ignores Pharaoh's reproof

---

[4] Genesis Apocryphon, cols. XIX, 7–XX, 32. cols. II–XXII retell Gen. 5:28–15:4.

[5] Demetrius, *FGrH*, 722 F 1 = Euseb. *Praep. Ev.* IX, 21, 16, gives the number of years from Abraham to the Exodus. Demetrius' chronology for the Abrahamic period was as detailed as that of Jacob's (722 F 1).

[6] Artapanus, *FGrH*, 726 F 1 = Euseb. *Praep. Ev.*, IX, 18, 1.

[7] Pseudo-Eupolemus, *FGrH*, 724 F 1 = Euseb. *Praep. Ev.*, IX, 17, 6–8.

[8] *Ibid.*

[9] *AJ*, I, 166; Philo, *De Abr.*, 69 ff. Cf. Tosefta, Qiddushin 5, 17; Bab. Shabbath, 156a; Bava Bathra, 16b, 91a–b; Gen. Rabbah, 44, p. 433; *Saadyana* (ed. Schechter), 93 f. See also Wacholder, "Pseudo-Eupolemus' Two Greek Fragments on Abraham," *HUCA*, XXXIV (1963), 83–113.

[10] Jub. 13:11–12 (Charles, *Apocrypha and Pseudepigrapha*, II [Oxford, 1913]).

to Abram: "Why did you say, 'She is my sister' " (Gen. 12:18–19). Abram returned to Canaan in the forty-first Jubilee, in the third year of the first week, i. e., 1963 A. M.[11] Jubilees then repeats Gen. 12:11–20, except that its author a) adds the chronology; b) omits the possible blemish on the patriarch's character;[12] and c) quotes Num. 12:22, that Hebron was built seven years before Zoan (Tanis).

The account of Abram's stay in Egypt in the Book of Jubilees raises several questions. If the author did not particularly admire the patriarch's activities in Egypt, why did he make him stay there seven years, contrary to the impression in Genesis? What is intended by the citation of Num. 13:22? Is it merely to yield the number seven? As a result of the successful decipherment of the account of Abram's stay in Egypt in the Genesis Apocryphon we have a better understanding of Jubilees' version of the same event. Like Jubilees, Genesis Apocryphon says, as pointed out by the editors, that Hebron was just completed when the patriarch was entering the Negeb, dwelling there two years before leaving for Egypt.[13] In Egypt, he successfully concealed Sarai for five years; when found, she was in the royal palace two years.[14] The chronology and sequence of events are the same in both works. However, only from Genesis Apocryphon can we determine the exact meaning of Jubilees' citation of Num. 13:22, quoted also by Josephus.[15] We learn that the citation of Num. 13:22 was not intended, as might be interpreted in Jubilees 13:11, to refer to the number of years that the patriarch spent in Egypt, but to the two years of his stay in Hebron plus the five years

[11] Jub. 13:13–15.

[12] That Jub. 13:11–15 intentionally conceals Abram's deception of Pharaoh has been frequently pointed out. See Charles' comments.

[13] Genesis Apocryphon, XIX, 9–10, reading, with Fitzmyer, *Catholic Biblical Quarterly*, 22 (1960), 287, . . . חמן] ין[שׁ תרתין], in the beginning of line 10.

[14] Genesis Apocryphon, XIX, 23; XXII, 28–29.

[15] *AJ*, I, 170: λαβὼν δ'αὐτὸς τὴν ὑπ'ἐκείνου καταλελειμμένην ὑπώρειαν ᾤκει ἐν τῇ Ναβρῶ πόλει· παλαιοτέρα δὲ ἐστιν ἔτεσιν ἐπτὰ Τάνιδος τῆς Αἰγύπτου. Josephus' words do not necessarily imply that these two cities were being built when the patriarch visited them, still this is probably Josephus' meaning, unless we assume that he copied the reference to Num. 13:22 without understanding it. In *BJ*, IV, 530, Josephus says that Hebron is not only older than any other Canaanite city but also older than Memphis, built 2300 years ago, counting from A. D. 68, Hebron being older by seven years. Josephus' failure to mention that the city was built when Abram settled there (*BJ*, IV, 530 f.), though he does mention the patriarch, indicates that unlike Jubilees and Genesis Apocryphon he understood Num. 13:22 to refer merely to the relative age of Hebron and Tanis (Memphis in *BJ*, IV, 530). This is also the view of the talmudic tradition, indicating that Josephus was sometimes influenced by the rabbinic tradition rather than by the exegesis preserved at Qumran.

when Sarai was concealed in Egypt. The patriarch lived in Zoan two years after its foundation just as he did in Hebron. As neither Gen. 12:9–20 nor Num. 13:22 hints at such a time scale, the time balance in the patriarch's sojourns must be credited to the author of Genesis Apocryphon.

Jubilees merely adds a chronology to the scriptural account, but Genesis Apocryphon weaves also a romance around Gen. 12:11–20. The author of the Aramaic scroll gives the exact route of the patriarch's itinerary and tells of a dream informing him of the impending kidnaping of Sarai.[16] We are not told anything of the events that happened during the five years of Sarai's concealment.[17] Evidently, nothing did. However, a substantial part of column XIX and the entire column XX are devoted to the adventures that occurred during the two years of Sarai's seizure. Though the text is missing, it seems that the completion of Zoan, named after Pharaoh Zoan,[18] ultimately caused Sarai's appearance. During the festivities, as the patriarch was entertained, in an Eastern fashion, by three Egyptian officials, "wisdom" as well as drinks was exchanged.[19] Having found Sarai's place of concealment, they admired her extraordinary beauty as they beheld her naked, which they unanimously reported to Pharaoh Zoan.[20] Taken to the house of the king, El Elyon's[21] punishment was swift and very severe, including plagues for which the royal magicians and healers could find no remedy. It was only when Sarai was restored to her husband and when Abram placed his hand on

---

[16] Genesis Apocryphon, XIX, 8–22.

[17] Genesis Apocryphon, XIX, 23.

[18] Pharaoh Zoan is the name given to the king (Gen. Apocryphon, XIX, 24; XX, 14. XIX, 22: וֹשֹׁרי למספנה לצען "...and Sarai towards Zoan," evidently refers to the city built by Pharaoh Zoan rather than to the prince. The author may have made a slip as Zoan was not yet completed (XIX, 23), but as the context is missing, it is not entirely clear what is meant.

[19] Genesis Apocryphon, XIX, 24 ff. "Three men from the princes of Egypt," (XIX, 24), one of whom is subsequently identified as חרקנוש (ḤRQNWŠ). It is generally assumed that ḤRQNWŠ is a proper name, sometimes identified as one of the Tobiads or Hasmoneans. This is unwarranted for the scroll does not otherwise contain contemporary names. ḤRQNWŠ is possibly the title of the leading officer who found Sarai and an early transcription of ἄρχον or, as is more likely, ἀρχώνης. The latter signifies a collector of revenue, a meaning that conforms to 'aggadic traditions that Sarai was seized by custom officers (Gen. Rabbah, 40, pp. 384 f.; Sefer Hayashar, [Warsaw, 1928], 42). See also Wacholder, HUCA, XXXIV (1963), 109 f.

[20] Genesis Apocryphon, XIX, 24–27; XX, 2–8.

[21] The use of Elyon throughout the scroll (XII, 17; XX, 12, 16; XXI, 2, 20), excluding the passages where its usage is expected (XXII, 15, 16 bis, 21), indicates that Genesis Apocryphon is to be dated during the second century B. C., perhaps, because of its affinities with, at the same time as Daniel.

Pharaoh Zoan's head that the evil spirit disappeared. Upon leaving Egypt, the patriarch was showered with gifts, not the least of which was Hagar the Egyptian.[22]

Genesis Apocryphon is primarily a literary work. But like Jubilees, Genesis Apocryphon is deeply concerned with chronological problems. This becomes particularly evident from its paraphrase of Gen. 15:1: "After these things the Lord appeared to Abram in a vision and said to him: 'Ten years have been completed since the day you left Haran, two years you have passed here, seven in Egypt, and one year since you have returned from Egypt.' "[23] The author's heavy emphasis on the chronological problem is indicated by his making the Lord himself reiterate the scheme. Why this constant reiteration?

It is conceivable that the author of Genesis Apocryphon was aware of another chronological scheme that he attempts to refute. The talmudic and midrashic literature follow a completely different scheme from that found in Jubilees and in the Genesis Apocryphon. The rabbinic dating is said to be implied in the Mishnah: "A man must not refrain from procreation, unless he already has children; the School of Shammai says, two males; the School of Hillel says, a male and a female, for it is written: 'Male and female he created them.' If a man married a woman and lived with her ten years, but she had not given birth to a child, he may no longer refrain from procreation,"[24] i. e., he shall marry another woman. To which the Tosefta adds: "Although there is no proof for this, there is an allusion to it: ['and Sarai the wife of Abram took Hagar the Egyptian, her maid], at the end of ten years that Abram had dwelt in the land of Canaan, [and she gave her to Abram her husband to be his wife'] (Gen. 16:3). Incidentally, we learn that the time of living outside of the Holy Land is not to be counted in the computation."[25] The argument of the Tosefta, repeated in the Bab. and Yer. Talmud, is that the patriarch spent ten full years in Canaan.[26] The proof text is Gen. 16:3: "At the end of ten years that Abram dwelt in the land of Canaan." And as Abraham was seventy-five years old when he entered Canaan (Gen. 12:4); and as he was eighty-six when Ishmael was born (Gen. 16:16), it follows that he could not have stayed in Egypt seven years and at the same time have spent ten full years in Canaan.

To the objection that the patriarch spent at least part of these

[22] Genesis Apocryphon, XX, 8–34.
[23] Genesis Apocryphon, XXII, 27–29.
[24] Mishnah, Yevamoth, 6, 6.
[25] Tosefta, Yevamoth, 8, 4.
[26] Yer. Yevamoth, 6, 6; Bab. Yevamoth, 64a; Gen. Rabbah, 45, p. 449.

ten years in Egypt, the Seder 'Olam[27] offers a detailed chronology: "Abraham our ancestor was seventy years old when He spoke to him of the covenant 'between the pieces,'[28] for it is written: 'And it was at the end of thirty and four hundred years, on that very day, the hosts of the Lord left Egypt.' (Exod. 12:41). After He had spoken to him, Abraham went down to Haran and spent there five years, for it is written: 'And Abram was seventy-five years old when he left Haran' (Gen. 12:4). . . . That year when Abraham our father left Haran was also the year of the famine, and he went down to Egypt, where he spent three months. And he went up and arrived and settled in the Plains of Mamre which was in Hebron. And that year was also the time that he defeated the kings. And he dwelt there ten years before marrying Hagar, for it is written: 'And Sarai the wife of Abram took Hagar the Egyptian her maid, at the end of ten years that Abram had dwelt in the land of Canaan, and gave her to Abram her husband to be his wife' (Gen. 16:3). And it is also written: 'And Abram was eighty and six years old when Hagar bore Ishmael to Abram.' " (Gen. 16:16).[29]

As a rule the Seder 'Olam cites familiar verses either to bring out an obscure point or to refute a rival chronological scheme. Otherwise this work assumes that the reader is familiar with the relevant scriptural references. It is possible then that its citations of Gen. 16:3, 16, were intended to refute the chronology found in Genesis Apocryphon and Jubilees. As already indicated, the Genesis Apocryphon makes the Lord himself attest to the correctness of its chronology.

Whether or not the hypothesis of a dialogue between the chronographers found in the Seder 'Olam and the traditions preserved in the Genesis Apocryphon is correct, there is no doubt that the rabbinic literature — Mishnah, Tosefta, Bab. and Yer. Talmud, Midrash Rabbah — presume the detailed chronology of Seder 'Olam.[30] Accord-

[27] Seder 'Olam Rabbah, ed. B. Ratner (Wilno, 1897), inadequate as it is, has been used. See Albeck's comments in his Hebrew edition of Zunz, *Die gottesdienstlichen Vorträge der Juden historisch entwickelt* (Jerusalem, 1947), 267 f. For the authorship of Seder 'Olam, see below note 44.

[28] For the rabbinic reasoning that assumed two journeys from Haran, see below.

[29] Seder 'Olam, I, pp. 4–6.

[30] In addition to the sources cited in note 26, see Mekhilta, *Bo*, 14; Tanhuma, *Bo*, 9; Middot deRabbi Eliezer, 32; Pirkei deRabbi Eliezer, 48; *Sefer Hayashar* (Warsaw, 1927), 38; Midrash Tadshe ed. Jellinek, *Beit Hamidrash*, III (Leipzig, 1855), 173; ed. Epstein (Vienna, 1887), p. XXV. This section of *Tadshe* evidently emanates from the rabbinic tradition rather than from the sectarian part, to which many sections of this Midrash belong. See below. This chronological scheme remained the basic belief of Jewish chroniclers throughout the mediaeval period. It was first challenged by Azariah dei Rossi, *Me'or 'Einayyim* (Wilno, 1866), 289 ff.,

ing to the rabbinic school, immediately after his second arrival to Canaan from Haran[31] Abram left for Egypt, where he stayed only three months. Returning to Hebron, he made war against Chedorlaomer and his allies; ten years later he married Hagar the Egyptian.[32] However, according to the Rabbis, God's covenant with Abram, described in chapter 16 of Genesis, refers to the patriarch's *first* visit to Canaan at the age of seventy.[33] Possibly, it was the complete lack of biblical evidence for the talmudic assumption of two visits to Canaan, that discredited this theory in the eyes of ancient chronographers. It is certain, however, that talmudic chronography for the patriarchal period differed substantially from that of the Genesis Apocryphon and Jubilees.[34]

Aside from being considered the first date of Hebrew history, the dating of Abram's journey to Haran and Egypt was also the starting point of the entire biblical chronology. It was the basis for determining the date of the Exodus. As is well known, the masoretic text of Exod. 12:40 gives 430 years as the length of the Israelites' sojourn in Egypt. This is emended in LXX and Samaritan versions, and is interpreted in the rabbinic tradition, to refer from the time of Abram. The main difficulty is that in Gen. 15:13, the Lord tells Abram: "Your seed shall be a stranger in a land that is not theirs and they shall serve them and they shall oppress them 400 years." The biblical writers, as pointed out by ibn Ezra, were not too concerned with dates.[35] But beginning with the Hellenistic period when chronography became a specialty, the difference between Gen. 15:13 and Exod. 12:40 was a stumbling block for establishing a chronology of the early period

---

who also cites the mediaeval authors who dissented from the chronology of the Seder 'Olam.

[31] The date of Abram's supposed first exit from Haran is not mentioned in the Seder 'Olam, but is preserved in the talmudic literature, an indication that the Seder 'Olam, as we know it, contains but a part of the rabbinic chronographic tradition. See 'Avodah Zarah, 9a; *Sefer Hayashar*, 27; cf. Ratner, note 22 on Seder 'Olam, p. 4.

[32] Seder 'Olam, I, pp. 5–6.

[33] Seder 'Olam, I, p. 4; III, pp. 13 ff. See also Mekhilta, *Bo*, 14, p. 50 (ed. Horowitz-Rabin); Pirkei deRabbi Eliezer, 48; Tanḥuma, on Exod. 12:40; *Sefer Hayashar* (Warsaw, 1927), 38; Targum Pseudo-Jonathan, Exod. 12:41; Yalkut, *Lekh lekha*, 77.

[34] See the sources cited in the previous note.

[35] Ibn Ezra on Exod. 12:40, pointing out that many biblical dates are obscure because the starting point is not known. Thus the precise starting point of the 430 years is not given. That it could not have referred to Jacob's coming into Egypt was shown by the rabbinic commentators that even assuming the maximum possible number of years of Qehath, Amram and Moses (133+137+80=350), it would still be short 80 years for the number of 430.

of the Israelites. The rabbis reconciled these differences by postulating 430 years from the time of Abram's vision, when he was seventy years old, to the Exodus; from the time of Isaac's birth, 400. The Book of Jubilees, however, gives 430 years from Isaac's birth to the Exodus.[36] We do not know whether the author of Genesis Apocryphon discussed the date of the Exodus or even whether his account treated the period of Egypt. But the odds are that he did and that his chronology was identical with that of Jubilees.[37] As the date of the vision in Gen. 15:1 ff., determined the time of the Exodus in Egypt, Genesis Apocryphon makes the Lord himself confirm the chronology.[38]

It follows that the differences between the chronologies of the Seder 'Olam and Genesis Apocryphon represent two schools of pentateuchal chronography. Not only is the Book of Jubilees part of the sectarian school, but works such as the Testament of the Twelve Patriarchs, *Midrash Tadshe*, and *Sefer Hayashar* have preserved some of the sectarian traditions.[39] It is no coincidence that the life spans assigned to Jacob's twelve sons by these works are roughly identical.[40] It may be assumed that the author of Genesis Apocryphon's dating for the later period, if his account continued to the times of the Exodus, corresponded to chronology of the sectarian school.

The existence of a Graeco-Jewish school of biblical chronography first becomes evident in LXX, Exod. 12:40, where the date given in the masoretic text is emended.[41] A detailed presentation of the text as emended has been preserved. Demetrius computed that the number given in Exod. 12:40, 430, is to be divided into two equal parts, 215 years from Abram's arrival to Canaan until Jacob's descent into Egypt

[36] According to Jubilees, Isaac's birth occurred in, or within a year of, 1980 A. M. See Jub. 15:1, accepting, with Charles, Dillmann's emendation; 16:13; 17:1. For some of this author's chronographic negligence, see E. Wiesenberg, "The Jubilee of Jubilees," *Revue de Qumran*, III (1961), 34–36. This negligence would seem to suggest that the writer was copying a chronological scheme he did not understand fully. For the date of the Exodus, 2410 A. M., see Jub. 50:4; cf. 48:1.

[37] In the absence of an indication to the contrary, it must be assumed that Genesis Apocryphon's account continued to the Exodus. That the Exodus was the termination point may be drawn from the treatment in the Book of Jubilees.

[38] Genesis Apocryphon, XXII, 27–29.

[39] See Albeck in Zunz, *Gottesdienstliche Vorträge* [Hebrew ed.], 136–40.

[40] See the dates of Jacob's twelve sons as given in Jub., Test. of XII Patriarchs, and Midrash Tadshe, arranged in tables by Charles, *The Book of Jubilees* (London, 1902), 28:11–24, n., pp. 170–72.

[41] Also in the Samaritan text. That Exod. 12:40 was revised by LXX is frequently mentioned in the talmudic literature; Yer. Megillah, I, 71c; Bab. Megillah 9a; Mekhilta, *Bo*, 14 (Horovitz-Rabin), p. 50; Soferim, V, 7–8; Sefer Torah, I, 8; Tanḥuma, *Shemoth*, 22; (Buber), 19.

and 215 years to the Exodus.[42] The chronographers of this school lengthened the time of Abram's stay in Egypt, perhaps comparing it to Jacob's journey to Egypt. And since the time from Abram's to Jacob's journey was almost the same as from Jacob's journey to the Exodus, chronologically speaking, Egypt became the apex of an equilateral triangle.[43]

In some respects we know less of the history of sectarian or rabbinic chronography than that of the Graeco-Jewish school. The talmudic writers had as their source the chronographic work preserved mainly in the Seder 'Olam.[44] Though generally attributed to Rabbi Jose ben Ḥalafta (circa A. D. 150), the Seder 'Olam must instead be considered a depository of pharisaic chronographic traditions.[45] But nothing is known of the original authors of these traditions.[46] We are somewhat better informed concerning the Hellenistic school. Chronography became an important field of study during the third century B. C. in Alexandria and elsewhere when Greek and Egyptian chronicles were subjected to a close and systematic scrutiny. The works of Eratosthenes of Cyrene, Manetho of Sebennystus, and perhaps Berossus of Babylon,[47] may have been among those writings which inspired the Jew

---

[42] Demetrius, 722 F 1 = Euseb. Praep. Ev., IX, 21, 16–19, counts 25 years from Abram's entrance into Canaan to Isaac's birth; 60 years of Isaac till Jacob's birth; and 130 years, the age of Jacob when entering Egypt, making a total of 215 years in the land of Canaan. Demetrius' chronology for the stay in Egypt is more complex; Levi was 43 years old when Jacob and his sons entered Egypt, 17 years later Qehath was born; Qehath begat Amram at the age of 40; Amram, Moses, at the age of 78; Moses' age during the Exodus was 80, making a total of 215. There is little doubt that Demetrius had a preconceived total into which he fits his dates. Rabbinic tradition maintained that the stay in Egypt lasted 210 years. This was based on the assumption that Abram's first entrance into Canaan was at the age of 70. Hence, Abram stayed there 30 years; Isaac, 60; Jacob, 130, making a total of 220 years in Canaan, remaining 210 years for the stay in Egypt, for the grand total must be 430 (Exod. 12:40); see Seder 'Olam, III, pp. 13 f. In AJ, II, 318, Josephus follows Demetrius' chronology, but otherwise he is either not consistent or negligent or follows different sources. See Freudenthal, Hellenistische Studien, 49, n.; von Destinon, Die Chronologie des Josephus (Kiel, 1880), 9–11.

[43] The Graeco-Jewish chronographers evidently assumed that the patriarch left for Egypt immediately after entering Canaan, which conforms to the rabbinic tradition and the impression of Gen. 12:1–20.

[44] Ratner maintains that the Mishnah and Tosefta made use of the Seder 'Olam. See his Mavo lehaseder 'Olam. But see Zunz and Albeck in Gottesdienstliche Vorträge [Hebrew ed.], p. 43, n. 8, pp. 267 f.

[45] See Yevamoth, 82b; Niddah, 46b; Ratner, Mavo, pp. 3 ff.

[46] Whether or not rabbinic chronography was influenced by the Hellenistic school is still an open question.

[47] For the history of Hellenistic chronography, Jacoby, FGrH, IID, 661 ff. For Eratosthenes, see FGrH, IIB, No. 241; Manetho, IIIC, No. 609; Berossus, No. 680.

Demetrius to undertake a searching study of the chronology of Genesis and possibly of the entire biblical period.[48] The date of Abram's journey to Canaan became to the Hellenistic Jewish writers what the fall of Troy was to the Greeks.

However, little is known of the sequence of the sectarian historiographic works. The Book of Jubilees was written, it is generally assumed, at the end of the second century B. C.; the date of Genesis Apocryphon is still an open question.[49] Which of the two sectarian works, the Genesis Apocryphon and Jubilees, is dependent on the other?[50] Or must we postulate an unknown work used by both?

Although the chronology is the same in both works, the presentation is different. The most obvious difference is that Genesis Apocryphon uses a relative system of dating; Jubilees, an absolute one. Less obvious, but nevertheless real, differences are that in the former the dating is an integral part of the narrative; in the latter it is superimposed. The author of Genesis Apocryphon still feels the need to defend his chronology by invoking the Lord himself; the author of Jubilees takes the chronology for granted.[51] When the author of Jubilees does defend his scheme, it is the calendar which, he says, was "ordained on the heavenly tables."[52] It is evident that Jubilees invokes the authority of the "heavenly tables" on issues that need emphasis or that he considered controversial.[53] That the authority

[48] The extent of Demetrius' work is not known. But 722 F 6 would seem to indicate that it extended at least to the destruction of the first Temple in 586.

[49] For the date of Jubilees, see Charles, *The Book of Jubilees*, pp. LVIII–LXVI. For that of Genesis Apocryphon, see Birnbaum, in *Bulletin of the School of the Oriental and African Studies*, 21 (1958), 185, who dates the script as of the third quarter of the first century B. C.; E. Y. Kutcher, "Dating of the Language of Genesis Apocryphon," *JBL*, 76 (1957), 288–92; "The Language of Genesis Apocryphon, a Preliminary Study," *Scripta Hierosolymitana*, 4 (1958), 1–35, assigns the language to the first century B. C., a view also maintained by J. A. Fitzmyer, *Catholic Bible Quarterly*, 22 (1960), 277–91. H. H. Rowley, "Notes on the Aramaic of Genesis Apocryphon," in *Hebrew and Semitic Studies . . . . Driver* (Oxford, 1963), 116–29, maintains that its Aramaic antedates that of Daniel.

[50] The editors of Genesis Apocryphon, p. 38, concluded that it "may have served as a source for a number of stories told more concisely" in Enoch and Jubilees. Fitzmyer, see previous note, however, says: "we are inclined rather to regard the scroll as dependent on Jubilees and the Enoch literature," p. 277.

[51] Genesis Apocryphon, XXII, 27–29. Jub. 14:1, merely gives the date, without comment.

[52] Jub. 6:29; 31; cf. 3:10.

[53] For the meaning of "heavenly tables," see Charles, *The Book of Enoch* I (Oxford, 1912), 47:3; Jub. 3:10. The phrase usually is invoked (En. 47:3; 81:1, 2; 93:2; 103:2; Test. Levi 5:4; Asher 2:10; 7:5, some texts; Jub. 3:10, 31; 4:5, 32; 5:13; 6:17, 29–35; 15:25–26; 16:9, 29; 18:19; 23:32; 24:33; 28:6; 30:9, 20; 31:32; 32:15;

is not invoked in regard to his chronology indicates that Jubilees believed it to have been authoritative. It follows that the author of Jubilees made use of a chronology that had already gained support. The author of Genesis Apocryphon, however, was not certain that his chronology would be accepted. Hence it must be assumed that he was writing when the chronology was either still recent or was being challenged. However, the fact that Genesis Apocryphon did not make use of the calendar found in Jubilees indicates that he did not know that work. Since the chronology in the two works is identical, it follows, if one made use of the other, that Jubilees was dependent on Genesis Apocryphon. Certainly, Genesis Apocryphon is more "primitive," for it does not make use of an absolute era. The evidence thus far indicates that Genesis Apocryphon was written before the Book of Jubilees.

Although older, it does not follow that Genesis Apocryphon was the direct source of Jubilees' chronology. Concerned as the author of Genesis Apocryphon is with chronological problems, he is not a chronographer like some of the Hellenistic professionals in this field. That there were biblical chronographers we know from Demetrius and Justus of Tiberias and the Seder 'Olam. It must then be presumed that there still is missing a work with chronological tables used by both of these sectarian authors. The presumption of a missing link, however, is not very helpful. On the basis of available works, the chronology of Genesis Apocryphon is either directly or indirectly the source of Jubilees. And there is no question that there flourished a sectarian school of biblical chronography that differed in some respects from that of the Graeco-Jewish or the rabbinic writers.

As to the length of the patriarch's stay in Egypt, the rabbinic school maintained that it lasted only three months; the Graeco-Jewish writers, long enough to introduce the sciences into that country; the sectarians, a total of seven years, five during Sarai's concealment and two in Pharaoh's palace. Certainly, the rabbinic and the sectarian views are too different to be reconcilable.[54] But what about the

---

33:10, 13) in Jub. to give emphasis to a point, either invoking the Pentateuch or to point out special punishment or authority.

[54] The chronographic differences between the rabbinic and Qumran schools seem to indicate that caution should be exercised before similarities between the schools are taken to be parallels, or even identical views. Cf. S. Hahn, "Zur Chronologie der Qumran-Schriften," *Acta Orientalia*, 9 (Budapest, 1960), 181–89, where the chronography of the Zadokite Documents is taken to be identical with that of the Seder 'Olam. The differences pointed out here are also intended to balance the impressions made by M. R. Lehmann, "1Q Genesis Apocryphon in the Light of the Targumim and Midrashim," *Revue du Qumran*, I (1958), 163–86.

Graeco-Jewish and the sectarian? Do they not present a similar position? The answer is yes. The patriarch's stay in Hebron and in the royal palace lasted two years, respectively, according to the sectarians. This view coincides with the statement of Pseudo-Eupolemus (200–150 B. C.), that the patriarch introduced the sciences first to the Canaanites and then to the Egyptians.[55] Since Gen. 12:11–20 gives the impression, confirmed by Gen. 16:3, that Abram's stay in Egypt was of a very short duration, the sectarians' presumption that it lasted many years must have been based on a strong belief that tended to invalidate these scriptural intimations. It is reasonable, then, to assume that the sectarians, like the Graeco-Jewish writers, believed in the patriarch's religious and educational mission to Canaan and Egypt. And it was this belief that influenced the sectarian chronographers. This assumption is now partially confirmed by Fitzmyer's decipherment of line XIX, 25, of Genesis Apocryphon: ". . . goodness, wisdom and truth and I [Abram] read to them [Egyptian officials] the book of the writings of Enoch."[56] As in several other instances, the wording is similar to Pseudo-Eupolemus, who says that Abraham, when instructing the Egyptians, attributed the scientific discoveries to Enoch. The assumption that the similarities are accidental is unwarranted. However, we do not know enough of the Graeco-Jewish and sectarian lore to describe the mutual influences. Only a rigorous dating of the relevant sectarian and Hellenistic Jewish literature could offer a solution.[57]

However, the differences between the sectarians and the Graeco-Jewish writers must not be forgotten. Pseudo-Eupolemus says that during his journey in Egypt the patriarch lived in Heliopolis.[58] As Genesis is silent on the exact location, what was the evidence for this identification? Parallels were drawn from Joseph and Moses. According to Gen. 41:50, Potiphar was the priest of On, in LXX, Heliopolis.[59]

---

[55] Pseudo-Eupolemus, 724 FF 1–2; *AJ*, I, 166–68. See also my comments, *HUCA*, XXXIV (1963), 83–113.

[56] מלי חנוך [כתב]ל קודמיהון וקרית וקושטא וחכמתא טבתא Genesis Apocryphon, XIX, 25, as deciphered by Fitzmyer, *Catholic Bible Quarterly*, 22 (1960), 288. My hypothesis that there was a connection between Pseudo-Eupolemus' mention of Enoch in his account of Abraham (724 FF 1–2) and Genesis Apocryphon's version of the patriarch's stay in Egypt (*HUCA*, XXXIV [1963], 109), was made before I became aware of Fitzmyer's decipherment.

[57] Cf. G. Vermes, *Scripture and Tradition* (Leiden, 1961), 80–82, 97.

[58] Pseudo-Eupolemus, 724 F 1, p. 679, line 10 = Euseb., *Praep. Ev.*, IX, 17, 8.

[59] See also Demetrius, 722 F 1 = Euseb. *Praep. Ev.*, IX, 21, 12; Artapanus, 726 FF 2–3 = *Praep. Eccl.*, IX, 23, 3; 27, 8.

Manetho said, if Josephus is to be trusted, that Osarsiph (Moses) was a native of Heliopolis.[60] To the reasoning of the Hellenistic Jewish writers it followed that Abram also visited that place. Since Heliopolis was a famous priestly and intellectual center, the patriarch must have founded it.[61]

The sectarians, however, claimed that the patriarch stayed in Zoan (Tanis), as already indicated, citing Num. 13:22 as evidence. This conforms to the traditions preserved in Ps. 78:12, 43, as well as in the rabbinic literature. Ps. 78:12, 43, parallels the "field of Zoan" with Egypt. The talmudic and midrashic literature cites Isa. 30:4 that Zoan was the residence of Egypt's princes.[62] It would seem to follow that the Rabbis, too, assumed that the patriarch founded Zoan, or at least visited this town in Egypt.

A search of the talmudic and midrashic sources, however, has failed to substantiate this assumption, though the treatment on this point is abundant. In fact, Num. 13:22, taken by the sectarians to refer to the times of the patriarch, is interpreted in rabbinic works to suggest the times of Ham. The Rabbis take it for granted that Ham was the builder of both Hebron and Zoan. Num. 13:22, stating that Hebron was built seven years before Zoan, according to the talmudic writers, proved the superiority of Canaan over Egypt. In this argument, Zoan is presented as being the most fertile area of Egypt (Isa. 30:4); Hebron, as the least fruitful of Canaan, for it was chosen to be the patriarchal burial ground.[63] Since Ham built Hebron before he did Zoan and since it was inconceivable to the Rabbis that he would have utilized the less desirable land first, it followed that Hebron, the least fertile land of Canaan, was still superior to the best of Egypt. And since Egypt contained the most desirable land in the world (Gen. 13:10, probably reading Zoan),[64] the worst of Canaan is better than the best anywhere in the world. So certain were the talmudists of their argument that they reversed the order of birth of Ham's sons. Gen. 10:6 reads: "The sons of Ham are Cush and Miẓrayyim and Put and Canaan." This sequence, the Rabbis argued, could not be correct, for it would follow that Ham built a city for the youngest

---

[60] C. Apion, I, 250 = Manetho, 609 F 10, p. 96, lines 6–9, app. crit., Jacoby cites the literature questioning whether the identification of Osarsiph with Moses is that of Manetho. Cf. Contra Apion, I, 238, where Moses is not mentioned.

[61] Cf. Herod., II, 3.

[62] Kethuvoth, 112a; Soṭah, 34b; Sifre, 'Eqev, 37.

[63] Cf. Gen. 23:1 ff.

[64] See Kittel in Biblia Hebraica, Gen. 13:10. The rabbinic sources (cited in next note) indicate that the reading was Zoan, attested in the Syriac.

before he did for his second son (Num. 3:22). Hence, Canaan was not the youngest, they said, but the oldest son of Ham.[65]

Although this study is limited to a minor episode, it is reasonable to argue that the views reflected here mirror roughly the three schools of ancient biblical historiography. All three schools accepted the thesis of Canaan's superiority over Egypt. The Hellenistic Jewish writers were sometimes the farthest removed from the literal history of Genesis. They expanded or contracted the account of Genesis to conform to contemporary concepts of the world. The wish to make the history of Genesis more current is also evident in the sectarian literature. But unlike the Hellenistic Jewish literature contrary passages are not silenced. Genesis Apocryphon and Jubilees attempt to reconcile the passages that seemed to indicate a different view from that which they presented. Rabbinic exegesis, though very subjective, was the least *au courant*. Interested in exegesis rather than in history, the reconciliation of contradictory verses became an end in itself, no matter how improbable these reconciliations were. Rabbinic thought was farther removed from Graeco-Jewish than were sectarian interpretations. It is remarkable that there is such a close parallel between the Graeco-Jewish and sectarian biblical exegesis.

[65] Kethuvoth, 112a; Soṭah 34b; Sifre, '*Eqev*, 37; Num. Rabbah, 16; Tanḥuma, Shelaḥ, 8.

VISIBILITY OF THE NEW MOON IN CUNEIFORM AND RABBINIC SOURCES*

BEN ZION WACHOLDER AND DAVID B. WEISBERG

THE problem of the visibility of the new moon in Ancient Mesopotamia[1] is now almost a century old. Closely connected with it is the problem of the evolution of the 19-year intercalary cycle, whose fixed points are determined by sightings of the lunar crescent. In the closing decade of the 19th century following the important work of Epping and Strassmaier,[2] Eduard Mahler posited a 19-year cycle for the Babylonian calendar adopted by Nabû-nāṣir in 747 B. C. E.[3] Mahler's conjecture was made on the basis of his knowledge of the rabbinic calendar that came into use during the first millennium of the present era. Moreover, he was the first one to see the relationship between the rabbinic and ancient Babylonian calendars.[4] But, as shown below, some of Mahler's views are clearly unacceptable while others remain as controversial today as they were at the turn of the century.

In this paper, the authors present evidence on the visibility of the moon from cuneiform sources as well as from talmudic texts from the

---

* Parts of this paper were read at the 181st Meeting of the American Oriental Society in Cambridge, Mass., on April 7, 1971.

[1] See J. K. Fotheringham, "The Visibility of the Lunar Crescent," *The Venus Tablets of Ammizaduga*, S. Langdon, C. Schoch, and J. K. Fotheringham (Oxford U. press: Oxford, 1928), pp. 45–49.

[2] Joseph Epping, "Astronomisches aus Babylon oder das Wissen der Chaldäer über den gestirnten Himmel," unter Mitwirkung von J. N. Strassmaier, *Ergänzungshefte zu dem Stimmen aus Maria-Laach, 44* (Freiburg, 1889); Epping and Strassmaier, *ZA* 5 (1890), 341 ff.; 6 (1891), 89–102, 217–244; 8 (1893), 149–178.

[3] See Eduard Mahler, *SKAW 101/II* March, 1892, 1–17, and "Das Kalenderwesen," in *9th ICO*, 1892; "Der Schaltcyclus der Babylonier," *ZA* 9 (1894), 42–61; "Der Saros-Canon der Babylonier und der 19-jähriger Schaltcyclus derselben," *ZA* 11 (1896), 41–46; "Der Schaltcyclus der Babylonier," *ZDMG* 52 (1898), 227–246; "Der Kalender der Babylonier," in *Hilprecht Anniversary Volume* (Chicago, 1909), 1–13.

[4] M. Jastrow, *Die Religion Babyloniens und Assyriens*, Giessen, 1912, Pt. II, pp. 540 ff. Almost 90 pages are devoted to a summary of the cuneiform evidence relating to the ominous portents associated with the visibility of the moon which he had culled from R. F. Harper, *Assyrian and Babylonian Letters . . .* (London, 1914), and from R: C. Thompson, *Reports of the Magicians and Astrologers of Nineveh and Babylon* (London, 1900).

first centuries C. E. We shall note a remarkable similarity in the procedures for determining the new month by the method of sighting the
lunar crescent. We believe that our results will show Mahler's conclusions to have been substantially correct. Important insights on the
related problem of the evolution of the luni-solar calendar and the
institution of the regular 19-year intercalary cycle are also obtained.[5]

Observation of the movements of the sun and the moon plays a
controlling part in the systematization of time-reckoning and is,
apparently, one of the oldest recorded features of civilization.[6] But
astronomy is only one of the ingredients — the others are social and
religious — that enters into the makeup of the calendar. And of all
civilization's institutions, the calendar is perhaps the most important
for regulating public life. We may assume that Babylonian mathe-
matics and astronomy reached the peaks that they did partially
because of the need to determine the time of the appearance of the
new moon. There was, at least in the beginning, a magical element too.
The mythology concerning the disappearance of the moon and its
reappearance reveals the anxiety that ancient man felt at this ominous
period.

The Babylonian calendar was luni-solar. Originally, actual sightings
of the moon determined the new month in this system.[7] It was observed that the interval between one lunation and the next was 29½
days. For practical purposes, this was changed to months having either

[5] Note also the following basic works: E. J. Bickerman, *Chronology of the Ancient
World* (Ithaca, N. Y.: Cornell U. Press, 1968), especially pp. 18 f., and p. 97, nn. 11
and 14 (Correct "Nŏ. 303" to "No. 298."); S. Gandz, J. Obermann, and O. Neugebauer, "Sanctification of the New Moon,'' from The Code of Maimonides, Book 3,
Treatise 8, *Yale Judaica Series, Volume 11* (New Haven: Yale U. Press, 1956), particularly the astronomical commentary of Neugebauer, pp. 113–149, bibliography,
pp. 151–2; Ernest Wiesenberg, "Elements of a Lunar Theory in the Mishnah, Rosh
Hashanah 2:6, and the Talmudic Complements Thereto," *HUCA* 33 (1962), pp. 153–
196; Neugebauer, *ACT* (London, 1955); Julian Morgenstern, "The Three Calendars
of Ancient Israel," *HUCA* 1 (1924), 13–78; 3 (1926), 77–107; 10 (1935), 1–148.

[6] See Alexander Marshack, "Lunar Notation on Upper Paleolithic Remains,"
Science 146 (1964), pp. 743–45. According to Marshack, there is evidence for luni-
solar lore in the early agricultural civilizations of Eurasia in the Paleolithic period.
The evidence consists of accurate lunar notations on bones and stones from the Ice
Age. These discoveries date from about 34,000 to about 10,000 years ago, in widely
ranging sites. If Marshack's interpretation of these notations is correct, our estimates
of the body of knowledge of our distant forebears will have to be revised — and the
traditions in Mesopotamia about which we are speaking will have to be placed much
farther back than anyone would have supposed. The writers would like to thank Miss
Margaret Currier, Librarian of the Peabody Museum, for her kind help in securing
this reference.

[7] See S. J. de Vries, "Calendar," in *IDB* Volume 1 (1962), pp. 483–488, with
bibliography. The "probable etymologies" are not convincing.

29 or 30 days. But whether a month was hollow (29 days) or full (30 days) was determined by sighting. Although it was not necessarily always so, on the average, a hollow month was followed by a full month, which made for six hollow months plus six full months of 354 days. Thus, some 11 ¼ days were lacking in the lunar year as compared with the solar. To make up this discrepancy, certain years, by edict of the king, contained an additional month. Custom determined that the intercalated month was either Ullulu or Addaru. This haphazard system of determining the time of the new moon was replaced in the first half of the 5th century B. C. E. by a calendar known in the west as the Metonic calendar.[8] This calendar, we believe, had its origin in Babylonia.

When the system of sighting was replaced by tables that predicted the position of the moon, a calendar was established which fixed the length of each month and year. The lists have been compiled by Richard Parker and Waldo Dubberstein; they run to about 100 C. E.[9]

The questions confronting us are the following:

(1) How did the system of sighting the new moon work?
(2) When did the standard 19-year cycle emerge in Babylonia?
(3) At what point did rabbinic authorities change the pre-exilic (biblical) calendar, possibly a solar one which had its origin in Egypt, to a Babylonian luni-solar one?
(4) How was the talmudic system of calendation related to that of the cuneiform tradition in Babylonia?

It should be pointed out at the outset that this study does not claim to be exhaustive, but is, rather, a preliminary effort at highlighting the relationship between the two traditions of calendation.

Cuneiform evidence relating to the problem of visibility will now be presented. This comes partially from Neo-Assyrian and Neo-Babylonian letters which contain actual examples of the sighting of the lunar crescent, reflecting the procedures in force at the time of their writing.

A Neo-Assyrian text from the Harper Collection, *ABL* 894, reads:

Sîn ūm 30 atamar šāqia ša ūm 30 ina pitti išāqia kī ša ūm 2 izzaz šumma ina pān šarri bēlia maḫir ina pān ša āl Aššur šarru lidqul ḫaramima šarru bēli ūmu lūkin

---

[8] The ancient testimony on Meton: Diodorus Siculus, XII, 36, 2; Aelian, *Var. Hist.* X, 7; Scholion on Aristoph. Av. 997 = F. Jacoby, *FGrH* IIIB, pp. 135 f., 328 F 122. Modern Literature: Diels and Rehm, Bischoff, "Kalender," *R.E.*, XX (1919), 1569; W. Kubitschek, *Grundriss der antiken Zeitrechnung* (Munich, 1928); Meritt. The Athenian Calendar (London, 1928), 101.

[9] Parker and Dubberstein, *Babylonian Chronology*, Brown U. press, 1956.

"I observed the moon on the thirtieth day of the month — it was in a high position. Concerning the thirtieth day, it will soon be as high as it stands on the second day. Therefore, if it is pleasing to the king, my lord, may the king wait for (the messenger) from Ashur, at which time the king, my lord, can fix the date."

The following facts would seem to follow from this letter:

1. The lunar month was determined by the sighting of the new moon and not by a predetermined calculation.
2. A messenger arrived from an important city bringing word about the sighting (*ina pān* (PN) *dagālu* — always used of people).
3. The date was fixed by the king after hearing from this messenger (i. e., it was officially proclaimed).

Many texts, especially from the Neo-Babylonian period, allude to the fact that the scholars determined the period for the intercalation of the month (based upon the visibility of the new moon), informed the king of this, who in turn instructed the Babylonian temple as to the official proclamation of the month, and they, the officials of the Babylonian temple, instructed those of neighboring cities.

From one text we learn that the king orders Addaru intercalated (*YOS 3* 115). In a second, six people write to the temple administrator, people qualified to enter the temple, and the assembly of Eanna, that the king has ordered Addaru intercalated. The recipients of the letter are to see that the proper rites are performed, and to be sure it is done promptly (*YOS 3* 152). A third text tells how the *qīpu*-officials of Esagil write to the temple administrator and another individual of Eanna: "For your information, we are now sending you the message that the month is an intercalary (month)" (*Yos 3* 15). This shows that royal instructions were sent to the various temples for the official proclamation of a month as intercalary. In this case, the instructions went from the king to the Babylonian temple, and from the officials of the Babylonian temple to those of Eanna in Uruk. A fourth text informs us that "For your information: Ullulu is an intercalary month" (*YOS 3* 196).

The following text would seem to demonstrate the intricate connection that exists between the establishment of the visibility of the moon and the proper performance of the religious rites which were based upon its appearance:

parṣīkunu ina Addari ša itti Nisanni tību akī ši ipšā "Perform your religious services in the month of Addaru that immediately precedes the month of Nisannu" (*YOS 3* 152; 16 ff.).

The recurring phrase in the letters telling about the observation

of the heavenly bodies is *maṣartu nitaṣar* ("we have kept the watch").
Many of these letters are written exclusively to inform the king that
the watch is being kept. For example, in *ABL* 141, the writers inform
the recipient that

maṣartu nitaṣar ūm 14 Sîn Šamaš aḫiš etamru

"We have kept the watch; on the 14th day the moon and sun appeared
together." Note that this is the exclusive subject of this letter. Watches
were kept in Akkad, Borsippa and Nippur for the eclipse of the moon
(*ABL* 337). It is safe to assume that they were kept there for the
appearance of the new moon and for the appearance of any noteworthy astronomical phenomena which might have ominous portent
(cf. also *ABL* 351).

That the practice of establishing the beginning of the month by
observation was in vogue at the time of the 7th and 6th centuries is
clear from the following letters:

ina ūm 29 maṣartu nitaṣar Sîn la nīmūr
Duzu ūm 2 limmu Belšunu piḫat Ḫindanu

"We kept watch for the new moon on the 29th day of the month,
but did not see the moon. [Dated] 2nd of Duzu in the *limmu* of Belšunu,
in the district of Hindanu" (*ABL* 671).

The watch described in this letter was kept on the 29th day of
Simanu. Because the crescent was not sighted on the 29th day, Simanu
was declared to have 30 days. The new month of Duzu was declared
to be on the 31st day. On the 2nd day of the new month, a report was
written. At Arba-el a watch was kept on the 29th day (*ABL* 423).
Because of cloudy conditions, the moon was not sighted. What the
implication is of the phrase ITI *Addaru ūm 1 pān 1 ūmu* is not clear,
unless this is an indication of a practice of predating.

We turn now to selections of Mishnah and Tosephtah from the
tractate Rosh Hashanah ("New Year's Festival") which deal with the
setting up of the rabbinic calendar. Mishnah RH 1:3–3:1 outlines the
procedure of verification. It is mainly from here that we can reconstruct
the pattern of the evidence relating to the problem of visibility.[10]

כיצד בודקין את העדים? זוג שבא ראשון בודקין אותו ראשון, ומכניסין את הגדול
שבהן ואומרים לו: אמור, כיצד ראית את הלבנה, לפני החמה או לאחר החמה, לצפונה
או לדרומה? כמה היה גבוה? ולאין היה נוטה? וכמה היה רחב?[11] אם אמר לפני החמה

---

[10] See now Saul Lieberman, *Tosefta Ki-fshuṭa* Part 5, (New York, 1962), pp.
1026–1038, whose comments embrace most of the talmudic material and who also
cites the secondary literature.

[11] For a discussion of the technical vocabulary, see Wiesenberg, *HUCA* 33 (1962),
152–196. The difficulty with Wiesenberg's commentary is: a) it runs counter the

TABLE I

Comparison of Akkadian and Rabbinic Procedures

Procedure	Akkadian	Rabbinic
1. witnesses sight new moon	1. "We have kept the watch" (*ABL*, passim) 2. "I saw the moon on the 30th day; it was high." (*ABL* 894)	1. "Was its appearance like this or this?" (RH. 2:8) 2. "It was two ox-cart-lengths high" (Tosephta)
2. bring information to authorities	1. "Let the king, my lord, wait for (the messenger from) Aššur." (*ABL* 894, 522)	1. "They bring in the pair that came first — they question the senior man . . ." (RH. 2:6)
3. witnesses cross-examined		
4. authorities proclaim new moon	1. "Let the king fix the day." (*ABL* 894) 2. King orders date fixed (*YOS* 3 115) 3. "Establish your festivals" (*YOS* 3 152:16) 4. "The intercalary month . . ." (*YOS* 3 15, 52)	1. "The head of the court proclaims, 'It is sanctified' . . ." (RH. 2:7) 2. (Letter of R. Gamaliel)
5. messengers are sent out	1. "We are now sending you the message . . ." (*YOS* 3 15)	1. ". . . messengers go out . . ." (RH. 1:3)

לא אמר כלום. ואחר כך היו מכניסין את השני ובודקין אותו. אם נמצאו דבריהן
מכוונים עדותן קיימת. (ר"ה ב:ו)

"How are the witnesses cross-examined? The pair that comes first
is cross-examined first. They bring in the senior man and say to him:
'Tell us, how did you see the moon? Was it facing the sun or turned
away from it? To the north or to the south? How high was it? To which
side did it lean? And how wide was the crescent?'

"If he said, 'Facing the sun,' his testimony is invalid. Afterwards
they brought in the second witness and cross-examined him. If their
testimony is found to agree, it was accepted."

דמות צורות לבנות היו לו לרבן גמליאל בטבלא ובכותל בעליתו, שבהן מראה
את הדיוטות ואומר: הכזה ראית או כזה? (ר"ה ב:ח)

"Rabban Gamaliel had drawings of the phases of the moon on a
tablet and on the wall of his attic. He used to show them to the laymen[12] and ask, 'Did you see it this way or that?' "

ראש בית דין אומר מקודש וכל העם עונין אחריו מקודש מקודש. (ר"ה ב:ז)

"The head of the court proclaims, 'The month is hallowed!' and all
the people answer after him, 'It is hallowed, it is hallowed!' "[13]

על ששה חדשים השלוחין יוצאין, על ניסן מפני הפסח, על אב מפני התענית, על
אלול מפני ראש השנה, על תשרי מפני תקנת המועדות, על כסלו מפני החנוכה, ועל
אדר מפני הפורים. (ר"ה א:ג)

"On six months agents would go out to proclaim the new month:

On Nisan, on account of Passover;
On Ab, on account of the Fast;

---

talmudic exegesis; and b) it assumes too great a mastery of astronomical lore on the
part of laymen, perhaps even of the average member of the court, unless one were a
professional moon-watcher.

[12] The implication is that Rabban Gamaliel was a professional astronomer, who
could calculate the presence of the new moon without the witnesses. See Bab. Talmud
Rosh Hashanah, 25a: "Rabban Gamaliel said to the Sages: 'Thus I have received
from the school of my grandfather: "(The interval between the conjunction and the
time the moon becomes visible) sometimes appears after a long time (42 hours in
September); at other times it appears after a short interval (16½ hours in March)." ' "
Ibid., "Rabban Gamaliel said to them . . .: 'The interval between one lunation and
another is not less than 29 days, and a half day, two thirds of an hour, and 73 parts
(73/1080 of an hour), which in standard computation is 29 days, 12 hours, and
793/1080 (or 44 minutes plus 3 and 1/3 seconds).' " It has been plausibly argued
(David Ganz, Neḥmad We-na'im, (Jessnitz, 1743), Par. 113) that "73 parts" is a
post-talmudic addition. But see now M. M. Kasher, Torah Shelemah, XIII (New
York, 1949), 101–109.

[13] See also Maimonides, Mishneh Torah, "Sanctification of the Moon," II, 8–9.

On Elul because of The New Year;[14]
On Tishri because of the order of the holidays;
On Kislev because of Hannukah;
and on Adar because of Purim."

אחד אומר ראיתיו נבוה שתי מרדעות ואחד אומר שלשה, עדותן קיימת . . .
(תוספתא ר"ה פרק א § 16, שורות 69–70)

"If one witness says, "I saw it (the moon) two oxcart-lengths-high,' and the other says, 'three oxcart-lengths-high,' their testimony is accepted . . ."[15]

A different type of cuneiform evidence involves calendrical dates culled from astronomical tables and administrative texts by J. N. Strassmaier, F. X. Kugler, and F. H. Weissbach, which revealed the detailed workings of the Babylonian luni-solar calendar. The most complete lists presently available, however, (to some degree based upon unpublished texts) are those of Parker and Dubberstein (note 9), which are the basis for our reconstruction of Tables II and III, given below.

The reader is warned nevertheless to be aware of the hypothetical nature of these two tables, partly due to the uncertainties of unclear readings, that have divided the savants since the 1890's.

Based on Epping and Strassmaier's publication of cuneiform planetary tables, as has been mentioned, Eduard Mahler wrote a series of articles beginning in 1892 which claimed that:

(a) Nabû-nāṣir introduced the permanent calendar on the 21st of April, 747 B. C. E., whose 19-year cycles remained unchanged until the first century B. C. E.;

(b) The Babylonian 19-year cycle was identical with the rabbinic calendar used by the Jews today; and

(c) on the basis of admittedly slight and in some cases fragmentary evidence it was possible to convert cuneiform dates into Julian ones, with an error of plus or minus one day, beginning with 747 B. C. E.

In 1895, Mahler published what he regarded as the Babylonian calendar of 747–100 B. C. E. in the *Denkschriften der königlichen Akademie der Wissenschaften* (Volume 62, pp. 641–664). The extravagant claims contained therein divided the scholars of that day. Eduard Mayer (*ZA* 9 (1894), 325–328) and C. F. Lehmann (*ZA* 11 (1896), 110–116), found amazing confirmation of Mahler's calendar in the Chaldean dates recorded by Ptolemy in his *Almagest* and in the verified statements mentioning eclipses in cuneiform records. On the other hand, Jules Oppert (*ZA* 8 (1893), 56–74), and F. H. Weissbach

[14] See below, note 17.
[15] See also Yer. Talmud Rosh Hashanah, II, 9, p. 58b; Bab. Talmud Rosh Hashanah, 24a.

(*ZDMG* 55 (1901), 195–220), pointed out that a number of years said by Mahler to have been intercalated were found in cuneiform texts to have contained only twelve months and vice versa. Reviewing the evidence in 1906, Ginzel (*Handbuch der Chronologie* I, 132) found that of the 51 attested dates, 33 confirmed Mahler's hypothetical calendar whereas 18 negated it; of the 16 eclipses recorded in the Babylonian tablets, one half proved Mahler right and the other half showed him wrong. Mahler's achievement must be considered quite remarkable given the meagre evidence which he then had at his disposal.

To some extent, the criticism levelled against Mahler's calendar is partially valid with regard to Parker and Dubberstein's tables as well, particularly for the data before the 4th century B. C. E. As Professor Abraham Sachs pointed out in a communication to us, some of the readings of intercalary months recorded in Parker and Dubberstein's tables may not be quite reliable, while a handful are admittedly hypothetical. But even assuming the essential correctness of Parker and Dubberstein's tables, Professor Sachs maintains, the supposition of a 19-year cycle prior to 386 B. C. E. may be reading into the evidence something which possibly is not there.

Despite these reservations, we find it difficult to believe that the discovery of the equivalence of 235 lunar months with 19 solar years and its implementation into the calendar were a sudden development. It is probable that centuries of experimentation led to this remarkable discovery and that more time passed before the Babylonian astronomers felt confident enough to convince the king that a permanent calendar was practicable. Tables II and III, even if somewhat hypothetical, seem to reflect roughly this period of experimentation.

The first table (Table II) shows our interpretation of the emergence of the standard 19-year cycle as seen in cuneiform records. We detect three stages of development, in which a trial-and-error procedure was adopted until the data had been systematized.

The second (Table III) shows how the Babylonians experimented with various positions of intercalary years in the 19-year cycle. It will be seen that in the cycle of 557–539 B. C. E. ("Period 11"), only 3 of the final 7 positions of the standard cycle were employed. In the cycle of 538–520 ("Period 12"), 4 of the 7 positions were employed. In the cycle of 519–501 ("Period 13"), the number was raised to 5. In the cycle of 500–482 ("Period 14"), the "standard cycle" had been adopted, with the exception that the first year of the cycle was kept as an intercalary one, thus making 8 intercalary years in the cycle. This, however, was the last time such an absence of regularity may be noted in the calendar; from 481 on, the seven years were regularly intercalated in the sequence 3 – 6 – 8 – 11 – 14 – 17 – 19.

TABLE II

The Emergence of The Standard 19-Year-Cycle As Seen in Cuneiform Documents
Based On Parker and Dubberstein, "Babylonian Chronology," Plate I (p. 6)

	STAGE I 747–634 B.C.E.	STAGE II 633–482 B.C.E.	STAGE III 481 B.C.E. — 71 C.E.
Preference for Addaru II or Ululu II?	No preference	Preference Emerging for Addaru (34) over Ululu (20)	Addaru (with Ululu as 17th yr.)
7 months intercalated in 19-year-cycle?	No	Experimentally (5,8,7,6,7,7,7,8)	Yes
Predictable pattern for intercalary years in cycle?	No	Yes	Yes — "standard" cycle.

TABLE III

Table Showing Experimentation With Intercalation of
Seven Years in 19-Year-Cycle*

	Position of Intercalary Years in 19-Year-Cycle
Period 11 (557–539)	1 — **3** — 5 — **8** — 12 — **14** — **17**
Period 12 (538–520)	2 — **3** — **6** — 9 — 12 — **14** — **17**
Period 13 (519–501)	1 — **3** — **6** — 9 — **11** — **14** — **17**
Period 14 (500–482)	1 — **3** — **6** — **8** — **11** — **14** — **17** — **19**
"Standard Cycle"	**3** — **6** — **8** — **11** — **14** — **17** — **19**

* (Bold face numeral indicates position of intercalary year is the same as that of the "Standard Cycle.")

Some scholars maintain that Ullulu II was occasionally intercalated during Second Temple days, while others deny this (see David Sidersky, *REJ* 58 (1909), 293–296). In the opinion of the writers, the state of affairs in the Talmud reflected a procedure in which it was still conceivable to intercalate Ullulu II as one of the intercalary months, though this was officially discouraged. For some reason which is not clear to us, the rabbis wanted to suppress this custom. But from Sanhedrin 12a and Rosh Hashanah 19b, the implication is clear: speculation about, perhaps even the practice of, the intercalation of a second Elul never ceased.

In Bab. Talmud Sanhedrin 12a, the following principle is enunciated: "The year is not intercalated immediately before Rosh Hashanah (i. e., one does not intercalate Elul to make Tishri fall in the proper season); but in case of an emergency, they intercalate immediately after Rosh Hashanah. Nevertheless, they intercalate only the month of Adar (but no other month)."

This unambiguous ban against proclaiming a second Elul is quite striking. No other month is specifically named, suggesting that we have here an allusion to, perhaps a disapproval of, the Babylonian calendar that regularly added another Ullulu each seventeenth year of the nineteen year cycle.

What is even more striking is that Bab. Talmud Sanhedrin 12a, quoting from a coded message from Tiberias to the fourth century Amora, Rabba, clearly asserts that the rabbis assembled "in the month that Aaron died" and added another "governor." The meaning is that they met in the month of Ab to proclaim an extra Elul.[16] Admittedly,

---

[16] See Rashi, *ad locum*, making it clear that the rabbis deliberated in the month of Ab to make Rosh Hashanah coincide with the fall equinox.

the action here involved an emergency because of some unknown clash with the Byzantine authorities. Nevertheless it is no accident that when a month other than Adar was added it happened to be Elul.

Another passage, frequently quoted and attributed to Rab (died in 247), also seems to deal with the problem of a second Elul: — מימות עזרא ואילך לא מצינו אלול מעובר "Since the time of Ezra we have no record of Elul me'ubar."[17] This word is taken to mean "full," i. e., that the month of Elul was always hollow, having only 29 days. That me'ubar could not mean "full" here is clear from the use of this term that only marginally refers to the length of a month, and as a rule refers to intercalation. Moreover, as the Babylonian Talmud points out, Rab's dictum, if interpreted to refer to the question whether Elul was hollow or full, would contradict a number of mishnaic traditions. Certainly, the talmudic answers do not remove the serious objections.

In the light of our discussion, however, it is possible that the statement attributed to Rab was no longer understood by the talmudists. It is likely that me'ubar here referred to the intercalation of an extra Elul rather than the number of days of the month. If so, the statement "Since the days of Ezra we have no record of an intercalated Elul" may retain a vague memory of a time when the Jews adopted the Babylonian luni-solar calendar. For in rabbinic literature, Ezra always stands for the leader of the returning exiles. But while the exiles borrowed the Babylonian system of calendation, only Adar, not Elul, was subject to intercalation.

A text preserved in Bab. Talmud Sanhedrin 11b, which informs the recipients about the intercalation of a month at the close of *Addaru*, is reminiscent of the typical Neo-Babylonian letter formula: "It once happened that Rabban Gamaliel was sitting on a step on the Temple-hill, and the well-known scribe Joḥanan was standing before him while three cut sheets were lying before him . . . He said: 'Take a sheet and write: "To our brethren the Exiles in Babylon and to those in Media, and to all the other exiled sons of Israel, thus: 'May your peace be great forever! We beg to inform you that the doves are still tender and the lambs are still young and that the crops are not yet ripe. It seems advisable to me and to my colleagues to add thirty days to this year.' " ' "[18]

---

[17] Bab. Talmud Betsah, 6a; 22b; Rosh Hashanah, 19b; 32a. Cf. also Yer. Talmud Shevi'it, X, 2, p. 39b; Rosh Hashanah, III, 1, p. 58c, where the wording is quite different.

[18] See also Tosefta, II, 6, p. 416 (Zuckermandl); Yer. Talmud Sanhedrin, I, 1, p. 18d. Bab. Talmud Sanhedrin 11b concludes the discussion with the words: דילמא בתר דעברוה which Rashi interprets: *"Possibly after they removed Rabban Gamaliel*

CONCLUSIONS

(1) The system of sighting in cuneiform and rabbinic records apparently worked as follows:

1. Witnesses saw the new moon;
2. They brought this sighting to the attention of the authorities;
3. They were cross-examined;
4. The authorities proclaimed the new moon;
5. Messengers were sent out bearing the official announcement of the beginning of the month.

(2) The standard 19-year cycle emerged in Babylonia in 481 B. C. E. after two distinct earlier stages had been passed through, beginning in about 747 B. C. E. (See Table III.)

(3) The Talmud still appears to preserve the older system of observation of the lunar crescent, if we may take the written record as reflecting actual procedure. It would seem, therefore, that the system of calendation preserved in 1st or 2nd century rabbinic texts preserves a system which was in use before 481 B. C. E. and continued in use even after a new one was introduced in Babylonia. The talmudic system could not have been adopted until — at the earliest — 359 C. E., and possibly as late as the seventh century of the Christian era.[19]

(4) The post-exilic calendar as presented in the Talmud was thus inconsistent with that of the cuneiform tradition in Babylonia after 481 B. C. E.; though bearing many resemblances, the two systems diverged until at least several centuries into the present era. The first clear exposition of the rabbinic standard 19-year cycle appears in the time of the historian Al-Biruni (973–1048), where we read of it in his "Chronology of Ancient Nations." Al-Biruni records what was in fact only one of several variants still then in vogue, which went out of practice by the 12th century. The philosopher Abraham bar Ḥiyya (12th cent. C. E.) mentions the cycle now in use in his "Book of Intercalation" (3–6–8–11–14–17–19).

---

from his office of *nasi*." Perhaps a better interpretation is that (mentioned by Z. H. Chajes in his commentary, *ad locum*, in the Romm editions) Rabban Gamaliel's letter was written after they "intercalated it" (the month of Adar).

[19] Hai Gaon (died in 1038) is the first authority who is said to have mentioned that Hillel ben Judah, the patriarch, instituted the rabbinic calendar in the year 670 A. Sel. (359), according to Abraham bar Ḥiyya (*Sefer Ha'ibbur* (London, 1851), p. 97). For a more recent text, see now M. Kasher, *Torah Shelemah*, XIII, 24, who cites more evidence (pp. 24 ff.), defending the tradition against Bornstein's view that the present Jewish calendar started in 836 or in 865 (pp. 176–179).

Two of the most important questions which have not yet been answered concern Ullulu II:

(1) Why did the rabbis seek to suppress the practice of inserting Ullulu II as an intercalary month?
(2) Why did the Babylonian cuneiform calendar keep Ullulu II as the month which was always inserted in the 17th year of the 19-year intercalary cycle?

As Parker and Dubberstein have noted in *Babylonian Chronology* (p. 3, n. 4), Professors O. Neugebauer and A. Sachs have attempted to grapple with these difficult questions. Writing in the *Journal of Cuneiform Studies* 6 (1952), pp. 13–14, with reference to the astronomical series MUL.APIN, Professor Sachs observes that "the mean date for the rising of Sirius is IV 15 . . . This feature may well have been of prime importance in connection with the invention of the 19-year cycle." He suggests that

> at some moment before 380 B. C., the 19-year cycle was invented on the basis of a set of observed dates of the heliacal rising of Sirius. The seven intercalary months were distributed over the 19 years in such a way that these dates of the rising of Sirius always fell in month IV [Duzu]. Perhaps the unique intercalary month VI₂ [Ullulu II] was included to make sure that the dates of the apparent acronycal rising of Sirius should never fall outside IX [Kislimu] or X [Ṭebetu] . . .

On p. 110 of his article, Dr. Sachs concludes that "the first use of the 19-year cycle is dated around 380 B. C., specifically not before 381/0 B. C." He rejects the theory of O. Neugebauer presented in *Studies . . . Sarton* (1946), pp. 435–48, that the beginning of the 19-year cycle may have been somewhere around 418 B. C.

The conclusion of the present writers is that the seven years of the 19-year cycle were regularly intercalated from 481 B. C. E. on. How can this be squared with the evidence of the Sirius rising dates? — It may be that the observed dates of the heliacal rising of Sirius actually predate the "Sirius scheme" that is evident from Seleucid texts by a century or a century-and-a-half but that we have no written record of the earlier development of this scheme. Alternatively it may be that the construction of the 19-year cycle with its regularly intercalated 7 years was an independent development that had no associations with the heliacal rising of Sirius.

As we have noted above, it was Eduard Mahler who first proposed that the Babylonians formulated the 19-year cycle from which both the Greek (also called the Metonic cycle) and the Jewish (rabbinic) calendars were ultimately derived. This study has sought to illustrate the interdependence of the cuneiform and rabbinic texts, thereby confirming Mahler's hypothesis concerning the rabbinic tradition.[20]

As to the Greek calendar, however, it is now recognized that Meton's discovery did not result in a 19-year cycle in Athens in 432 B. C. E. or even thereafter. Meton's contribution was the publication of an astronomical tract for an Athenian audience which showed that 235 lunar months equal 19 solar years. But Meton was operating as an individual. He was a scholar without links with the rulers of the city, who would have been able to put his principles into practice.[21] A body of scientific knowledge such as this, which requires centuries of careful observation before principles can be formulated, cannot be assumed to have developed simultaneously in Greece as well as Babylonia. Barring a remarkable coincidence, then, Meton's cycle was a Greek version of the Babylonian institution.

In conclusion, it may be asked, "What was the link connecting the Mesopotamian, Palestinian, and Greek calendar traditions of the 19-year cycle?" It is our contention that the two Mediterranean systems, the Palestinian and the Greek, go back to a common origin, Mesopotamia. Some possible paths of transmission to the west might have been cultural links between Palestine and Mesopotamia during the pre-exilic period; the experience of the returnees in the Persian period; or the Phoenician bridge between Mesopotamia and the southern part of the Levant coast. Nor would it be difficult to envisage how the Greeks, who had extensive contacts in Mesopotamia in the pre-Christian centuries, might then have learned of the 19-year cycle. Table IV summarizes this hypothesis:

[20] For other studies that relate cuneiform and rabbinic traditions, see D. Weisberg, "Some Observations on Late Babylonian Texts and Rabbinic Literature," *HUCA* 39 (1968), pp. 71–72, nn. 1–15, to which should be added the important study by Baruch Levine, "*Mulūgu Melûg*: The Origins of a Talmudic Legal Institution," *JAOS* 88 (1968), 271–285; the comments of J. N. Epstein, *A Grammar of Babylonian Aramaic*, (Jerusalem: Magnes Press, 1960), pp. 105–115; and S. Greengus, "Old Babylonian Marriage Rites and Ceremonies," *JCS* 20 (1966), p. 68, n. 75.

[21] On Meton, see above note 8. As to the formulation and the possible adoption of the Metonic cycle in Athens, see now W. B. Dinsmoor, *The Archons of Athens* (1931), 217, 377 ff., who believes that Meton's observations were utilized. See, however, W. S. Ferguson, *Hellenistic Athens* (London, 1911), 122: "The demos, not the astronomers, ruled Athens"; Jacoby, *Atthis, the Local Chronicles of Ancient Athens* (Oxford: the Clarendon Press, 1949), 65; *FGrH,* IIIb (Suppl.), I, 497 f.; II, 402 f.

TABLE IV

Path of Transmission of the 19-year cycle in the Ancient Near East

Akkadian Language texts

[Aramaic texts]

Greek Sources (Meton, 432 B. C. E.)   [Babylonian Exiles]

Palestinian Tannaitic

Palestinian and
Babylonian Amoraic

PSEUDO-EUPOLEMUS' TWO GREEK FRAGMENTS
ON THE LIFE OF ABRAHAM

THIS essay is essentially a commentary on two Greek fragments that treat with the life of Abraham.[1] They are from the monograph *On the Jews* by Cornelius Alexander Polyhistor of Miletus (*circa* 80–35 B. C. E.).[2] A tireless researcher, Alexander Polyhistor excerpted a remarkably large number of Hellenistic biblical writers.[3] None of these writers has survived, and most of them must have already been obscure in Alexander Polyhistor's time. Our knowledge of these writers comes exclusively from Alexander Polyhistor or the sources dependent on him. Even Josephus (37–100) retained but a vague and faulty memory of writers such as Theophilus, Theodotus, Philo the Elder and Eupolemus.[4] Alexander Polyhistor's works are no longer extant, but Eusebius in the ninth book of his *Praeparatio Evangelica*[5] made extensive excerpts from Alexander's account of the Jews, including the two fragments discussed here.[6] These depict not only Abraham's ancestry and his travels into Phoenicia and Egypt, but also what

---

[1] F. Jacoby, *Die Fragmente der griechischen Historiker*, IIIC, Pt. 2 (Leiden, 1958), pp. 678 f., No. 724 FF 1–2. Hereafter this work is cited as "*FGrH*."

[2] *FGrH*, 273 F 19a–b; Nos. 722–33; C. Mueller, *Fragmenta Historicorum Graecarum*, III (Paris, 1849), pp. 211–30; J. Freudenthal, *Hellenistische Studien⁹ Alexander Polyhistor und die von ihm erhaltenen jüdischen und samaritanischen Geschichtswerke* (Breslau, 1875). For Alexander Polyhistor's date, see G. F. Unger, "Wann schrieb Alexander Polyhistor," *Philologus*, XLVII (1889), 177–83, who argues that Polyhistor wrote his works in the 40's and 30's B. C. E. Unger's view is generally rejected: Susemihl (*Geschichte der griechischen Litteratur in der alexandriner-zeit* [Leipzig, 1892] II, 357 f.), dates Polyhistor's birth *circa* 105 B. C. E., and his death after 40 B. C. E. Jacoby, who cites the secondary literature, gives 80–35 B. C. E. as the time of Alexander Polyhistor's writings (*FGrH*, IIIa, 248 f.).

[3] At least thirteen writers were quoted by Alexander Polyhistor in his monograph *On the Jews*. See Wacholder, "Greek Authors in Herod's Library," *Studies in Bibliography and Booklore*, V (1960), 104–109; *Nicolaus of Damascus* (Berkeley and Los Angeles, 1962), 81–86.

[4] *C. Apion*, I, 216–218, confuses these Jewish writers with heathen authors.

[5] *Praep. Ev.* IX, 17–41.

[6] *Praep. Ev.* IX, 17 = *FGrH*, 724 F 1; *Praep. Ev.* IX, 18, 2 = 724 F 2.

83

were believed to be his civilizing and educational activities. These fragments preserve not only a Hellenistic image of the Hebrew patriarch, but also a little known school of Hellenistic biblical historiography.

The first fragment, containing a page and a half of Greek text, Alexander Polyhistor ascribed erroneously to Eupolemus.[7] As shown by Freudenthal, Eupolemus wrote in 158/7 B. C. E., and was Judah Maccabaeus' envoy to Rome in 161 B. C. E.[8] The fragments that truly belong to Eupolemus show him to have been a Jewish writer who embellished biblical traditions with Greek rhetoric.[9] Eupolemus probably did not deal with Abraham at all, because some of the virtues that Pseudo-Eupolemus' fragment ascribes to Abraham are credited by Eupolemus to Moses.[10] The style of the fragment on Abraham, moreover, is concise and free of rhetoric, and frequently departs from the biblical traditions; its author probably was not a Jew, but a Samaritan.[11] Furthermore, the second fragment, containing but several lines of text, and merely summarizing the content of the first, is ascribed by Alexander Polyhistor not to Eupolemus but to an anonymous work.[12] Following Freudenthal, Jacoby labeled the two fragments "Pseudo-Eupolemus (Anonymous)."

Alexander Polyhistor gives the title of the work as *On the Jews of Assyria*, Περὶ Ἰουδαίων τῆς Ἀσσυρίας.[13] Both parts of the heading are incorrect. It is unlikely that an account dealing with the patri-

---

[7] 724 F 1, line 13. Jacoby printed the ascription in petite, indicating that he suspects the tradition.

[8] Eupolemus, 723 F 4; Freudenthal, *Alexander Polyhistor*, 126 f. The peculiarity of the name makes it very likely that Eupolemus the writer is the same man mentioned in I Macc., VIII, 17; II Macc., IV, 11; Jos., *AJ*, XII, 415 ff.; 723 T 1.

[9] Eupolemus, 723 F 2, concocts an extensive correspondence between Solomon and the kings of Egypt and Tyre. Although based on Kings and Chronicles, these letters are characteristically Hellenistic exercises (Freudenthal, *Alexander Polyhistor*, 106 ff.).

[10] According to Eupolemus, 723 F 1a–b, Moses was the first wise man who invented writing, which the Jews transmitted to the Phoenicians and they in turn taught the Greeks. 724 F 1, however, credits Abraham and even Enoch with the invention of the sciences.

[11] See 724 F 1, p. 679, line 1, which makes Freudenthal's identification of the author as a Samaritan almost certain (*Alexander Polyhistor*, 82–103), a view now generally accepted: Graetz, *Geschichte d. Juden*, III[5] (1905), 46; Schürer, *Geschichte d. jüd. Volkes im Zeitalter Jesu Christi*, III[4] (1909), 476; Susemihl, *Gesch. d. griech. Litt.*, II, 652; Stearns, *Fragments from Graeco-Jewish Writers* (Chicago, 1908), 67. A. Schlatter, *Geschichte Israels von Alexander dem Grossen bis Hadrian*[2] (Calw and Stuttgart, 1906), II, 140 ff., however, dissents from this point of view.

[12] ἐν δὲ ἀδεσπότοις εὕρομεν (*Praep. Ev.*, IX, 18, 2 = 724 F 2.).

[13] 724 F 1, p. 678, line 13 = Al. Polyh., 273 F 19a, line 14.

76

archs would have been titled "of Assyria." Kuhlmey maintained that by "Assyria" the author meant Syria, the two being frequently confused among the ancients.[14] This might have been possible, were it not that our author always refers to the land as Phoenicia.[15] The more reasonable explanation, generally agreed upon, is that "of Assyria" does not modify "On the Jews," but the next word, "polis."[16] However, the first part of the title is equally erroneous. It is inconceivable that a Samaritan author would have entitled a work concerning Abraham: *On the Jews*. Freudenthal suggested that perhaps the original heading was Περὶ Ἑβραίων, "On the Hebrews."[17] This is very doubtful, for no such title has come down from the Hellenistic period.[18] It must then be assumed that Alexander Polyhistor erred both in ascribing the fragment to Eupolemus and in crediting him with a work *On the Jews*. A possible solution is that περὶ Ἰουδαίων, used very frequently in the Hellenistic literature, does not refer to the title of Pseudo-Eupolemus' work but to its contents.[19] Unaware of the rift between the Jews and the Samaritans, Alexander Polyhistor assumed that a work dealing with Abraham must have the Jews as its subject matter.

The date of Pseudo-Eupolemus is unknown, except that he wrote after 293/2, the approximate date of Berossus' *Babylonica*, and before 63 B. C. E., when Alexander Polyhistor composed his monograph on the Jews.[20] Based on the fact that Eupolemus lived in the middle of

[14] C. Kuhlmey, *Eupolemi Fragmenta prolegomenis et commentario instructa* (Berlin, 1840), 46.

[15] 724 F 1, p. 678.

[16] Εὐπόλεμος δὲ ἐν τῷ περὶ Ἰουδαίων τῆς Ἀσσυρίας φησὶ πόλιν Βαβυλῶνα (724 F 1, p. 678, lines 13–14). That τῆς Ἀσσυρίας does not modify Ἰουδαίων, but πόλιν, was pointed out by Freudenthal [*Alexander Polyhistor*, 207] and accepted by Gifford, the editor of Eusebius [*Praep. Ev.*, Vol. IV, 299]; Susemihl, *Gesch. d. griech. Litt.*, II, 652, n. 87.)

[17] Freudenthal, *Alexander Polyhistor*, 207.

[18] See *FGrH*, IIIC, "Juden," Nos. 722–37, pp. 666–713. From Hecataeus of Abdera (322 B. C. E.) to the second century C. E. the title Ἰουδαῖοι or its modifications constantly recur, but never Ἑβραῖοι.

[19] The title Περὶ Ἰουδαίων is credited by Jacoby to the following authors: Pseudo-Hecataeus of Abdera (264 FF 21–24); Aristeas (725 F 1); Artapanus (726 FF 1–3); Cleodomus-Malchus (727 F 1); Alexander Polyhistor (273 F 19); Damocritus (730 F 1); Nicarchus of Ammonius (731 F 1); Theodotus (732 F 1); Philo of Byblos (790 FF 9–11). The variety of the subject matter treated in these works, such as Damocritus' diatribe against the Jews or Aristeas' Job, suggests that in some cases Περὶ Ἰουδαίων merely denotes a generic name rather than an actual title.

[20] For the date of Alexander Polyhistor's monograph *On the Jews*, see Jacoby, *FGrH*, IIIa, 269, lines 14 ff. Jacoby rejects Unger's dating of Alexander's work after

the second century B. C. E., Pseudo-Eupolemus is frequently assigned the same date,[21] though this does not follow at all. Jacoby cautiously dates Pseudo-Eupolemus in the second century B. C. E., but adds a question mark.[22] Nevertheless, there are a few indications that he flourished between the end of the third century and the early part of the second century B. C. E. Some evidence, but not much, in support of the early dating is the fact that Alexander Polyhistor, writing *circa* 63 B. C. E., already referred to Pseudo-Eupolemus' work as anonymous; while the literary activities of Demetrius and Eupolemus, also quoted by Alexander, were dated 221–204 and 158/7, respectively.[23] If this argument has any force, Pseudo-Eupolemus antedated Eupolemus and Demetrius. But there are other somewhat more reliable considerations. Alexander Polyhistor quotes from a section of the Jewish Sibylline Books which, it is generally assumed, is directly indebted to Pseudo-Eupolemus.[24] It follows that Pseudo-Eupolemus preceded Alexander by at least two generations. And if we accept the consensus of the scholars that the third book of the Oracula Sibyllina was written *circa* 140 B. C. E., Pseudo-Eupolemus must be placed at least in the middle of the second century B. C. E.[25] Furthermore, Pseudo-Eupolemus' reference to "Argarizin," the Samaritan temple, would seem to indicate that it was still in existence when the author was writing.[26] As the Samaritan shrine was destroyed by John Hyrcanus (134–104 B. C. E.), it may perhaps be assumed that Pseudo-Eupolemus wrote before that date. But his syncretistic tendencies, which Pseudo-Eupolemus presents freely and unapologetically, point to a period when the forces of syncretism in Samaria were powerful

---

40/39 B. C. E. as fantastic. That Pseudo-Eupolemus made use of Berossus' *Babylonica*, written after 293/2 B. C. E., see below n. 117.

[21] M. Friedländer, *Geschichte der jüdischen Apologetik* (Zürich, 1903), 110 f.; H. St. J. Thackeray, *Josephus*, Vol. IV (1930), 82, n. a.

[22] 724 F 1, margin. Unfortunately, Jacoby's commentary on this F has not as yet been published.

[23] For the date of Demetrius, see 722 F 6; for that of Eupolemus, 723 F 4. The weakness of the argument presented here is that anonymity does not necessarily imply antiquity.

[24] Alexander Polyhistor quotes the Or. Sibyll. (III, 97 ff.); Berossus, 680, F 4a–b, pp. 382 f. That the Or. Sibyll. followed Pseudo-Eupolemus, see J. Geffcken, *Or. Sibyll.* (Leipzig, 1902), n., on III, 97, p. 53; III, 218, n., p. 59; Jacoby, 680 F 4b, p. 382, lines 22–23, app. crit.

[25] The relevant passages of the Or. Sibyll. are generally dated 150 or 140 B. C. E. (Geffcken, *Komposition und Entstehungszeit der Or. Sibyll.* [Leipzig, 1902], 7; R. H. Charles, *The Apocrypha and Pseudepigrapha of the Old Testament* [Oxford, 1913], II, 372).

[26] 724, F 1, p. 678, lines 1 f.

and unchallenged, i. e., before the Maccabaean revolt in 167 B. C. E.[27] However, Pseudo-Eupolemus' use of the Septuagint, discussed below, indicates that he could not have lived before the middle of the third century B. C. E.[28] Furthermore, his thrusts against Egypt and his defense of Babylon seem to reflect a period when the Seleucids and the Ptolemies competed for the annexation of Coele Syria. If, then, we assume that Pseudo-Eupolemus lived in the first half of the second century B. C. E., his fragments are among the oldest remnants of the treatment of the Abraham-theme written originally in Greek.[29]

In addition to the Bible, Pseudo-Eupolemus made use of Hellenistic sources. He used the Hebrew text of Genesis together with the Septuagint translation as the basis of his account. The use of the LXX is attested by the transliteration of names such as Enoch, Methuselah, Cham, Chanaan, Abraam and Melchisedek.[30] It is possible to argue

[27] II Macc., VI, 2; *AJ*, XII, 257–264; cf. XI, 344, blame the Samaritans for their acquiescence to Antiochus IV's Hellenization. Freudenthal, *Alexander Polyhistor*, 87 ff., maintains that these sources indicate that the Samaritans were less monotheistic than the Jews (see Ḥullin, 6a). For this there is no evidence, at least not after the Maccabaean revolt. The anti-Samaritan passages in Josephus reflect the Jewish attitude towards that sect. For though it is true that the Samaritans did not participate in the revolt, neither did they welcome Antiochus IV's policies. The king evidently expected resistance in Samaria, for he appointed a new governor (*AJ*, XII, 261). See J. A. Montgomery, *The Samaritans: The Earliest Jewish Sect* (Philadelphia, 1907), 78. Certainly, Freudenthal's argument, that syncretistic tendencies by themselves are sufficient to identify writers such as Cleodomus-Malchus (727 F 1) or Thallus (256 FF 1–8) as Samaritans, must be rejected. Artapanus' extreme syncretistic account of Moses (726 FF 1–3), reproduced partially by Josephus (*AJ*, II, 238–253), indicates that the Samaritans had no monopoly on mixing Jewish with heathen worship. That Cleodomus-Malchus was not necessarily a Samaritan, see Graetz, *Gesch. d. Juden*, III⁵, 609; Schürer, *Gesch. d. jüd. Volkes*, III¹, 481 f. Although Thallus is generally identified as a Samaritan (Freudenthal, 100 f.; Schürer, III¹, 494 f.; Wachsmuth, *Einleitung in das Studium der alten Geschichte* [Leipzig, 1895], 146 f.). Jacoby, *FGrH*, IID, 835 f., seems to be correct in rejecting this view. Both the Jews and the Samaritans appear to have had their Hellenistic factions during the reign of Antiochus IV. The rout of syncretism in Judaea undoubtedly had the same result in Samaria.

[28] Despite the fictional nature of the Letter of Aristeas, it is generally agreed that the LXX translation of the Pentateuch dates from the period of Ptolemy II Philadelphus (285–247 B. C. E.). For a summary of the evidence and the secondary literature see M. Hadas, *Aristeas to Philocrates* (Philadelphia, 1951), 1 ff.

[29] Except for the LXX itself (see previous note), Demetrius the chronographer (221–204) is the oldest known Greek writer on a biblical theme (722 F 6); unless Aristobulus the Peripatetic is taken to have lived during the reign of Ptolemy Philadelphus (Eusebius, *Hist. Eccl.* VII, 32, 16). But it is agreed that Aristobulus flourished under Ptolemy Philometer (Schürer, *Gesch. d. Jüd. Volkes*, III¹, 512 f.).

[30] Ἐνώχ, 724 F 1, p. 679, lines 12, 19; Μαθουσάλα, line 19 (LXX, Gen. 5:21–26);

that a medieval scribe retouched the names to conform with the LXX. But this is unlikely, as Polyhistor's fragments frequently preserve forms that differ from those of LXX.[31] Two times Pseudo-Eupolemus gives the Hebrew terms with his renditions into Greek, indicating strongly that he made use, though incorrectly, of the Hebrew text.[32] In fact, several interpretations found in the fragments become intelligible only in light of the Hebrew version of Genesis. Pseudo-Eupolemus' radical departures from the traditional texts, then, cannot be explained, as suggested by Freudenthal, by carelessness or ignorance.[33] The explanation of the differences lies in the author's attempt to integrate the Genesis tradition with that of Babylonian and Greek sources. Phrases such as "the Babylonians say,"[34] "but the Greeks say,"[35] "which some call,"[36] "recorded in history"[37] — meaning no doubt recorded in non-biblical sources — suggest that Pseudo-Eupolemus made use of Babylonian and Greek works. That the author made use of the pseudepigraphical Book of Enoch, and of Berossus, the priest of Bel in Babylon who dedicated his *Babylonica* to Antiochus I, will be shown below. To these we may add Hesiod, and perhaps Ctesias, Artaxerxes Mnemon's physician, who flourished in the beginning of the fourth century B. C. E.[38] Whether Pseudo-Eupolemus was the first to fuse the biblical account with the Greek sources or whether he was indebted to an older tradition is not known. But to assume that such an integration of sources existed much earlier than at the end of the third century B. C. E. presupposes the existence of a Greek school of biblical historiography at a time when there is no reason to believe there was one.

Χάμ, line 15 (Gen. 5:32 and *passim*); Χαναάν, line 15 (Gen. 9:18 and *passim*); Ἀβραάμ, p. 678, line 19 and *passim*; Μελχισεδέκ, p. 679, line 2 (Gen. 14:18). Pseudo-Eupolemus' spelling of Μεστραείμ, line 17, conforms with many LXX MSS. of Gen. 10:6, 13. See Freudenthal, *Alexander Polyhistor*, 98.

[31] The transliteration of כוש as Χοὺμ, instead of Χοὺς, the description of the invading armies as Armenians, as well as other departures from traditional exegesis, seem to indicate that the fragments were not retouched by a conformist scribe. In Eupolemus (723 FF 1–5), for example, the transliteration of the Hebrew names frequently departs from that of LXX.

[32] 724 F 1, p. 678, lines 18–19: אור כשדים = Χαλδαίων πόλις; p. 679, lines 1–2: הר נריים = ὄρος ὕψιστος.

[33] Freudenthal, *Alexander Polyhistor*, 96; 187.

[34] Βαβυλωνίους γὰρ λέγειν (724 F 1, p. 679, lines 13–14).

[35] Ἕλληνας δὲ λέγειν (724 F 1, p. 679, line 18).

[36] ἥν τινας λέγειν (724 F 1, p. 678, line 18).

[37] οἰκοδομεῖν δὲ τὸν ἱστορούμενον πύργον (p. 678, lines 15–16).

[38] The use of Hesiod is discussed below. As for Ctesias (*FGrH*, No. 688), see Alfred von Gutschmid, *Kleine Schriften*, II (1890), 575 f.

Pseudo-Eupolemus began his story of Abraham with an account of the patriarch's ancestry and the foundation of the first city: "The Assyrian city of Babylon was founded by those who had escaped the flood. They were the giants who built the tower recorded in history. But when the tower was ruined by God's act the giants dispersed over the whole earth."[39] The pre-Noachite genealogy of Genesis is ignored by Pseudo-Eupolemus. The version of the flood and the tower, however, is scriptural,[40] except that Noah and his descendants, perhaps including Abraham, are considered giants. That this is the proper interpretation may be seen from the second fragment: "Abraham traced his ancestry to the giants, who were dwelling in Babylonia and were destroyed on account of their impiety by the gods, as one of them, Belus, escaping death, settled in Babylon and having built a tower he ruled over it, which was named Belus after its builder Belus."[41] The account in Genesis of the נפילים, which LXX renders γίγαντες, provides ready confusions. We are told that the "sons of God" took the daughters of man and they bore the "giants," who were responsible for the flood.[42] Nimrod, the third generation after Noah, dubbed the first *gibbor* — translated by LXX as "giant" — ruled in Babylon.[43] But the story of the tower and the foundation of Babylon by those who were dispersed contains no reference to any name in Genesis except that of Peleg, the fourth generation after Noah, in whose time it is mentioned that the confusion of the tongues occurred.[44] Pseudo-Eupolemus, however, seems to be the first, as far as we know, who made Nimrod the chief of the giants and the architect of the tower, a tradition preserved also in Josephus and in the rabbinic literature.[45]

That Nimrod is identical with Belus is found only in the Anonymous fragment. The reasoning behind Pseudo-Eupolemus' identification is not hard to follow. As it is shown below, he tends to concoct

---

[39] 724 F 1, p. 678, lines 13–17: Εὐπόλεμος δὲ . . . τῆς 'Ασσυρίας φησὶ πόλιν Βαβυλῶνα πρῶτον μὲν κτισθῆναι ὑπὸ τῶν διασωθέντων ἐκ τοῦ κατακλυσμοῦ. εἶναι δὲ αὐτοὺς γίγαντες, οἰκοδομεῖν δὲ τὸν ἱστορούμενον πύργον· πεσόντες δὲ τούτου ὑπὸ τῆς τοῦ θεοῦ ἐνεργείας, τοὺς γίγατας διασπαρῆναι καθ' ὅλην τὴν γῆν. For the meaning of 'Ασσυρία and πόλις, see note 16.

[40] Gen. 11:1–9.

[41] 724 F 2.

[42] Gen. 6:1–8.

[43] Gen. 10:8–10.

[44] Gen. 11:1–9; 10:25.

[45] *AJ*, I, 113 ff.; *Antiquities of Philo*, VI, 3 ff. (cited by S. Sandmel, *Philo's Place in Judaism* [Cincinnati, 1956], 50 = *HUCA*, XXVI [1955], 171). Gen. Rabbah [ed. Theodor], XXIII, 227; XXVI, 246; *Pirkei d'Rabbi Eli'ezer*, XXIV. The name Nimrod was taken by the Midrash to imply rebel, from the root מרד.

etymologies from the biblical texts. Babel, the Hebrew equivalent of Babylon, which the Akkadians pronounced Babilu and popularly explained to mean "the gate of Ilu (god)," appears to be interpreted by Pseudo-Eupolemus as *ba bel*, "Bel came."[46] That seems to be the basis of the unknown author's emphasis that Belus settled in Babylon. Pseudo-Eupolemus' derivation of the Hebrew meaning of Babel differs of course from that given in Genesis, *balal*, "confused," but it is simpler Hebrew, though neither etymology need be taken seriously. The reasoning behind the equating of Nimrod and Belus was perhaps thus: Babel means Bel came; as Scripture says that Nimrod founded Babylon, Nimrod must be a variant of Belus. A more plausible explanation for Pseudo-Eupolemus' identification of Nimrod with Belus is that he equated Bel with Marduk and Marduk with Nimrod.[47]

The inspiration of Pseudo-Eupolemus' philological aberration, however, was based on Hellenistic sources. Ctesias and the sources dependent on him made Ninus — the son of Belus — and his wife Semiramis the founders of Babylon.[48] Christian and Parthian writers, therefore, equated Nimrod with Ninus.[49] But Berossus ascribed the foundation of Babylon to Belus.[50] The parallel between the biblical Nimrod and Berossus' Belus was not limited to the foundation of the first city. Castor of Rhodes (*circa* 50 B.·C. E.) tells that Belus was king of the Assyrians when the Cyclopes, with lightning and fiery rays, rendered aid to God in his battle against the giants.[51] Castor's account generally follows that of Ctesias, but his introductory passage that describes the battle between the Titans and Belus seems to be a mixture of Berossus and Hesiod.[52] Berossus credited Belus with the creation of the world as well as the foundation of Babylon and the construction of its walls.[53] But Castor's description of the battle between Belus and the Titans is clearly the struggle between Zeus

---

[46] For a similar view, see Ibn Ezra's Commentary to Gen. 11:9.

[47] For a similar equation, see Jer. 50:2: אמרו נלכדה בבל הביש בל חת מרדך; cf. Jer. 51:44. I am indebted to Professor Jonas C. Greenfield for many valuable suggestions and bibliographical notes.

[48] Ctesias, 688 F 1a = Cephalion 93 F 1; cf. Herod., I, 7.

[49] Eusebius, *Chronica*, I; *Chronic. Pasch.* (*Patr. Gr.* Vol. XCII), 36, p. 148. Cf. *The Chronicles of Jerahmeel*, ed. M. Gaster (London, 1899), XXXII, 3, which identifies Nimrod as the father of Bel. The Parthian literature is cited by G. Widengren, *Iranisch-semitische Kulturbegegnung in parthischer Zeit* (Cologne and Opladen, 1960), 42–50.

[50] Abydenus, 685 FF 1; 6, who follows here Berossus.

[51] Castor, 250 F 1.

[52] That Castor supplemented his Ctesias with Berossus, see E. Schwartz, *RE*, III, 314 = *Griechische Geschichtschreiber* (Leipzig, 1957), 197.

[53] [Berossus] in Abydenus, 685 FF 1a–b; 6; cf. Berossus, 680 F 1, 7–9.

and Kronos described by Hesiod.[54] That Kronos was the leader of
the Titans who battled Zeus, identical with Belus, is also recorded
by Thallus, a second century C. E. author of a chronological history.[55]
Castor and Thallus, however, were not the first to combine Berossus
with Hesiod. The Jewish author of the third book of the Oracula
Sibyllina, already cited by Alexander Polyhistor, supplemented his
description of the biblical tower with a long excerpt from Hesiod's
Theogony.[56] The oldest extant literary source, however, that contaminated the Genesis account of the tower with Berossus and Hesiod
is that of Pseudo-Eupolemus. For it is Pseudo-Eupolemus who made
Belus-Kronos the giant who founded the human race and Belus the
architect of the tower.[57]

There is a basic difference, however, between Pseudo-Eupolemus'
treatment of Belus and that of Berossus. Berossus, himself a priest
of Bel, regarded Belus as the deity who created the world; according
to Pseudo-Eupolemus, however, Belus, Kronos, Atlas and the Babylonian and Greek pantheons are none other than pagan names for
the ancestors of Abraham.[58] In typical Hellenistic fashion Pseudo-
Eupolemus utilized exegesis to fuse biblical traditions with pagan
mythological accounts.[59]

Schnabel's reconstruction of the sources differs from that presented here. Schnabel started with the assumption that Pseudo-
Eupolemus' entire account of the tower and the foundation of Babylon
was, directly or indirectly, dependent on Berossus.[60] In a postscript
to his work, however, Schnabel came to believe that Pseudo-Eupolemus
made no use of Berossus, but that an oral tradition prevalent among

---

[54] Hesiod, *Theog.* 421 ff.

[55] Thallus, 256 F 2.

[56] Or. Sibyll. III, 97–154; Hesiod, *Theog.*, 421 ff.; Alexander Polyhistor in
Berossus, 680 F 4a–b, pp. 382 f., quoting Or. Sibyll. (III, 97 ff.).

[57] Despite Alexander Polyhistor (see previous note), there is no evidence that
Berossus mentioned the tower and the divine punishment of its builders. In Berossus,
Belus creates the heavens and the earth out of a chaotic mass (680 F 1, 7); Kronos
forwarns Xisuthrus of the impending flood (680 F 4a–b). According to Pseudo-
Eupolemus, Kronos-Belus is the first creature and Belus is the villain who rebelled
against the gods (724 FF 1, 8; 2). The use of θεοί in 724 F 2, despite Pseudo-
Eupolemus' monotheistic beliefs, to describe Belus' punishment strengthens the
evidence that he was following Hesiod's description of Kronos' fall.

[58] 724 F 1, 9.

[59] For the contamination of biblical traditions with pagan mythology, see
Artapanus, 726 FF 1–3; Cleodomus-Malchus, 727 F 1; Theodotus, 732 F 1, p. 692,
line 15; Or. Sibyll., III, 97 ff.

[60] P. Schnabel, *Berossos und die babylonisch-hellenistische Literatur* (Leipzig und
Berlin, 1923), 67 ff.

BEN ZION WACHOLDER

the Samaritans coincided with that of the Babylonian priest.[61] Both
of these assumptions are unlikely. As noted above, Pseudo-Eupolemus'
wording such as "some say," "the Babylonians say," "called by the
Greeks," indicates that the author made use of literary sources.[62]
Several passages of the fragment, as will be shown below, also show a
coincidence of phrasing in Pseudo-Eupolemus and Berossus which
can be accounted for only if one assumes direct dependence. Schnabel's
original assumption that Pseudo-Eupolemus' account of the foundation of Babylon and the tower is but a paraphrase of Berossus must
equally be rejected.[63] For there is reason to believe that Berossus was
entirely dependent on Babylonian traditions.[64] The euhemeristic color-
ing of these traditions and their fusion with Genesis must be credited
to Pseudo-Eupolemus.

Pseudo-Eupolemus' suggestion that the biblical tower of Babel is
somehow related to Hesiod's account of the battle between Zeus and
Kronos became a leading motif in world literature. The first to ex-
pand Pseudo-Eupolemus' theme was the Jewish author of the third
book of the Oracula Sibyllina.[65] As far as we can tell, Pseudo-
Eupolemus merely said that the builders of the tower were un-godly
giants, led by Belus, the Greek Kronos.[66] It is conceivable that
Pseudo-Eupolemus referred directly to Hesiod's *Theogony*, which was
omitted in Alexander Polyhistor's excerpts. Be that as it may, the
author of the Oracula Sibyllina, who made use of Pseudo-Eupolemus,
quoted Hesiod's *Theogony* as if it were but intended to supplement
the biblical version of the confusion of the tongues. Inspired perhaps
by Pseudo-Eupolemus' fusion of the Bible with Berossus and Hesiod,
Alexander Polyhistor, in his turn, contaminated Berossus with a cita-

[61] Schnabel, *Berossos*, 246; Lehmann-Haupt, *Reallexikon der Assyrologie*, II
(1938), 9a.
[62] See above notes 34–37. It is unreasonable to assume that these phrases refer
to oral traditions. That Pseudo-Eupolemus did not manufacture them himself,
see notes 63; 67–68.
[63] Schnabel, *Berossos*, 67 f., cites Pseudo-Eupolemus (Eusebius, *Praep. Ev.*,
IX, 17 = 724 F 1) to prove that Berossus mentioned the tower and Camarina, because other passages of the two authors coincide. In his postscript, Schnabel (p. 246)
gives no reason for abandoning this hypothesis. But it may perhaps be assumed
that he was aware of the circular reasoning contained in his original assumption.
This in turn led him to the assumption that Pseudo-Eupolemus did not make use
of Berossus at all.
[64] That Berossus was not aware of the Genesis account is suggested even by
Josephus, who cited the Babylonian priest to corroborate the historicity of Abraham
(*AJ*, I, 158 = Berossus, 680 F 6).
[65] Or. Sibyll., III, 97 ff.
[66] 724 FF 1, 9; 2.

tion from the Sibylline Oracles.[67] The attempt to synthesize Babylonian, biblical and Greek themes, as well as Pseudo-Eupolemus'
euhemeristic views, must have been especially attractive to Alexander
Polyhistor, one of the most learned men of a learned age. Castor,
Thallus, Eusebius, Moses of Khoren, and, in turn, Milton — to cite a
few — either repeated or expanded upon the theme begun by Pseudo-
Eupolemus.[68] Curiously, it is now generally agreed that the link between the Babylonian traditions and Genesis was much more profound
than conceived by either Pseudo-Eupolemus or Alexander Polyhistor.
Some scholars argue that Iapetus, in Hesiod's *Theogony* the son of
Earth and Heaven, was originally somehow connected with Japheth,
the son of Noah; and that Hesiod's cosmogony was not unrelated to
similar Near Eastern traditions.[69]

Pseudo-Eupolemus' reconstruction of the Noachite descendants
also contains a mixture of Babylonian and Greek mythology: "The
Babylonians say that the first [giant] was Belus, who is Kronos, who
begat Belus [?] and Cham. This [Cham] had a son named Chanaan,
the father of the Phoenicians. His son was Chum, who is called by
the Greeks Asbolus, the father of the Ethiopians and brother of
Metsraeim, the father of the Egyptians."[70] The reader should be
warned that the Greek text is somewhat ambiguous. But the translation given here, based on Gutschmid's reconstruction, is plausible.[71]
That Pseudo-Eupolemus equated Belus with Noah and these two with
Kronos is strange, but in light of the author's euhemeristic nuances,
not surprising. It is perhaps possible to detect contempt for paganism
in the identification of the biblical hero of the flood with Kronos, who
according to Hesiod was the father of Zeus, and Belus, whom Berossus
described as the creator of the world.[72] Kronos, it may be recalled,
was according to Berossus directly involved in the flood: Kronos
advised Xisuthrus, in a dream, of the impending deluge.[73] Pseudo-

[67] Berossus, 680 F 4, pp. 382 ff.; Abydenus, 685 F 4a–b.

[68] Castor, 250 F 1; Thallus, 256 FF 2–3; Eusebius, *Praep. Ev.*, IX, 14 (see previous
note); Moses of Khoren, *Arm. Hist.*, I, 6; Schol. ad Plat. *Phaeder.*, 244 B; Theophilus,
Ad Autol., II, 31.

[69] Hesiod, *Theog.*, 134; 507 ff. See Rose in *OCD*, 448a; G. S. Kirk and J. E.
Raven, *The Presocratic Philosophers* (Cambridge, 1960), 35–37. Hittite sources now
confirm this view: H. G. Gütterbock, *Kumarbi: Mythen von Kurritischer Kronos*
(Zurich-New York, 1946); "The Hittite Version of the Kumarabi Myths: Oriental
Foreruners of Hesiod," *AJA*, LII (1948), 123–134.

[70] 724 F 1, 9.

[71] See Jacoby's app. crit. to 724 F 1, 9.

[72] Hesiod, *Theog.*, 137 f.; 154 ff.; Berossus, 680 F 1a–b, 7–9.

[73] Berossus, 680 F 4a–b. Xisuthrus corresponds to the Sumerian Ziusudra

Eupolemus, it would seem, in a single sentence intended to parallel the Noah story with Babylonian and Greek mythology, at the same time pointing out the inferiority of these traditions when compared with the Bible. For the biblical tradition, unlike the pagan, maintained that the progenitor of the human race, as well as the hero of the flood and the founder of Babylon, was a mere mortal.

In his attempt to fuse Hebrew with Babylonian and Greek traditions, Pseudo-Eupolemus was forced to stretch thin his exegesis of Genesis. He had two, perhaps three, giants named Belus. The second fragment identifies Nimrod with Belus. In the first fragment, however, we find Belus-Kronos-Noah. Then we have Belus II, identical either with Belus-Nimrod of the second fragment, or with Shem, the son of Noah. The latter interpretation is more likely. Pseudo-Eupolemus could not have identified Belus II with Nimrod, since Genesis says that Nimrod was the son of Cush, the son of Cham. It is also strange that Belus-Kronos-Noah's son bears the same non-biblical name as his father. The solution to this problem appears to be that Pseudo-Eupolemus, here as elsewhere, played on the Hebrew etymology of words. As "Shem" in Hebrew denotes "name," it may have occurred to Pseudo-Eupolemus that Shem really bore his father's name, Belus, Shem being an alternate designation to distinguish the son from the father. A rabbinic tradition identifies Shem with Melchisedek, confirming the circumstance that Shem was known by another name.[74] Pseudo-Eupolemus follows Genesis that Chanaan was the son of Ham and the father of the Phoenicians.[75] However, Pseudo-Eupolemus says that Chum and Metsraeim were the sons of Chanaan; in Genesis they are the brothers of Chanaan. It is possible that there was an error in the transmission of the text. But it is conceivable that Pseudo-Eupolemus, a Phoenician patriot, as shown below, intentionally altered the biblical genealogy in favor of Chanaan. By making Chanaan the father of Metsraeim and Chum, instead of their brother as recorded in Genesis, he seems to suggest the precedence of Phoenicia over Egypt and Ethiopia.

Pseudo-Eupolemus' assertion that Chum (Χοὺμ) was the ancestor of the Ethiopians conforms with the traditional biblical interpretation of Cush. The variant Χοὺμ, however, where Χοὺς is expected, is strange because the fragment as a rule transliterates the Hebrew meticulously and follows the LXX. Gutschmid's emendation

---

(J. Pritchard [ed.], *Ancient Near Eastern Texts Relating to the Old Testament*[2] [Princeton, 1955], 42–44); and Utnapishtim of the Gilgamesh epic (pp. 88 ff.).

[74] Gen. Rabbah, 26, p. 246; *Midrash Tehillim*, 76:3.

[75] Gen. 10:6, 15.

to read Χοὺς is conceivable, but lacks authority.[76] Equally puzzling is Pseudo-Eupolemus' identification of Chum with Asbolus. Following Neibuhr, it is generally assumed that Asbolus is none other than Chomasbelus, the second post-diluvian king of Babylon, recorded in Berossus.[77] Zimmern has suggested that Chomasbelus was perhaps Berossus' spelling of Gilgamesh; Jacobsen argues that Chomasbelus equals Lugal-banda.[78] But despite the general acceptance of this view, the identification of Asbolus with Chomasbelus remains doubtful. For Pseudo-Eupolemus does not otherwise mention any of the names of the kings listed by Berossus. Moreover, as Pseudo-Eupolemus says that Asbolus is the Greek name for Chum, it is unlikely that his source here was Berossus' genealogy of the Babylonian kings. A more likely solution is that for etymological reasons Pseudo-Eupolemus intentionally changed the transliteration of Χοὺς to Χοὺμ. As in several other cases in the fragment, he liked to play with similar-sounding Hebrew roots. Attempting to account for the derivation of כוש (Kush), he seems to have confused it with חמם (ḥmm), or חום (ḥum), denoting blackened by the sun or heat, which would explain the pigmentation of the Ethiopians. Strange as it may seem, ancient and medieval scholars, such as Jerome and Isidorus, maintained that חם and כוש were etymologically related.[79] Thus Χοὺμ was preferable to the traditional Χοὺς and Ἄσβολος, soot, apparently was a perfect equivalent to Χοὺμ. Asbolus, moreover, appears in Hesiod's *Shield*, 185, as an augur. Hesiod, it is true, did not connect Asbolus with Ethiopia, but others may well have done so. It is conceivable that Pseudo-Eupolemus, or his source, by identifying Chum with Asbolus attempted to show once again that the Greeks borrowed from the Bible.

Having stated that Metsraeim was the ancestor of the Egyptians, Pseudo-Eupolemus digresses to deal with his favorite theme, the discovery and dissemination of the astral sciences: "The Greeks say that Atlas discovered astrology. Atlas is the same as Enoch. And

---

[76] See app. crit. to 724 F 1, p. 679, line 16. The letters Σ and M are easily confused, however.

[77] Berossus, 680 F 5a–b, p. 384a, lines 6–7; 384, 12. For the identification of Chomasbelus with Asbelus, see M. Neibuhr, *Geschichte Assurs*, 472, cited by Freudenthal, *Alexander Polyhistor*, 208; Schnabel, *Berossos*, 68; cf. F. Hommel, *Ethnologie und Geographie des alten Orients* (Munich, 1926), 184, n. 1; 1021.

[78] H. Zimmern, "Die altbabylonischen vor (und nach-) sintflutlichen Könige nach neuen Quellen," *ZDMG*, LXXVIII (1924), 31, n. 4, identified Gilgamesh either with Εὐήχοιος (cf. Aelian, *De Nat. Anim.*, XII, 21,) or with Χωμάσβηλος; Th. Jacobsen, *The Sumerian King List* (Chicago, 1929), 88, n. 122.

[79] Jerome, *De nom. Hebr.*, 4: 7; Isidorus, *Etymologiae*, IX, 2, 39; 127.

Enoch had a son Methuselah, who learned all things through the angels of God, and thus we gained our knowledge."[80] It may be noted that Pseudo-Eupolemus had already mentioned Enoch's contribution: "And Abraham lived with the Egyptian priests in Heliopolis, teaching them many things. And he introduced astrology and other sciences to them, saying that the Babylonians and he himself had discovered them, but he traced the discovery to Enoch, and he [Enoch] was the first to discover astrology, not the Egyptians."[81] It is evident that Pseudo-Eupolemus' repeated digressions into the origin of the astral sciences are primarily intended to deflate the Egyptian claims for pre-eminence in fields of endeavor then regarded as the greatest achievements of man. In Pseudo-Eupolemus' scheme, the Babylonians were the first cultured people, followed by the Phoenicians; but the Egyptians were rather latecomers.

The Greek claim that Atlas discovered astrology, a favorite theme of Hellenistic mythology, Pseudo-Eupolemus refutes indirectly. In Hesiod Atlas is the son of Iapetus, who holds up the sky to keep it from falling, though in Homer Atlas is a mere guardian of the pillars of heaven.[82] But Herodorus of Heracleia (400 B. C. E.), Xenagorus of Heracleia (150 B. C. E.), and Dionysius Scytobrachion of Alexandria (second century B. C. E.), among others, credited the discovery of astrology to Atlas.[83] Pseudo-Eupolemus disposed of these claims by the simple device of identifying Atlas with Enoch. The contamination of Semitic heroes with Greek mythology has its parallel in the writings of Philo of Byblos (54–142 C. E.), who claimed that he was merely transmitting the writings of the ancient Sanchuniathon: Uranus (Heaven) begat four sons by his sister Ge (Earth): Elus-Kronos, Baetylus, Dagon-Siton, and Atlas.[84] But Pseudo-Eupolemus had even less respect for Greek mythology than Philo of Byblos. According to Pseudo-Eupolemus, Atlas and Kronos were but Greek adaptations of biblical heroes.

That Enoch was the discoverer of the astronomical sciences was a major theme of the extra-canonical literature. Genesis, it is true,

[80] 724 F 1, p. 679, lines 18–20.

[81] 724 F 1, 8.

[82] Hesiod, *Theog.*, 517; *Od.* I, 53.

[83] Herodorus, 31 F 13; Xenagorus, 240 F 32; Dionysius Scytobrachion, in Diod., III, 60, 2 = 32 F 7.

[84] Philo of Byblos, Eusebius, *Praep. Ev.*, I, 10, 16 = 790 F 2. Cf. Eissfeldt, *Taautos und Sanchunjaton* (Berlin, 1952); *Sanchunjaton von Beirut und Ilumilku von Beirut* (Halle, 1952); "Art und Aufbau der Phönizischen Geschichte des Philo von Byblos," *Syria*, XXXIII (1956), 88–98; C. Clemen, *Die Phönikische Religion nach Philo von Byblos* (Leipzig, 1939).

merely says that he disappeared at a relatively young age, having been 365 years old, "for God had taken him."[85] This mysterious passage gave rise to, or was based on, descriptions of secrets revealed by Enoch.[86] The Book of Enoch devotes a major part of the work to the hero's heavenly revelations, and references to Enoch's astronomical discoveries are found in the Book of Jubilees and in the midrashic literature.[87] The Book of Enoch is a composite work, and the dating of its various parts is still debated among scholars. But there is good reason to believe that the astrological parts of the Book of Enoch were already written down in the third century B. C. E.; certainly they antedate the Maccabaean revolt.[88] It may then be assumed that Pseudo-Eupolemus' attribution of the discovery of astrology to Enoch was taken from the Book of Enoch or a work dependent on it.[89] The suggestion that Pseudo-Eupolemus here followed an oral legend rather than a literary source must be rejected,[90] for the fragment attests to the author's wide acquaintance with the contemporary literature.

The interdependence between Pseudo-Eupolemus and the Enochite legendary literature can be demonstrated by textual analysis. The passage in Pseudo-Eupolemus: "And Enoch had a son Methuselah,

---

[85] Gen. 5:18–24.

[86] During the Hellenistic period, and perhaps earlier, there seems to have been a belief that Oannes (Berossus, 680 F 1; Pseudo-Apollodorus, 244 F 84), the fish-man, and Enoch were not unrelated. In fact Enoch assumes in the pseudepigraphical literature the character of an all-wise mythological figure, such as Adapa or of semi-historical men as Gilgamesh, Aḥikar, or Zoroaster.

[87] Enoch, VI–XVI; XXIII–XXXVI; LXII–XC; Jub., IV, 17–32; *Midrash 'Aggadah* on Gen. 5:24; *Pirkei d'Rabbi Eli'ezer*, 8; S Schechter. *Saadyana* (Cambridge, 1903), 93.

[88] Fragments of the original Enoch have been uncovered at Qumran (Milik, *Qumran Cave I* [Oxford, 1955], 84–86; 152). Charles, *Apocrypha and Pseudepigrapha*, II, 163 f., sums up the consensus of scholars that major portions of Enoch are pre-Maccabaean. D. Flusser, *Encyclopedia Biblica*, III (Jerusalem, 1958), 207–209, however, believes that none of its portions should be assigned that early and regards the work as a product of the Qumran sect. Flusser's argument is not convincing. Certainly Pseudo-Eupolemus' mention of Enoch attests to an early composition of the astronomical sections of the Book of Enoch. Cf. Ben Sira's possible references to the Enochite legends (Ecclus. 44:16; 49:14).

[89] H. Ewald, *History of Israel*, V (London, 1874), 347, n. 2; *Abhandlung über des äthiopischen Buches Henokh: Entstehung, Sinn und Zusammensetzung* (Göttingen, 1845), 76.

[90] A. Dillmann, *Das Buch Henoch* (Leipzig, 1853), p. L; A. Hilgenfeld, *Die jüdische Apokalyptik in ihrer geschichtlichen Entwickelung* (Jena, 1857), 145, n. 3, assumes that, contrary to Ewald (see previous note), Pseudo-Eupolemus did not make use of the Book of Enoch, but of an oral tradition. The parallel wording of Pseudo-Eupolemus and Enoch, discussed below, excludes such a possibility.

who learned all things through the angels of God, and thus we gained our knowledge,"[91] is ambiguous. The text seems to say, and was so interpreted by Hilgenfeld, that Methuselah, not Enoch, was the discoverer of the sciences.[92] The context, however, makes it clear that the meaning of this passage is that Methuselah transmitted his father's knowledge to posterity.[93] That this interpretation is correct may be seen from related passages in the Book of Enoch and the recently discovered Genesis Apocryphon. Chapter 106 of the Book of Enoch says that when Noah was born, his father Lamech was in a great state of shock. The child's appearance resembled more that of an angel than a human. Suspecting that the prodigious baby was the offspring of the angels, Lamech implored his father Methuselah to learn the truth from Enoch, whose "dwelling-place is among the angels."[94] Genesis Apocryphon's Aramaic text, though mutilated, is even more dramatic: "Then I, Lamech, hastened to Methuselah my father and [I told] him all . . . his father; and he will know everything in truth, because he [Enoch] is beloved and . . . [with angels] his lot is shared and to him they tell everything."[95] Pseudo-Eupolemus evidently transmits a tradition found in the Book of Enoch and Genesis Apocryphon that the angels revealed all knowledge to Enoch, which was handed down to subsequent generations through his son Methuselah:

Pseudo-Eupolemus, 724 F 1, 9	Gen. Apocryphon, Col. II
	רטת
τοῦ δὲ Ἐνὼχ γενέσθαι υἱὸν Μαθουσάλαν, ὃν πάντα δι' ἀγγέλων θεοῦ γνῶναι, καὶ ἡμᾶς οὕτως ἐπιγνῶναι.	19. באדין אנה למך על מתושלח אבי וכולא לה̄]
	20. אבוהי וכולא מנה ביצבע ינדע בדי הוא רחים ור̄]
	21. עדבה פליג ולה מחוין כולא

Although the Greek fragment uses a phrase that is dependent on the traditions found in the Book of Enoch and Genesis Apocryphon, Pseudo-Eupolemus' aim differs substantially from the pseudepigraph-

[91] 724 F 1, 9.

[92] Hilgenfeld, *ibid.*, 145, n. 3.

[93] The repeated assertions of the fragment: "Abraham attributed the original discovery of astrology to Enoch"; "Enoch discovered astrology, not the Egyptians"; "Atlas is the same as Enoch," make it evident that the meaning of the passage is that Methuselah merely transmitted Enoch's discovery.

[94] Enoch, CVI, 1–12.

[95] N. Avigad and Y. Yadin, *A Genesis Apocryphon: A Scroll from the Wilderness of Judaea* (Jerusalem, 1956), Col. II, 19–21.

90

ical writers. The authors of the Book of Enoch and Genesis Apocryphon were primarily concerned with interpreting certain ambiguous passages of Genesis. The account which denies Noah's divine ancestry suggests that this was an attempt to refute a belief that the builder of the ark was indeed the offspring of the sons of God.[96] Berossus tells that Xisuthrus, having escaped the deluge, was raised by the gods to be one of them, as was Ziusudra in the Sumerian account.[97] Utnapishtim of the Gilgamesh epic, the Mesopotamian hero of the flood, was like-wise a semi-divine being.[98] The account of Genesis, which tells of sexual intercourse between the "Sons of God" and the daughters of men, as it immediately precedes the story of Noah, must have given rise to similar beliefs in the hero's divinity.[99] This the authors of Enoch 106 and Genesis Apocryphon vehemently deny; Noah was a mortal and the son of a mortal, though his facial features were indeed ex-traordinary and though the possibility of cohabitation between divine and human is not excluded. Do we perhaps have here an ancient refer-ence to a debate among Jewish writers as to whether any of the biblical heroes was of divine progeny, an argument which was sub-sequently to bring about a major schism in the Jewish ranks?

The Hellenistic writers, however, were less inhibited by the con-flict between biblical accounts and pagan mythology.[100] This was especially true before the Maccabaean revolt. By identifying Noah with Kronos or Belus, Pseudo-Eupolemus apparently was satisfied that he had undermined the polytheistic creeds. But Pseudo-Eupolemus' main object was to glorify Abraham, by pointing out that the patriarch descended from the giants, a popular view among Hellenistic Jewish writers.[101] Freudenthal's view that Noah-Belus-Kronos or Enoch-Atlas represented a Samaritan concession to polytheism needs modifica-tion.[102] To Pseudo-Eupolemus, it seems, these identifications served to reenforce the veracity of the account of Genesis.

"In the tenth generation, he [Pseudo-Eupolemus] says, in the Babylonian city of Camarina, which some call Urie (Οὐρίη), and

---

[96] Enoch, CVI; Genesis Apocryphon, Col. II.

[97] Berossus, 680 F 4a–b, p. 381, lines 1 ff.; Pritchard, *Ancient Near Eastern Texts*, 44.

[98] Pritchard, *ibid.*, 88 ff.

[99] Gen. 6:1–8. In the rabbinic exegesis these difficult passages were reinterpreted to minimize the personalities of Enoch, Methuselah and even Noah (see Gen. Rabbah, XXV and Theodor's notes, p. 238; Sanhedrin, 108a).

[100] Cf. Artapanus, 726 FF 1–3; Cleodomus-Malchus, 727 F 1.

[101] Cf. Josephus, *AJ*, I, 241 = Cleodomus-Malchus, 727 F 1; Philo the Elder, 729 F 1.

[102] Freudenthal, *Alexander Polyhistor*, 82 ff.

which is in translation the city of the Chaldaeans, in the thirteenth generation, Abraham was born."[103] Various suggestions have been proposed to answer the contradiction as to the generation in which the patriarch was born. Neibuhr and Kuhlmey believed the phrase "in the thirteenth generation," which Jacoby puts in brackets, to be a gloss.[104] But Freudenthal is probably correct in arguing that Pseudo-Eupolemus gave two alternative versions: Abraham was born in either the tenth or the thirteenth generation. But a phrase such as "or some say," frequently used in the fragment, was omitted from the text.[105] However, it is far-fetched to say, as does Freudenthal, that the tradition which placed Abraham's birth in the thirteenth generation was based on a view preserved by Apollonius Molon.[106] Molon, an anti-Semitic writer of the first century B. C. E., says that Abraham was born in the third generation after the flood.[107] According to Freudenthal, Pseudo-Eupolemus may have added the three generations found in Molon's source to his own ten as an alternative view.[108] But aside from the fact that Molon lived probably a century after Pseudo-Eupolemus, Molon's account displays ignorance of the sources. Having received his information from a secondary source, Molon probably confused the three patriarchs with three generations between the flood and Abraham. It is not impossible that the thirteen generations represent not a different tradition, but a different system of computation, perhaps beginning with Enoch, a major hero in Pseudo-Eupolemus. In other words, counting from Noah-Belus-Kronos, Abraham was born in the tenth generation; but if one begins with the generation after Enoch, he was born in the thirteenth.

Like modern scholars, Pseudo-Eupolemus speculated as to the etymology of Ur Kasdim, Abraham's birthplace. He offers two views, either Camarina or Urie. Urie he renders from עיר כשדים, the city of the Chaldaeans.[109] But no Babylonian city by the name of Camarina

---

[103] 724 F 1, 3: δεκάτῃ δὲ γενεᾷ φησὶν ἐν πόλει τῆς Βαβυλωνίας Καμαρίνῃ, ἥν τινας λέγειν πόλιν Οὐρίην (εἶναι δὲ μεθερμηνευομένην Χαλδαίων πόλιν), [ἐν τρισκαιδεκάτῃ] γενέσθαι Ἀβραὰμ [γενεᾷ].

[104] Kuhlmey, *Eupolemi Fragmenta*, 49; Neibuhr, *Geschichte Assurs*, 506; Gifford in Eusebius, *Praep. Ev.*, IV, 300.

[105] Freudenthal, *Alexander Polyhistor*, 94; Mras, cited by Jacoby, app. crit., p. 678, line 19.

[106] Freudenthal, *Alexander Polyhistor*, 93 f.

[107] Apollonius Molon, 728 F 1 = Eusebius, *Praep. Ev.*, IX, 19, 2.

[108] Freudenthal, *Alexander Polyhistor*, 94; Gifford, in Eusebius, *Praep. Ev.*, IV, 300.

[109] 724 F 1, 3. The location of אור כשדים, rendered in LXX χώρα Χαλδαίων, has been the subject of numerous studies. T. G. Pinches in Hasting's *Dictionary of*

is known. However, modern editors since C. Alexandre have filled a lacuna in the third book of the Oracula Sibyllina with the name taken from Pseudo-Eupolemus: "There is a city [Camarina] down in the land of Ur of the Chaldees, from which comes a race of most righteous men."[110] Scholars usually explain the meaning of Camarina as derived from the Arabic *qamar*, moon, as Ur was in the third millenium B. C. E. the residence of the moon god Sin Nannar.[111] Modern opinion is equally divided as to the original meaning of Ur. Some say it is based on the Sumerian *uru*, city; others, on the Babylonian *uru-uniki,* the seat of light.[112] Both views cite Pseudo-Eupolemus in support of their opinions — a rather unreliable witness.[113] Speiser believes, however, that Ur and Uruk may be of Elamite rather than of Semitic or Sumerian origin.[114] Schnabel cites Pseudo-Eupolemus' mention of Camarina as evidence that the Samaritan author made use of Berossus, for Arabs had settled in Babylon and named it Ur Camarina, the city of the moon.[115] This presupposes that Berossus mentioned Camarina, for which there is no evidence. Whether or not Pseudo-Eupolemus' speculations have a sound basis must be left to the Orientalists, but there is no doubt that he attempted to integrate information collected from diverse sources.

The first fragment characterizes Abraham as one "who surpassed all men in nobility and wisdom, who also discovered astrology and

---

the Bible, IV (New York, 1902), 835–37, sums up the evidence of those who maintain that Ur refers to Urfa (Edessa), near Haran, citing as their authority Isidorus, *Comm. in Gen.*, 296 (Migne); cf. Naḥmanides' Commentary on Gen. 11:28; 12:1. Pinches himself, however, believes that Ur of the Chaldees refers to Mukayyar, the modern site of the famous Sumerian city. This view is now supported by C. J. Gadd, *History and Monuments of Ur* (New York, 1930), 233, 254 f.; L. Wooley, *Ur of the Chaldees*[2] (London, 1952), 22 and *passim*. For attempts to locate Ur elsewhere, see C. H. Gordon, *JNES*, XVII (1958), 28–31; a view rejected by H. W. F. Saggs, *Iraq*, XXII (1960), 200–9.

[110] C. Alexandre, ed., *Orac. Sibyll.* (Paris, 1841), III, 218. Charles, *Apocrypha and Pseudepigrapha*, II, 382, follows Alexandre. The basis for filling the lacuna of Or. Sibyll. with Pseudo-Eupolemus is the supposition that Or. Sibyll., III, 218–35 is a polemic against Pseudo-Eupolemus. Or. Sibyll. denies that the people of Ur of Chaldaea engaged in the foolishness of astrology, but were a race of righteous men.

[111] Alexandre, on Or. Sibyll., II, 218; Kuhlmey, *Eupolemi Fragmenta*, 47; Ewald, *Gesch. d. Volkes Israel*, VII[3], 481; Langdon, *AO*, XXVI (1926), 19–55; Kohler, *Lexicon Vet. Test. Libr.* (Leiden, 1958), 23.

[112] See Hommel, *Ethnologie und Geographie*, 373 f.; S. Yeivin, *Encyclopedia Biblica*, I, 170 f.

[113] Yeivin, *Encyclopedia Biblica*, I, 171; Pinches in Hasting's *Dictionary of the Bible*, IV, 835–37; Gadd, *History and Monuments of Ur*, 254 f.

[114] E. Speiser, *Mesopotamian Origins* (Philadelphia, 1930), 38; 92 f.

[115] Schnabel, *Berossos*, 69.

Chaldaean [science (?)] and who on account of his piety was well-pleasing to God."[116] As Freudenthal has shown, the description of Abraham is a close paraphrase of Berossus, as quoted by Josephus: "In the tenth generation after the flood there lived among the Chaldaeans a just man and great, and versed in the celestial lore."[117] The parallel between Berossus and Pseudo-Eupolemus is close enough to dispose of the doubt voiced by Schnabel as to whether the latter was dependent on the former.[118] There is, however, no reason to believe that Berossus alluded to Abraham.[119] Pseudo-Eupolemus, and Josephus after him, used the work of the Babylonian priest as an independent source to substantiate the account of Abraham in Genesis.[120]

Although the description of Abraham follows a formula derived from Berossus, its spirit is that of LXX. Abraham's εὐσέβεια, piety, is probably intended to contrast with the giants' ἀσέβεια, impiety or ungodliness.[121] The phrase εὐαρεστῆσαι τῷ θεῷ, well-pleasing to God, is the usual LXX rendition of התהלך את האלהים, describing the piety of Enoch, Noah and Abraham.[122]

Abraham's piety is not neglected, but the emphasis throughout the fragment is on his scientific contributions. The patriarch's chief claim to fame, according to Pseudo-Eupolemus, was the discovery and dissemination of the astronomical sciences: "By the command of God, this man went to Phoenicia to dwell there and he pleased the king by teaching the Phoenicians the changes of the sun and the moon and all things of that kind."[123] The account in Genesis ascribes to Abraham materialistic or nationalistic goals[124] which did not satisfy the Samaritan author. Pseudo-Eupolemus apparently believed that Scripture's description of Abraham's vision of the stars revealed the patriarch's real objective.[125] Thus, Pseudo-Eupolemus constructed an image of

---

[116] 724 F 1, 3.

[117] *AJ*, I, 158 = Berossus, 680 F 6. Freudenthal, *Alexander Polyhistor*, 94.

[118] Schnabel, *Berossos* 246, correcting his earlier view (67–69) that Pseudo-Eupolemus is basically a paraphrase of Berossus.

[119] *AJ*, I, 158 = 680 F 6, clearly states that Berossus did not mention Abraham.

[120] Since Josephus cites Berossus' work under a wrong title — Χαλδαϊκά instead of Βαβυλώνικα — it follows that he possibly knew Berossus only through Alexander Polyhistor: Schnabel, *Berossos*, 20–21, 166–67; A. Schalit (ed.), *AJ* (Hebrew edition), I, p. XLV. Freudenthal, *Alexander Polyhistor*, 26 f., however, argues that Josephus used Berossus directly.

[121] 724 F 1, p. 678, line 21; F 2, p. 678, line 23.

[122] LXX, Gen. 5:24; 6:9; 17:1; 24:40. Cf. Liddell-Scott-Jones, *s.v.* εὐαρεστέω.

[123] 724 F 1, 4.

[124] Gen. 12:1–3; 15:13–20.

[125] Gen. 15:5.

Abraham that conformed with the scientific spirit of the Alexandrian age. Pseudo-Eupolemus' great interest in astral sciences suggests that he himself, like Berossus, was an ardent student of this field.[126]

That Abraham was a great astrologer is a common theme in ancient Jewish sources. According to Josephus, the patriarch inferred the monotheistic doctrine from observing the celestial bodies.[127] Josephus also says that Abraham introduced arithmetic and astronomy to the Egyptians, a view also maintained by Artapanus.[128] Philo of Alexandria grants that Abraham was a great astrologer, but argues that the patriarch's migration from Chaldaea implied the departure from the world of the senses to enter into the harmony of the universe.[129] The talmudic scholars were, as usual, divided. Some regarded Abraham as an astrologer; but the predominant opinion seems to be that God advised Abraham to abandon his astrological pursuits.[130] As there is no reason to believe that either Artapanus or Josephus was dependent on Pseudo-Eupolemus, it must be assumed that the belief concerning Abraham's mastery of the Chaldaean science was a major motif of Jewish folklore.[131] Pseudo-Eupolemus differs, however, from the Hellenistic and rabbinic sources in making astrology the main theme of Abraham's accomplishment.

Another departure from the Jewish tradition is Pseudo-Eupolemus' repeated reference to the land of Canaan as Phoenicia.[132] Technically, the designation of Canaan as Phoenicia is correct. Phoenician and biblical sources attest that the two terms are equal.[133] Even LXX occasionally renders the Hebrew Canaan into Phoenicia.[134] Still, it is

---

[126] Berossus, 680 TT 3; 4–6; 9; FF 15–22.

[127] *A J*, I, 156.

[128] *A J*, I, 167 f.; Artapanus, 726 F 1.

[129] Philo, *De Abr.*, 69 ff. Cf. S. Sandmel, *Philo's Place in Judaism*, 144 = *HUCA*, XXVI (1955), 265.

[130] Tosefta, Qiddushin, 5, 17; Bava Bathra, 91a–b; Shabbath, 156a; Gen. Rabbah, 43.

[131] Schechter, *Saady…ana*, 93–94, maintains that astrology was Abraham's chief virtue. Cf. also Genesis Apocryphon, XIX, where the patriarch appears as an interpreter of dreams.

[132] 724 F 1, 3–4.

[133] Philo of Byblos, 790 F 1, p. 813, line 10 = Eusebius, *Praep. Ev.*, I, 10, 39; Chna was the first who changed the name of the land to Phoinix (cf. *Iliad*, XIX, 311); the name Canaan appears on Phoenician coins, N. Slouschz, *Thesaurus of Phoenician Inscriptions* (Tel-Aviv, 1942), No. 30; Augustine, *Ep. ad Rom. incoata expos.*, XIII, cited by Eissfeldt, *RE*, XX (1941), 354. See also B. Maisler, "Canaan and the Canaanites," *BASOR*, 102 (1946), 7–12. Gen. 11:19.

[134] LXX always transliterates the Hebrew of Canaan when referring to the land of the patriarchs or the Jews; it sometimes employs Φοινίκη instead of Canaan

unlikely that a Jewish author of the third or second century B. C. E. would have written that God commanded Abraham to go to Phoenicia.[135] Despite the historical justifications that might be marshalled for such a statement, the implication that the Lord promised Phoenicia, and not Canaan, to Abraham's descendants would probably have been offensive to one believing that the divine promise referred to Jerusalem. Here we have additional evidence for Freudenthal's view that Pseudo-Eupolemus was a Samaritan.[136] According to Josephus, the Samaritans, addressing Alexander, claimed that they were Hebrews, but called themselves Sidonians of Shechem.[137] In an exchange of letters with Antiochus IV, the Samaritans are also addressed as Sidonians of Shechem.[138] This designation led Rostovtzev to believe that semi-Greeks from Phoenicia settled during the Hellenistic period in Judaea and Samaria.[139] According to Abel, Phoenician migration to Palestine had begun during the reign of Eshmunazar of Sidon.[140] It is possible, then, that Pseudo-Eupolemus was either a descendant of the Greek settlers or a Hellenized Phoenician. This may explain his propensity towards identifications such as Noah-Belus-Kronos, Nimrod-Belus, and Enoch-Atlas. Phoenician patriotism would also shed light on Pseudo-Eupolemus' insistence on the pre-eminence of Babylonia and Phoenicia over Egypt.

Despite his syncretistic tendencies, Pseudo-Eupolemus was a firm believer in the literal account of Genesis: "Later [after Abraham's arrival into Phoenicia] the Armenians marched against the Phoenicians, and being victorious they took captive his nephew. Abraham together with his servants came to the rescue, overcame the captors and made their wives and children prisoners. And when ambassadors came to Abraham to ransom the prisoners for money, he chose not to take advantage of the unfortunates, but after providing food for

---

when referring to the produce of the land or when relating to non-Jews: Exod. 6:15; Josh. 5:1; Prov. 31:24. Cf. E. Bickerman, "Un document relatif à la persécution d'Antiochus IV Épiphane," *RHR*, CXV (1937), 204–6.

[135] The only possible exception is the phrase in the Assumption of Moses, I, 3, "profectionis fynicis." But as the reference seems to be to the exodus from Egypt rather than from Phoenicia, this passage is doubtful and no proof can be deduced that the meaning is here Canaan.

[136] Freudenthal, *Alexander Polyhistor*, 96.

[137] *AJ*, XI, 344.

[138] *AJ*, XII, 258 ff.

[139] Rostovtzev in *CAH*, VII, 191; Bickerman in Finkelstein, *The Jews: Their History, Culture and Religion* (New York, 1960), I, 87; Bickerman, *RHR*, CXV (1937), 206–9.

[140] Abel, *Histoire de la Palestine depuis la conquête d'Alexandre jusqu'à l'invasion arabe* (Paris, 1952), I, 56.

his servants he restored the booty."[141] Essentially, this is a brief
summary of Gen. 14. But there are several departures from the
biblical account. In Genesis the four invading armies are led by the
kings of Elam and Shinar (Sumer?); the Sodomite city kings were
the victims. But according to Pseudo-Eupolemus, it was the Armenians
who marched against the Phoenicians. The identification of the
Sodomites as Phoenicians is consistent with Pseudo-Eupolemus' rendition of Canaan as Phoenicia. But the view that the invaders were
Armenians is, if not unique, at least contrary to tradition. Freudenthal
may or may not be right in maintaining that Pseudo-Eupolemus
intentionally avoided identifying the four kings as Babylonians (or
Assyrians, as found in Josephus),[142] on account of the close ties between
the Samaritans and Babylonia.[143] Whether or not Freudenthal's reasoning is correct, there is no doubt of Pseudo-Eupolemus' pro-Babylonian
bias throughout his account. It is possible that Pseudo-Eupolemus
here attempted to defend the patriarch from the charge of making war
against his own kin. It might also have detracted from his account
of Abraham's magnanimity towards the Babylonian captives if the
patriarch was himself a native of that country. Plausible as this
explanation is, for it conforms with the pro-Babylonian bias of the
author, it is not conclusive. Ancient sources, such as the Genesis
Apocryphon, Gen. Rabbah and Symmachus, locate the kingdom of
at least one of the invading armies as far away as the Pontus or
Cappadocia.[144] Pseudo-Eupolemus' claim, however, that the four kings
came from Armenia, though perhaps related to these sources, departs
more radically from Genesis and may reflect a personal view.

Despite his brevity, Pseudo-Eupolemus makes Abraham a greater
hero and a somewhat more generous victor than does the Genesis
account. Genesis says that Abraham defeated the enemy, freed the
Sodomite captives, and restored to the Sodomites the booty taken
from them during the war.[145] Pseudo-Eupolemus relates that Abraham
took captive the wives and children of the Armenians, which seems
to imply that he had invaded the territory of Armenia. In the Greek
fragment, moreover, Abraham accepts the plea of the enemy's ambassadors to free the prisoners, refusing to accept ransom, and re-
storing to the Armenians the spoils taken during the war.[146]

---

[141] 724 F 1, 4–5.   [142] *AJ*, I, 172.
[143] Freudenthal, *Alexander Polyhistor*, 97, referring to II Kings 17:24–41.
[144] Genesis Apocryphon, col. XXI, 23, identifies Elasar (Gen. 14:1) as king of
Cappadocia; see the comments of the editors, p. 34. Pseudo-Jonathan and Symmachus, Gen. 14:1, identify Elasar with Pontus.
[145] Gen. 14:14–17; 21–24.   [146] 724 F 1, 4–5.

Of greater significance is Pseudo-Eupolemus' reconstruction of Gen. 14:18–20: "Being entertained as a guest by the temple of the city of Argarizin, which may be translated as the Mount of the Most High, he [Abraham] received gifts from Melchisedek, who was its priest of God and king."[147] The relevant passage in Genesis is ambiguous, for it is not clear whether Abraham gave "a tenth" to or received it from Melchisedek.[148] Jewish exegesis, attested in the Genesis Apocryphon, Jubilees and the talmudic writers, interpreted Gen. 14:20b, because of the technical term מעשר, a tenth, to mean that Abraham offered Melchisedek a tenth of the spoil.[149] Thus they found support for the Mosaic legislation of tithing. Pseudo-Eupolemus, however, evidently understood the word מעשר to mean "gifts." And as Melchisedek is the subject of Gen. 14:20a, he is also the subject of 14:20b: "And he [Melchisedek] gave gifts to him [Abraham]."[150] Josephus, however, appears to have combined both interpretations. According to Josephus, Melchisedek entertained Abraham and supplied his army, but the patriarch, in return for the favors, gave a tenth of the spoil to Melchisedek.[151] Josephus' suggestion that the relations between Abraham and Melchisedek were business-like cannot be read into Pseudo-Eupolemus. For the Greek fragment mentions Melchisedek's reception of Abraham after the patriarch had already given away the booty and freed the prisoners. The context of Pseudo-Eupolemus' account, moreover, makes it clear that Melchisedek was honoring Abraham for his victory over the Armenians.

Pseudo-Eupolemus' designation of Melchisedek as king and priest

---

[147] 724 F 1, p. 679, lines 1–3: Ξενισθῆναι τε αὐτὸν ὑπὸ πόλεως ἱερὸν Ἀργαριζίν, ὃ εἶναι μεθερμηνευόμενον ὄρος ὑψίστου, παρὰ τοῦ Μελχισεδὲκ ἱερέως ὄντος τοῦ θεοῦ καὶ βασιλεύοντος λαβεῖν δῶρα. The joining of הרגריזים into one word is common in the Samaritan version of the Pentateuch (Deut. 27:4); cf. A. Merx, *Der Messias oder Ta'eb der Samaritaner* (Giessen, 1909), 77. Cf. Ἀρμαγεδών = הר מגדו (Rev. 16:16).

[148] Cf. M. R. Lehmann, "I Q Genesis Apocryphon in the Light of the Targumim and Midrashim," *Revue de Qumran*, I (1958), 262 f.

[149] Genesis Apocryphon, col. XXII, 17; Jubil., XIII, 25–27; Nedarim, 32b; Soṭah, 5a; Gen. Rabbah, 43, p. 422.

[150] Traces of a similar interpretation seem to be preserved in Gen. Rabbah, 43, p. 420, where Melchisedek king of Salem (Gen. 14:18–20) is paralleled with Ps. 45:13: "And daughter of Tyre, the wealthy of the people shall entreat your favor with a gift." According to the Midrash, the daughter of Tyre refers to Abraham for he brought distress to the kings (a play on צור, מיצר), thus Melchisedek's gift. Pseudo-Eupolemus' assertion that Abraham was received by the Phoenician king (724 F 1, 4) and that Melchisedek gave gifts to the patriarch makes this somewhat obscure passage of the Midrash more intelligible.

[151] *AJ*, I, 179–182.

of God follows Gen. 14:18. ἱρέως ὄντος τοῦ θεοῦ is a literal rendition of the Hebrew והוא כהן לאל עליון, except for the last word. Pseudo-Eupolemus evidently omitted the translation of עליון intentionally, because he had already given a technical meaning to the word: "Argarizin, which may be translated as the Mount of the Most High."[152] In Gen. 14:18, however, Melchisedek is the king of Shalem. The Jewish tradition maintains unanimously that Shalem is to be equated with Jerusalem.[153] However, Epiphanius cites two opinions as to the geographic location of Shalem: According to some, it is Jerusalem; according to others, it is in the valley of Shechem, now called Neapolis, a view now accepted by some scholars.[154] The Babylonian Talmud also mentions two Jerusalems, meaning no doubt two Shalems, and the Palestinian Talmud records Kefar Shalem in the vicinity of Shechem.[155] This interpretation is supported in Gen. 33:18, though the meaning of the Hebrew text is uncertain: ויבא יעקב שלם עיר שכם. The Septuagint renders this verse: "And Jacob came to Salem the city of Shechem." Rabbinic exegesis, however, possibly to avoid the Samaritan argument that Shalem usually refers to Shechem, interpreted the Hebrew "shalem" to mean perfect, i. e., in peace.[156] Curiously, the rabbinic exegesis of Gen. 33:18 finds its strongest support in the extant texts of the Samaritan Pentateuch.[157]

---

[152] 724 F I, p. 679, line 1 f. The equation גרזים = ὕψιστος is peculiar to Pseudo-Eupolemus, unless we assume that he equated גרזים with עליון. LXX usually renders עליון as ὕψιστος (Gen. 14:18; Deut. 32:8). The term was used to describe the Samaritan temple as late as the fifth century C. E. Damascius quotes Marinus, a Samaritan apostate and head of the Athenian Neo-Platonic academy, that in Neapolis (Schechem) on Argarizus Abraham worshiped ἐν ᾧ Διὸς ὑψίστου ἁγιώτατον ἱερόν (Reinach, Textes d'auteurs grecs et romains relatifs au judaïsme [Paris, 1895], 212). See Cumont, "Hypsistos," RE, IX, 445. Cf. Philo of Byblos, Mueller, FGH, III, pp. 566 f., Fr. 2, 7, 12 = FGrH, 790 F 2, pp. 808, line 8; 809, line 14, for Ὑψουρανίος and τις Ἐλιοῦν καλούμενος Ὕψιστος.. On Elyon, see further J. Lewy, "Les textes paléo-assyriens et l'Ancien Testament," RHR, CIX (1934), 59 f., M. H. Pope, El in the Ugaritic Texts (Leiden, 1955), 55–58.

[153] Ps. 76:3; 110:4; Genesis Apocryphon, col. XXII, 13; Targumim on Gen. 14:18; Gen. Rabbah, 43, p. 420.

[154] Epiphanius, C. Haer. (ed. Dindorf), II, 55. Cf. Jerome, Onom.; Ambrose, Epist. ad Hebr., VII. Modern scholarship is equally divided: C. Mackey, "Salem," PEQ, 1948, 121–30, argues that Shalem must be placed in Samaria (cf. Judith, 4:5); J. Simons, Geographical and Topographical Texts of the O.T. (Leiden, 1959), 216 f., favors the Jewish tradition that Shalem equals Jerusalem.

[155] 'Arakhin, 32b; cf. Yer. 'Avodah Zarah, 5, 4.

[156] Targum on Gen. 33:18; Shabbath, 33b; Gen. Rabbah, 79, 5.

[157] The Samaritan version, Gen. 33:18, reads שלום, peace, instead of the Masoretic שלם. This might suggest that the extant Samaritan versions of the Pentateuch were influenced by rabbinic exegesis or that the ancient Samaritan versions differed from

Following the account of Melchisedek's reception of Abraham, Pseudo-Eupolemus relates the journey of Abraham and Sarah to Egypt.[158] This sequence of events is a reversal from that found in Genesis, where the story of Pharaoh's seizure of Sarah precedes the war between the four and the five kings.[159] Why did the Samaritan author reverse the sequence of events related in Genesis? The brevity of the Greek fragments makes it impossible to give a definite answer. It is reasonable to assume, however, that Pseudo-Eupolemus' departure from the biblical version was intentional. In Genesis Abraham's stay in Canaan following his arrival from Haran was brief. It was only upon his return from Egypt that the patriarch settled in Canaan permanently. Such a reconstruction of events apparently would have weakened Pseudo-Eupolemus' thesis that the patriarch brought culture first to Phoenicia and only thereafter to Egypt.[160] For if Abraham's stay in Phoenicia was but of short duration, his instruction of astrology and other sciences to its inhabitants could not have had as profound an effect as the author makes us believe. To support his thesis that the Phoenicians mastered the Chaldaean sciences before the Egyptians, Pseudo-Eupolemus lengthened considerably the patriarch's stay in Phoenicia before describing his departure to Egypt. The precedence of the Phoenicians over the Egyptians, it is true, was only a matter of a few years; but evidently for the Phoenician patriot it was a priority nonetheless.

Alexander Polyhistor quotes Pseudo-Eupolemus' reconstruction of the patriarch's journey to Egypt in the following words: "There being a famine [in Phoenicia] Abraham and his whole household departed to Egypt and settled there. The king of the Egyptians married his wife, having been told by Abraham that she was his sister. He [Pseudo-Eupolemus] related even more extraordinary things, that the king was unable to have intercourse with her and that his people and his household were perishing. The diviners having been summoned, they said that the woman was not a widow. Thus the king of the Egyptians learned that she was Abraham's wife and he restored her to her husband."[161] Surprisingly, the account is not unfavorable to

the extant text. It is possible, however, that the Samaritans regarded Shalem as identical with Shechem. From this point of view the identification of Shalem with Shechem would appear superfluous; hence the reading of *shalom* instead of Shalem. The rabbis and the Samaritans, although for different reasons, came to the same conclusion. In the Samaritan Targum the reading is Shalem, however.

[158] 724 F 1, 6–7.
[159] Gen. 12:10–20; 14:1–24.
[160] 724 F 1, 4, 8; F 2.
[161] 724 F 1, 6–7.

צ 53.7%

Pharaoh. Alexander Polyhistor was impatient, however, with Pseudo-Eupolemus' long list of miracles, shortening it considerably.

It is also certain that Pseudo-Eupolemus, in common with the midrashic literature, embellished the account of Genesis to preserve Sarah's chastity as well as to make her deliverance even more miraculous than in the Bible. The detail that Pharaoh became impotent is recorded in Gen. Rabbah.[162] As noted above, Pseudo-Eupolemus' description of Enoch and Methuselah coincides with that of the recently discovered Genesis Apocryphon. Pseudo-Eupolemus and Genesis Apocryphon use almost the same wording in relating the incident of Pharaoh's inability to have intercourse with Sarah:

Pseudo-Eupolemus, 724 F 1, line 6	Genesis Apocryphon, Col. XX, 17
ὅτι οὐκ ἠδύνατο αὐτῇ συγγενέσθαι	ולא יכל למקרב בהא ואף לא ידעהא

That the account of Abraham in Genesis Apocryphon coincides in several details with Pseudo-Eupolemus has been independently deduced by G. Vermes.[163] Vermes has raised the question as to whether Genesis Apocryphon was "influenced by Hellenistic Judaism, or did Jewish writers of the Greek Diaspora adopt and partly modify Palestinian tradition?"[164] He concludes that "the literature of Hellenistic Judaism was built upon Palestinian Judaism."[165] I believe, however, that it might be argued that Genesis Apocryphon and Pseudo-Eupolemus were products of Palestinian scholarship. Both of these sources mention the tradition that Pharaoh summoned the diviners to advise him why God had afflicted him and his household with plagues.[166] But Genesis Apocryphon has a further refinement of the story. According to the Aramaic scroll, "all the physicians and all the wizards and all the wise men were not able to rise and heal him, for a spirit[167] smote all of them and they ran away. חרקנוש (ḤRQNWŠ)

---

[162] Gen. Rabbah, 40, p. 389; Yer. Kethuvoth, 7, 10: דטלטסן למנע בסמא דמטרונה (for he dared to touch the body of a matron). As pointed out by Krauss (Griechische und lateinische Lehnwörter im Talmud, Midrash und Targum, II, 268; 332; 297); and Lieberman (Greek in Jewish Palestine [New York, 1942], 39 ff.), the text is an Aramaic admixture of a Greek phrase containing the words of ἐτόλμησεν, σῶμα, ματρᾶνα.

[163] G. Vermes, Scripture and Tradition in Judaism (Leiden, 1961), 80–82; 97, n. 2; 101, n. 1; 115, n. 1.

[164] Ibid., 123.

[165] Ibid., 124.

[166] Pseudo-Eupolemus, 724 F 1, 7; Genesis Apocryphon, col. XX, 16–18.

[167] Genesis Apocryphon, col. XX, 20, רוחא in the context appears to mean spirit, not wind, as translated by the editors; see A. Dupont-Sommer, Les écrits esséniens découverts près la Mer Morte² (Paris, 1960), 300, n. 2.

then came to me [Abraham] that I pray for the king."[168] Who is this ḤRQNWŠ?[169] It is generally taken for granted that ḤRQNWŠ is a proper name.[170] This assumption, I believe, has given rise to fruitless speculations. As the account of Abraham in Genesis Apocryphon contains no names except those mentioned in Genesis, there is no reason to assume that this puzzling word is one. It is likely, however, that ḤRQNWŠ is an early form of transliteration of ἀρχώνης.[171] A detailed presentation of the linguistic evidence would lead us from the main topic. It is sufficient to say here that ἄρχων and ἀρχώνης appear in a variety of forms in the talmudic and midrashic literature.[172] The author of the Genesis Apocryphon appears to say that when all the wise men of Egypt failed the king, the archon, the head of the household, by consulting Lot, finally arrived at the source of Pharaoh's afflictions.[173] If our rendition of ḤRQNWŠ is correct, it would indicate that the Genesis Apocryphon employed a loan word from the Greek. This is not the only instance where the author of Genesis Apocryphon borrowed a Greek term. The Aramaic scroll designates Mount Tauros (טור תורא) as the northern border of Palestine, which is a loan translation of Ταῦρος ὄρος.[174] The mention of כפתור, probably Cappadocia, as pointed out by the editors of Genesis Apocryphon, is another example of the scroll's use of Greek geographic terms.[175]

Does Genesis Apocryphon's use of loan words from the Greek indicate Hellenistic influence? And how shall we interpret the remarkable parallels between Genesis Apocryphon and Pseudo-Eupolemus?

---

[168] Genesis Apocryphon, col. XX, 20 f.

[169] ḤRQNWŠ appears in col. XX, 8, 21, 24.

[170] The editors of *Genesis Apocryphon*, English section, 26; Hebrew, 22. H. E. Del Medico, *L'énigme de manuscrits de la Mer Morte* (Paris, 1957), 520, identifies ḤRKNWŠ with Hyrcanus, either the Tobiad or the last king of the Hasmonaeans; J. Finkel, in *Essays on the Dead Sea Scrolls* (Jerusalem, 1961), 174 f., agrees but adds that the puzzling name is Rikayon of the *Sefer ha-yashar*. Dupont-Sommer, *Écrits esséniens*, 300, does not attempt to identify the name.

[171] Gen. 12:15 says that שרים, the princes or officers of Pharaoh praised Sarah's beauty to the king. LXX renders שרים as ἀρχόντες,; Pseudo-Eupolemus uses μάντεις (724 F 1, p. 679, line 7); Josephus, ἱερεῖς, priests (*AJ*, I, 164).

[172] Tosefta, Giṭṭin, 6, 6; *Yer.* Yevamoth, 8, 8; Shir ha-Shirim Rabbah, 7, 3, commenting on Daniel 3:2. Cf. S. Krauss, *Griechische und lateinische Lehnwörter im Talmud, Midrash und Targum*, II, 129.

[173] Genesis Apocryphon, col. XX, 24–26. It is worth noting that it is said that three officials seized Sarah (XIX, 24; XX, 8). This conforms to the Greek political structure of three *archontes*, the highest of whom was called the Archon.

[174] Genesis Apocryphon, XXI, 16; pp. 19; 25 (Hebrew section); 22; 30 (English section). See also Dupont-Sommer, *Écrits ess.'niens*², 306, n. 3.

[175] Genesis Apocryphon, XXI, 23, כפתוך undoubtedly means כפתור (p. 34).

Verbal borrowings from a foreign tongue sometimes reflect merely superficial association, and do not necessarily imply an acquaintance with or an imitation of the foreign literature or culture. Daniel (written in 164 B. C. E.), Megillath Ta'anith (written before 70 C. E.), and especially the Talmud and the Midrash absorbed an abundant number of Greek terms, while retaining a distinctive pattern of thought far removed from Hellenistic influence.[176] Paradoxically, Plato and Aristotle penetrated Jewish intellectual life only during the Middle Ages, but hardly affected the main stream of Judaism during the centuries when Greek was the second language of the Jews.[177] The Greek terms in Genesis Apocryphon may indicate nothing except that it was written during the Hellenistic period. Nevertheless, some features of Genesis Apocryphon do indicate certain characteristics found in the Hellenistic Jewish literature. The erotic depiction of Sarah's body in Genesis Apocryphon recalls the description of Bilhah in the Testament of Reuben, or of Potiphar in the novels preserved by Josephus.[178] The incorporation of a chronological scheme by the author of Genesis Apocryphon into his account of Genesis may also indicate Hellenistic influence.

Despite the possibility that Genesis Apocryphon was influenced by Hellenistic literature, and despite the common traditions found in both the Genesis Apocryphon and Pseudo-Eupolemus, it does not necessarily follow that either was dependent on the other. Both anonymous authors, one a Hellenized Samaritan and the other possibly a member of the Qumran sect, made use of the Enochite literature. But the Enochite works were basically apocalyptic, whereas the authors of the Greek fragments and the Aramaic scroll believed that

[176] Dan. 3:5, 10; Megillath Ta'anith, 23rd of Iyar; 25th of Sivan; 5th of Kislev. Krauss, *Griechische und lateinische Lehnwörter*, has assembled thousands of Greek terms adopted by the Rabbis. Lieberman, *Greek in Jewish Palestine*; and *Hellenism in Jewish Palestine* (New York, 1950), attempts to show that the rabbis had a profound knowledge of Greek letters and culture. (See next note.)

[177] D. Daube, "Rabbinic Methods of Interpretation and Hellenic Rhetoric," *HUCA*, XXII (1949), 239 ff., argues that the hermeneutic rules adopted by the rabbis were borrowed from Hellenistic jurisprudence; Y. Baer, "Ha-yesodoth ha-historiyyim shel ha-halakhah," *Luaḥ ha-areẓ* (1951–1952), 130 ff.; *Israel among the Nations* (Jerusalem, 1955), 36 ff., likewise parallels rabbinic with Hellenistic law. Granted that these studies open new fields of research that may widen our understanding of rabbinic Judaism, Lieberman (see previous note), Daube and Baer have not proven a close relationship between Hellenistic and rabbinic cultures.

[178] Genesis Apocryphon, XX, 2–8; cf. Test. of Reuben, III, 11–13; Test. Joseph, III–VI; Josephus, *AJ*, II, 39 ff. See M. Braun, *History and Romance In Graeco-Oriental Literautre* (Oxford, 1938), 44-104. Cf. Flusser, *Kirjath Sepher*, XXXII (1957), 381 f.

they were writing history. Indeed a wide gulf separates the two works. Genesis Apocryphon was written in the tradition of Jewish historiography. It employs the first person throughout the narrative, a characteristic of Jewish history writing. Its author is convinced that the biblical account as well as his own embellishments are not only true, but need no external corroboration. Josephus drew a distinction between Jewish and Greek historiography: The one was based on reliable and undisputed records; the other contained differing and contradictory accounts of the same event.[179]

According to Josephus' definition, Pseudo-Eupolemus was, as far as we know, the first author to write biblical history in the Greek tradition. Abraham was born either in Camarina or, as some say, in Ur. Pseudo-Eupolemus did not commit himself as to which of these traditions is correct. The biblical account was no longer history that must be followed to the last dot. Frequently, Pseudo-Eupolemus preferred Babylonian or Greek names to those found in Genesis. He wove Babylonian and Greek mythology into his account of biblical history. But the historicity of Genesis never remained in doubt. By glorifying Babylonia, disparaging Egypt, and dismissing Greek claims as mere adaptations of the Hebrew, the anonymous author believed he had vindicated the essential truth of ancient biblical history. That his philology was often faulty, his parallels absurd and his hypotheses apologetical, cannot be denied. That his syncretistic tendencies were not unique is attested in the fragments of Artapanus and Cleodomus-Malchus.[180] But Pseudo-Eupolemus' level of sophistication was superior to that of any other known Hellenistic biblical historian. His was a conscious effort to integrate the traditions of Genesis with those of the Mediterranean culture.

If we assume that the fragments of Pseudo-Eupolemus are remnants of a work written in Samaria *circa* 200 B. C. E., we learn something of the nature of Palestinian Hellenism before the Maccabean revolt. Our knowledge of the outlook of the Hellenistic party during this critical period is limited to what is related in Daniel and I and II Maccabees, which say little of the intellectual background of Antiochus IV's partisans and nothing of their attitude towards the traditions of the Pentateuch.[181] It may be assumed that the so-called Hellenizers

[179] *C. Apion*, I, 6–41.

[180] Artapanus, 726 FF 1–3; Cleodomus-Malchus, 727 F 1 = *AJ*, I, 238–241; cf. Philo the Elder, 729 F 1.

[181] Erwin R. Goodenough, "The Rabbis and Jewish Art in the Greco-Roman Period," *HUCA*, XXXII (1961), 272, parallels the syncretistic tendencies found in Alexander Polyhistor's fragments with the pagan symbols appearing in Jewish

produced their own literature, now lost. The fact that Pseudo-Eupolemus was a Samaritan seems to be less significant than that his work possibly reflected the Hellenizers' approach to Genesis. There are indications that the Hellenizers attempted to interpret the Pentateuch to conform to their own cosmopolitan outlook. Like the other contemporary factions, the Hellenizers claimed that they alone were the authentic adherents of the Mosaic traditions.

tombstones and synagogues, indicating that normative Judaism did not hold sway over the entire Jewish population. Although Goodenough has built a strong case for his point of view, Alexander Polyhistor's fragments in general and Pseudo-Eupolemus' radical syncretism in particular, being based on third and second century B. C. E. sources, do not necessarily corroborate contentions for the rabbinic period. There is, moreover, a difference between the verbalized and sometimes flagrant paganisms found in the Hellenistic Jewish literature and the symbolic heathenisms of the talmudic period. It is possible to argue that the rabbinic discouragement of Jewish art left artistically inclined Jews little choice but to borrow symbolic representations from their pagan environment.

Postscript: This paper was read before the Los Angeles Society of Jewish Research in June, 1962.

BIBLICAL CHRONOLOGY IN THE
HELLENISTIC WORLD CHRONICLES*

CHRONOGRAPHY became a discipline of its own during the Alexandrian age. Herodotus and Thucydides still reckoned the remote past by generations. But from 300 B.C. onward learned men of Alexandria attempted to assign more or less precise dates for notable events. Homeric scholars dated the fall of Troy 407 years prior to the first Olympic games in 776 B.C., i.e., 1184 B.C. Eratosthenes of Cyrene asserted that this was the first datable event of human history, giving an unmistakable demarcation line between mythology and history. For the Orientals, whose records reputedly went back to the time when gods and semi-gods held sway over man, Eratosthenes' Greek-colored view of ancient history appeared myopic. Perhaps to match the Orientals, Greek writers manufactured genealogical tables which traced the pedigrees of famous Greek cities to remote antiquity with their autochthonous progenitors. To create order among the conflicting claims, during the second century B.C., the universal chronicle made its appearance. In the universal chronicles the Greek and Oriental genealogical lists followed each other, were synchronized, or even tabulated.

The brilliant contributions of Eduard Schwartz and Felix Jacoby have outlined some of the main trends of Hellenistic chronography. This essay explores the stages through which biblical chronography passed prior to its absorption by Christian chronologists, in the second half of the second century.

An immense intellectual effort was expended during the Hellenistic period by both Jews and pagans to date creation, the flood, exodus, building of the Temple. With the data available to these early scholars, however, this was an impossibility. The putative

* This study was made possible through the generosity of a 1966 Summer Fellowship of the Frank L. Weil Institute for Studies in Religion and the Humanities, for which the author expresses his profound gratitude. I am also indebted to Samuel Sandmel, whose suggestions have improved this paper.

Jewish era adopted by the rabbis began in 3761 B.C.; the Byzantine, in 5509 B.C.; Archbishop James Ussher's, in 4404 B.C. The Hellenistic and medieval chronographers, whether Jewish, pagan, or Christian, could not agree on some of the most basic biblical dates. As independent studies led nowhere, a consensus slowly developed among various groups, which, with the passage of time, sometimes assumed a sacred character.

This study, however, is limited to the very beginnings of Graeco-Jewish biblical chronography — from 250 before the common era to 150 after. Christian and Jewish annalistic works after this period are outside our purview. But the writings of the Church Fathers on this subject are of vital significance. In the course of their studies, men such as Tatian of Antioch (flourished in 180), Clement of Alexandria (died before 215), Hippolytus of Rome (died in 235), Julius Africanus of Jerusalem (died after 240), Eusebius of Caesarea in Palestine (260–340), and Pseudo-Justin frequently quoted their Hellenistic predecessors. It is through the dim light of these partly preserved extracts that the shadows of the more distant pagan and Jewish scholarship can sometimes be discerned.

First Stage — Reconciling Biblical Dates

Traces of a biblical chronological school are perhaps evident already in the Septuagint version of the Pentateuch, i.e., in the first half of the third century B.C. The Hebrew text of Ex. 12:40 records that the Israelites stayed in Egypt 430 years. The Greek translation, however, apparently because only four generations are accounted for, emended the passage to read "in the land of Egypt *and* in the land of Canaan," halving the Israelites' stay in Egypt to 215 years.[1] The Hebrew and the Greek versions diverge also in regard to the number of years which had elapsed from

---

[1] The *Codex Alexandrinus*, Ex. 12:40, emends further: [the Israelites] "and their ancestors," to make sense out of the corrected text, which, anachronistically, alludes to the patriarchs as "Israelites." Like LXX and the Samaritan versions, talmudic exegesis interprets the 430 years to be referring to their stay in both Canaan and Egypt. However, the rabbis counted 220 years for Canaan and 210 for Egypt (*Seder Olam* 2–3). For the evidence that LXX means to split the 430 years in equal halves, see below, p. 455f. The Samaritan text contains another gloss: "and in the land of Goshen."

Adam to Abraham.[2] When the years given in the Hebrew text are added, the flood occurred 1656 after Adam, Abraham was born 292 years after the flood, making a total of 1948 years from Adam to Abraham. According to the Septuagint, however, the antediluvian period adds up to 2264 years and the pre-Abrahamic epoch totals 3334 years.

The significant divergence of 1396 years between the Hebrew and Greek texts did not escape the notice of the ancients. Josephus shows awareness of the differing chronological schemes, and the Church Fathers commented upon the question at length.[3] In fact, for the latter the problem of the differing texts was of immediate and vital concern. The Christians had believed firmly that Jesus Christ would rise again soon after the world entered the sabbatical millennium. The larger the age of the world, the sooner appeared the New Age. Christian chronographers, therefore, beginning with Clement of Alexandria, Judas, Julius Africanus, Hippolytus, and Eusebius, accepted the Septuagint version as authentic.[4] The problem how to explain the lower numbers of the Hebrew version moved the Monophysite Bishop of Edessa, Jacob (died in 708), to charge that the Jews had altered the Hebrew text to discredit the Christian belief in the imminent

---

[2] Gen. 5:3–31; 11:10–25; LXX repeating the generation of Cainan of Gen. 5:9f.

[3] JOSEPHUS' chronology for the antediluvian period conforms with LXX (*A.J.*, I, 82–88), but for the Noachites he used the Hebrew (*A.J.*, I, 148–150). All witnesses, except RO, which represent here a compromised emendation, attest that JOSEPHUS used the Hebrew. Unhappily, NIESE chose to print RO in the body. THACKERAY (Loeb Classical Library) was quite wrong in defending NIESE. See JUSTUS VON DESTINON, *Die Chronologie des Josephus* (Kiel, 1880), 5–9. The Samaritan text, disregarded in our discussion, diverges from both the Masoretic and LXX versions in respect of the Adamite generations, but conforms mostly with the Greek tradition as to the Noachites. It is not the intention of this study to exhaust the problems involved in solving the origins of the chronological schemes as they appear in the various LXX, Samaritan, Julibee recensions. See the commentaries *ad locum*, e.g., SKINNER, *Genesis* (*ICC*, New York, 1925); OLOF LINTON, Synopsis Historiae Universalis, in *Festskrift udgivet of Københavns Universitet* (1957), 7–41.

[4] For CLEMENT, see *Stromata*, I, 125; JUDAS in EUSEB. *H.E.*, VI, 7 = JACOBY, *FGrH* 261 F 1, writing in 202; on AFRICANUS, see GELZER, *Sextus Julius Africanus und die byzantinische Chronographie* (Leipzig, 1880), I, 24–26; HIPPOLYTUS' Commentary on Daniel, *passim*; cf. note 3. The statement in *Seder Eliyyahu* (FRIEDMANN, ed.), 6f.; *Bab. Avodah Zarah* 9a; *Sanhedrin* 97a, announcing the messianic age in the sabbatical millennium, makes sense only if it is supposed that it was taken from a text which had followed the readings of LXX. For only according to a chronological scheme based upon the LXX was the sixth millennium rapidly approaching. According to the rabbinic chronology, these writers were living only in the beginning of the fifth millennium, too remote from the messianic age.

Second Coming of Jesus.[5] Heinrich Graetz, equally perplexed, reversed the charges, accusing the Church Fathers of having intentionally lengthened the number of years by falsifying the texts of the Septuagint.[6] However, since Josephus was already aware of the diverging Hebrew and Greek numbers here, they must have antedated the Christian period.[7]

We are, then, confronted with the problem, often debated, whether the Greek rendition reflects a Hebrew proto-text or the differing numbers in the Septuagint resulted from an alteration made in the Greek version. It should be noted that the presumption of diverging Hebrew proto-texts merely rephrases the difficulty into how they had come into being.

In this case the argument between a proto-Hebrew copy and a Greek alteration of the original text can be resolved on the basis of external evidence. The existence of a biblical chronographical school during the third century B.C. is indicated in the remnants of the Hellenistic Jewish writer named Demetrius. Demetrius flourished during the reign of Ptolemy IV Philopator (221–204 B.C.) and wrote a work called *On the Kings of Judaea* dealing with biblical exegesis, mainly chronology. The advanced stage of the hermeneutic art in his fragments as well as such an expression as "some ask" suggests that Demetrius ought to be considered as a representative of an exegetical and chronographical school rather than as an isolated writer. We gain an insight into this exegetical school from questions such as why did Joseph neglect to report to Jacob of his rise in Egypt? Because, says Demetrius, he was afraid lest his family's occupation of shepherding would disgrace him in Egypt. Whence did the departing Israelites receive weapons (Ex. 13:18) after having left Egypt unarmed? From the drowned men (Egyptians?).[8] But the subtlety of this

---

[5] See EPHRAEM Syrus, in ASSEMANI, *Bibliotheca Orientalis* (Rome, 1719), I, 65f. Cf. also EUSEBIUS, *Chronik* (ed. Karst, Leipzig, 1911), 27ff.

[6] H. GRAETZ, Fälschungen in dem Texte der Septuaginta von christlicher Hand zur dogmatischen Zwecken, *MGWJ*, II (1853), 432–36.

[7] See note 3. Confronted with two chronological systems, JOSEPHUS resolved the problem by using LXX for the Adamite generations but the Hebrew for the Noachites. See also below, p. 454.

[8] EUSEBIUS, *Praeparatio Evangelica*, IX, 19, 21, 29; *Hist. Eccl.*, VI, 13, 7; CLEMENT Alex., *Strom.*, I, 141, 1. The fragments are collected by MUELLER, *FHG*, III (Paris, 1888), 208ff.; FREUDENTHAL, *Hellenistische Studien* (Breslau, 1875), 219–23; JACOBY, *FGrH*, IIIC 2 (Leiden, 1958), No. 722 FF 1–7, 666–71. N. WALTER

school becomes discernible mostly in its chronological schemes. Some calculations appear at first glance to have been based merely on simple additions of biblical numbers. A close reading of the fragments, however, indicates that each computation was but part of general explanations intended to make the Scriptural events appear "rational" and part of a preconceived plan. Thus the chronology of Abraham is formulated to show that Zipporah and the "Kushite woman" (Num. 12:1) were but different designations of the Midianite wife, the sixth generation after Abraham and Keturah, of the monogamous Moses.[9] Jacob, according to Demetrius, begat twelve children within seven years in Laban's house,[10] apparently because seven was a sacred number. Contrary to 2 Kings 17:3, 18:9, Demetrius ascribed the destruction of the Northern Kingdom of Samaria, which had occurred in 722/1, to Sennacherib (705–681)[11] — to contrast the fate of Judah with its more wicked neighboring state. In other words, Demetrius' datings were partly derived from Scripture and partly from extra-biblical hypotheses.

Demetrius set out to demonstrate the exact date of the exodus. He showed that from Abraham's entry into the land of Canaan to Jacob's descent into Egypt there elapsed 215 years. For this he had biblical support.[12] His detailed presentation, however, that from Jacob's descent to Egypt to the exodus there had also elapsed 215 years was fanciful: Levi was forty-three years old when he was brought to Egypt and he was sixty years old when he begat Kohat; Kohat was forty years old when he begat Amran; Amran

---

is preparing a new edition of the fragments under the auspices of the Deutsche Akademie.

[9] EUSEB., *P.E.*, IX, 21, 13 = 722 F 1; *P.E.*, IX, 29, 3 = 722 F 2. That the "Kushite woman" was identical with Zipporah, see EZECHIELUS, *Exagoge* (ed. Wieneke, 1931), 8, here probably dependent on DEMETRIUS; and Sifre on Num. 12:1 (FRIEDMANN, 99). It does not necessarily follow, though, that DEMETRIUS was the midrash's source.

[10] 722 FF 1–6; see note 8, but specially *P.E.*, IX, 21 = 722 F 1.

[11] CLEM. Al., I, 141 = 722 F 6. *Mishnah Yadayyim*, IV, 4; *Tos. Qiddushim*, V, 4 (Zuckermandel), 342, 9–11. This does not necessarily imply that rabbinic chronology followed DEMETRIUS' scheme, though the coincidence is hard to explain (see note 9). Cf. M. GASTER, Demetrius und Seder Olam, in *Festskrift Simonsen* (Copenhagen, 1923), 243–52.

[12] Abraham settled in Canaan when 75 years old (Gen. 12:4), begat Isaac at 100 (21:5), who begat Jacob at 60 (25:26), who in turn came to Egypt at the age of 130 (47:9): 25 + 60 + 130 = 215.

was seventy-eight when Moses was born, in whose eightieth year occurred the exodus $[(60–43) + (40 + 78 + 80) = 215]$.[13] The scheme to give the year and month of the birth of each of Jacob's sons appears to have been intended to present proof that the Israelites' sojourn in Egypt equaled exactly the time of the patriarchs' stay in the land of Canaan.[14] Demetrius' detailed and repetitive concoction of evidence makes sense if it is assumed that the Septuagint reading of Ex. 12:40, crediting a part of the 430 years in Egypt to Canaan, was of recent origin, if not an invention of Demetrius himself.[15]

Demetrius computed the date of the flood as 2264 years and the birth of Abraham 3334 years after Adam, exactly as in the Septuagint text.[16] There is no direct proof that Demetrius had tampered with the biblical texts to lengthen the antediluvian and pre-Abrahamic periods. But the chances are that, as in the dates of the Israelites' stay in Egypt, Demetrius (or chronographers of a similar school) emended the text to make it conform to a preconceived chronological scheme.[17]

This interpretation differs from Freudenthal's, who regarded Demetrius as a precursor of the midrashic literature. Demetrius, says Freudenthal, was a close reader of the Bible, presenting occasionally bits of information that differed with the Hebrew text, but never one to depart from the Greek version, which must have been already fixed in the form we have it during the last decades

---

[13] EUSEB., *P.E.*, IX, 21, 19 = 722 F 1.

[14] See WACHOLDER, *HUCA* 35 (1964), 43–56.

[15] The permissive attitude in regard of changing patriarchal datings can be seen in the different biblical versions and the Book of Jubilees. The identity of the numberings in the LXX and DEMETRIUS surely shows dependence. Since the latter displays the rational behind these numberings, it follows that he (or his school) was the originator of this scheme rather than a mere commentator.

[16] DEMETRIUS counted from Adam to the coming of Jacob into Egypt 3624 years; from the flood to the same time, 1360; from then to the exodus, 215 years (*P.E.*, IX, 21, 18 = 722 F 1), 3624 − 1360 = 2264. It becomes clear that he was concerned almost as much with the date of Jacob's arrival into Egypt, his native country, as with the Israelites' departure.

[17] See also LXX III Kingdoms 6:1, where the Greek gives 440 years from the exodus to the commencing of the temple's construction, instead of 480 in the Hebrew text. It is generally agreed that the Greek chronological departures from the Hebrew were deliberate corrections (see, for example, J. MONTGOMERY, *Critical Commentary on Books of Kings* [New York, 1951], 143; S. J. DE VRIES, Chronology, in *Interpreter's Dictionary of the Bible* [1962], I, 581). An old but useful study is E. PREUSS, *Die Zeitrechnung der Septuaginta* (Berlin, 1859).

of the third century B.C.[18] However, it was shown above that Demetrius gave Egypt as Kohat's place of birth contrary to Gen. 46:11. The dates of Jacob's sons, Kohat and Amran, are Demetrius's inventions. It may be assumed that though Demetrius frequently followed Scripture closely, he was not a literalist. He did not hesitate to modify the text when some passages contradicted his chronological schemes.[19]

What was Demetrius' (or some other Hellenistic Jewish chronographer's) possible motivation in lengthening the pre-Abrahamic period from 1948 years found in the Hebrew to the Greek 3234? Perhaps, though unlikely, the explanation lies in the state of contemporary Alexandrian historical scholarship. Some of the techniques used by Eratosthenes of Cyrene (275–194 B.C.) are also evident in Demetrius, such as a consistent chronological scheme and minute textual analysis.[20] But Eratosthenes had spurned attempts to assign dates to the mythical period of Greece, thus founding scientific chronography. Demetrius, however, dated creation and the flood. For the ancients, it should be noted, the longevity of the Adamite and Noachite generations as recorded in Genesis was consistent with their outlook that early man was somehow a half-god or a superman. The credibility of the biblical tradition was the inverse of what confronts the modern reader. Babylonian and Egyptian writers, such as Berossus and Manetho,[21] ascribed to these semi-divinities reigns of myriads of years.

[18] FREUDENTHAL, *Hellenistische Studien*, 35–82; H. B. SWETE, *An Introduction to the Old Testament in Greek* (Cambridge, 1902), 17f., 369f.; SCHÜRER, *Geschichte d. jüdischen Volkes* (Leipzig, 1909), III⁴, 426, 473; STÄHLIN, in CHRIST's *Griechische Literaturgeschichte* (Munich, 1920), II⁶, 588f.

[19] Conceivably, but unverifiably, DEMETRIUS, whose chronology was written during the last two decades of III century B.C., was himself one of the so-called "Seventy" translators. That the name DEMETRIUS is not found in the *Letter of Aristeas* among the seventy-two names is no proof one way or the other, as the list is pure fiction, appended to the text by another hand. I am now inclined to doubt any direct nexus (see sources cited in the previous note) between DEMETRIUS and the midrashic methods, except that both showed an amazingly close knowledge of the Scriptural text. The Book of Jubilees, written perhaps nearly a century after DEMETRIUS, and the recently discovered Genesis Apocryphon (Jerusalem, 1956) both follow a schematic chronology that often overrides the Pentateuchal traditions. The idea that nonlegal texts (even the Pentateuch) of Scripture were authoritative and unalterable is evidently post-Maccabean. Cf. EUPOLEMUS's account of the Temple (*FGrH* 723 FF 1–5).

[20] On ERATOSTHENES, see JACOBY, *Apollodors Chronik* (*Philologische Untersuchungen*, XVI [1902]), 10 ff.; *FGrH* 241 FF 1–48.

[21] E. SCHWARTZ, Berossos, *RE*, III (1897), 309–16; *FGrH* 680 FF 1–22. Mane-

The relative short duration of this period in the Pentateuch appeared rather incredible. Influenced by this view, it would seem, Demetrius lengthened the reign of the giants by adding consistently a century to the age of the patriarchs when their first son was born. In making the world somewhat older, Scripture appeared closer to reality.

The writings of Demetrius mark the first stage of Hellenistic biblical chronology. He established the so-called *annus Adami*, divided the biblical history into epochs, assigning absolute dates to the flood, the patriarchs, the exodus, and the destruction of the Northern and Southern kingdoms. It is possible, even likely, that the chronological alterations adopted in the Septuagint version of the Pentateuch were a product of Demetrius' chronographic schemes. Although it is speculated above that Demetrius was influenced by the contemporary Alexandrian chronographic schools, it should be noted that the evidence for such claims is precarious. Demetrius probably lived in Alexandria, as did Eratosthenes; both were professional chronographers. There is no direct proof, however, of non-Jewish influence in Demetrius' chronology.

Second Stage — Fusion of Biblical and Greek Myth

The essential characteristic of the second stage of biblical chronography is the fusion of the Hebrew accounts with Oriental and Greek mythology. As far as is known, Pseudo-Eupolemus, a Samaritan, who lived possibly about 200 B.C., marks the first attempt to identify the Noachite generations of Genesis with what seemed to him their Babylonian and Hellenic equivalents.[22] The progenitors of Abraham, according to Pseudo-Eupolemus, were the giants, the "Sons of God" who had escaped the flood and built the tower of Babel. Babylon, the first city in history, was also constructed by them, which they had originally named Belus,

---

tho, ed. Waddell (*LCL*, 1940); *FGrH* 609 FF 1–28. See, also, J. PRITCHARD, *Ancient Near Eastern Texts Relating to the Old Testament* (Princeton, 1955), 265f.

[22] On PSEUDO-EUPOLEMUS, see FREUDENTHAL, *Hellenistische Studien*, 35–82; GUTSCHMID, *Kleine Schriften*, II (1890), 180–95; WACHOLDER, *Hebrew Union College Annual* 34 (1963), 83–113; N. WALTER, Zu Pseudo-Eupolemos, *Klio* (1965), 282–90.

after their leader. Belus' father was also named Belus.[23] The older Belus, it is evident, equaled Noah; and the younger, Nimrod. The Greek equivalent of the Babylonian Belus (Nimrod) was Kronos. And the Hellenic Atlas was identical with Enoch of Genesis, the discoverer of the astral sciences.[24] Pseudo-Eupolemus' set of equivalents were syncretistic rather than synchronistic. It should not be forgotten, however, that Belus was regarded as a datable figure and that Enoch, Noah, Nimrod, and Abraham were usually assigned absolute time scales. Even so sober a historian as Eusebius followed the mendacious Ctesias in making Ninus the son of Belus the first Assyrian king (in whose 43rd year, says Eusebius, Abraham was born).[25] The set of equivalents of biblical and Hellenic mythical figures, in addition to the synchronism, prompted the Jewish author of the Third Book of the Sibylline Oracles (140 B.C.?) to fuse Hesiod's *Theogony* with Genesis. It resulted in a scene that depicts the battle between Yahweh and the Titans. In a sense this was a fusion of chronography and Euhemerism.[26]

Artapanus, writing probably in the second century B.C., named the pharaohs who, he said, lived in the days of Abraham, Joseph, and Moses. When the patriarchs came to Egypt, the name of the king was Pharethothes[27] — an obvious concoction of Pharaoh and Thoth. The name of another pharaoh, evidently during Jacob's arrival into Egypt, was Mempsasthenoth. His son Palmanothes initiated the enslavement of the Jews, forcing them to build Heliopolis and Tanis.[28] Palmanothes' daughter Merrhis, who rescued Moses, was married to Chenephres, the king of Thebes and the pharaoh of the exodus.[29] It is otiose to speculate

---

[23] EUSEB., *P.E.*, IX, 17; 18, 2 (Anonymous) = *FGrH* 724 FF 1–2.

[24] EUSEB., *P.E.*, IX, 17, 9 = 724 F 1.

[25] CTESIAS is preserved primarily in DIODORUS II, 1–28, NICOLAUS of Damascus, 90 FF 1ff., and PHOTIUS. The fragments are collected in JACOBY, *FGrH* 688 FF 1–74. It is doubtful that CTESIAS had assigned an absolute date for Ninus, though the presumed 52-year reign usually credited to Ninus was made up by CTESIAS. For a recent attempt to exonerate CTESIAS, see R. DREWS, Assyria in Classical Universal Histories, *Historia* 14 (1965), 129–42. EUSEBIUS' chronology of Assyria follows CTESIAS', as did that of CASTOR (EUSEB., *Chronik*, 26ff.; *FGrH* 688 F 1a).

[26] *Or. Sibyll.*, III, 106–60. See WACHOLDER, *HUCA* 34 (1963), 92f.

[27] EUSEB., *P.E.*, IX, 18, 1 = 726 F 1.

[28] *P.E.*, IX, 27, 1 = 726 F 3.

[29] *P.E.*, IX, 27 = 726 F 3a. In CLEMENT (*Strom.*, I, 154, 2 = 726 F 3b), the name is spelled Νενεφρέους, but emended, on the basis of EUSEBIUS, Χενεφρέους.

on what basis Artapanus had made up these names. Joshua Gutman suggests that Artapanus had sound historical reasons for
identifying Chenephres, whom Gutman designates as of the
Thirteenth Dynasty in the eighteenth century,[30] as the contemporary of Moses. This assumption has no basis, however. Mueller,
emending slightly Manetho, finds Chenephres to have been the
ninth king of the Second Dynasty (roughly 2800–2700 B.C.).[31]
But this is rather unlikely, if for no other reason than that Artapanus would not have chosen a pharaoh of whom Manetho had
remarked that nothing worth saying occurred during his reign.[32]
Because the name of this pharaoh reads Nechephreus in Clement,
Jacoby cites as a possible identification the first king of the Third
Dynasty, Necherophes (2700 B.C.).[33] (Note Eupolemus' date
of the exodus in the manuscripts in 2738 B.C.) Of greater significance than these speculations, however, is the fact that to
make credible his fantastic attribution of the Egyptian religion
to Moses, Artapanus supplied Egyptian-sounding names for the
pharaohs recorded in the Pentateuch.[34] Artapanus synchronized
biblical and Egyptian figures, but there is no evidence that he was
interested in assigning to either absolute dates.

In the aftermath of the Maccabean revolt, it would seem, the
trend toward assimilation among Hellenized Jews declined. Artapanus' synchronization was not taken seriously by subsequent

[30] Y. GUTMAN, *The Beginnings of Jewish-Hellenistic Literature* (Jerusalem,
1963), 135 [in Hebrew]. GUTMAN dates Chenephres on the basis of ARTAPANUS'
statement that there then were many pharaohs in Egypt, a rather weak proof.

[31] C. MUELLER, *Fragmenta Historicorum Graecorum*, III (Paris, 1883), 221;
MANETHO, in *FGrH*, FF 2–3a–b, IIIC, p. 20, 19, where the text reads Χενερὴς, see
app. crit., line 19.

[32] See previous note. EUSEB., *Chronik* (Armenian), p. 65.

[33] MANETHO, in *FGrH* 609 F 2, IIIC, p. 22; ARTAPANUS, 726 F 3b, p. 684, app.
crit.

[34] Except that he lived before ALEXANDER POLYHISTOR (flourished 85–35 B.C.),
no attempt has been made to date ARTAPANUS. O. LINTON, *Synopsis Historiae
Universalis*, 74, dates him in 30 B.C., which must be a misprint. His extreme syncretism coupled with the knowledge of the book of Exodus seems to place him
during the first half of the second century B.C., before the Maccabean rebellion
reaffirmed the monotheistic belief. A somewhat stronger indication of ARTAPANUS'
date is his statement that the pharaoh of the exodus was the first to have been
afflicted with elephantiasis (EUSEB., *P.E.*, IX, 27, 20 = 726 F 3, p. 684, 10f.). This
disease was apparently first named circa 200 B.C. by BOLOS DEMOCRITUS. ART-
APANUS, whose writings show a kinship with those of BOLOS, attributed the malady
to the Egyptian king in line with the traditional interpretation of Ex. Rabbah, 1,
34 (DIELS-KRANZ, *Die Fragmente der Vorsokratiker*, II⁶ [1952], 216, 9ff.).

writers. In Palestine, at the end of the second century B.C., we see the anonymous authors of Genesis Apocryphon and the Book of Jubilees construct a biblical chronology independent of, but along the lines of, Demetrius. There is nothing in these texts, however, to indicate an interest in the synchronization of biblical events with those of the outside world. But for Greek-reading Jews such a synchronization was of paramount significance.

Eupolemus, a Palestinian Jew and a friend of Judah Maccabee, writing in 158 B.C., had laid down the principle upon which all subsequent synchronization was based: "Moses was the first wise man, and he was the first who had imparted the alphabet to the Jews, the Phoenicians received it from the Jews, the Greeks from the Phoenicians. Moses was also the first to have written laws for the Jews." [35] Now, boasts for one's own people such as these were quite common in antiquity. What was remarkable about Eupolemus' claim was that with the passage of time even some pagan and atheistic chronographers accepted its premise. The Church Fathers phrased this view by quoting Numenius, the second-century A.D. heathen precursor of Neo-Platonism: "Who was Plato except Moses speaking in an Attic dialect?" [36]

The Mosaic origin of civilization is the principle that underlies the third stage of Hellenistic biblical chronology. Its basic premise was that none of the mythical Hellenic kings could have antedated the Jewish lawgiver. What to do with the long lists of Babylonian and Egyptian kings in Berossus and Manetho presented a problem, but not a serious one. These Oriental authors could be ignored, reinterpreted, so somehow made to fit into a world chronicle which placed Moses at a time when man was just emerging from barbarism or semi-divinity, depending on one's view of early man. [37] Increasingly, as in Alexandria and in Rome,

---

[35] CLEMENT Al., *Strom.*, I, 153, 4; EUSEB., *P.E.*, IX, 25, 4 = 723 F 1a–b. FREUDENTHAL, *Hellenistische Studien*, 105–30.

[36] CLEMENT Al., *Strom.*, I, 150, 4; EUSEB., *P.E.*, IX, 6, 9 = MULLACH, *FPh*, III, 166.

[37] MANETHO, according to EUSEBIUS, counted 13,900 years for the period of the gods' rule, 24,900 years for the semi-gods, followed by the 30 dynasties lasting (according to AFRICANUS) 1050 years totaling 39,850 years (EUSEB., *Chronik*, 63ff.; *FGrH* 609 FF 2–32; *Anlage* I, 56–63). These numbers of years were in part reduced by the Jewish chronographers to months (see GELZER, *Sextus Julius Africanus*, II, 59ff.).

interest in matters Babylonian or Egyptian declined while the past of the Jews assumed greater significance.[38]

It is not known whether Eupolemus was the first historian who synchronized biblical and Greek history in accordance with the theory of the Mosaic origin of culture. According to Clement of Alexandria, the chronology of Eupolemus and a certain Philo diverged from that of the above-mentioned Demetrius.[39] Conceivably, the difference between these two schools was that whereas the latter used the Septuagint, the former based its dates on the Hebrew text. If the manuscript reading is correct, Eupolemus dated the exodus 2569 anno mundi in contrast to Demetrius' 3839. This would indicate that Eupolemus based his chronology partly on the Hebrew text of Genesis. But modern editors have emended the number, increasing the year of the exodus from 2569 to 3569, bringing it closer to, though not quite in consonance with, the Septuagint's date of 3849.[40] Eupolemus assigned Joshua a rule of thirty years, perhaps with some proof from the Book of Joshua.[41] But his attribution to Saul of a reign of twenty-one years, the claim that Solomon ascended to the throne at the age of twelve, and that he had begun the building of the temple in the second year of his reign, is either without or contrary to the biblical tradition.[42] Unfortunately, there is nothing in the fragments of Eupolemus to indicate that he synchronized Jewish with universal history, though there is no doubt that he made use of Manetho, Ctesias, and Graeco-Phoenician historians.

[38] CTESIAS, in DIODORUS (Book II; 688 F 1b); PLUTARCH (688 FF 15a; 17–23; 26; 28–29) became the authority of Babylonian history, while BEROSSUS of Babylon (290 B.C.) was ignored. MANETHO (609 FF 1–28) had been preserved only by Jewish and Christian writers. The interest in Egypt, however, never ceased completely in the Graeco-Roman world, but declined sharply from its high point in the 4th and 3rd centuries. See Aegypten in JACOBY, *FGrH*, IIIC, pp. 1–277.

[39] CLEMENT Al., *Strom.*, I, 141, 3–4 = PHILO, 729 T 2; 723 F 4. For DEMETRIUS' chronology see above.

[40] STÄHLIN, *Clemens Alexandrinus* (*Stromata*, Berlin, 1960), II, 88; FREUDENTHAL (*Hellenistische Studien*, 213, 230); JACOBY (723 F 4); and WALTER (forthcoming publication). This emendation, however, is perhaps not justified. For the manuscript's date of the exodus according to EUPOLEMUS, 2569 anno mundi is not much different from that of the Book of Jubilees, 2410 anno mundi, and the rabbinic 2448. If so, the problem is why EUPOLEMUS dated the exodus 2738 B.C.

[41] EUSEB., *P.E.*, IX, 30, 1 = 723 F 3b. For Joshua's rule, see Josh. 24:29 (30); 14:7; Num. 14:30–34.

[42] EUSEB., *P.E.*, IX, 30, 2, 8 = 723 F 3b; cf. LXX III Kingdoms 2:12.

Third Stage — Biblical Events Part of World Chronicle

It is certain, however, that within a century after Eupolemus a world chronicle which synchronized Jewish and Greek history had gained international circulation. That the synchronization was based on Jewish calculations is presumed because it favored the antiquity of Moses and because it is attested by authors who are known to have used Jewish sources. But only the names of pagan writers have been preserved: Alexander Polyhistor (flourished in 85–35 B.C.), Varro (116–27 B.C.), Ptolemy of Mendes (50 B.C.), Apion (first century A.D.), Thrasyllus (before A.D. 36), and Thallus (first century A.D.), all cited chronicles which had incorporated the dates of the Noachite flood and the exodus. Since Alexander Polyhistor, writing in the sixties B.C., already takes such a chronicle for granted, its existence during the second century B.C. is indicated.

A few words must be said about the state of Greek chronography before its fusion with Oriental history. The Oriental peoples possessed relatively authoritative lists of kings assembled through the centuries by their priesthoods. The Greeks had had none. But eager to prove their own antiquity, since the fifth century B.C., mythographers constructed hastily genealogical tables going back to divine progeny. Antiquarians, in turn, collected these tables, remnants of which have been preserved. These lists counted by generations and had made no attempts to assign absolute dates.[43] Timaeus of Tauromenion (c.357–260 B.C.) established the Olympic era, dating it in 776 B.C., which became popular among historians.[44] Eratosthenes preferred the Trojan era, beginning with the fall of Troy, in 1184 B.C., reputedly the first datable event in Hellenic history.[45] Anything before 1184 was regarded as mythical. From the point of view of Greek history Eratosthenes' method was a brilliant achievement. But the Babylonian (Berossus), Egyptian (Manetho), Phoenician (Me-

[43] JACOBY, FGrH, IIIb (Suppl.), I, 380–83. See also, on the whole subject, JACOBY, Atthis: The Local Chronicles of Ancient Athens (Oxford, 1949).

[44] POLYBIUS, XII, 11, 1 = Timaeus, 566 T 10. This was the first use of an era for historical purposes. Cf. T. S. BROWN, Timaeus of Tauromenium (Berkeley and Los Angeles, 1958), 10–13.

[45] JACOBY, Apollodors Chronik, 75–77.

nander, Dius), Jewish (Demetrius, Philo, Eupolemus) historians correctly disregarded the fall of Troy as the beginning of recorded history.

The existence of a world chronicle during the second century B.C. is attested also in the so-called Pseudo-Apollodorus. Apollodorus of Athens (150 B.C.) wrote a chronicle, following the footsteps of Eratosthenes, which was limited to Hellenic history beginning with the Trojan date of 1184 B.C.[46] But soon thereafter there appeared a history that fused Berossus' history of Babylonia and Manetho's annals of Egypt and a royal papyrus of ancient Egypt with Apollodorus' chronographic account of Hellas.[47] Thus a world chronicle was spread that boasted of the great antiquity of the Oriental states compared to the late appearance of the Greeks in the history of civilization.

To refute such boasts, it would seem, Castor of Rhodes, circa 60 B.C., concocted a world chronicle that attempted to restore Greek parity with, if not superiority over, the Orient.[48] Castor ignored Manetho and Egyptian history altogether and replaced the rather reliable Berossus with the mendacious Ctesias as the authority on Babylonian antiquities. He introduced dates into the mythical period of Greek history, manufacturing a long list of kings of Sicyon, the oldest of whom (Egialeus) ascended the throne the same year as Ninus, the first king of Assyria, in 2123 B.C.[49]

Castor's chronicle made no mention of the Jews. The reason, as suggested by Gelzer, was perhaps because of the rampant anti-Semitism in Rhodes.[50] But since Castor's annals ignored Egypt as well and since they viewed Babylonia through the Greek eyes

[46] JACOBY, *Apollodors Chronik*, 1ff.; *FGrH* 244 FF 1–87.
[47] 244 FF 83–87. E. SCHWARTZ, *Königlisten* (see next note), dated PSEUDO-APOLLODORUS in 100 B.C.; GUTSCHMID, *Kleine Schriften*, I (Leipzig, 1889), 164, in 63 B.C. But, as noted above, the use of the chronicle by ALEXANDER POLYHISTOR makes a second-century B.C. date probable. Conceivably, this world chronicle had been a Jewish fabrication, as is indeed suggested by *FGrH* 244 FF 83–87.
[48] E. SCHWARTZ, *Königlisten des Eratosthenes und Kastor* (Göttingen, 1894); KUBITSCHEK, Kastor, *R.E.* 10 (1919), 2347–56; JACOBY, *FGrH* 250 FF 1–20.
[49] EUSEBIUS, *Chronik*, 26ff., 81ff.; *FGrH* 250 FF 1–4; see also JACOBY's comment in IIIb (Suppl.), I, 380–90. The invention of the Sicyonic kingdom's supposed antiquity indicates that CASTOR revised the traditional Greek chronology to make it as ancient at least as Assyria.
[50] GELZER, *Sextus Julius Africanus*, II, 89; cf. POSIDONIUS, 87 FF 69–70; APOLLONIUS MOLON, 728 FF 1–3.

of Ctesias, it seems that Jewish history was ignored not because of anti-Semitism, but because of pro-Hellenism.[51] At any rate, Castor's chronicle cannot be cited as evidence that it was customary to disregard biblical history in the current world histories.[52]

It is not certain that the above-mentioned universal chronicle of Pseudo-Apollodorus had incorporated Jewish history. But Alexander Polyhistor (flourished 85–35 B.C.), the first historian who cited Pseudo-Apollodorus, quoted a world chronicle that had synchronized the biblical flood with the one recorded in Berossus. Berossus, said Alexander Polyhistor, had reported that a flood occurred during the reign of Xisuthrus, the tenth mortal king of Babylonia, who ruled 64,000 years.[53] Alexander Polyhistor added that this was "the first and great flood" about which Moses had written.[54] Chances are that Alexander Polyhistor copied the admixture of Genesis and Berossus from the universal chronicle of Pseudo-Apollodorus.[55] The credit for equating Noah-Xisuthrus-Utnapishtim belongs not to the modern decipherers of cuneiform texts, but to a second- or first-century B.C. chronographer.

The name of the Jewish chronicle as it became known to the heathen world may have fortunately been preserved by Alex-

[51] A disliked people was usually not ignored, but vilified. There is nothing to indicate that CASTOR attacked the Jews in his writings.

[52] The treatment of Jewish history by pagan historians during the second and certainly the first century was quite extensive, considering the political insignificance of the Jewish state. POSIDONIUS (87 FF 69–70), TEUCRUS of Cyzicus (274 T 1), TIMAGENES (88 FF 4–6), DIODORUS, XL, 3, to mention a few, either wrote monographs on Jewish history or summed up their history. See *FGrH* 737 FF 1–23; and below, note 100.

[53] BEROSSUS in EUSEBIUS, *Chronik* (Karst), 4ff.; 680 F 32, pp. 374–77. Cf. also ABYDENUS, in EUSEB., *Chronik*, 15f.; CTESIAS, 688 F 2.

[54] EUSEB., *Chronik*, 4, 26ff. (680 F 3, p. 374a), in Karst's translation, quotes: "von Alores [*scil.* Assyriens] dem ersten Konig, bis zum Xisuthron, unter welchem, sagt er, die grosse und erste Sintflut gewesen sei, deren auch Môses Erwähnung tut." "*Sagt er*" can here refer to either BEROSSUS or ALEXANDER POLYHISTOR, from whose work EUSEBIUS was quoting BEROSSUS. JACOBY, *FGrH* IIIb (Suppl.), II, 282, n. 50, differentiates between *die grosse und erste* flood (p. 4, 27), which he attributes to ALEXANDER POLYHISTOR, and *die grosse* flood (pp. 5, 22; 10, 24), which JACOBY ascribes to BEROSSUS. But it is more reasonable to assume that the epithet "the first" antedates ALEXANDER, and was found in a world chronicle, where it was quite fitting. See also next note and note 89.

[55] PSEUDO-APOLLODORUS is cited by EUSEBIUS (*Chronik*, 4, 18; 244 F. 83a–b) as having identified the Xisuthrus flood with that recorded by Moses. Conceivably, PSEUDO-APOLLODORUS, composed during the end of the second century B.C., was a work written by a Jewish author. See note 47.

ander Polyhistor. He parallels (see below, note 89) the *Atthides* with the *Syria*. The former were annalistic histories of Athens, written by natives or sympathizers, the most renowned of whom were Hellanicus of Lesbos (fifth century) and Philochorus (c. 340–263). Despite their questionable origin, brilliantly illuminated in Jacoby's *Atthis*, these works were reputed to have been authoritative in matters of genealogy and customs. Apparently, the *Syria* were for Jewish history what the *Atthides* were for Athenian. In Alexander Polyhistor's time, it would seem, Greek and Oriental chronicles were already fused.

In his *History of Chaldea*, citing as authority the third book of the Jewish Sibylline Oracles, Alexander Polyhistor also mentioned the tower of Babel.[56] He synchronized the builders of the biblical tower with Titan and Prometheus. Here, too, Alexander Polyhistor apparently was quoting a Jewish writer who in an Euhemeristic vein had fused Genesis with Berossus and Hesiod.[57] The Babylonian contemporary of the tower has unhappily not been preserved. Conceivably, though, Alexander Polyhistor was alluding here to his own citation from Pseudo-Eupolemus in the monograph *On the Jews*, naming Belus II as the builder of the tower and founder of Babylon.[58] That Ninus, the son of Belus, was a contemporary of Abraham became a common synchronism since antiquity.[59]

Alexander Polyhistor set the date of Moses during the reign of Ogygus, the first autochthonous Attic king, in whose day the flood of Deucalion occurred, 1020 years before the first Olympiad (776 B.C.), i.e., 1796 B.C.[60] Since, as mentioned above, Eupole-

---

[56] EUSEBIUS, *Chronik*, 12f.; ALEXANDER POLYHISTOR, 273 F 79, IIIA, p. 110; BEROSSUS, 680 F 4, IIIC 382f.; ABYDENUS, 682 F 4; *Orac. Sibyll.* 3:97ff.; cf. JOSEPHUS, *A.J.*, I, 118.

[57] See previous note. HESIOD, *Theogony*, 421ff.

[58] See *FGrH* 724 FF 1–2; WACHOLDER, *HUCA* 34 (1963), 90–94.

[59] DIODORUS, II, 1, 4ff.; EUSEB., *Chronik*, 28 = 688 F 1a–b; EUSEB.-JEROME (ed. Helm, Berlin, 1956), 20a–b, 6.

[60] EUSEB., *P.E.*, 10 (see MRAS, I, 592, on lines 9–18) = ALEXANDER POLYHISTOR, 273 F 101a–b. In this passage AFRICANUS cites quite an array of authorities: ACUSILAUS (2 F 23), DIODORUS (?), THALLUS (256 F 7), CASTOR (250 F 6), POLYBIUS (254 F 3), HELLANICUS (323a F 10), PHLEGON (257 F 6), in addition to ALEXANDER POLYHISTOR. See also Ps.-JUSTIN, *Coh. ad Graec.*, 9. JACOBY (*FGrH* IIIb, Suppl., I, 385–87, on PHILOCHORUS, 328 F 92) regards ALEXANDER POLYHISTOR as the author who had dated Moses 1020 years before the Olympic games. Instead, ALEXANDER POLYHISTOR must be viewed as the first transmitter of this tradition.

mus dated the exodus about 1738 B.C.,[61] the question arises whether Alexander Polyhistor followed here this Hellenistic Jewish historian or whether he arrived at this date independently. And if the latter, what was his basis for dating Moses in 1796 B.C.?

The answer, conceivably, lies in the divergent genealogical treatments of the mythical period. Herodotus and Thucydides named Cecrops as the first human king of Attica.[62] For them, as for Castor and Strabo, Ogygus was a term used for the primeval period of immortal kings.[63] It had never occurred to Herodotus or Thucydides to assign absolute dates for the mythical period. During the Hellenistic period, however, "scientific" chronography demanded precise time tables for the genesis of Hellenic history. Thus Cecrops, the first mortal king of Attica, according to the *Marmor Parium*, ascended the throne in 1581 B.C., but according to Castor, in 1556 B.C.[64]

Another school of chronographers, however, though disputed by Philochorus (340–263 B.C.), pushed back the autochthonous rule of Attica to Ogygus. Ogygus, it was said, had died 189 years before Cecrops, the next known monarch, gained dominion over Attica.[65] Alexander Polyhistor evidently followed this tradition.[66] If so, he must have dated Ogygus' death either in 1770 (*Marmor Parium*) or in 1745 (Castor). The date of Ogygus's ascent to kingship, however, is nowhere directly recorded. But, as shown above, Alexander Polyhistor maintained that in 1796 B.C. Ogygus was the contemporary Attic king when the Israelites departed from Egypt. It follows that the reputedly first king of Attica must have ruled, according to *Marmor Parium*'s computation, at least twenty-six years; but according to Castor's, fifty-one years.[67] Theoretically, either number is acceptable, but the larger one is

---

[61] See, however, *supra*, note 40, where the Ms. reading of EUPOLEMUS' text would seem to date the exodus in 2738 B.C.

[62] HEROD., VII, 141; THUC., II, 15, 1.

[63] STRABO, IX, 1. 18; CASTOR, *FGrH* 250 F 4.

[64] *Marmor Parium*, *FGrH* 239, IIB, p. 993, 3f.; CASTOR, 250 F 4, IIB, p. 1140, 11ff.

[65] PHILOCHORUS, *FGrH* 328 F 92 (IIIb, Suppl., I, 383–85).

[66] According to *Marmor Parium*, *FGrH* 239 A 1, Cecrops died in 1770 B.C.; CASTOR, 250 F 4, apparently dated his death in 1745 B.C.

[67] See previous note.

more likely. Autochthonous kings were habitually assigned long reigns, and the cipher fifty-one or so for the first monarch appears to have been customary.[68]

Biblical Dates in Heathen Chronicles

It follows that Ogygus, the first mortal Attic king, ascended to the throne in 1797 B.C. It follows further that Alexander Polyhistor's dating of the Hebrew exodus from Egypt a year later in 1796 is explainable in terms of Hellenic dating.[69] There is no need, then, to posit a link between Eupolemus and Alexander Polyhistor. Such a link, moreover, would have to account for the discrepancy between Eupolemus' date of the exodus in about 1738 B.C. and Alexander Polyhistor's in 1796. The basis of the latter's date appears to have been the premise, introduced by Eupolemus, that the Jewish civilization was at least as old as the Hellenic one. Hence Moses was a contemporary of Ogygus.

Nevertheless, a conclusion that Alexander Polyhistor had a consistent chronology of biblical events would be erroneous. The opposite is true. Part of the confusion stemmed from his attempt to synchronize Hebrew, Babylonian, and Attic mythologies. A popular record of Athenian chronology is preserved in the *Marmor Parium*, inscribed in 264 B.C.[70] It begins, as mentioned above, with Cecrops in 1581 B.C., during whose reign King Deucalion of Mount Parnassus survived a flood.[71] It goes without saying that in the Greek tradition the flood of Deucalion did not have the paramount significance as the one recorded in the Babylonian and Hebrew texts. But, consistent with the style of parallel-

---

[68] Thus CASTOR, following partially CTESIAS, ascribed a reign of 52 years to Ninus (250 F 1d) as well as to the first king of Sicyon, the oldest Greek monarch (EUSEB., *Chronik*, 30; 81). Inachus, the first king of Argos, is assigned but 50 years (p. 83).

[69] Is there a relationship between JOSEPHUS' dating of the bondage of the Jews during the Hyksos period of the XVII Dynasty (1800–1550 B.C.) and ALEXANDER POLYHISTOR's date of the exodus in 1796? Unfortunately, nothing remains of his monograph on Egypt, where ALEXANDER POLYHISTOR may have treated the issue again. For a recent review of the evidence in JOSEPHUS, see O. EISSFELDT, in *Cambridge Ancient History*, rev. ed., II, Ch. XXVI(a) [Cambridge, 1965], 1–32, who dates the exodus in the XIII century.

[70] JACOBY, *Das Marmor Parium* (Berlin, 1904); *Rh. M.*, LIX (1904), 63–107; *FGrH* 239, IIB, 992–1005; IID, 665–709.

[71] *Marmor Parium, FGrH* A 1–2, IIB, 993.

123

ing the Oriental and Greek mythology, Pseudo-Apollodorus and Alexander Polyhistor identified the flood of Deucalion, said to have occurred in the days of Ogygus (instead of Cecrops), with that of the Oriental Noah and Xisuthrus (Utnapishtim).[72] It is difficult to see how Alexander Polyhistor could have reconciled the dating of Noah as well as Moses in the days of Ogygus. Possibly, though, he was merely quoting Pseudo-Apollodorus' chronicle when he made Noah a contemporary of Ogygus, but his own view was that the latter lived in the days of Moses. Moreover, as a compiler there was no need for Alexander Polyhistor to be consistent. The main point, however, is unquestionable. Both Pseudo-Apollodorus (circa 100 B.C.) and Alexander Polyhistor, who flourished a generation later, had incorporated biblical history into the world chronicles.

The synchronization of biblical with general history is also attested in the writings of Varro (116–27 B.C.). Varro was sympathetically inclined to Judaism, remarking once that he had found the true god of philosophy only in the Roman Jupiter and in the imageless One honored by the Jews.[73] Varro's interest in ancient chronography, like that of some Jews, stemmed from his desire to synchronize Roman history with that of the Greeks. In a work written in 43 B.C., *De gente populi Romani*, fragments of which have been preserved in Censorinus, Varro divided the past into three periods: a) the unknown ($\mathring{\alpha}\delta\eta\lambda ov$); b) the mythical; and c) the historical.[74] The first period began with the first man, whose time could not be determined, and ended with the "first flood" of Ogygus. The second period began with Ogygus and ended in the first Olympiad, lasting 1600 years — 400 years from Ogygus (2376 B.C.) to Inachus (1976), from the latter to

---

[72] ALEXANDER POLYHISTOR, 273 F 101.

[73] VARRO, in AUGUSTINE's *City of God*, IV, 31, 2. Cf. NORDEN, Varro über den Gott der Juden, in *Festgabe für Harnack* (Tübingen, 1921), 298f.; DAHLMANN, Varro, *R.E.*, Suppl. VI (1935), 1235.

[74] CENSORINUS, *De die natali*, 21, quoting VARRO, "Hic enim tria discrimina temporum esse tradit. Primum, ab hominum principio ad cataclysmum priorem, quod proter ignorantiam vocetur $\mathring{\alpha}\delta\eta\lambda ov$; secundum, a cataclysmo priore ad Olympiadem primam, quod quia in eo multa fabulosa referentur, $\mu\upsilon\theta\iota\kappa\grave{o}\nu$ nominatur; tertium, a prima Olympiade ad nos, quod dicitur $\iota\sigma\tau o\rho\iota\kappa\acute{o}\nu$." There is no reason to assume that CENSORINUS was quoting here ERATOSTHENES (so JACOBY, *FGrH*, IID, 709, 20ff.; LINTON, *Synopsis Historiae Universalis*, 72f.), because VARRO and ERATOSTHENES differ here.

the fall of Troy 800 years (1176 B.C., in round numbers, actually 1184), and from the fall of Troy to the Olympic era 400 years (776 B.C.). Accurate information was available only for events after 776 B.C.[75]

In marking the flood as the dividing point between the first and second epoch of human history, Varro shows that he was influenced by the biblical tradition.[76] But the apparent equation Noah-Ogygus indicates, as suggested by Jacoby, that he may have received the account of the flood from the writing of Alexander Polyhistor.[77] Both Varro and Alexander Polyhistor speak of the "first flood," hinting that there was another one. The basic divergence is that the Deucalion flood occurred in Alexander Polyhistor during the days of Ogygus and Moses, while Varro dated Ogygus during the days of the first flood, referring apparently to Noah.

It is not known whether Varro dated Moses in his detailed description of the mythical period of history. The odds are that he did. The fact that the Church Fathers do not cite Varro is no evidence to the contrary, as they rarely quoted Latin works. Augustine apparently was the first Christian author to perceive that Varro's scheme of history was somehow related to Scripture. If Varro did mention Moses, he must have synchronized him with the Argive king Inachus (1976 B.C.), who in his view marked a new epoch in the mythical period of history.

Varro's rating of Moses remains a question mark. But the synchronization of Moses-Inachus is attested in the writings of Ptolemy of Mendes (40 B.C.), Apion of Alexandria (A.D. 40), Justus of Tiberias (flourished 60–100), and perhaps by Thrasyllus of Rhodes (before A.D. 36), Polybius (before A.D. 46), Thallus

[75] CENSORINUS, De die natali, 21.

[76] See note 73. Whether or not the Graeco-Roman writers were acquainted with the Greek translations of Hebrew Scripture or received their information from pro- or anti-Jewish propagandists is still an open question (cf. HEINEMANN, Antisemitismus, R.E., Suppl. V, 3ff.). There is no doubt, however, that VARRO's chronological scheme was based on some earlier chronographer, rather than from a reading of Genesis.

[77] DAHLMANN (R.E., Suppl. VI, 1240) assumed that VARRO's source was CASTOR, whom VARRO cited once. This limiting of VARRO to a single source is rightly challenged by JACOBY (FGrH, IIIb, Suppl., I, 387, 12–18), who suggests ALEXANDER POLYHISTOR as an additional antecedent, because of the mention of Ogygus. The divergence between VARRO and ALEXANDER POLYHISTOR, however, is sufficient to presume that both made use of a world chronicle.

(first century A.D.), and Phlegon of Thralles (A.D. 150), as well as in Christian chronography.[78] Unhappily, little is known of Ptolemy, the oldest authority that Moses lived in the days of Inachus, the first king of Argos. Ptolemy was the priest in an Egyptian temple of Mendes and he wrote a chronicle of Egyptian history in three books.[79] That Ptolemy flourished during the pre-Christian century is deduced from the fact that Apion of Alexandria, whose activity stretched throughout the first century A.D., was quoting Ptolemy.[80] Conceivably, Ptolemy of Mendes is the anonymous historian who in 40 B.C., according to Clement of Alexandria, adjusted Eupolemus's *annus Adami* to the equivalent of 5269 B.C.[81]

Ptolemy synchronized Moses not only with Inachus, the king of Argos, but also with Amosis, the king of Egypt.[82] An old chronicle, quoted by Clement and attributed by Jacoby to Ptolemy, gives the date of the exodus: "The exodus took place during the reign of Inachus, for Moses left Egypt more than 345 [Pessl emends, 445] [83] years before the Sothic cycle [i.e., 1676 or 1666 B.C.]. From the time of Moses' leadership and Inachus to the flood of Deucalion — I mean the second flood — and the conflagration of Phaethon, which had occurred in the time of Crotopus, forty generations are counted, a century being three generations." [84] The account, citing Thrasyllus, goes on to detail

---

[78] PTOLEMY of Mendes, preserved in the writings of TATIAN (38), CLEMENT of Alexandria (*Strom.*, I, 101, 3), EUSEBIUS (*P.E.*, X, 10, 15–20), and PSEUDO-JUSTIN (*Cohortatio ad Graec.* 9 = FGrH 611 F 1).

[79] 611 TT 1–2b.

[80] APION of Alexandria wrote his work circa 39 A.D., before he headed the Alexandrian delegation against the Jews (JOSEPHUS, *A.J.*, XVIII, 257–59 = 614 T 6).

[81] See EUPOLEMUS in CLEMENT, 141, 4 = 723 F 4; GUTSCHMID, *Kleine Schriften*, II, 192, emends the text to refer to a certain CASSIAN (*Strom.*, I, 101), whom Clement was supposedly citing. This view is rightly rejected by N. WALTER, Der angebliche Chronograph Julius Cassianus, in *Studien ... Erich Klostermann* (Berlin, 1961), 177–92. In my forthcoming study on EUPOLEMUS, I argue that the anonymous historian quoted by CLEMENT in *Strom.*, I, 141, 4, is perhaps PTOLEMY of Mendes.

[82] 611 F 1a–c.

[83] UNGER, *Chronologie des Manetho* (Berlin, 1867), 54, 167, emends 435; PESSL, *Das chronologische System Manethos* (Berlin, 1878), 56, reads 445.

[84] CLEMENT, *Strom.*, I, 136, 3–4 = THRASYLLUS, FGrH 253 F 1; TH. REINACH, *Textes d'auteurs grecs et romains relatifs au Judaïsme* (Paris, 1895), 113f. See next note.

events of 310 years to the fall of Troy (dated here in 1194) and continues with 417 years to the first Olympiad in 776 B.C.[85]

The use of the Sothic cycle suggests an Egyptian provenance, justifying Jacoby's speculation that the author of this passage was Ptolemy of Mendes, known for his synchronistic Egyptian history, rather than Thrasyllus, who is cited at the end of the quotation and about whom nothing is known. Whoever he was, the author was a heathen specializing in synchronistic history.

In dating the exodus in 1676 (or 1666) there is a striking similarity between our author and Varro. Ptolemy (?) counted 900 years from Inachus to the Olympic era (776 B.C.), while Varro computed roughly 800 years to the fall of Troy. Ptolemy (?) also diverges from Alexander Polyhistor, who calculated 1020 years from Ogygus to 776, i.e., 1796 B.C. This difference would almost vanish, however, if Pessl's emendation of Clement's text be accepted, yielding the date of the exodus a neat millennium before the Olympic era.[86] One must guard, though, from the temptation to tamper with manuscripts in order to manufacture remarkable coincidences.

Fortunately, we have independent testimony for Ptolemy of Mendes' date of the exodus. As was already said, he had synchronized Moses-Inachus-Amosis. In Manetho's Egyptian history Amosis is listed as the first pharaoh of the XVIII dynasty, dated by Eusebius in 294–319 *anno Abrahami*, or 1723–1698 B.C.[87] This is somewhat, but not seriously, out of joint with the Sothic date, attributed by Jacoby to Ptolemy of Mendes, of 1676 (or 1666) B.C. For though Eusebius' most remarkable book on the chronology of the ancient world was based on the Hellenistic chronicles, it must be considered largely an independent work. This cannot be said of Africanus, for example, who, though quoting Ptolemy, dated the exodus, as did Alexander Polyhistor, in 1797/6 B.C.

The somewhat divergent dates of the exodus, deduced from

[85] Jacoby, *FGrH*, IID, 830, 2f., 5, citing Gutschmid (*Kl. Schr.*, I, 154f.), believes that the passage quoted in the previous note may have emanated from Ptolemy of Mendes, rather than from Thrasyllus. Only *Strom.*, I, 135, 5, is ascribed to Thrasyllus. Unfortunately, too little is known of either to be certain; in this paper the hypothesis is tentatively accepted.

[86] See note 83.

[87] Manetho (in *FGrH*), 609 FF 2–3c, IIIC, pp. 36f.

composite quotations in the writings of the Church Fathers, need not becloud the bits that are known of biblical chronography during the first century B.C. Alexander Polyhistor, quoting, no doubt, Jewish and Samaritan historians, identified Enoch with Atlas, Noah with Belus I and Xisuthrus, and Nimrod with Belus II. He synchronized Moses with the Athenian king Ogygus, in whose time the flood of Deucalion took place. The date of the exodus in Alexander Polyhistor seems to have been 1797/6. A tradition attributed to Eupolemus, however, gave 1738 B.C. as the year of the Israelites' departure from Egypt. 1676 (or 1666) and 1723–1698 B.C. were perhaps among the other proposed datings of Moses. The different solutions suggested indicate an intense interest in the subject matter though no means to solve the problem.

In contrast to Alexander Polyhistor's synchronization of Moses with Ogygus, Ptolemy of Mendes (and perhaps Varro) placed the Jewish legislator in the days of Inachus, the first king of Argos. The artificial feature of both synchronisms is that Ogygus and Inachus appeared rather late in the respective Athenian and Argive genealogies of mortal kings. The older Greek tradition had listed Ogygus and Inachus as Titans. When and by whom these names were transformed into humans is still an open question. Jacoby attributes the change to Castor, who flourished in the middle of the first century.[88] The fact is, however, that in the first century the name of Moses was already linked with Ogygus *or* Inachus. The synchronization of Moses with Ogygus is even attested in the first half of the first century, in the fragments of Alexander Polyhistor and Pseudo-Apollodorus. Conceivably, the same chronographer who classified Ogygus as the first mortal king also dated him in the days of Moses. It is more likely, however, that the shift of Ogygus from the immortals to the mortals and his timing in the days of the exodus were consecutive developments in Hellenistic chronography.[89] Circumstantial evidence

[88] See JACOBY, *FGrH*, IIIB (Suppl.), I, 386f.

[89] JACOBY, *FGrH*, IIIb (Suppl.), I, 387, 18ff.: "The question may remain open whether it was he [Alexander Polyhistor] who created the syncretistic combination of Greek and Oriental tradition which counts the floods and puts the first under the name of Ogygus, or whether the Jewish chronographers preceded him, the knowledge of whom in Christian chronography may entirely derive from Alexander

suggests, then, that during the second century B.C. an unknown author composed a universal world chronicle.

From the writings of Tatian, Clement, and Africanus it would seem that Alexander Polyhistor's dating of Moses in the days of Ogygus and Ptolemy's dating in the period of Inachus were identical.[90] There is no doubt, however, that the learned Church Fathers were in error. For Inachus and Ogygus represented two rival schools of Hellenic antecedence. Some genealogists, like Castor, who named Inachus, regarded Athens (Ogygus) as a late comer in the Hellenic scene.[91] The invention of Ogygus as the first autochthonous king, on the other hand, was intended to ante-date Attica before Argos. The synchronism Moses-Ogygus-Inachus was, therefore, a contamination of two mutually exclusive chronographic approaches. Dionysius of Halicarnassus asserts flatly that Inachus of Argos was the first mortal king.

Ptolemy of Mendes's addition of the pharaoh of the exodus created a triangular synchronism Moses-Inachus-Amosis.[92] The link became almost universal when an unknown chronicler supplied the Babylonian (Assyrian) contemporary of Moses: Belochus, the eighth king after Ninus in Ctesias' manufactured list of Assyrian kings, who supposedly reigned 35 years, and in whose 32nd year the exodus occurred, 402 years after the founding of the Assyrian empire.[93] This suggests that a biblical chronographer had synchronized the patriarchal period of the Jews with the

---

Polyhistor." The first alternative, that ALEXANDER POLYHISTOR had fused Jewish and Greek mythology, must be rejected. For, as far as we can judge from the fragments, his works consisted of gluing together diverse quotations rather than of concocting the material himself. Moreover, there is nothing to suggest that a heathen on his own would have put Moses in such favorable light. The synthesis of Greek and Jewish chronology antedates ALEXANDER POLYHISTOR. The Jewish chronicles, it would seem, were known as οἱ τὰ Σύρια, paralleling οἱ τὰς Ἀτθίδας (EUSEB., P.E., X, 10, 8 = ALEXANDER POLYHISTOR [273 F 101]). For the vulgar forms, see MRAS, Rh.M., XCII (1944), 226F.

[90] TATIAN, Oratio adversus Graecos, 38; CLEMENT Al., Strom., I, 101 (EUSEB., P.E., X, 12, 2–4); AFRICANUS in P.E., X, 10 (Ps.-JUSTIN, Coh. ad Graec., 9) = ALEXANDER POLYHISTOR, 273 F 79; PTOLEMY of Mendes, 611 F 1; APION, 616 F 2a–c.

[91] CASTOR in EUSEB., Chronik (Karst), p. 86 (FGrH 250 F 4, p. 1140), makes Cecrops the first Athenian king, as does the Marmor Parium (JACOBY, FGrH 139 A 1–2). CASTOR, however, antedated Sicyon before Argos.

[92] PTOLEMY of Mendes in EUSEBIUS, quoting AFRICANUS, P.E., X, 10, 16ff. = 611 F 1.

[93] CLEMENT Al., Strom., I, 102, 4; EUSEB., P.E., X, 12, 8; Chronik, 31, 3; 85, 14.

widely read Assyrian history of Ctesias.[94] To do so, the ancient Jewish historian was forced to juggle Ctesias' figures, at least as they are attested in Castor. The basic assumption of the biblical chronicler was the synchronism of Abraham-Ninus, a view that remained the starting point of the entire Byzantine chronography.[95] Since Moses was the seventh generation after Abraham, the parallel Assyrian king in Ctesias' list might have been Amramithes, the seventh after Ninus. But since the exodus occured in the 80th year of Moses and 430 years after Abraham's arrival into Canaan, the eighth generation after Ninus, Belochus, seemed preferable. In Castor, according to Eusebius, Belochus ascended the throne 271 years after the birth of Assyria. The Jewish chronicler changed this number to 402 so that in Belochus' 32nd year the biblical 430 years (Ex. 12:40 LXX) would have been completed. Thus the contamination of Argive and Athenian claims plus the additions from Manetho and Ctesias resulted in a neat universal synchronism: Moses-Ogygus-Inachus-Amosis-Belochus. This list represented, respectively, the Jews, Attica, Argos, Egypt, and Babylonia (Assyria).

Since Gelzer and Gutschmid, the unified synchronism of the exodus is ascribed to Justus of Tiberias, the renowned rival of Josephus,[96] dating the universal chronicle at the end of the first century. Justus was the author of a chronicle which had begun with Moses and ended with the reign of his patron Agrippa II in the year 100.[97] This work was still available in the middle of the ninth century to Photius. Unfortunately, the two fragments of

---

[94] CTESIAS, as preserved in CASTOR (see previous note) 250 1c–d; CEPHALION, 93 F 1. None of these sources mention CTESIAS by name. But there is no question he was the ultimate authority for both CASTOR and CEPHALION, as indicated by DIODORUS (II, 23, 1 = CTESIAS, 688 F 1) and NICOLAUS of Damascus (90 F 2).

[95] EUSEBIUS-JEROME, Chronik (Helm), pp. 14, 20a; EUSEBIUS, P.E., IX, 10, 11; X, 9, 10; MALALAS, V, 7c; EPIPHANIUS, Pan. Haer., III, 12.

[96] GELZER, Sextus Julius Africanus, I, 4, 20, 118, 265; GUTSCHMID, Kl. Schr., II, 203; WACHSMUTH, Einl. der alten Geschichte (Leipzig, 1896), 439; cf. SCHÜRER, Gesch. d. jüd. Volkes, I⁴, 61f.

[97] On JUSTUS, see the inadequate study of H. LUTHER, Josephus und Justus vom Tiberias (Halle, 1910). Known mainly from JOSEPHUS' Vita, he is cited also (aside from passages quoted below) in PHOTIUS, Bibl. 33. Since VALESIUS, it is assumed that the Suda, s.v. Phlegon, contains a reference to JUSTUS' work (GUTSCHMID, Kl. Schr., IV, 349; SCHÜRER, I, 61). But, if the text of the Suda needs emendation, the reading of Josephus perhaps makes more sense than Justus (see JACOBY, FGrH 737 F 3, app. crit. to 19–20).

Justus dealing with the date of the exodus are of inferior quality, which makes it impossible to verify the attribution to him of the universal synchronism.

The two passages of Justus, moreover, diverge. According to Eusebius, Justus repeated the synchronism Moses-Inachus.[98] Africanus, preserved in Syncellus, said that Justus made Moses the contemporary of Phoroneus and his successor Apis, the two first kings of Argos, and Amosis of Egypt.[99] Now Justus may have dated Moses either in the days of Phoroneus, the first king of Argos in the old tradition; or in the time of Inachus, a name added by second- or first-century chronographers. But Justus would not have synchronized Moses with *both* Phoroneus and Inachus. All that can be said of Justus' chronology is that, unlike Josephus, Justus seems to have made full use of the Hellenistic universal chronicles.

The assumption, maintained by Gelzer, that whatever the Church Fathers report of Hellenistic biblical chronology had filtered through Justus is untenable also on general grounds. Africanus' biblical chronology may or may not have been based on Justus. But there is enough evidence to suggest that biblical chronology was a subject not limited to Jews. Already in the first century B.C., treatments of Jewish antiquities had become standard in universal histories.[100] The pagan chronographers Polybius (A.D. 47) and Phlegon of Tralles (under Hadrian) synchronized Moses with Assyrian, Athenian, Argive, or Egyptian history.[101] The third-century Porphyry, whose chronographic technique enabled him to date the Book of Daniel accurately, said

---

[98] EUSEBIUS-JEROME, *Chronik* (Helm), 7b (SYNCELLUS) = 734 F 2.

[99] SYNCELLUS, p. 116 = 734 F 3. Both fragments (see previous note) are marked by JACOBY as defective.

[100] The treatment of Jews in Greek heathen texts had begun with HECATAEUS of Abdera, in the end of the fourth century B.C. (DIOD., XL, 3 = FGrH 264 F 6). MEGASTHENES, writing in the period of the Diadochi, likewise glorified the Jews (JOSEPHUS, *A.J.*, X, 227 = 715 F 1; CLEMENT Al., *Strom.*, I, 72, 4f. = 715 F 3). THEOPHRASTUS discussed the priestly code (W. PÖTSCHER, *Theophrastos* [Leiden, 1964], Fragment 13, pp. 172–76). Aside from ALEXANDER POLYHISTOR, TEUCRUS of Cyzicus also wrote a monograph on the Jews in the first century B.C. (274 T 1); and so did CONON (26 F 4). For other treatment, see the now inadequate work of REINACH, *Textes d'auteurs grecs et romains relatifs au Judaïsme*; and JACOBY's *FGrH*, *passim*. Cf. above, n. 52.

[101] POLYBIUS, *FGrH* 254 FF 1–4; THALLUS, 256 FF 1–8; PHLEGON of Tralles, 257 F 16. See also supra, notes 55–56; 73–75; 78–80, and *passim*.

that the Assyrian Semiramis had lived after Moses but 150 years before Inachus and that Moses flourished about 1984 B.C.[102] Porphyry, no doubt, merely echoed the dates given in the Hellenistic world chronicles. By and large, pagan chronologists before the spread of Christianity placed Moses in an honored place, accepting implicitly the most extreme antiquity of Judaism they could imagine.[103]

Anti-Semitic Biblical Chronology

Anti-Semitic authors, therefore, had to contend not only with Jewish propagandists but also with the rather favorable attitude to Jews reflected in heathen chronography. The synchronism Moses-Inachus-Ogygus-Belochus must have been rather displeasing to Alexandrian Jew-baiters, struggling to deny the rights of citizenship to the Jews. Is it not paradoxical, then, that Apion, the author of a diatribe against the Jews, himself acknowledged the antiquity of the Jewish people when he reiterated Ptolemy of Mendes' synchronism of Moses-Inachus-Amosis? [104]

There was, however, another side to Apion's dating of Moses. The development of Alexandrian heathen treatment of ancient Jewish history is still obscure. Manetho, as claimed by Josephus, had given the first Egyptian account of the Hebrews' stay in the land of the pharaohs. Despite Josephus, though, it appears that Manetho merely described the Hyksos, whom the Jewish historian identified with the Jews. Manetho may not have alluded to the Jews at all.[105] Conceivably, though, Manetho did mention

---

[102] PORPHYRY in *Adversus Christianos*, Harnack ed. (Berlin, 1916), fragment 40; JACOBY, *FGrH* 260 F 33; EUSEBIUS-JEROME (Helm ed.), p. 8: "Porphyrius... post Mosem Semiramin fuisse adfirmat, quae apud Asyrios CL ante Inachum regnavit annis. Itaque iuxta eum DCCC paene et quinquaginta annis Troiano bello Moyses senior inuenitur." JACOBY, *FGrH*, IID, p. 878, on F 33, points out that PORPHYRY merely repeated the older tradition, since his own chronicle began with the Trojan Wars.

[103] The view gained from JOSEPHUS' *Contra Apionem* and repeated by REINACH (*Textes d'auteurs grecs et romains*, VIII–XX) that, with a few exceptions in the early period, the Greek heathen writers were anti-Jewish is decidedly misstated and overstated. The dominant treatment was decisively pro-Jewish.

[104] APION, 616 F 4a–c.

[105] GUTSCHMID, *Kl. Schr.*, IV, 402, 439f.; R. LAQUEUR, Manetho, *R.E.*, XIV, (1928), 1064ff., proposes that JOSEPHUS (*C. Apionem*, I, 74–92) utilized a PSEUDO-MANETHO written by a polytheistic author, whom Josephus believed to have been

the exodus of the Israelites, which he dated in the reign of Tuth-mosis, the seventh king of the XVIII dynasty (1626–1618).[106] If so, Ptolemy of Mendes' timing of Moses in the days of Amosis (1776 B.C.) was by the nature of the material only a slight cor-rection.[107] Not so the chronology of Lysimachus (flourished be-fore Apion), who dated Moses in the reign of Bocchoris.[108] Wit-tingly or unwittingly, Josephus' remark that Bocchoris lived near-ly "1700 years ago," has falsified Lysimachus's intent to show that the appearance of the Jews on the historical scene occurred at a late date.[109] In fact, the date of Bocchoris in Manetho's tables, mentioned in Diodorus, was the only pharaoh of the XXIV dynas-ty, in 770–635 B.C.,[110] nearly a millennium later than the time assigned by Josephus. Lysimachus as well as Apion dated the exodus in the eighth century B.C. Apion further refined Lysi-machus' timing of the exodus, making it occur in the eighteenth year of Bocchoris' reign, i.e., in 753 B.C.[111]

Josephus' testimony, as shown above, is contradicted by the Church Fathers's attribution to Apion of the synchronism Moses-Inachus-Amosis.[112] Gutschmid reconciles the contradictory evi-dence by assuming that Apion had merely synchronized Inachus with Amosis, referring to the period of the Hyksos, to which Justus and the Church Fathers had appended the name of Moses.[113] This explanation is not satisfactory, as Apion was

real. See JACOBY, *FGrH*, IIIC, 84, app. crit. Cf., also, E. MEYER, *Aegyptische Chronologie* (Berlin, 1904), 71; R. WEILL, *La fin du moyen âge Egyptien* (Paris, 1918), 68ff.

[106] *Contra Apionem*, 86–90 = *FGrH* 609 F 8, pp. 87f. See the authorities cited in the previous note, especially, MEYER, *Nachträge* (1907), 34, n. 5.

[107] PTOLEMY of Mendes, 611 F 1a–c.

[108] LYSIMACHUS is known only through JOSEPHUS, *C. Apionem*, I, 304–11; II, 16f., 20, 145, 236 = 621 FF 1–4. He antedates APION, but is later than PTOLEMY of Mendes.

[109] *C. Apionem*, II, 16 = 621 F 2.

[110] MANETHO in EUSEBIUS, *Chronik*, p. 68, "under whom the lamb spoke" (609 FF 2–3c, pp. 46f.). DIOD., I, 45, 2; 65, 1; 79, 1; 94, 5, makes him the greatest lawgiver of Egypt or even the world.

[111] APION in *C. Apionem*, II, 17 = 616 F 4.

[112] TATIAN, 38; CLEMENT Al., *Strom.*, I, 101; EUSEBIUS, *P.E.*, X, 10 = JACOBY, APION 616 F 2a–c.

[113] GUTSCHMID, *Kl. Schr.*, IV, 362. MUELLER, *FGH*, III, p. 509, F 3, suggested that this fragment (*C. Apionem*, II, 16 = *FGrH* 616 F 4a) was not in APION's fourth book of his history of Egypt, where the anti-Semitic texts were collected. JACOBY (616 F 4) also questioned the title of the book in which APION dated the exodus.

clearly quoting Ptolemy of Mendes, who certainly had synchronized the Jewish lawgiver with Amosis and Inachus.

A possible solution seems to be that Josephus and the Church Fathers were quoting different parts of Apion's work. Apion, indeed, had mentioned the synchronism Moses-Inachus-Amosis, but only to refute it. This fact the Christian chronologists evidently did not bother to cite. Apion's own date of the exodus, however, is undoubtedly that ascribed to him by Josephus, i.e., 753 B.C. It is not known why Josephus failed to allude to the synchronism Moses-Inachus-Amosis, mentioned not only by Apion but also in the current universal chronicles as well.[114] Of course, chronology *per se* was of little interest to the Jewish historian. He was primarily bent on refuting the charges that the Jews were expelled from Egypt because of leprosy, rather than the date of the exodus. Conceivably, though, Josephus' failure to allude to the Moses-Inachus-Amosis synchronism was due to the fact that it had been the corner stone of Hellenistic chronicles, works he refused to acknowledge, even if indirectly.[115] At any rate, after A.D. 70 the anti-Semitic synchronism Moses-Bocchoris gained wide currency in Rome, as attested in Tacitus.[116]

Apion's dating of the exodus in 753 B.C. is noteworthy. It was constructed to synchronize, according to Josephus, with the foundation of Carthage, which Apion placed in the same year as the exodus. The traditional year of the foundation of Carthage was 814 B.C., a view stated by Timaeus and repeated by Dionysius of Halicarnassus, the Roman historian.[117] Apion apparently

---

[114] Because JOSEPHUS' biblical chronology has been subjected to several studies, its treatment has been excluded from this essay. M. BUEDDINGER, Die Exodus nach Manetho, *Sitzungsber. d. k. Akad. d. Wissensch.*, LXXV (Vienna, 1873); JUSTUS VON DESTINON, *Die chronologischen Systeme im alten Testament und bei Josephus* (*Mitteilungen der Vorderasiatischen Gesellschaft*, 1908, 2, Berlin); LINTON, *Synopsis Historiae Universalis*, 76–86; as well as in discussions of Josephus and the Bible relating to chronology. Moreover, as evidently felt by the Church Fathers, JOSEPHUS' chronology was frequently contradictory and unrelated to the main stream of biblical historiography antecedent to him.

[115] See *C. Apionem*, I, 218, where JOSEPHUS groups several Graeco-Jewish historians with those heathen writings. At any rate, it is clear that JOSEPHUS made no use of his Graeco-Jewish predecessors, including PHILO of Alexandria, whom he mentioned once (*A.J.*, XVIII, 259f.).

[116] TACITUS, *Hist.*, V, 3, 1.

[117] *C. Apionem*, II, 17 = 616 F 2a; TIMAEUS, 566 F. 60 = DIONYSIUS of Halicarnassus, *A.R.*, I, 74, 1. TIMAEUS had placed the foundation of Carthage and

had intended to correct Dionysius, whose reputation he coveted,[118] pointing out the remarkable coincidence that Rome and Carthage had been built within one year. Ironically, by dating the exodus in the same time as the founding of Carthage and Rome, Apion unwittingly assigned greater world significance to this event than he had perhaps intended.

It has been taken for granted that in antiquity interest in biblical chronology was restricted to the Jews and Christians. This study has demonstrated that heathen historians — Alexander Polyhistor, Varro, Ptolemy of Mendes, and others — were likewise eager to date the main events recorded in the Bible. Interest in biblical chronology during the first century B.C. went hand in hand with the incorporation of ancient Jewish history as part of universal history. The writings of Posidonius, Diodorus, Nicolaus of Damascus, and Strabo contained lengthy accounts about Moses, far exceeding the political or geographical significance of Judaea. In part, the widening of the horizons of the universal historians resulted from the ecumenical nature of the Roman state. But monotheism and the majestic description of creation and the flood in the Book of Genesis were beginning to attract the attention of the heathen learned community. It is doubtful, though not impossible, that the heathen writers read the Book of Genesis. The odds are that they received their knowledge of the Bible through Hellenistic Jewish reworkings of biblical events, of which there were many. The incorporation of biblical chronology into the world chronicles explains the honored position given to Moses by heathen historians centuries before Christian chronography made its appearance. In fact, philo-Semitic chronography antedated its anti-Semitic variety.

That despite these immense efforts the Jewish and heathen attempts to date the flood or the exodus ended in complete failure is not surprising. Modern scholars with all the advantages of scientific tools have not been more successful. The significance of the synchronistic world chronicle is twofold. Biblical tradition

---

Rome in the same year (814 B.C.), a view which rightly mystified DIONYSIUS. APION followed TIMAEUS in the synchronism of the foundation of Carthage and Rome, but modified the date.

[118] Cf. the *Suda*, *s. v. Apion*, 616 T 1.

had penetrated heathen historiography through the works of Graeco-Jewish writers. And when Christian learned men subsequently attempted to prove the greater antiquity of the Jews in relation to the Greeks, they invoked the testimony of heathen authors who had but echoed the Graeco-Jewish writers: "Who was Plato, except Moses speaking in Attic?"

PROLEGOMENON

A HISTORY OF THE SABBATICAL READINGS OF SCRIPTURE FOR THE "TRIENNIAL CYCLE"

1. *Introduction*

This essay offers an outline of the use of Scripture in the synagogue from the time of the Second Temple to the thirteenth century when a process of standardization resulted in a high degree of uniformity throughout Jewry. The recitation of Scripture on the mornings of the Sabbaths and festivals is no doubt the oldest segment of synagogal liturgy and deserves attention because of its intrinsic significance. It merits attention, moreover, because it fathered two respectable offspring: the midrash and the piyyut. Midrash is the rabbinic use of Scripture for halakah and aggadah. The midrashic homilies, ancient and medieval examples of which fill hundreds of volumes, originated as lessons derived from the portion of Scripture recited during a particular Saturday morning, with which they have remained partly linked to this day.

Piyyut, a rabbinic borrowing of the Greek word *poetes,* is a peculiar synagogal hymn that combines rhyme with customary alphabetic acrostics. Attesting to one of the first uses of rhymed poetry in the world, these rabbinic hymns utilize the rich midrashic lore to combine the themes of the introductory sections of the Shemoneh 'Esreh ("Eighteen Blessings") with the Scriptural portions of the week. The oldest surviving specimens of the piyyut are those of Yannai and his disciple Eleazar Ha-Qalir, who appear to have flourished at the end of the sixth and the beginning of the seventh centuries.[1] The midrashic homilies, the weekly hymns, and the biblical readings dominated the Sabbath morning service. The fixed prayers constituted but a small, though significant part of the day's liturgy.

137

It is rather surprising how little we know of the ancient Palestinian customs. The halakah as codified by Alfasi, Maimonides, and Karo reflects the Babylonian rite, which diverged considerably from that practiced in the West. This essay, therefore, may be read as an attempt to trace the liturgic divergence in the light of the weekly readings of Scripture.

The appearance of this volume in 1940 marked a new stage in our knowledge of the Palestinian tradition of the reading of Scripture. Although some of the leading scholars of the nineteenth century, such as Rapoport (Shir), Zunz, and Friedmann (Ish Shalom) discussed the subject, it was not until Büchler's publication of a Geniza fragment that students of the subject became aware of a list of Prophetic readings completely different from the one read now in the synagogues.[2] Prior to the publication of this list, the question often debated was whether the Palestinian cycle of readings lasted three years or three and a half years. After its publication the problem shifted to the question of what precisely were the Pentateuchal and Prophetic passages recited. Volume I of *The Bible as Read and Preached in the Ancient Synagogue* supplied the chapter and verse for the weekly lections of the Books of Genesis and Exodus. In 126 essays Mann identified the Scriptural readings for 73 Sedarim and 53 sub-Sedarim, claiming that there was an intimate link between the first verse of the Prophetic lections and the halakic problems raised in the midrashic homilies. In other words, Mann was concerned not only with facts, but also with discovering the underlying principles that link synagogal liturgy with midrash and halakah. In Volume II, which appeared posthumously in 1966,[3] Mann carried the discussions to Seder 105 pertaining to Num. 6:1.[4] Simply stated, this hypothesis assumed that the weekly Prophetic portions were of greater significance for the development of the sermon than were the readings of the Torah.

It is easy to point out that Mann failed to prove his daring hypothesis. The homilies of the so-called Tanhuma type of midrash were not consistently, or even frequently, as Mann claimed, inspired by the haftara's first verse. It is also true that Mann's view of the actual workings of the so-called "Triennial Cycle" was essentially faulty. He assumed that it was almost identical with the

Annual Cycle, except that the cycle lasted longer and that the sections recited were smaller. In fact, however, as we shall see, the very term "Triennial Cycle" is questionable since it implies that it operated like the Annual Cycle. It is also possible to show that Mann occasionally listed Sedarim that never existed, and that many of the "Triennial" haftarot named in this volume are erroneous.[5]

Yet it should be noted that the criticism leveled against him is to a large degree based on the tools supplied by Mann's own work, for it is Mann who identified most of the Geniza fragments of the "Triennial Cycle." It is this volume that has shown the way to the principles that lie behind the Prophetic selections of the "Triennial Cycle," proving that they diverged completely from the criteria which determined the Prophetic selections of the Annual Cycle. It was Mann who opened the field and guided the students who have followed him. The publication of the list of the haftarot for the "Triennial Cycle," appearing here for the first time in Appendix I of this essay, has been made possible by Mann's keen insights.

It should be stressed, moreover, that the rejection of Mann's claim of an intimate link between the Scriptural weekly portions and the midrashic sermons does not necessarily imply a denial of unity. On the contrary, there are many threads which seem to bind the midrash to the Sabbath and Festival liturgy. In the review that follows, some of them will be identified. But the basic facts concerning both the "Triennial Cycle" and the midrash await solution before the synthesis that Mann aimed for can be achieved. Mann's work is a milestone in our understanding of this rabbinic liturgy of the Sabbath, though it needs considerable modification in the light of new knowledge.

2. The Reading of Scripture during the Second Temple

Although we know little of the liturgy for this period, it is possible to assert that the reading of Scripture on the mornings of the Sabbaths and festivals constitutes the oldest segment of the synagogal liturgy. Jewish tradition (Philo, Josephus, the New Testament, the Talmud) ascribe the weekly lessons to Moses.[6] Deut. 31:10 ff., however, seems to ordain the reading of Scripture only once in seven years.

Of the ten innovations ascribed by the talmudists to Ezra, one refers to the recitation of a Torah portion on the mornings of Mondays and Thursdays and on the afternoon of the Sabbath.[7] Although the historicity of this tradition may be questioned, it is a fact that the first and only ancient account of the use of the Bible for public worship does link the Torah service with Ezra. It is reported in Nehemiah 8 that Ezra the Scribe, having recently arrived from Babylonia, assembled the people on the first day of the seventh month (Rosh Hashanah) and presented the book of the Law (Torah) of Moses to the congregation in a solemn service. Standing on a wooden platform, and assisted by a dozen or so Levites and other literate men, Ezra blessed the Great Lord God, as the people, shouting amens, in turn rose and prostrated themselves. Neh. 8:8 offers a technical, if obscure, description of the service: "And they (i.e., Ezra and his assistants) read from the book, the Law (*torah*) of God, clearly (*meforash*); and they gave the sense (*wesom sékhel*), so that they (the people) understood the reading."

The Revised Standard Version offers "with interpretation" as an alternate rendition of *meforash,* which some commentators, following Bab. Megillah 3a, assume to refer to an Aramaic translation from the Hebrew, the vernacular of the returnees from Babylonia; "gave the meaning" may suggest the simplification of the technical points of the text so that the people would understand, but it may refer instead to instructional embellishments. Enough has been said to show why we conjecture that this verse may record the use of both the targum and the midrashic sermon.[8]

Whatever the precise meaning of this verse, it is clear that Ezra recited only a portion of the Mosaic Law, though the service lasted from dawn to noon. What was the Scriptural selection for the occasion? From a careful reading of Neh. 8:14-15, when a smaller group of people met and read from the *torah* (Law) on the second day, it would seem to follow that he recited Lev. 23:25-27: "And they found it written in the Law (*torah*) that the Lord had commanded by Moses that the people of Israel should dwell in booths during the feast of the seventh month, and that they (Ezra and his assistants) should publish and proclaim in all their towns and in Jerusalem, 'Go out to the hills and bring branches of olive, wild

140

olive, myrtle, palm, and other leafy trees to make booths, as it is written.'" Since this is almost a direct quotation, with some amplification and in reverse order, of Lev. 23:40-42, which prescribes the ritual for the festival of Sukkot, it appears likely that on the preceding day the passage of Lev. 23:25-27, pertaining to the celebration of the first day of the seventh month (Rosh Hashanah), found in the beginning of chapter 23, had been recited.

It is possible to argue, then, that the custom of reciting the related Pentateuchal passages on the festivals dates back to the time of Ezra, though Megillah III, 6 interprets Lev. 23:44 as originating in a Mosaic precept: "And Moses *read* (*wayyedabber;* RSV and JPS: declared) to the Israelites (the passages of) the set times of the Lord." Rooted in Ezra's time, it would seem, was also the reading of Lev. 23:23 prescribed in the same Mishnaic text, though this procedure was changed during the Amoraic period. The same may be true of the ordinance in Megillah IV, 4 that requires a minimum of three verses of text to fulfill the duty of reading. The passage relating to the first of the seventh month— Lev. 23:23-25—actually contains three verses. Bab. Megillah 21b, however, rationalizes the number, either because of the three divisions of the Hebrew Scriptures or because of the parallel with the Priests, Levites, and Israelites—the three classes of Israel.

It is an indication of the paucity of our sources that we must move from a passage in the book of Nehemiah to the accounts of the Gospels. But we have to dispose first of a medieval legend that ascribed the origin of the custom of reciting several verses from the Prophets, called *haftarah*,[9] to the fourth decade of the second century B.C.E. When Antiochus IV, it is said, prohibited the reading of the Torah, the edict was evaded by a recitation of a Prophetic portion; and this substitute survived the persecution.[10] There is nothing in our sources to substantiate the legend, except to say that the haftara originated in the days of the Second Temple.[11]

Two possible hypotheses as to the period when the haftara originated may be proposed: that the ritual of Scriptural readings was set at a time when there was only a twofold division of the Hebrew sacred texts, thus explaining the presence of the Torah and Prophets but the absence of the Hagiographa in the Sabbath morning ritual;

alternately, it is possible that as "the other books of our fathers"—the phrase used in the prologue to the Greek translation of Ben Sira for the Books that became part of the division later called "Hagiographa" were gaining official acceptance, they were incorporated into the Sabbath and Festival liturgy. But the custom of using selections from the Psalms and other Hagiographic texts, though it never vanished entirely, as will be shown below, was later discouraged. The first alternative seems more plausible.

Jesus, according to Luke 4:16-19, upon returning to Nazareth and visiting a local synagogue, "was given to him the book of the Prophet Isaiah to read. He opened the book and he found the place that was written"—Is. 61:1-2. The passage seems to imply that though the choice of the Biblical Book was determined by custom or by the synagogal authorities, Jesus was free to select any text within that Book that he wished. This is so because, miraculously it seems, according to Luke, the scroll unrolled precisely on the spot that summed up Jesus' mission. I am not sure whether the fact that Jesus is said to have read two verses—the minimum length of the haftara as recorded in a later period—is significant; though, as mentioned above, the requirement of three verses for the public recitation of the Torah may be rooted in the passage chosen by Ezra.

Of some interest to our subject is Acts 13:15, which reports Paul's participation in the Sabbath service of a synagogue in Antioch. Upon the conclusion of the reading of the Law and the Prophets, Paul delivered the sermon, filled as usual with learned allusions to Scripture. First he quotes verses directly from the book of Psalms, intermingled with a citation from Isaiah (Acts 13:33-35, quoting Ps. 2:7; Is. 55:3; Ps. 66:10), and he concludes the sermon with a discussion of Hab. 1:5. It is an intriguing question whether Paul's sermon is an example of a formula of citing various parts of Scripture, attested in the later midrashic and liturgical texts. Essentially, however, Paul's speech appears to be a Jewish version of the Hellenistic homily rather than a type of homily found in the Qumran or midrashic texts.

Unfortunately, it is impossible to reconstruct the respective readings of the Torah and Prophets for the Sabbaths when Jesus and Paul appeared in the synagogues of Nazareth and Antioch.

Adolph Büchler's article (see n. 2 above) claiming to do so has misled some scholars into believing that our present knowledge permits us to reconstruct the cycles for the Scriptural selections during the pre-70 period, thus making it possible to fix seasons for events recorded in the Gospels.[12] Except for the Festival readings, and even here much doubt remains, there is no evidence of a cycle of Scriptural readings linked with the calendar. The so-called "Triennial Cycle," as we shall see, is probably of a later date, and was not tied to a particular season of the year.

3. *The Mishnaic Period (70-c. 220 C.E.)*

The Mishnah is the first source that contains a number of passages dealing with our subject. The problem in these passages is not so much how to interpret them as how to relate them in time and space. Does the testimony of the Mishnah reflect essentially the period of its formation between the destruction of the Second Temple in the year 70 and the death of Rabbi Judah Hanasi about 220? Can it be used as a guide to trace practices during the time of the Second Temple? Is it correct to assume that the customs attested in this text reflect the situation in Palestine as a whole or should they be regarded as practices of the academies of Yabneh and Tiberias? And, finally, are the ordinances of the Mishnah intended to stress their normative importance or merely to record their innovative or controverted nature? These questions are raised here because too often a quotation from this ancient text is considered to be authoritative and unimpeachable testimony instead of, as it should be, the beginning of an inquiry into a historical situation. We know that during talmudic and even post-talmudic times variety rather than uniformity prevailed in the practice of the Sabbatical readings of Scripture. For the purpose of this study it is assumed that the Mishnah's accounts reflect merely a version of the rite as recommended and observed in tannaitic circles. The mishnaic evidence is, however, of paramount significance because soon after its publication, the Mishnah became authoritative for the amoraic tradition, and began to displace the customs not recorded in it.[13]

Of basic significance for the understanding of the mishnaic

143

lections of Scripture is the twofold division of the biblical text:
the *pasuk* or verse, and the *parashah* or paragraph. The term *seder*
in the sense of *parashah* is post-mishnaic and perhaps post-talmudic.
Two verses made up a small *parashah,* three the normal, more
than three a large *parashah.*[14] A *parashah* may therefore be defined,
in mishnaic parlance, as a unit of content or as the minimum
passage recited in the formal reading of Scripture without a stop.[15]

Mishnah Ta'anit, IV, 3, records the paragraphing of Gen. 1:1-
2:3 (a total of 34 verses) as they were divided during the week of
the *ma'amad,* the Israelite prayer sessions associated with the
priestly "watches" (*mishmarot*):

Paragraph	Gen.	No. of verses
1.	1:1-5	5
2.	:6-8	3
3.	:9-13	5
4.	:14-19	6
5.	:20-23	4
6.	:24-31	8
7.	2:1-3	3

The Mishnah says that daily *ma'amad* readings were as follows:

Day of the Week	Paragraph	No. of verses
Sunday	1 and 2	8
Monday	2 and 3	8
Tuesday	3 and 4	11
Wednesday	4 and 5	10
Thursday	5 and 6	12
Friday	6 and 7	11

This text suggests that the requirement of three verses per reader,
as reported in Mishnah Megillah IV,4, was not observed, for on
the first two days of the week only a total of 8 verses was recited
for the three men called up. The third-century amora, Samuel of
Nehardea, insisted that there was nothing wrong with stopping

in the middle of a verse, thus dividing the five verses into two paragraphs of two and a half verses each.[16]

How many verses were read on Saturday morning? According to Mish. Megillah IV, 2, seven men recited the weekly portion, three verses each, for a total of 21.[17] The Mishnah suggests that the Torah reading was normally continuous from Sabbath to Sabbath. This is to say that the sections read on Saturday afternoons and weekdays were not counted as part of the cycle, though some authorities maintained that they were.[18] Since our masoretic text of the Pentateuch contains 5,845 verses,[19] it would have taken 278 Sabbaths of 21 verses to complete the cycle of readings. In practice, however, as on the Sabbath of Genesis, when 34 verses were recited, the average weekly lectionary was larger than the minimum.[20] Somtimes the required length was not reached, at least in some localities; thus Seder 5 in Appendix I began with Gen. 8:1 and ended with 8:14.[21]

When a feast or other commemorative day fell on a Saturday, the cyclical reading was ignored and an appropriate portion was substituted. The Mishnah lists the Pentateuchal selections for a number of Sabbaths—including the festivals, the New Moon, Hanukah, and Purim—fast days, Ma'amadot, and the four Saturdays between the first of Adar and the first of Nisan.[22] During these Sabbaths, the number of verses sometimes—as during Parashat Amalek, the Sabbath before Purim, Exod. 17:8-16—did not reach the prescribed number.[23] The same is true of the festivals, when only five readers sufficed, presumably because the *parashiyot* were normally smaller. On the Day of Atonement six readers were required, and during the reading, it is said, the high priest recited Lev. 16 and skipped to Lev. 23:26 ff. This, as noted in Yoma, 69b, violated the rule of Mishnah Megillah IV, 4, which proscribes skipping in the recitation of Torah passages althogether. Does it follow, then, that the stricture against skipping originated only in post-70 times?[24]

The Pentateuchal lections required Aramaic translations, suggesting that, as apparently in the days of Ezra, the people as a whole were not adequately familiar with the Hebrew of the Bible. During this period the translation was certainly oral, with the use of a written targum forbidden. The readers of Hebrew were laymen, but a professional *meturgeman* gave a verse-by-verse rendition in the Aramaic vernacular.[25] Certain sections, such as the one that deals with Reuben's cohabitation with Bilhah (Gen. 35:22), were considered unsuitable for translation. The tannaim likewise discouraged allegorical and interpretative renditions, or the use of euphemisms for passages, such as Chapter 18 of Leviticus that records the laws of incest.[26]

As far as the haftarot are concerned, the rules were not rigid. The reader, as we have seen during the pre-70 period, could choose an appropriate Prophetic passage, skipping either within the same Book or to another Book. He was free to recite as many verses as he desired, and to translate or not. Certain sections, such as the account of Tamar's rape (II Sam. 13), however, were regarded as taboo. The rabbis of the Mishnah disagreed as to whether it was permitted to recite the first chapter of Ezekiel describing the prophet's vision of the heavenly chariots.[27] Although Mish. Megillah IV, 1, asserts that the Torah readings on the afternoons of the Sabbaths or the mornings of Mondays and Thursdays are not to be followed by any Prophetic lesson, we know that in some communities this was the case and that such customs were still common in some localities in the Geonic period.[28]

Differing norms also prevailed in regard to the recitation from the Hagiographa. M. Shabbat, XVI, 1, says: "Why are they not read? Because of the loss of time in the house of study." The mishnaic prohibition notwithstanding, certain psalms, or other Hagiographic selections, considered apt for a particular Sabbath used to be recited, evidently preceding the Prophetic portions. We know that this was so from the New Year liturgy, from lists of Hagiographic portions found in works such as the Pesikta Rabbati, the Tractate Soferim, and Aggadat Bereshit, as well as from manuscript collections.[29] This, as suggested above, may reflect an attempt, after the incorporation of the Writings (Ketubim) into the Holy Writ, to gain synagogal recognition for the third division of Scripture.

4. *The Talmudic Period* (*c. 220-550 C.E.*)

Soon after its publication about 220, the Mishnah assumed an importance second only to the Pentateuch for Jewish law.

146

Many passages which were only recommendations or of local significance became almost normative by virtue of having been recorded in this tannaitic source. The rules for reading the Torah and Prophets as recorded in the Mishnah were subjected to intense and frequently divergent interpretation in the academies of Palestine and Babylonia. It should be stressed, however, that neither of these centers should be regarded as a halakic unit. The academies of Sura and Pumpedita frequently differed in their interpretation, and in Palestine's districts a diversity, rather than uniformity, of customs prevailed. Nonetheless, by the end of the talmudic period, in the sixth century, we can speak of essentially two rites as far as the recitation of Scripture is concerned, the Palestinian and the Babylonian.[30] This divergence between West and East is also known as the so-called "Triennial Cycle" and the Annual Cycle. In the Annual Cycle, as practiced today, the Torah is divided into 53 or 54 pericopes (*parashiyot*); in the "Triennial Cycle" the number of sections was less consistent, but we are not wrong in assuming that it ultimately came to have 154 sections (*sedarim*).[31]

It should be noted that the term "Triennial Cycle" misrepresents the Palestinian Sabbatical readings of Scripture.[32] As has been pointed out above, seven men were called up for the readings and each of them read a minimum of three verses, making a total of at least twenty-one verses for each Sabbath service. Had this computation been followed, it would have taken some five and a half years to complete the Pentateuch. But according to Ta'anit IV, 3 cited above, the section of Genesis recited during the first Sabbath of the Palestinian cycle, consisted of 34 verses (Gen. 1:1-2:3), exceeding the minimum by thirteen lines; and if we take 34 verses as the average weekly reading, it would have taken almost 172 Sabbaths, more than three and a half years, to complete the cycle. This is so because while, on the average, there are 52 Sabbaths during the year, the Palestinian custom of omitting the cyclical readings during festivals and on such special Sabbaths as Hanukah and the New Moon lengthened the cycle by about six weeks each year. It is likely, then, that the Palestinian readings lasted closer to four years rather than to three. The terms of a three-year or of a three-and-a-half-year cycle found in the sources must be interpreted to mean simply a cycle of four years.[33]

It is, further, inaccurate to speak of a "Triennial Cycle" in the same sense that the term is used for the Annual Cycle. The latter was bound to the seasons of the year from one Simḥat Torah to the next. In the former, the reading of Genesis 1:1-2:3 could occur during the summer of one cycle but during the winter of the next cycle. Zunz, followed by Mann, maintained that the "Triennial Cycle" began in Tishre; Büchler argued for the month of Nisan. Both scholars, as pointed out by Heinemann, were mistaken because they supposed that the Palestinian system of Scriptural readings closely resembled the one in practice today. In fact, as pointed out below, Simhat Torah in the Palestinian liturgy was not associated with the last day of Sukkot, but was celebrated at the completion of the book of Deuteronomy, whether this occurred in the summer (*tal*) or in the winter (*geshem*).[34] Despite these objections, the term "Triennial Cycle" is retained in this essay because of its convenience, though it is always enclosed in quotation marks.

It may be supposed that this split between Babylonia and Palestine in the divisions of the Torah occurred during the talmudic period. The Palestinian sources—Tosefta, the halakic and aggadic midrashim—do not mention the cycles at all. In the Babylonian Talmud (Megillah 29b), however, the Annual Cycle is taken for granted, and it is once contrasted with that of the "Westerners, who complete the Torah in three years." Does it follow, then, that the Annual Cycle originated in Babylonia?

Mann argued that this was indeed the case. The difficulty with this position is that Megillah 31b cites a statement by Rabbi Simon ben Eleazar, a contemporary of Judah Ha-Nasi, which not only presumes the Scriptural readings of the Annual Cycle but ascribes their origin to Ezra.[35] Mann counters that since this quotation is found only in the Babylonian Talmud, this Baraitha is spurious and was not known in Palestine. This may or may not be true, but Mann is not averse to quoting Babylonian testimony when it supports his position relative to conditions in Palestine. It is one thing to regard a certain class of baraithot as unauthentic, but another to dismiss as spurious the one text that contradicts the author's hypothesis.

But even if this Baraitha is disregarded, the question of the relationship between the two cycles remains. As Appendix I shows, 43 out of the 54 pericopes of the Annual Cycle happen to be identical with those of the "Triennial Cycle." Such an identity may not be explained as the result of coincidence. A reasonable supposition is that the two cycles were interdependent. Which one was original and which secondary is the question. My own conjecture is that Palestine was the ultimate source of both cycles. As was pointed out above, the diversity of *minhagim* within Palestine was frequently quite profound. It is possible that Rabbi Simon ben Eleazar's reference to the Annual Cycle reflects a local Palestinian custom, in contrast to that of Galilee where the divisions of the "Triennial Cycle" prevailed. This may be so because he appears to be sometimes associated with the southern part of Palestine.[36]

The interdependence of the two Cycles may be seen from another point of view. The number of pericopes in the Annual Cycle has been either 52, 53, or, more consistently, 54. These numbers show that each was based either on the average number of Sabbaths of a 365-day year or on the longest possible intercalated Jewish year of 385 days. And it is curious that, though the manuscripts vary, the number of sections in the "Triennial Cycle" numbered 154. Is it mere coincidence, then, that in the most common listings the last two digits of both are identical?

5. *The Haftarot during the Amoraic Period*

In contrast to the Mishnaic period, when there was considerable freedom in the selection of Scriptural passages, the texts became more and more set during the days of the amoraim. Thus although Mishnah Megillah III, 4 ordains the reading of the *parashah* of Shekalim, it fails to specify the Pentateuchal passage to be recited. Rab and Samuel, who flourished in Babylonia during the first half of the third century, differed as to the selection. The former chose Num. 28:1 ff., which deals with the daily morning and afternoon sacrifices, while the latter chose Exod. 21:1 ff., which recorded the contribution of half-shekels for the wilderness census.[37] The Palestinian Talmud and the Tosefta uphold the position of Samuel.[38] Here, too, Rab seems to have followed a practice not current in Galilee.

The authorities could not agree, moreover, as to the haftara for Shabbat Shekalim. The Tosefta and the Talmudic texts prescribe chapter 12 of II Kings. Yet, a Palestinian practice, as preserved in the Romanian rite, reads instead Ezek. 45:12. Other Palestinian haftarot for Shabbat Shekalim are also recorded: I Kings 4:20 (Pesikta Rabbati), Hos. 2:1 (Qalir), Isa. 43:3 (Qalir). As for the other special Sabbaths, the differences appear to be minor, but are nevertheless significant since the Palestinian practice diverged from that recommended in both the Babylonian Talmud and the Tosefta.[39]

Despite the differences as to the haftara of Shekalim, what ought to be stressed is the relative consensus of both the Babli and the Yerushalmi in regard to the Prophetic selections for the Festivals and special Sabbaths.[40] This consensus must have taken place prior to the time of the liturgical schism between the two communities. We know that in the third and fourth centuries there was a constant flow of students between Tiberias-Caesarea and Sura-Pumpedita. Thus the Babylonian Talmud quotes Palestinian amoraim of this period as frequently as it does the native scholars. This interchange of rabbinic authorities, however, ceases at the end of the fourth century—a cessation that seems to have lasted well after the Arab conquest of the East. It follows perhaps that the haftarot for the Festivals, unknown in the mishnaic period, made their first appearance during the first half of the amoraic era. As partial confirmation of this position it is worth recalling that it is during the second half of the third century that we hear first of *Haftara Scrolls,* which because of their novelty were regarded as controversial texts.[41] The appearance of haftarot collections in Palestine and Babylonia suggests that they were filling a need and were becoming an independent literary unit.

As suggested by the very name, the haftarot had always been regarded as supplementary to the weekly portions of the Torah. During the amoraic period, however, though only occasionally mentioned in the Talmuds, some selections were assigned independent significance. The Prophetic selections for the three Sabbaths before the Fast Day of Ninth of Ab and the seven weeks thereafter related to the periods of mourning and consolation rather than to the weekly pericopes of the Torah. The selections from Jeremiah and Isaiah for these Sabbaths were identical for both Palestine and Babylonia, which seems to indicate that they originated when there existed a free interchange between the two centers, i.e. in amoraic times. Their relative antiquity is also attested by the fact that the Pesikta d'Rab Kahana contains homilies for these portions. On the Sabbath preceding, or following, Rosh Hashanah, depending on custom, the theme of the day was repentance. Private celebrations also sometimes interrupted the routine of Prophetic lessons. On the Sabbaths preceding a wedding the haftara was appropriately taken from Isa. 61:10 to harmonize with the nuptial celebrations.[42]

6. *The Post-Talmudic Sedarim*

In the third century and the first half of the fourth, Palestine in general and Galilee in particular exercised considerable authority over the academies of Sura and Pumpedita. This influence, by no means one-sided, appears to have ceased during the latter part of the fourth century, as a result of the deterioration of the political and economic conditions in Palestine. The two great centers of talmudic Judaism continued to produce masterpieces, but in isolation from each other, developing different systems of vocalization, divergent halakic codes and the like. It was not until the ninth and tenth centuries that contact between the two centers resumed. By this time the wilted academies of Palestine were in no condition to contest the superiority of Babylonia.

The divergence in the reading of Scripture, therefore, is but an illustration of the polarization of the two communities. A Geonic treatise—*The Differences Between the East and Palestine*—points out that in Babylonia the leader recited the Torah portion, whereas in Palestine the person called up to make the blessing recited the text. If this was so—and the text is not quite clear—it shows that Hebrew literacy was more common in Palestine. This position finds support in a Baraitha of Qiddushin 49a: " 'On the condition that I am a reader'—if he has read three verses in the synagogue" —the condition is fulfilled. Rabbi Judah, though, argues that literacy implies also the ability to translate a biblical passage. The reader (*Qr'*) in Babylonia, however, appears to have been a professional who had mastered "Torah, Prophets, and Writings with perfection." [43] The need for specially trained men to read and translate the weekly Scriptural readings may explain the popularity, if not the origin, of the so-called Targum Onqelos, composed in Babylonia. In Palestine the Aramaic rendition had been exclusively oral. Our Palestinian Targums, as mentioned in n. 8 above, originated as embellishments of Targum Onqelos.

As has been noted, during both tannaitic and amoraic times, any division of Scripture other than that of the verse (*pasuk*) was called *parashah* in the singular and *parashiyot* in the plural. Though essentially a unit of content, it also came to be understood as a scribal mark to differentiate between the two types of paragraphing of the Holy Writ: the open paragraph (*parashah petuḥah*) and the closed paragraph (*parashah setumah*); hence the פ's and the ס's in the masoretic text. In Babylonia, however, the term *parashah* had come to designate one of the 53 or 54 pericopes of the Pentateuch. The Palestinian name for the weekly reading of the Torah was now *seder,* a term first recorded in Leviticus Rabbah III,6, but used in the treatises Soferim and *The Difference between the East and Palestine.* The Babylonians also appropriated the term haftara, for the Prophetic selections; but the Palestinians, evidently to stress the difference of their *minhagim* called them *'ashlamata.*[44]

An outstanding characteristic of the Annual Cycle is its harmony with the current Jewish calendar. Thus the Sabbath of the pericope *Ṣav* (Lev. 6:1), or *Meṣora'* (Lev. 3:17) during an intercalated year, always precedes Passover; *Bemidbar* (Num. 1:1) precedes Shabuot; *Debarim* (Deut. 1:1), the Ninth of Ab and *Niṣṣabim* precede Rosh Hashanah. That these rules, recorded first in the Geonic treatises of about 800, are never breached shows that they were incorporated into the very formation of the perpetual Jewish calendar. This, incidentally, also lends additional support to the contention that the Jewish calendar is of Babylonian, not Palestinian provenance.[45]

A basic difference between the Eastern and Western liturgies revolved about Simḥat Torah: "The Easterners observe Simḥat Torah each year, the Palestinians every three and a half years"; (one variant reading adds:) "And on the day of concluding it (viz., the Torah). The parashah recited in one district is not the same as in another." [46] The number three and a half years is more accurate than "Triennial," but it is still only an approximation of the time that it took Galileans to complete their Torah cycle. Simḥat Torah, however, was but a local festival, since there was no uniform reading of Scripture throughout Palestine. The statement that each district followed its own pace should not be taken literally, even though the country was divided into small districts. But this lack of concord probably weakened the Palestinian position vis-à-vis Babylonia, whose exilarch and academies enforced a discipline throughout the Diaspora.

The lack of uniformity in Palestine explains also the midrashic and manuscript divergences as to the number of the sedarim in the "Triennial Cycle." The treatise Soferim knows of 175 sedarim; the Leningrad Manuscript, 167; the Jerusalem Manuscript, as described by Joel, lists 154, but marks only 141 in the text.[47] Some of these numbers are corruptions but other manuscript testimony no doubt reflects local customs as to the divisions of the sedarim. Mann, rather than his critics, was basically right in assuming the existence of local sedarim. He erred, however, in his belief that he could easily identify the local haftarot, or that all the local sedarim had set Prophetic readings. Nonetheless, the most widespread number of sedarim was 154, for it appears again and again in the manuscripts and because it seems to harmonize with the divisions of the fragments of the haftarot of the "Triennial Cycle" as well as with the liturgical compositions. This suggests that even in Palestine the movement was toward unity, as will be discussed below, resulting, possibly, from the influence of the famous payyetanim. Thus although the "Triennial Cycle" never achieved the relative stability of its rival, the Annual Cycle, beginning with the seventh century and onward it is possible to speak of the standard sedarim.

The following table shows the comparative distribution of verses for the Palestinian sedarim and the Babylonian parashiyot:

	Verses	Sedarim	Average	Parashiyot	Average
Gen.	1,534	43	35.7	12	127.8
Exod.	1,209	29	41.7	11	109.9
Lev.	859	23	35.2	10	85.9
Num.	1,288	32	40.2	10	120.9
Deut.	955	27	35.4	11	86.8
Total	5,845	154	37.3	54	108.2

Although Appendix I, appearing at the end of this essay, tells what the readings of the two cycles were, the circumstances under which these divisions came into being are obscure, and more research is needed. For the moment let us remember that, as has been mentioned above, 43 out of 54 parashiyot coincide with the divisions of the sedarim, which suggests that the Annual Cycle was an adaptation of a Palestinian rite. And so, the question is: What was the source of those 11 parashiyot which lack sedarim? In some instances, such as Deut. 21:10, it is reasonable to assume that the Babylonian divisions of Scripture were based on a cycle of sedarim now lost.

A clue as to what may have sometimes happened may be gained from the origin of the last parashah of Genesis, *Vayyeḥi* (47:28). As is well known, and this needs emphasis, the beginnings of the parashiyot as well as the sedarim, though less consistently, coincide with the scribal paragraphing of the Pentateuch, which the Masoretes note either as פ ("open") or ס ("closed"). The parashah of *Vayyeḥi*, however, is an exception in that it does not constitute a separate section; and the Midrash Tanhuma and the vulgar edition of Genesis Rabbah at this verse ask why.[48] The solution rests with the late appearance of the parashah. Since Gen. 47:28 had not been marked either as a paragraph or as a seder, the older midrashim—and this includes the author of Genesis Rabbah—whose new paragraph and seder began with verse 48:1, could not have been aware of this problem. But sometime after the publication of the original Genesis Rabbah—but before the appearance of the Tanhuma—Gen. 47:28 (*Vayyeḥi*) was marked as a new pericope, failing however to mark either a *P* or an *S*. The change occurred probably because the normal

154

seder began with a verse that mentions either "death" (Gen. 47:20) or "sickness" (48:1), which was changed to a parashah with "life" (47:27). This seems to explain how new parashiot sometimes came into being.[49]

Incidentally, for relative dating it seems significant that the beginnings of the "triennial" sedarim never coincide with the beginnings of the portions read on Festivals and on special occasions. Certainly, if content alone were the deciding factor, Exod. 12:1 would have begun a new seder. It does not. The reason appears to be that this verse had been reserved for the Sabbath Haḥodesh. This explains why, for instance, Exod. 19:1 (Shabu'ot), 30:11 (Sheḳalim), Lev. 22:26 (First Day of Passover), 23:23 (Rosh Hashanah, in the mishnaic ritual), and Num. 7:1 (Hanukah) do not start new sedarim. Since some, if not all, of these verses would have been chosen as new weekly sections had they not been preempted, it follows that the Festival selections antedate the choice of the sedarim as they have been perserved.

It has been shown that the origins of "Triennial" sedarim and the Annual parashiyot were intertwined. This was not the case with the haftarot of the two cycles, however. Only less than a handful of Prophetic selections of the Annual Cycle coincide with those attested in the "Triennial Cycle."[50] These few instances must be explained as chance rather than as interdependence, since the principles by which the haftarot of the two systems were chosen were different. Interestingly enough, this is basically true only of the haftarot of the Sephardic and Ashkenazic rites, and the like, whose provenance was in Babylonia, but not of the so-called Romanian and Karaite minhagim whose selections overwhelmingly depended on those of Palestine.[51]

7. *The Post-Talmudic Haftarot*

It is only recently that we have gained some knowledge of the "Triennial" haftarot. As noted above in n. 2, Adolph Büchler was the first to reveal their existence, publishing a list of Triennial haftarot for Gen. 5:1-Lev. 6:12, reprinted by Mann (*infra* 561-67). Mann's work has remained thus far the only systematic analysis of the subject. Unfortunately, his premature death has left the study incomplete. The publication of Volume II in 1966, with Hebrew and English notes by the late Isaiah Sonne, does not fill the void, since Mann's essays end with seder 105a(6a) of Num. 6:1. The haftarot of the remainder of the books of Numbers and Deuteronomy have, with some exceptions, not been identified. Moreover, as a pioneer Mann often erred in his suppositions as to the identity and structure of the exceptional sedarim and haftarot. This led Mann to misjudge the very nature of the "Triennial Cycle." What is needed, then, is not only a continuation of Mann's work but also a complete revision of it in the light of more recent knowledge. A first step would be the publication of the remnants of a collection of "Triennial" haftarot, a few of which have appeared in print, but most of which are still scattered in the Geniza collections of Cambridge, Oxford, and Leningrad.[52] The payyetanic material, discussed below, is immensely helpful in the reconstruction of the lost haftara cycles, as are the old Romanian and Karaite Bibles and prayer books. Appendix I of this essay attempts to fill the void temporarily. It contains the first almost complete list of the "Triennial Cycle" of both sedarim and haftarot as this system developed in the post-talmudic period.

The basic difference between the haftarot of the two cycles is of course that of numbers. This is not only because there are 54 parashiyot but 154 (or, according to some 175) sedarim, but also because only 41 haftarot of the Annual Cycle relate to the contents of weekly Torah portions. The remaining 13, including those of the book of Deuteronomy, belong to the seasons of mourning, consolation, and repentance. This is not to say that these seasonal portions were not observed in the "Triennial Cycle"; on the contrary, they are native to it. But since the Palestinian Scriptural readings, as pointed out above, were not linked to the calendar, the special haftarot ran independently of the sedarim of the book of Deuteronomy.

Related to the difference in bulk are also the divergent principles of selection. Typical, possibly is the pericope of Noah (Gen. 6:9-11:32), for which five sedarim are recorded. The Annual haftara for this parashah begins with Isa. 54:1 and, depending on the rite or tradition, ends with 54:10, 55:3, or 55:8. The reason for this choice is the allusion of Isa. 54:9-10, which refers to God's promise to Noah never again to destroy the world (Gen. 9:8-17). The link to the Torah portion of the week may appear in any part of the Annual haftara.

Not so in the "Triennial" haftara; here the connection is immediate. The first verse of Prophetic selection for Seder 5, which begins with Gen. 6:9: "These are the generations of *Noah*," quotes Isa. 54:9: "For it is like in the days of *Noah* . . ." In this system there is always a verbal link between the first, sometimes the second, verse of the Torah and the first verse of the Prophetic lesson. Thus Seder 6 (Gen. 8:1): "But God *remembered* Noah" (*wayyizkor*) is linked with Hab. 3:2: "O Lord, I have heard . . . in wrath *remember* (tizkor) mercy." Seder 7 (Gen. 8:15): ". . . *come out* (*ṣe'*) from the ark" is joined with "To *bring out* (*lehoṣi'*) the prisoners from the dungeon" (Is. 42:7). Seder 8 (Gen. 9:18): "The sons of Noah *who came out* (*hayyoṣe'im*) from the ark" with "Saying to the prisoners 'Come forth' (*ṣe'*)" (Isa. 49:9). The account of the tower of Babel, introduced in Seder 9 by "All the earth had the same *language* (*safah*)" (11:1) was concluded with Zeph. 3:9: "For then (in the day of judgment) will I restore to the peoples a clear *language* (*sáfah*) that they may all call in the name of the Lord." The haftara of the "Triennial Cycle" links not the contents of the Torah portion with those of the Prophets, but the first significant words or phrases of the two divisions of Scripture.

The connection, though seemingly strictly verbal, is in addition eschatological. The messianic kingdom, rather than the related contents of the Torah lesson, is the dominant theme of the Palestinian haftarot. The Annual haftara for Gen. 1:1 is Deutero-Isaiah's description of creation (42:5 ff.); the "Triennial" selection for the same lesson is the prophet's vision of the new creation in the Lord's day, when the account of creation in Genesis would no longer be worth remembering (Isa. 65:17). Thus in Palestine, the haftara seems to have been conceived as a sort of peroration, which as in the later midrashic homilies usually conclude with messianic allusions.

The different principles of the haftara of the two cycles also account for the basic difference as to the choice of the Prophetic books.

157

PROLEGOMENON

The Distribution of Prophetic Books of the "Triennial Cycle" in the Haftarot

	Josh. No.	%	Judg. No.	%	Sam. No.	%	Kings No.	%	Isa. No.	%	Jer. No.	%	Ezek. No.	%	Min. Proph. No.	%	Total No.	No. of Sedarim
Gen.	2	4.0	1	2.0	3	6.0	2	4.0	29	58.0	3	6.0	1	2.0	9	18.0	50	43
Exod.	1	3.1	—	—	2	6.3	2	6.3	18	56.3	3	9.4	1	3.1	5	15.6	32	29
Lev.	1	3.3	1	3.3	1	3.3	—	—	14	46.7	2	6.7	5	16.7	6	20.0	30	23
Num.	4	9.3	3	7.0	—	—	2	4.7	18	41.5	1	2.3	2	4.7	13	30.0	43	32
Deut.	5	15.6	—	—	—	—	2	6.3	14	43.8	1	3.1	1	3.1	9	28.1	32	27
	13	2	5		6		8		93		10		10		42		187	154

The Distribution of Prophetic Books of the Annual Cycle in the Haftarot (Ashkenazic and Sefardic Rites)

	Josh. No.	%	Judg. No.	%	Sam. No.	%	Kings No.	%	Isa. No.	%	Jer. No.	%	Ezek. No.	%	Min. Proph. No.	%	Total No.	No. of Parashiyot
Gen.	—	—	—	—	—	—	4	33.3	3	25	—	—	1	8.3	4	33.3	12	12
Exod.	—	—	1	8.3	—	—	4	33.3	2	16.7	3	25	2	16.7	—	—	12	11
Lev.	—	—	—	—	1	9.1	2	18.2	1	9.1	3	27.3	3	27.3	1	9.1	11	10
Num.	1	10	2	20	1	10	1	10	—	—	2	20	—	—	3	30	10	10
Deut.	1	9.1	—	—	1	9.1	—	—	8	72.7	—	—	—	—	1	9.1	11	11
	2	3.6	3	5.4	3	5.4	11	19.5	14	25	8	14.3	6	11.7	9	16.1	56	54

(The number of haftarot exceeds those of the sedarim and parashi-yot because some doubtful selections have been included in these tables).

In the Annual Cycle only the haftarot of Deuteronomy show the same penchant for a certain biblical book as those of the "Triennial Cycle." The reason is of course that they were not selections linked with the Torah readings, but with the seasonal Sabbaths of mourning and consolation. They were in fact Palestinian choices for the extra Sabbaths, which the Babylonians adopted. It is no accident, therefore, that these haftarot were taken mostly from Deutero-Isaiah, whose prophecies had been interpreted to suggest a messianic message. Excepting the supplementary readings for Deuteronomy, the Annual Cycle shows no preference for one biblical book over the others, as related content alone determined the selection.

Almost half of the "Triennial" haftarot were taken from the book of Isaiah, some two-thirds of them from chapters 40-66. The book of Jeremiah, whose total number of verses exceeds that of Isaiah, and Ezekiel, which is only somewhat shorter, appear to have been quite ignored in the Palestinian cycle. Only the historical books, with the exception of the book of Joshua, were read less. Also favored were the Twelve Minor Prophets, which together with Isaiah account for more than three-fourths of the known "Triennial" haftarot.

The verbal link between the beginning of the Torah lesson and that of the Prophetic selection, combined with the messianic message, accounts for more than four-fifths of the Palestinian readings. There are, however, quite a number of haftarot for which no apocalyptic exegesis is apparent. The verbal links alone, it would seem, are not a satisfactory explanation for the selection of certain passages from the historical books. For the Palestinian scholars who made the choices seem to have possessed both the ability of total recall and a remarkable sensitivity for linking words that might, at first sight, seem incongruous, but which after reflection suggest profound homiletic possibilities. Thus the Prophetic readings for the book of Leviticus and other priestly texts rarely relate to sacrifices. The inventory of the desert tabernacle (*Pekude*, Exod. 38:21) is supplemented by a prophetic paraphrase of Num. 24:5— the Lord's promise to restore the tents of Jacob and his tabernacles (Jer. 30:18). The first word of Leviticus—"And he called" links with "The Lord called the city" to impose honest weights and measures (Mic. 6:9). Many of the haftarot, then, show a tendency to allegorize Torah passages into which later generations infused new meanings. In one instance the Prophetic se· lection was made as if to protest the cruelty of the weekly lesson. Influenced by the exegesis of Gen. Rabbah LVI, the haftara tells of the angels crying (Isa. 33:7) at the account of Abraham's binding of Isaac (Gen. 22:1).

The paramount meaning attached to the link between the primary verses of the "Triennial" seder and the haftara may have been the reason for the Palestinian halakic indifference to the length of the selections. On this point there is a difference between the two Talmuds. Bab. Megillah 23b requires that a haftara have a minimum of twenty-one verses, but adds that Rabbi Yohanan, when an Aramaic translation was necessary, reduced the number to ten.

Pal. Megillah, IV, 1, 75a, however, claims that the same Rabbi
Yoḥanan fulfilled the obligation of the haftara with three verses.
In fact, some texts list a number of haftarot with two verses only.
Not merely were the Palestinian haftarot relatively brief, but the
skipping of superfluous passages, as stressed by Mann, was quite
prevalent. The messianic message of the Prophet, rather than length
or continuity, mattered more than anything else.

8. *The Sedarim and the Midrash*

Both the halakhic and the aggadic midrashim presuppose the
Palestinian divisions of the Torah. The Mekilta of Rabbi Ishmael
opens with a commentary on Exod. 12:1 because this was the first
verse of the portion recited on the Sabbath of, or before, the
New Moon of Nisan, when the lore relating to Passover became the
theme of the day.[53] This explains the different nomenclature of the
Mekilta's first section—*Pasḥa*—in contrast to the other sections of
this book which are named after the first catchword. Other parts
of the Mekilta, such as *Shirata* on Exod. 15:1-19, and *Amalek* on
Exod. 17:8-18, were the respective Palestinian readings for the
seventh day of Passover and the Sabbath preceding Purim. The
section *Baḥodesh* (Exod. 19:1-20:26) has been the biblical reading for Shabuot. The tractate *Kaspa* (Exod. 22:24-23:20) coincides precisely with the length of a Palestinian seder, but would
be unexplainable in the light of the Babylonian divisions of Scripture. The usual reasoning for the Mekilta's beginning—the first
legal section of the Torah—is not really cogent as this work contains an abundance of texts, including the treatises of *Shirata,
Vayyassa'*, and *Amalek*, made up entirely of aggada.[54]

The divisions of the Sifra, the oldest midrashic work, no doubt
originally corresponded to the Palestinian sedarim. But in the
process of "Babylonization," the pervasive influence of the Talmud
Babli, evident so strongly in the change of the spelling, determined
also most of the names of the parashiyot. Traces of the ancient
divisions are still found in the manuscripts: Vatican 66 of the
Sifra calls the second treatise of the Sifra "The Scroll of *Nefesh*,"
the catchword of the Palestinian seder commencing with Lev. 4:1.[55]

The traces of the Palestinian sedarim are more obvious in the

Sifre on Numbers, though the formal divisions have become obscured. It seems that the author of the Sifre comments more extensively on the first verses of the apparent sedarim than on the remainder of the text. He also, almost mechanically, raises the question, "Why is there a need for this section (parashah)—*lamah ne'emar?*" precisely at the points where tradition tells us that the "Triennial Cycle" began a new seder.[56] It is clear, then, that an awareness of the liturgical use of Scripture may shed considerable light upon the structure and contents of the halakic midrashim.

I have dealt at some length with the relationships between the halakic midrashim and the "Triennial Cycle" because this matter needs further investigation and may be of some assistance in dating the publication of these texts. As far as the aggadic midrashim are concerned, such as Genesis Rabbah and Leviticus Rabbah, the investigations of Theodor, Lerner, and Albeck have shown that the economy of midrashic chapters presupposes the Palestinian readings of the Torah.[57] The Genesis Rabbah is in its own way a running commentary on the book of Genesis. But certain favored verses gained a rhetorical prominence by being introduced with the so-called *petihtot*. A scholar, usually anonymous but often associated with a famous preacher, to enhance the authoritativeness of the homily, "opened" (*patah*) the exegesis of the seder. The citation is seemingly unrelated, but more often than not it is taken from the Hagiographa and frequently from the Prophets, occasionally even from the Pentateuch. After having expounded at length on this "surprise" passage, the scholar artfully shows that it sheds considerable light on the announced text of the sermon. Many chapters of Genesis Rabbah begin with one *petihta,* though most have several; but all *petihtot* introduce the first (sometimes the second, and occasionally the third) verse of a section. Thus a verse that is the subject of a *petihta* was almost invariably the beginning of a paragraph (the so-called "Petuhah" or "Setumah"). The link between the paragraphing by the author of Genesis Rabbah and the Palestinian Cycle of readings becomes evident when we note that, with possibly one exception, all of the verses of the forty-five sedarim of the book of Genesis, listed in Appendix I below, have *petihtot.* Of the hundred chapters of this

Book, nearly a half is clearly interdependent with the "Triennial Cycle" of Torah readings listed in Appendix I.

The majority of chapter headings, however, do not coincide with our sedarim. It is therefore by no means certain that *our* lists of the Palestinian divisions of sedarim antedate those of Genesis Rabbah. In other words, even if we assume, as we must, that the so-called "Triennial Cycle" of biblical readings is the basis upon which the author of Genesis Rabbah constructed his work, it does not follow that the weekly portions of readings coincided with the ones that have come down to us as standard sedarim.

Leviticus Rabbah differs basically from Genesis Rabbah in that it treats only the introductory verses of a Scriptural paragraph. It was therefore, if anything, more closely linked with the Palestinian liturgy of Scriptural readings than Genesis Rabbah was. Of the 37 chapters that make up our editions of Leviticus Rabbah, 18 (nearly the same proportion as Genesis Rabbah) follow the divisions of the sedarim listed in Appendix I. Fortunately, an allusion, the only one of its kind, to a divergent set of sedarim is reported in this text: "Rabbi Hananyah bar Rabbi Aha (an amora of an unknown date) went to a certain place where he found that this verse was the beginning of the seder: 'And the remainder of the gift offering' (Lev. 2:3). What verse did he 'open'? (answer: Ps. 17:14)." [58] It follows that a) communities diverged as to the start of a seder, and that b) whereas each beginning of a seder called for a *petihta,* the reverse was not true; one could construct a *petihta* for a section which had no seder. This may explain why more than half of the chapters of both Genesis Rabbah and Leviticus Rabbah do not harmonize with our lists of sedarim.

It is apparent, however, that the weekly readings of the Torah play a greater part in the composition of Leviticus Rabbah than they do in Genesis Rabbah. The author of the former still felt obligated to expound upon almost every passage of the book, though the *petihtot* stressed the introductory verses of the paragraphs. The author of the latter, however, as far as his exegesis is concerned, ignored verses other than the one that began new sections as though they did not exist. The Pesikta d'Rab Kahana, a work consisting of a collection of festival and occasional homilies, reflects the same relationship with the "Triennial Cycle" of Scriptural readings as Leviticus Rabbah does. Both of these midrashim seem to be characteristic of the second stage of rabbinic homiletical literature.[59]

A third stage of midrashic development appears to be reflected in the so-called Tanhuma works (Exodus Rabbah, Deuteronomy Rabbah, Tanhuma [standard], Tanhuma Buber). Whereas only about half of the chapters of the older midrashim coincide with the sedarim listed in Appendix I, the composition of the Tanhuma midrashim is built almost entirely upon our list of the "Triennial Cycle."[60] The occasional departures, as assumed by Mann, no doubt reflect local customs that have not been perpetuated in our available traditions.

It is likely, then, that halakic midrashim and Genesis Rabbah reflect the earliest stages, Pesikta d' Rab Kahna and Leviticus Rabbah the middle, and the Tanhuma or, as they are sometimes called, the Yelamdenu midrashim, the last stage of the development of the "Triennial Cycle." The Mishnah and Tosefta and the Palestinian Talmud still presume a continuous reading of the Torah. It is only in the fourth- or fifth-century layers of the Babylonian Talmud that we encounter for the first time the only mention of a three-year cycle of readings in the West. We do not know, however, whether this reference alludes to the early or late development of the "Triennial Cycle."

Incidentally, the Palestinian cycle of Scriptural readings may help solve the puzzle as to the relationship between Targum Pseudo-Jonathan and Targum Yerushalmi. Since the latter is virtually an abridged version of the former, the question is what was the purpose of the abridgement? An analysis of Targum Yerushalmi suggests that its author copied primarily, though not exclusively, the passages of Pseudo-Jonathan that either conclude or begin a "Triennial" seder. Some of these selections, however, have been omitted in the current editions of Targum Yerushalmi, though enough are left to indicate a definite pattern.

The Palestinian cycle of Scriptural readings had a powerful, perhaps decisive influence on the development of the aggada. By virtue of the fact that they were the beginnings of the sedarim, some verses became the subjects of sermons; other verses, because they were in the middle or at the end of the weekly readings were ignored. Unfortunately, the modern editors of the midrashim have not taken cognizance of this fact, and have aggravated the problem already present in the manuscripts by imposing the parashiyot of the Annual Cycle on works that presuppose the "Triennial" system of Pentateuchal divisions. One may hope that in the future these editorial aberrations will be remedied.

9. *The Haftarot and the Midrash*

The hypothesis that the "Triennial" sedarim gave rise to many, perhaps most of the sermons recorded in the midrashic texts brings up the problem of the "Triennial" haftarot. The question before us is independent of Mann's thesis that the haftara determined the halakic issue raised in the Yelamdenu passages. As I see it, the scope of the problem extends to all midrashic works: Were some of the rabbinic homilies conditioned by the haftarot, or were the haftarot inspired by the homilies, or were the two unrelated?

This is not the place to deal at length with such a complex problem. Suffice it to say, however, the Mekilta, *Mishpatim* XVIII, links Exod. 21:1 with Isa. 56:1 and Pasha XII connects Deut. 32:1 with Isa. 1:2, precisely as do the "Triennial" haftarot. Genesis Rabbah, I, for example, connects Gen. 1:1 with the "Triennial' reading of the creation of the new heavens (Isa. 65:17); Leviticus Rabbah XIV finds a nexus between the seder of Lev. 14:2 and Isa. 57:17 f., its Palestinian haftara. These and similar references might be taken as proof that the midrashic works were familiar with the "Triennial" list of haftarot, at least with a number of them.

Although the issue should not be regarded as closed, present evidence does not seem to support such a conclusion. Considering the midrashists' remarkable mastery of Scripture and the constant rabbinic search for connecting texts, several citations are not enough to prove that authors of the Mekilta, Genesis Rabbah, or Leviticus Rabbah linked certain passages because they were the Sabbatical readings. It is conceivable that the presence of the same connecting passages in the midrash and "Triennial Cycle" is due either to coincidence or to the fact that the men who chose the haftarot were influenced by the homiletical links found in Genesis Rabbah and Leviticus Rabbah.[61]

As far as the Tanhuma or Yelamdenu midrashim are concerned, however, there is no doubt that certain homilies presuppose the underlying "Triennial" haftarot. Tanhuma Mishpatim, sections 3-4, are homilies on the Prophetic reading of Isa. 56:1 rather than on the Torah readings. The same is true of Tanhuma, Kedoshim, 11, 14, whose *petihtot* relate to Isa. 54:22, the "Triennial" seder of Lev. 19:23. Many passages of the Yelamdenu-type texts seem to take for granted the weekly Prophetic readings. Nonetheless, a review of these texts as a whole does not justify the conclusion that the Tanhuma midrashim were consistently aware of the "Triennial" haftarot. More often than not the authors of these homilies seem to be oblivious of passages which, had they been synagogal readings, the rabbis would in all likelihood have quoted. A possible explanation for this contradictory evidence is that the type of sermon now labeled Tanhuma was only in the process of formation at the time that the Prophetic lections were just beginning to become standardized.

Present evidence does seem to suggest that one difference between the oldest of the extant midrashim—Genesis Rabbah—and the youngest ones—Tanhuma-Yelamdenu—is the increased use of the "Triennial" haftarot, as these have become known to us. A major stumbling block in midrashic studies, however, is our ignorance of absolute (or even relative) dates of formation of the major halakic and aggadic midrashim. We are fortunate, therefore, that the Palestinian system of readings sheds some light on this most important problem. For at, or after, the close of the Talmudic period, a new mode of liturgical expression, related to the Sabbatical Scriptural lessons came into being, which preserved the names of the payyetanim because of the desire to recognize literary creativity.

10. *The Poetry of Yannai*

Yannai used to be cited as a medieval payyetan (poet) whose work had perished and whose significance was problematical. Thanks largely to the Geniza, the publication in 1919 of *Mahzor*

Yannai by Israel Davidson, and in 1938 the *Piyyute Yannai* by Menahem Zulay, Yannai has been turned from a ghost into the first and best known Palestinian payyetan.[62]

Yannai's amazing productivity is astonishing since it is now certain that he composed at least one—sometimes several—Kerobah Kedushta (or Shib'ata) for every Sabbath of the 154 sedarim, not counting the festivals and special occasions. A Kedushta is an integrated and highly stylized poem of nine stanzas, consisting of 140-odd rhymed lines to be recited as part of the three blessings of the Sabbath morning "Shemoneh Esreh," and introducing the Sanctification of God's name (*Kedushah*). The contents for the Kedushtot were gleaned from the halakah and aggadah of the weekly readings of Scripture. Yannai shaped into poetry the rabbinic lore from the Mishnah, the Palestinian Talmud, and the midrashim.[63] The first stanza of Yannai's Kedushta weaves around, and concludes with, the first verse of the weekly Torah reading of that Sabbath or festival; the second stanza cites the second verse of the seder; the third stanza, whose acrostic spells the author's name, concludes with the first verse of the "Triennial" haftara.

Yannai's kerobot, therefore, have been of immense help for the reconstruction of the "Triennial Cycle." Since he often merely added a poetic form to the passages he found in rabbinic sources, many of the works which Yannai used may be identified.[64] The trouble is, however, that Yannai's date is a problem. The oldest reference to him, found in Al-Qirqisani, is connected with that of Anan, the eighth-century founder of the Karaite sect, who is said to have used Yannai's poems. Davidson, therefore, dates Yannai in the seventh century. Schirmann, however, placed him in the fourth century, though some scholars favor the fifth.[65] A searching analysis of Yannai's sources by Rabinowitz seems to indicate that though the Mishnah is the only rabbinic work quoted by name, this payyetan may have used the Palestinian Talmud, the Mekilta of Rabbi Ishmael, Genesis and Leviticus Rabbah, and the Pesikta d'Rab Kahana, but evidently not the Tanhuma homilies. If so, Yannai must have flourished at the earliest about the year 600, as there is no reason to date the Pesikta or the Leviticus Rabbah before the sixth century. On the other hand, the internal evidence suggests that Yannai lived in Palestine under Byzantine rule but he seems to have been totally unaware of the Moslem world. There is a tradition, perhaps historical, that more famous Eleazar Ha-Qalir was Yannai's pupil, one legend [66] having it that the master in a fit of jealousy killed his supposedly more talented disciple. Qalir's poetry apparently reflects the turbulence caused by the Arab invasion of Palestine in the fourth decade of the seventh century. We must, therefore, date Yannai, at the earliest, at the end of the sixth century, but more likely at the beginning of the seventh, essentially confirming Davidson's hypothesis.

11. *Conclusion*

Yannai's date also yields the time when the "Triennial Cycle," as we know it, was a flourishing institution. Yannai is also the oldest witness that the masoretic lists of sedarim and the fragmentary collections of the "Triennial" haftarot go back at least to the beginning of the seventh century. To be sure, in many instances these lists of the Sabbatical readings diverge among themselves as well as from those of Yannai. These differences, significant as they are, do not affect their basic uniformity.

Yannai's poems, however, do not help determine when the "Triennial Cycle" came into being. For it is possible that the piyyutim attest to Sabbatical readings that had been long established; or that the sedarim and haftarot of the piyyutim reflect only local customs, and that Yannai's poems were instrumental in making what had been essentially regional into standard.

As a proposed solution, this essay differentiates between the sedarim and the haftarot. The former probably had reached an advanced stage of relative uniformity long before the latter did. It should be recalled that the mishnaic evidence reflects a time when the parashah still constituted primarily a unit of content. During the early amoraic period, however, a process of standardization of the Pentateuchal divisions came into being. Of the divergent customs, two systems gained more than local importance: the Annual Cycle, which had originated possibly in southern Palestine, became the Babylonian tradition, and ultimately gained universal acceptance; as for the "Triennial Cycle," also called Palestinian but evidently native to Galilee, the first stages are presupposed in the earliest halakic and aggadic midrashim. The Tanhuma texts, however, weave their homilies about a set of sedarim that to a large extent is identical with the standard list.

The trend toward the standardization of the "Triennial" haftarot, however, apparently gained momentum only after Yannai's piyyutim had enjoyed wide popularity. To be sure, some Prophetic selections—Obad. 1:1 on Gen. 32:4; Josh. 2:1 on Num. 13:1, for example—may have been customary lections even in the amoraic period. This may be the reason that they are choices of both Cycles. Some "Triennial" haftarot certainly antedate the appearance of Genesis Rabbah and Leviticus Rabbah. These are exceptions, however. The authors of these and other exegetical works seem to have been ignorant of the bulk of the "Triennial" haftarot. They do not appear to be older than Yannai.

Thus far we have discussed the date of the "Triennial' haftarot. But the date of the Annual haftarot, independently developed from those of Palestine, requires further investigation. The only haftara cited is that of Jer. 7:21 for Ṣav (Lev. 6:1), attributed to Raba,[67] the famous amora of Nehardea the year of whose death is given by Sherira as 351. Does it follow then that in the middle of the fourth century the cycle of the Babylonian haftarot had been set, or is this a reference to an isolated selection? Incidentally, our lists of the "Triennial Cycle" know neither of a seder beginning with Lev. 6:1 nor of a haftara of Jer. 7:21. Rabba's allusion to the Annual haftara seems to suggest the possibility that the Babylonian Prophetic selections were established in amoraic times, more than two centuries before we hear of standardized "Triennial" haftarot. One suspects, therefore, that although the Palestinian haftarot are independent selections, the tendency to move from individual or regional preferences to standardization was an adaptation of a Babylonian *minhag*.

Competition between the "Triennial" and Annual Cycles continued until the thirteenth century. But after the Arab conquest of the East, and when Baghdad became the capital of the Moslem empire, the Annual Cycle practiced in Babylonia gained a foothold in Northern Africa and Western Europe. In fact, the victory of the Annual Cycle reflects the pervasive influence of the Babylonian Talmud. The halakah of the East became canonized by

the Geonim and that of the West came to be either supplemental
or completely ignored.

Despite the hegemony of the Babylonian halakah, the Palestinian
readings of Scripture remained a living tradition until the days
of Maimonides. The traveler Benjamin of Tudela, who visited
Egypt about 1170, reports that the two synagogues of Cairo—the
Palestinian and the Babylonian—differed widely in their Scriptural
liturgy. "For the Babylonians read a parashah every week, like in
Spain, completing the Torah each year. The Palestinians, however,
make three sedarim of each parashah, concluding the Torah every
three years. There is a custom and an ordinance to meet and pray
on Simhat Torah together".[68] The last sentence means that, unlike
the Babylonians, who celebrated this festival on the last day of
Sukkot, the Palestinian synagogue proclaimed a special festival
to celebrate the completion of the Pentateuch. It should be noted,
however, that his wording suggests that the learned traveler understood the "Triennial Cycle" only vaguely. Both Maimonides
and his son Abraham confirm the "Triennial" readings in Fustat.
And it is the former's disparaging allusion in the Mishneh Torah
which seems to have given the death blow to the "Triennial Cycle"
of Scriptural readings.[69] Ironically, although the "Triennial"
sedarim have disappeared from the Sabbath morning liturgy, the
haftarot have in part remained a living tradition. The Karaites and
the Jews who follow the Romanian *minhag* (Byzantium, Corfu)
have adopted the Pentateuchal readings of the Annual Cycle, but
recite the former "Triennial" Prophetic selections of Galilee. In
recent times, some Conservative and Reconstructionist congrega-
tions have introduced a division of readings that complete the
Pentateuch in three years; but this division is a modification of
the Annual Cycle rather than an adoption of the ancient Galilean
"Triennial Cycle."

NOTES

1. For a discussion of Yannai's date, see below pp. XL.

2. A Büchler, "The Reading of the Law and Prophets in a Triennial Cycle," *JQR,* O.S., 5 (1893), 420-68; 6 (1894), 1-73. For a select bibliography, see below p. L. For the older bibliography, see Mann, *infra,* pp. 3-14, esp. p. 6, n. 11.

3. By Jacob Mann and Isaiah Sonne (Cincinnati: The Hebrew Union College—Jewish Institute of Religion, The Mann-Sonne Publication Committee, 1966). P. IX of Volume II lists the members of the Committee who made possible its publication. Victor E. Reichert has contributed eloquent biographical sketches of Jacob Mann (II, pp. xi-xvii) and Isaiah Sonne (xviii-xx). Sonne's contribution to Volume II is greater than is indicated. His "Preface" and "Supplementary Preface" review the scholarly opinions in regard to Mann's thesis and, in addition, redefine Mann's thesis itself. Sonne theorizes that the midrashic homily has a unity which links the Petihta, the body of the Sermon, with the peroration. Sonne illustrates what he calls the "magnetic field" theory in his notes (II, pp. 154-74, 236-55). And some of the perceptive comments on rabbinic texts, in the Hebrew footnotes to the Midrash Hadash—the headings on the inside pages erroneously identify it as Geniza—and on the Geniza Fragments (II, Hebrew Section, pp. 167-239), are Sonne's, not Mann's.

4. For a summary of the critical review of this work see Sonne, in II, pp. xxi-xxxviii; Ch. Albeck in Zunz-Albeck, *Ha-derashot Be-yisrael* (Jerusalem, 1947), 473-74.

5. N. Fried, "Haftarot'alternatibiyyot be-piyyutei Yannai," *Sinai,* 61 (1967), 271, n. 23, accuses Mann of inventing haftarot wholesale, promising an article on the subject. S. Lieberman, in *Studies in Memory of M. Schorr,* ed. L. Ginzberg (New York, 1944 [in Hebrew]), 186 f., on the other hand, applauds enthusiastically Mann's thesis. Cf. S. Baron , *A Social and Religious History of the Jews* (Philadelphia, 1958), VI, 405, n. 13.

6. Philo, *De Opificio Mundi,* 128; Josephus, *Contra Apionem,* II, 175; Acts 15:21; Mish. Megillah, III, 6; Yer. Megillah, IV, 1, p. 75a.

7. Yer. Megillah, I, 3, p. 70b; Baba Qamma 72a.

8. The reference is of course to free oral Aramaic renditions rather than to any of the extant Targumim. The Genesis Apocryphon, found in Qumran, the earliest extant Targum, is not a translation, but an independent composition. Targum Onqelos, as it has come down to us, is a Babylonian work of the fifth or sixth century; and the Palestinian Targumim (Pseudo-Jonathan and Yerushalmi) are midrashic expansions of Targum Onqelos. The so-called Neofiti version, recently published by Diez Macho, seems to be of late medieval or Renaissance vintage, being primarily an embellishment of Palestinian Targumim.

9. For the etymology of the word as "to take leave", see S.Y. Rapoport, *Kerem Ḥemed,* 3 (1838), 42 f.; *'Erek Millin* (Warsaw, 1914), 321 ff. Another explanation is the synonym *'ashlamta,* "completion." Cf. Yer. Sanhedrin, I, 2, 19a; and below, p. 561 ff. For other conjectures, see "Haftarah," in *Talmudic Encyclopedia,* X (1961), col. 1.

10. Abudraham, 47a; E. Levita, *Tishbi* (Grodno, 1805), *s.v. pṭr,* p. 45a.

11. Persecution as a reason for liturgical portions whose origin is unknown is a favorite rabbinic explanation. Yehudai Gaon, for example, attributed the recitation of the *Shema* in the repetition of "Eighteen Blessings" as a result of Byzantine persecution (L. Ginzberg, *Ginze Schechter* [New York, 1929], II, 551, and cf. p. 100; Mann, "Changes in the Divine Service of the Synagogue due to Religious Persecutions," *HUCA*, 4(1927), 241-302, who however places too much faith in these traditions.

12. Cf. H. St. J. Thackeray, *Journal of Theological Studies,* (1914), 194, 197; R. G. Finch, *The Synagogue Lectionary and the New Testament* (London, 1939), *passim,* esp. pp. 6-9.

13. The matter requires fuller treatment; here it is only a working hypothesis on which I hope to elaborate. Meanwhile, see Ch. Albeck, *Mabo' Le-Mishnah* (Jerusalem-Tel-Aviv, 1958), 65 ff.

14. M. Ta'anit, IV, 3. See below, p. XXI.

15. M. Sotah, VII, 1-8, lists *inter alia* the "parashah of the king" (Deut. 17:14-20). Cf. the priestly blessings of Num. 6:24-27.

16. Bab. Ta'anit, 27b; Megillah 22a. Rab, however, followed the view of Yer. Megillah, IV, 5, 75b, citing a Baraitha that a section of five verses may be recited by two men, as the one reads three verses and the other repeats the last verse and adds two more.

17. On the afternoon of the Sabbath and on Mondays and Thursdays, three men are called up; on Rosh Hodesh, four; on Festivals, five; on the Day of Atonement, six; on the Sabbath mornings, seven.

18. Mish. Megillah, III, 6, seems to imply that reading was continuous. Yer. Megillah, IV, 8, p. 74c, cites an anonymous opinion of "Some" that the readings on the Sabbath afternoons and on Mondays and Thursdays were continuous, rather than identical with those of the next Sabbath morning, but decides against this view. In Megillah 31b, and Tosefta, III, 10, p. 355 (ed. Lieberman), Rabbi Judah and an anonymous opinion (Rabi Meir in the Babli) debate this question. But the Babylonian Talmud, like the Yerushalmi, concludes that the readings were continuous from one Sabbath to the next. Cf. G. F. Moore, *Judaism* (Cambridge: Harvard University Press, 1966), I, 299-302.

19. For a different computation of verses, see, for instance, Qiddushin 30a.

20. M. Ta'anit, IV, 3. This appears to be the oldest evidence for the length of a *seder*.

21. See Mann, *infra,* pp. 76 f., whose explanation that seder 6 (Gen. 8:1) and seder 7 (Gen. 8:15) exclude each other is unsatisfactory. The minimum of 21 verses was not required when a *parashah* was a self-contained unit. See Yer. Megillah, IV, 2, 75a, citing the Palestinian Parashah Amalek (Exod. 17:8-16), which contained only 9 verses but was recited by seven men. It is possible, though unlikely, that the following seder of *Yitro* was read to reach the full length. But as far as we can tell, the weekly and the festival portions were kept apart.

22. M. Megillah, III, 4-6.

23. See n. 21 above.

24. Mish. Yoma, VII, 1; Sotah, VII, 7. In Yer. Yoma, VII, 1 p. 44a and Megillah, IV, 5, 75b, the skipping by the high priest is described as exceptional, but this does not seem to be a satisfactory explanation.

25. See n. 8 above. Cf. Yer. Megillah, IV, 1, 74d; Bab. Gittin 60a.

26. M. Megillah, IV, 9; cf. M. Hagigah, II, 1; Tos. Megillah, III, 31-41, 362-64 (ed. Lieberman); Bab. Qiddushin 49a.

27. M. Megillah, IV, 9; Tos. Megillah, III, 37-41. p. 36 (ed. Lieberman.)

28. See Shabbat 24a, which contradicts the Mishnah. Hai Gaon asserts that in the eleventh century in Persia and Elam (Susania?) a haftara was recited on

Saturday afternoons; see Lewin, *Otzar Ha-Geonim,* vol. II (Haifa, 1930), i, pp. 26 f.

29. See the Babli and Yerushalmi on this Mishnah; Tosefta Shabbat, XIII, 1-3, p. 57 (ed. Lieberman). Cf. Albeck, *Introduction to Bereshit Rabba* (Jerusalem, 1965), 13 f. [in Hebrew]. The readings from the book of Psalms are recorded in Soferim, XVIII, 1-4, 11; Pesikta Rabbati contains homilies on the Sabbatical psalms which often coincide with those prescribed in Soferim: Hanukkah, Ps. 30 (Soferim, XVIII, 3; Pesikta Rabbati, 2). This, incidentally, suggests a common source of Pesikta Rabbati and Soferim. British Museum, Or. 2531, published here as Appendix II, contains a Karaite list of Damascus of Haftarot and Psalms adjusted to the Annual Cycle.

30. The difference between Palestine and Babylonia as far as the reading of Scripture is concerned, is first alluded to in Megillah 29b, which attributes to the former a "three-year cycle." The Geonic treatise (see ed. Margulies in n. 43 below, p. 88) mentions a "three and a half year cycle." There is a vast literature on the subject; see below, nn. 32, 34, 47. The divergence between the two rites was of course but one aspect of the halakic and liturgical divisions between Babylonia and Palestine. Cf. now J. Heinemann, *Prayer in the Period of the Tanna'im and Amoraim* (Jerusalem, 1966), 25 f. [in Hebrew].

31. Abraham bar Ḥiyya, *Sefer Ha-'ibbur,* 70, lists 52 pericopes for the Annual Cycle; Saadia Gaon in his *Seder*[3] (Jerusalem, 1970), 364, has 53 *parashiyot,* as does Maimonides, in his Seder Tefillot. For the variety of customs in the division of *parashiyot,* see note to line 12) of *Ibid.,* p. 364; L. Zunz, *Die Ritus des Synagogalen Gottesdienstes* (Berlin, 1859), 170, n. 1.

32. J. Heinemann, *Tarbiẓ,* 33 (1963-64), 362-68; N. Fried, *Sinai,* 61 (1967), 269-90; 62 (1968); 50-66.

33. See n. 30 *above.*

34. See the poem by the Palestinian payyetan Rabbi Pinehas published by E. Fleischer, *Sinai,* 59 (1966), 209-27, esp. p. 213. A. Yaari, *The History of the Simḥat Torah Festival* (Jerusalem, 1964 [in Hebrew]), 13 f., misinterprets a passage in Benjamin of Tudela's *Travels* (ed. Adler, London, 1903), p. 63; see below, XLIII. B. Mandelbaum, ed. *Pesikta d'Rab Kahana* (New York, 1962), II, 437, basing himself on the erroneous assumption that the celebration of Simḥat Torah in Palestine referred to the festival of the last day of Sukkot, unjustifiably concluded that the homily for Simḥat Torah (437-51) is not an authentic Pesikta.

35. "Rabbi Simon ben Eleazer says: 'Ezra ordained that Israel read the curses of Leviticus (26:15-31—שבתורת כהנים) before the festival of Shabu'ot and the curses of Deuteronomy (27:15-26; 28:15-68—שבמשנה תורה) before Rosh Hashanah' " (Megillah 31b; Mann, *infra,* p. 5). This presents the Annual Cycle in a nutshell.

36. See Deut. Rabbah, II, 33; but this reference is doubtful, because the parallel source in Yer. Abodah Zara, V, 44d, is anonymous. Moreover, Simon ben Eleazar is frequently linked with towns in Galilee; cf. Yer. Mo'ed Katan, III, 81d; Erubin 29a; Tosefta *ibid.* VI, 4 (ed. Lieberman), p. 119.

37. Megillah 29b.

38. "They read the haftara of the section of Shekalim, that of Joiada the High Priest" (Tosefta, Megillah III, 1, p. 353 [ed. Lieberman]; Yer. Megillah, IV, 75b; Lieberman, *Tosefta Ki-fshutah,* 1164, *ad loc.*), following the *Naḥalat Ya'akov,* differentiates between the reading of Vienna Ms., which he says recommends the reading of II Kings 12:5, in accordance with the Spanish rite, on the one hand, and on the other hand between the Ehrfurt Ms. and the Vulgar editions, and the Babylonian Talmud, which he says commence with II Kings 11:17, the Ashkenazic rite. The Tosefta accordingly, indirectly refutes Rab's position that Shekalim's Torah portion deals with the daily offering. This

is doubtful since II Kings 12:5 (or 12:1) does not contain any direct reference to Joiada. It is moreover unlikely that the Tosefta here shows any awareness of the controversy between Rab and Samuel, as reported in Megillah 29b. Whatever the first verse of the haftara, the text never mentions the daily sacrifice. II Kings 11:17 f. records the destruction of the idols only.

39. The sources are listed by N. Fried, in *Encyclopediah Talmudit*, X, cols. 721 f.

40. See Fried's list, *idem.*, cols. 717-22, which embraces the Palestinian haftarot for the festivals and special occasions.

41. Y. Megillah, IV, 5, 75b; Gittin 60a. Jastrow, *s.v.* *'Aftarta*, following S.Y. Rapoport, *Erek Millin* (Warsaw, 1914), p. 328, explains the term "as a book containing homiletic notes for toasts, etc." But this construction is impossible in the Palestinian Talmud. Geonic testimony suggests that the reference is to haftara collections rather than necessarily to Aramaic renditions, as maintained by Rapoport on the basis of the reference to the Palestinian Talmud; see *Otzar Ha-Geonim*, II, p. 26, on Shabbat 24a.

42. Even in the post-talmudic period, on significant occasions, the Sabbatical readings of Scripture were canceled in order to record an appropriate passage. Saadia (*Abudraham*, 82b) says that on the Sabbath after the death of a sage the proper haftara is I Sam. 4:21. Upon Sherira Gaon's death in 1006, the Torah portion Num. 27:15-23, and the haftara of I Kings 2:1-13 were read, to harmonize with the transfer of the gaonate from the deceased to his son Hai. The haftara recited on the Sabbath following Maimonides' death (20th of Tebet, 1204, whose haftara should have been I Kings 2 was Josh. 1:1 (*ibid.* 82b): "After the death of Moses, the servant of the Lord . . ." On the Sabbath preceding a wedding, Gen. 24, the selection of Rebekah as Isaac's wife, followed by Isa. 61:10, were read (Judah bar Barzilai, *Sefer Ha-'Ittim* [Berlin, 1902], 278. This custom seems to go back to a period when one could choose an appropriate biblical text for the occasion.

43. *The Differences Between Babylonian and Palestinian Jews,* ed. Margulies (Jerusalem, 1938 [in Hebrew]), 88. On p. 170, n. 3, Margulies rejects this interpretation, originally proposed by Miller, as unlikely. However, it still seems more plausible than his own, though the text is obviously corrupt. Cf. Yer. Megillah, IV, p. 75a: "The men who use the vernacular (הלעוזות —Greek, Aramaic?) follow a different custom, one recites the entire parashah." The correct procedure, however, the text seems to say, is: "if there is only one man who can read the entire parashah, he reads it all; seven men, each knowing three verses, all read; one who knows but three verses, he reads and rereads again." It is clear that in Palestine the men called up to make the blessings recited the Scriptural readings. Cf. Qiddushin 49a-b. Yer. Megillah, IV, 7, p. 74d; J. Karo, *Bet Yosef* on Tur Oraḥ Ḥayyim, Sections 139 f.

44. See Y. Sanhedrin, I, 1, 18a; Mann, *infra,* p. 558 ff.

45. See, however, n. 35 above.

46. The version published at the end of *Yam Shel Shelomoh* on Baba Kamma by Solomon Luria (Prague, 1613); Margulies, *Differences,* 88, variae lectiones.

47. Soferim, XVI, 8, misquoting Yer. Shabbat, XVI, p. 15c. Esther Rabbah, Introduction, 3 p. lc (Romm ed.), quoting Rab, appears to assume 155 sedarim— the numerical equivalent of the Hebrew word קנה (Deut. 28:68, last word). For the older literature, see A. Epstein, *Works,* ed. by A. M. Habermann (Jerusalem, 1957 [in Hebrew]), II, 54 ff.

48. See Gen. Rabbah, XCVI, p. 1192 (Albeck) on Gen. 47:28: ; ולמה פרשה זו סתומה מכל פרשיות שבתורה, Cf. Albeck's introductory notes on pp. 1185, 1231.

49. This offers a relative dating of Genesis Rabbah and the two editions of Tanhuma and the Masorah of Sedarim:

Masorah of Sedarim—Seder Gen. 47:29
Genesis Rabbah, XCV-XCVII (Vatican Ms. [Albeck], pp. 1231-49)
New Parashah called Vayyeḥi (Gen. 47:28)
Tanḥuma Vayyeḥi (ed. Buber)
Genesis Rabbah Vayyeḥi (Vulgar editions and pp. 1199-1230)

Even the Babylonian haftara for this parashah—I Kings 2:1—was chosen as a consequence of the seder that had begun with Gen. 47:29, not 47:28. That there had been such a seder see Gen. Rabbah (Vatican), p. 1235; cf. also Mann, *infra*, pp. 340-45.

50. Genesis has two haftarot common to both the "Triennial" and Annual Cycles: 28:10—Hos. 12:13; 32:4—Obad. 1; Ex. and Lev. have none; Num. has 8:1—Zech. (doubtful); 13:1—Josh. 2:1; 30:2—Jer. 1:1 (doubtful). Deut. 33:1— Josh. 1:1 was originally a Palestinian reading, but has become attached to the last day of Sukkot in the Annual Cycle.

51. Except for haftarot of the book of Deuteronomy, which as explained above were originally Palestinian. How the Karaites adopted the Annual Cycle of Torah readings and the Byzantine haftarot is still puzzling. Anan had ordained the completion of the Pentateuch twice a year on Sukkot and on Passover. See Mann, "Anan's Liturgy and His Half-Yearly Cycle of the Reading of the Law," *Journal of Jewish Lore and Philosophy*, I (1919), 329-353, esp. p. 352; see also Z. Ankori's Introduction to the *Aderet Eliyyahu* (Jerusalem, 1966). S. Goldberg, *Karaite Liturgy and Its Relation to Synagogue Worship* (Manchester University Press, 1957), 93 f., unaware of the dependence on the Byzantine and ultimately Palestinian readings, ascribes the Karaite selections to the peculiar theological tenets of this sect.

52. A few fragments have been published. I. Yeivin, *Textus*, 3(1963), 121-27; Fried, *ibid.*, 128 f. There are a number of photographs which have not been edited: E. N. Adler, *Catalogue* (Cambridge, 1921), 96; A. I. Katsh, *Catalogue of Hebrew Manuscripts Preserved in the USSR* [Antonin Collection], New York, 1958, II, 14. For allusions to some other extant fragments, see Fried, *Sinai*, 61 (1967), 267, n. 4.

53. See Yer. Pesaḥim, I, 1, 27b: The view of Rabban Gamaliel, "For Moses instructed the laws of Passover on the New Moon [of Nisan]." Cf. also parallels: Tos. Megillah, III, 5, p. 354 (ed. Lieberman). Pesaḥim 6a, Megillah 29b, etc., are secondary.

54. Cf. Lauterbach, "The Arrangement and the Divisions of the Mekilta," *HUCA*, I (1924), 427-66; *Mekilta*, Introduction, pp. xxvi f., who gives a different explanation for the make-up of the Mekilta.

55. See p. 66 of the facsimile edition of *Sifra*, Vatican 66 by L. Finkelstein (New York, 1956). Incidentally, this Ms. is of great interest for the "Babylonization," the scribal changes introduced under the influence of the Babylonian Talmud, evident for instance on pp. 26, line 4; 27, 12, 19; 28, 4.

56. See, e.g., Sifre Num. at 5:1 (Piska 1); 6:1 (22); 8:1 (59); 10:1 (72); 10:35 (84).

57. See Epstein (n. 47 above); Theodor, *MGWJ*, 28(1879), 97 ff.; M. Lerner, *Anlage und Quellen des Bereschit Rabba* (Berlin, 1882), 16 ff. Albeck, Introduction to Genesis Rabba, 96 ff.; "Midrash Vayyikra Rabbah," in *L. Ginzberg Jubilee Volume* (New York, 1946), 25 ff. [in Hebrew].

58. Leviticus Rabbah, III, 6, p. 69 (ed. Margulies). Margulies dates the passage in the third century, as Rabbi Ḥananyah bar Aḥa was a Palestinian amora of the second generation.

59. M. Margulies, in his Introduction to Leviticus Rabbah (Jerusalem, 1960), pp. xii ff., disputes Albeck's conclusion, *The Ginzberg Jubilee Volume* (note 57), that Leviticus Rabbah is later than Genesis Rabbah, and that the Pesikta d'Rab

Kahana borrowed some of its sections from Leviticus Rabbah. Margulies (p. xiii, n. 2) cites Genesis Rabbah, p. 1100-Leviticus Rabbah, p. 566 and Genesis Rabbah, 36 f.-Leviticus Rabbah 215, which ends with the messianic perorations in the latter, but not in the former. This shows that Genesis Rabbah is sometimes dependent on Leviticus Rabbah. But other contextual links indicate that the latter is here also dependent on the former.

As to Margulies' argument that the same man was author of both Leviticus Rabbah and the Pesikta—since several sections are identical in both—this must be rejected. The material that is common to both differs from that which differentiates them. But Albeck's conclusion (contrary to L. Zunz, S. Buber, J. Theodor, A. Epstein, and M. Friedmann) that the editor of the Pesikta d'Rab Kahana borrowed five sections, among other material, from Leviticus Rabbah is likewise unacceptable. First of all, the idea of themes is essentially rooted in the Pesikta, not in an exegetical work such as a supposed commentary on Leviticus. Secondly, Albeck's proofs (pp. 36-38) that the Pesikta is secondary are not conclusive. On the contrary; the praise of "the Book of the Priests" (Leviticus Rabbah. VII, p. 156; Pesikta I, p. 118) fits better for the reading of Rosh Hodesh (Num. 28) rather than for Lev. 6, where the title is out of place, and should have been used in the beginning of the book. Thirdly, we know that Yannai (see below, n. 63), who lived about the year 600, utilized the Pesikta. Fourthly, as pointed out above (pp.XXIX), Chapter 29 of Leviticus Rabbah on Lev. 23:23 f. is only conceivable as originating with the holiday, as no new seder was permitted to begin with this verse.

60. Mann, *infra*, pp. 11-15, tends to believe that the Yelamdenu is the oldest segment of the midrashic homilies. Unfortunately, Mann never told us his view as to the relationship between the Yelamdenu homilies and those of the other types. His statement is merely negative: "The Y[elamdenu] homilies are not as late as usually assumed . . ." (p. 14).

61. The "Triennial" haftara of Isa. 33:7, for the account of the binding of Isaac (Gen. 22:1), as alluded to above, is clearly dependent upon the link reported in Genesis Rabbah (LVI, p. 600).

62. Among the additional fragments of Yannai recently published: S. Widder, "Piyyute Yannai," in *Jubilee Volume, Bernard Heller* (Budapest, 1941), 32-65 (Hebrew Section); I. Sonne, "An Unknown Keroba of Yannai: A New Fragment of *Maḥzor Yannai* (A Supplement to *Piyyute Yannai*)," *HUCA*, 18 (1944), 199-221; Diez Macho and S. Spiegel, "Fragmentos de Piyyutim de Yannay en Vocalizacion Babylonica," *Sefarad,* 15 (1955), 286-334; Z. M. Rabinowitz, *Tarbiz,* 38 (1969), 384-93.

63. See now Z. M. Rabinowitz, *The Halakah and Aggadah in Yannai's Piyyutim* (Tel Aviv, 1965 [in Hebrew]). Cf. S. Lieberman, *Sinai,* 4 (1939), 221-50.

64. Rabinowitz, *ibid.,* lists the parallel passages. Only Yannai's use of the Mishnah (pp. 1-15) is certain, though his dependence on Genesis Rabbah (72-126) is also assured. Yannai's reworking of the Mishnah and Genesis Rabbah shows that he followed the original very closely, so closely that he may be used for textual emendations. This raises a question as to the validity of Rabinowitz's conclusions in regard to the other midrashic material.

65. Davidson, *Maḥzor Yannai,* pp. ix-xlix, treats the problem fully. A monograph on this subject is a desideratum. Cf. Schirmann, *JQR,* 44 (1953), 143; M. Zulay, *Meḥḳere Yannai* (Berlin, 1936), 267 f.; S. Lieberman, *Sinai,* 4 (1939), 243 f.; Rabinowitz, *The Halakah and Aggadah,* etc., 24 f.

66. Cited in the name of the twelfth-century Rabbi Ephraim ben Jacob of Bonn, as quoted by Zunz from a Ms., in a communication to S. J. Rapoport, in *Kerem Ḥemed* 4 (1836), 25; I. Davidson, *op. cit.,* p. xlix.

67. Megillah 23b.

68. *The Itinerary of Benjamin of Tudela,* ed. Adler (London, 1907), 63; cf. Joseph Sambari's Chronicle, in A. Neubauer, *Medieval Jewish Chronicles* (Oxford, 1887), I, 118.

69. Maimonides, *Yad, Tefillah,* XIII, 1: "The common custom of Israel is to complete the Torah every year . . . But there are those who do so in three years, but this is not a widespread *minhag."*

12. *A Select Bibliography*

Adolf Büchler, "The Reading of the Law and Prophets in a Triennial Cycle," *JQR,* O.S., 5 (1893), 420-68; 6 (1894) 1-73.

Israel Davidson, *Mahzor Yannai: A Liturgical Work of the Seventh Century,* etc. (New York, The Jewish Theological Seminary, 1919).

Mordecai Margulies, *The Differences Between Babylonian and Palestinian Jews: With Reference to Laws, Customs, and Ritual Observances of Jews During the Geonic Period* (Jerusalem, Rubin Press, 1938 [in Hebrew]).

Nathan Fried, "Haftarah," *Talmudic Encyclopaedia,* X (1961 [in Hebrew]), cols. 1-32; 701-24.

Issakar Joel, "A 'Keter' of the year 5,020 A.M. (1260)," *Kirjat Sefer,* 38 (1962-63 [in Hebrew]), 122-32.

Nathan Fried, "The Haftaroth of T.-S. B. 17, 25," *Textus,* 3 (1963), 128-29 (with reference to I. Yeivin, *ibid.,* 121 ff.).

Joseph Heinemann, "The 'Triennial Cycle' and the Annual Cycle," *Tarbiz,* 33 (1963-64 [in Hebrew]), 362-68.

Ezra Fleischer, "Simhat Torah of Palestine," *Sinai,* 59 (1966 [in Hebrew]), 209-27.

Nathan Fried, "Alternate Haftarot in the Piyyutim of Yannai and other Payyetanim," *Sinai,* 61 (1967 [in Hebrew]) 287-90; 62 (1968), 50-66.

Nathan Fried, "Some Further Notes on *Haftarot* Scrolls," *Textus,* 6 (1968), 118-126.

APPENDIX I

A LIST OF
"TRIENNIAL" SEDARIM AND HAFTAROT

The Symbols

A) SEDARIM

1: The Sedarim listed in the first edition of the Rabbinic Bible (Venice, Bomberg, 1524-25). 154 Sedarim.
2: The Sedarim marked in the Leningrad Manuscript of the Bible, as reported in Biblia Hebraica. 167 Sedarim.
3: A list in the Bible at the National Library, Jerusalem, of the year 1260. 154 Sedarim.
4: A different collation found in the body of the same Manuscript. 141 Sedarim.
5: Mann's collation of Sedarim in Volumes I and II of this work. 106 Sedarim to Num. 6:22.
Y: The Sedarim mentioned by Yannai in *Piyyute Yannai,* ed. M. Zulay (Berlin, 1938) and in other publications.
M: The Geniza fragments of lists of Sedarim and Haftarot published by Mann. See *infra,* pp. 561-74.
*: An asterisk at the beginning of a line indicates that the parashah of the Annual Cycle coincides with the beginning of this Seder.

B) HAFTAROT

1: Geniza fragments of "Triennial" Haftarot collections scattered among major libraries of the world.
2: The Geniza fragments of lists of "Triennial" Sedarim and Haftarot, published by Mann, *infra,* pp. 561-74.
3: The Haftarot mentioned in Yannai's piyyutim (see above).
4: The Haftarot of Minhag Romania.
5: The Karaite Haftarot.
6: The Haftarot of the Ashkenazim, Sefardim, etc.
7: Scholarly speculations.
8: Unknown.

Gen.	Heading	1	2	3	4	5	Y	M
* 1:1	בראשית	1	1	1	1	1	Y	
2:4	אלה תולדת הש׳	2	2	2	2	2		
3:22	הן האדם	3	3	3	3	3		
5:1	זה ספר תול׳	4	4	4	4	4		
* 6:9	אלה תול׳ נח	5	5	5	5	5		M
8:1	ויזכר א׳ את נח		6	6		6		M
8:15	צא מן התבה	6	7	(7)	6	7	Y	M
9:18	ויהיו בני נח	7	8	(8)	7	8	Y	M
11:1	ויהי כל הארץ		9			9	Y	
*12:1	לך לך	8	10	(9)	8	10	Y	M
12:10	ויהי רעב	9		10		10a		
14:1	ויהי בימי אמרפל	10	11	11	19	11	Y	M
15:1	במחזה לאמר	11	12	12	10	12	Y	M
16:1	ושרי אשת	12	13	13	11	13	Y	M
17:1	ויהי אברם	13	14	14	12	14	Y	M
*18:1	וירא אליו	14	15	15		15	Y	M
19:1	ויבאו שני	15	16	16	13	16		M
20:1	ויסע משם	16	17	17	14	17		M
21:1	וה׳ פקד	17	18	18	15	18		M
22:1	והא׳ נסה	18	19	19	16	19		M
24:1	ואברהם זקן	19	20	20	17	20	Y	M
24:42	ואבא היום	20	21	21	18	21		M
25:1	ויֹסף אברהם	21	22	22	19	22		M
*25:19	ואלֹה תולדת	22	23	23	20	23	Y	M
26:12	ויזרע יצחק					24		M
27:1	ויהי כי זקן	23	24	24	21	25		M
27:28	ויתן לך	24	25	25	22	26	Y	M
*28:10	ויצא יעקב	25	26	25	23	27	Y	M
29:31	וירא ה׳	26	27	27	24	28	Y	(M)

H A F T A R O T   S O U R C E S

Prophet	Heading	1	2	3	4	5	6	7	8
Is. 65:17	בורא שמים	1			4	5			
Is. 51:6	שאו לשמים	1							
Ez. 28:13	בעדן	1							
Is. 29:18	ושמעו	1							
Is. 54:9	כי־מי נח	1	2		4	5			
Hab. 3:2	ה' שמעתי	1	2						
Is. 42:7	לפקח	1	2	3					
Is. 49:9	לאמר לאסורים	1	2	3					
Zep. 3:9	אהפך אל עמים	1	2	3					
Jos. 24:3	ואקח את אביכם	1	2	3	4	5			
I Kings 8:37	רעב							7	8
Is. 41:2	מי העיר ממזרח	1	2						
Is. 1:1	חזון ישעיהו	1	2	3					
Is. 54:1	רני עקרה	1	2	3					
Jer. 33:25	אם לא בריתי	1							
Is. 54:10	ההרים ימושו		2						
Is. 33:17	מלך ביפיו	1	2		4	5			
Is. 17:14	לעת ערב	1	2						
Is. 61:9	ונודע בגוים זרעם	1	2						
I Sam. 2:21	כי פקד	1	2						
Is. 33:7	הן אראלים	1	2						
Is. 51:1(2)	שמעו אלי	1	2		4	5			
Is. 12:3	ושאבתם מים	1	2						
I Sam. 5:12	והאנשים	1	2						
Is. 65:23	לא יגעו לריק	1	2		4	5			
Is. 62:8	נשבע ה'		2						
Is. 46:3	שמעו אלי	1	2						
Mic. 5:6	והיה שארית	1	2						
Hos. 12:13	ויברח יעקב		2		4	(5)	6		
Is. 60:15	היותך עזובה		(2)	3					
I Sam. 1:2	ולו שתי נשים			(3)					

TORAH		SEDER					SOURCES	
Gen.	Heading	1	2	3	4	5	Y	M
30:22	ויזכר אל׳	27	28	28	25	29	Y	M
31:3	שוב אל ארץ	28	29	29	26	30	Y	M
*32:4	וישלח	29	30	30	27	31	Y	M
33:18	ויבא	30	31	31	28	32		M
35:9	וירא אל׳ אל	31	32	32v	29	33	Y	M
*37:1	וישב	32	33	33	30	34	Y	M
38:1	ויהי בעת ההיא	33	34	34	31	35	Y	M
39:1	ויוסף	34	35	35	32	36	Y	M
40:1	חטאו		36			36b		
*41:1	מקץ	35	37	36	33	37	Y	M
41:38	הנמצא	36	38	37	34	38	Y	M
42:1	כי יש שבר					38a	Y	
42:18	ויאמר אליהם	37	39	38	35	39	Y	M
43:14	וא׳ שדי	38	40	39	36	40		M
*44:18	ויגש	39	41	40	37	41	Y	M
46:28	ואת יהודה	40	42	41	38	42		M
48:1	אביך חלה	41	43	42	39	43	Y	M
49:1	ויקרא יעקב	42	44	43		44	Y	M
49:27	בנימין	(43)	45			45		M
Exod.								
* 1:1	ואלה שמות	1	1	1		46(1)	Y	M
2:1	וילך איש		2					
3:1	ומשה	2	3	2	2	47(2)	Y	M
4:18	וילך משה	3	4	3	3	48(3)	Y	M
* 6:2	וארא אל	4	5	4	4	49(4)	Y	M
7:8	כי ידבר	5	6	5	5	50(5)	Y	M
8:16	השכם בבקר	6	7	6	6	51(6)	Y	M
*10:1	הכבדתי	7	8	7	7	52(7)	Y	M
11:1	עוד נגע	8	9	8	8	53(8)	Y	M
12:29	ויהי בחצי	9	10	9	9	54(9)	Y	M

Prophet	Heading	1	2	3	4	5	6	7	8
I Sam. 1:11	ותדר נדר		2						
Mic. 6:3	עמי		2						
Jer. 30:10	ואתה אל תירא	1		3					
Ob. 1	חזון עבדיה	1	2		4	5	6		
Na. 1:12	אם שלמים	1	2	3					
Is. 43:1	בראך יעקב		2	3					
Is. 32:18	וישב עמי		2	3	4	5			
Is. 37:31	ויספה		2						
Is. 52:3	חנם נמכרתם		2	3					
Jud. 18:1	בימים ההם								8
Is. 29:8	והיה כאשר יחלם		2		4	5			
Is. 11:2	ונחה עליו		2						
Is. 55:1	הוי כל צמא			3					
Is. 50:10	מי בכם		2						
Jer. 42:12	ואתן לכם		2						
Josh. 14:6	ויגשו	1	2	3	4	5			
Zech. 10:6	וגברתי	1	2						
II Kings 13:14	ואלישע חלה	1	2	3	4	5			
Is. 43:22	ולא־אתי קראת	1	2	3					
Zech. 14:1	הנה יום בא	1	2						
Is. 27:6	הבאים ישרש	1	2	3	4	5			
									8
Is. 40:11	כרעה עדרו	1	2	3					
Is. 55:12	כי בשמחה	1	2						
Is. 42:8	אני ה׳	1	2		4	5			
Joel 3:3	ונתתי מופתים	1	2	3					
Is. 34:11	וירשוה	1	2		4	5			
I Sam. 6:6	ולמה תכבדו	1	2						
Mic. 7:15	כימי צאתך	1	2						
Is. 21:11	משא דומה	1	2	3					

Exod.	Heading	1	2	3	4	5	Y	M
13:1	קדש	10	11	10	10	55(10)	Y	M
14:15	מה תצעק אלי	11	12	11	11	56(11)	Y	M
16:4	הנני ממטיר	12	13	12	12	56c(11c)		
16:28	עד אנה מאנתם	13	14	13		57(12)	Y	M
*18:1	וישמע יתרו	14	15	14	13	58(13)	Y	M
19:6	ואתם תהיו לי	15	16	15	14	59(14)	Y	M
*21:1	ואלה המשפטים	16	17	16	15	60(15)	Y	M
22:24	אם כסף תלוה	17	18	17	16	61(16)		M
23:20	הנה אנכי שלח		19			61a(16a)		
*25:1	ויקחו לי תרומה	18	20	18	17	62(17)	Y	M
26:1	ואת המשכן תעשה	19	21	19	18	63(18)	Y	M
26:31	ועשית פרכת	20	22	20	19	64(19)		M
*27:20	ואתה תצוה	21	23	21	20	65(20)	Y	M
29:1	זה הדבר	22	24	22	21	66(21)	Y	M
30:1	ועשית מזבח	23	25	23	22	67(22)	Y	M
31:1	ראה קראתי	24	26	24	23	68(23)	Y	M
32:15	ויפן	25	27	25	24	69(24)	Y	M
34:1	פסל לך		28			69c(24c)		
34:27	כתב לך	26	28	26	25	70(25)	Y	M
35:30	ראו קרא ה׳		30			70b(35b)		
37:1	ויעש בצלאל	27	31	27	26	71(26)		M
*38:21	אלה פקודי	28	32	28	27	72(27)	Y	M
39:33	ויביאו את המשכן	29	33	29	28	73(28)		M
Lev.								
* 1:1	ויקרא	1	1	1	1	74(1)	Y	M
4:1	נפש כי תחטא	2	2	2		75(2)	Y	M
5:1	ונפש כי תחטא		3			76(3)	Y	M
5:14	נפש כי תמעל				2	—		
6:12	זה קרבן אהרן	3	4	3	3	77(4)	Y	M
8:1	קח את אהרן	4	5	4	4	78(5)		
10:8	יין ושכר	5	6	5	5	80(7)		

HAFTAROT		SOURCES							
Prophet	Heading	1	2	3	4	5	6	7	8
Is. 46:3	שמעו אלי	1	2	3					
Is. 65:24	טרם ישמעו	1	2						
Josh. 24:7	ויצעקו			3	4				
Is. 58:13	אם תשיב משבת	1	2						
Is. 33:13	שמעו רחוקים	1	2		4	5			
Is. 61:6	ואתם כהני	1	2						
Is. 56:1	שמרו משפט	1	2	3	4	5			
Is. 48:10	הנה צרפתיך	1	2						
Mal. 3:1	שלח מלאכי								8
Is. 60:17	תחת הנחשת	1	2	3	4	5			
Is. 66:1	השמים כסאי	1	2	3					
Ez. 16:10	ואלבישך רקמה	1	2		4				
Hos. 14:7	ילכו יונקותיו	1	2						
Jer. 11:16	זית רענן	1			4	5			
Is. 61:6	כהני ה׳	1	2	3					
Mal. 1:11	כי ממזרח שמש	1	2						
Is. 43:7	כל הנקרא	1	2		4	5			
II Sam. 22:10	ויט שמים	1	2	3					
I Kings 8:9	אין בארון								8
Jer. 31:31	לא כברית	1	2	3					
									8
I Kings 8:1	אז יקהל	1	2		4	5			
Jer. 30:18	שב שבות		2			5			
Is. 33:20	חזה ציון		2						
Mic. 6:9	קול ה׳	1	2	3					
Ez. 18:4	כל הנפשות	1	2	3					
Zech. 5:3	זאת האלה	1	2						
Ez. 14:12	בן אדם								8
Mal. 3:4	וערבה	1	2	3	4	5			
I Sam. 2:28	ובחר אתו	1							
Ez. 44:21	ויין לא ישתו	1			4 ?				

183

Lev.	Heading	1	2	3	4	5	Y	
11:1	זאת החיה	6	7	6	6	81(8)		
*12:1	אשה כי תזריע	7	8	7	7	82(9)	Y	......
13:29	בראש	8	9	8	8	84(11)	Y	
*14:1	תורת המצרע	9	10	9	9	85(12)	Y	......
14:33	ונתתי נגע	10	11	10		86(13)	Y	
15:1	איש איש כי	11	12	11	10	87(14)	Y	
15:25	ואשה כי יזוב	12	13	12	11	88(15)	Y	
17:1	אשר ישחט	13	14	13	12	89(16)	Y	
18:1	כמעשה ארץ	14	15	14		90(17)		
*19:1	קדשים	15	16	15	13	91(18)	Y	
19:23	ונטעתם כל עץ	16	17	16	14	92(19)		
*21:1	אמר אל	17	18	17	15	93(20)	Y	
22:17	אשר יקריב	18	19	18	16	94(21)	Y	
23:9	וקצרתם		20			95(22)		
23:15	וספרתם לכם	19		19	17	95a(22a)		
24:1	שמן זית		21			96(23)		
25:14	וכי תמכרו	20	22	20		97(24)	Y	
25:35	וכי ימוך	21	23	21	18	98(25)	Y	
*26:3	אם בחקתי	22	24	22	19	99(26)		
27:2	איש כי יפלא	23	25	23	20	100(27)	Y	

TORAH SEDER SOURCES

HAFTAROT SOURCES

Prophet	Heading	1	3	4	5	6	7	8
Is. 40:16	ולבנון	1						
Is. 9:5	כי ילד	1						
Is. 66:7	בטרם תחיל		3	4				
Is. 7:20	ביום ההוא יגלח	1						
Is. 57:17	בעון בצעו		3					
Jer. 30:17	אעלה ארכה		3					
Is. 5:8	הוי מגיעי בית	1	3					
Hos. 6:1	לכו ונשובה	1	3					
Ez. 16:9	וארחצך במים		3					
Is. 66:1(3 ?)	השמים כסאי	1	3 ?					
Jer. 10:2	דרך הגוים	1						
Is. 4:3	הנשאר בציון	1		4	5			
Is. 65:22	לא יבנו	1						
Ez. 44:25	ואל מת אדם	1		4	5			
Is. 56:7	והביאותים		3					
Joel 4:13	שלחו מגל	1						
Josh. 5:11	ויאכלו							8
Hos. 14:7	ילכו יונקותיו							8
Jer. 11:16	זית רענן							8
Is. 24:2	והיה כעם	1	3	4	5			
Is. 35:3	חזקו ידים	1	3					
Is. 1:19	אם תאבו	1	3	4	5			
Jud. 11:30	וידר יפתח	1						

TORAH		SEDER				SOURCES		
Num.	Heading	1	2	3	4	5	Y	M
* 1:1	במדבר סיני	1	1	1		101(1)	Y	··············
2:1	איש על דגלו	2	2	2	1	102(2)	Y	
3:1	ואלה תולדת	3	3	3	2	103(3)	Y	
4:17	אל תכריתו	4	4	4	3	104(4)	Y	··············
5:11	כי תשטה	5	5	5	4	105(5)	Y	
6:1	כי יפלא לנדר		6			105a(5a)		
6:22	כה תברכו	6	7	6	5	106(6)	Y	
7:48	ביום השביעי	7	8	7	6		Y	
* 8:1	בהעלתך	8	9	8	7		Y	··············
10:1	עשה לך	9	10	9	8		Y	
11:16	אספה לי	10	11	10	9			

HAFTAROT		SOURCES							
Prophet	Heading	1	2	3	4	5	6	7	8

.... ⌈ Hos. 2:16	לכן הנה אנכי	1		3					
⌊ Is. 35:1	יששום מדבר			3					
Is. 8:18	הנה אנכי והילדים								8
Is. 45:19	לא בסתר	1		3					
.... ⌈ Zeph. 3:17	ה׳ אלהיך בקרבך								8
⌊ Is. 56:5	ונתתי להם								8
Hos. 4:14	לא אפקד			3	4				
Jud. 13:2	איש אחד מצרעה								8
I Kings 8:54	ויהי ככלות								8
Jud. 5:14	מני אפרים								
.... ⌈ Zech. 4:2	ויאמר אלי			3					
⌊ Zech. 2:14	רני ושמחי				4	5	6		
Is. 27:13	ביום ההוא יתקע								8
Joel 2:16	אספו עם								8

187

| TORAH | | SEDER | | | | SOURCES |
Num.	Heading	1	2	3	4	Y
11:23	היד ה׳ תקצר	11	12	11		
*13:1	שלח	12	13	12	10	
14:11	עד אנה ינאצני	13	14	13	11	
15:1	כי תבאו אל הארץ	14	15	14	12	Y
*16:1	ויקח קרח·	15	16	15	13	Y
17:16	ויקח מאתם מטה	16	17	16	14	Y
18:25	ואל הלוים	17		17	15	
*19:1	זאת חקת		18			Y
20:14	וישלח משה	18	19	18	16	Y
*22:2	וירא בלק	19	20	19	17	Y ....
23:10	מי מנה	20	21	20	18	Y ....
25:1	וישב ישראל	21	22	21		Y
*25:10	פינחס בן אלעזר	22	23	22	19	Y
26:52	לאלה תחלק	23	24	23	20	Y
27:15	יפקד ה׳	24	25	24	21	Y
28:26	וביום הבכורים	25	26	25	22	
*30:2	ראשי המטות	26	27	26	23	....
31:1	נקם נקמת	27	28	27		
31:25	שא את ראש	28	29	28	24	Y
32:1	ומקנה רב	29	30	29	25	Y
*33:1	אלה מסעי	30	31	30	26	Y
34:1	זאת הארץ	31	32	31	27	
35:9	והקריתם לכם	32	33	32	28	Y

(29)

HAFTAROT		SOURCES						
Prophet	Heading	1	3	4	5	6	7	8
Is. 50:2	מדוע באתי							8
Is. 59:1	הן לא קצרה יד ה׳							8
Josh. 2:1	וישלח יהושע			4	5	6	7	
Is. 52:5	ועתה מה לי פה	1						
Is. 56:3	ואל יאמר	1						
Hos. 10:2	חלק לבם		3	4	5			
Is. 11:1	ויצא חטר		3					
Is. 62:8	נשבע ה׳ בימינו	1						
Jud. 11:1	ויפתח הגלעדי			4	5	6		
Ob. 1	חזון עבדיה	1	3					
⌐ Mic. 7:16	יראו גוים	1	3					
⌐ Is. 60:5	אז תראי		3					
⌐ Is. 49:23	והיו מלכים		3					
⌐ Mic. 7:17	ילחכו עפר		3					
Joel 4:18	ביום ההוא יטפו		3	4	5			
Mal.2:5	בריתי היתה אתו		3	4	5			
Is. 57:13	בזעקך יצילך						7	
Josh 13:7	ועתה חלק		3(?)				7	
Is. 40:13	מי תכן את רוח						7	8
Mal. 3:4	וערבה לה׳						7	8
⌐ Is. 45:23	בי נשבעתי	1						
⌐ Jer. 1:1	דברי ירמיהו			4	5	6	7	
Ez. 25:14	ונתתי נקמתי	1						
Is. 40:24	היקח מגבור	1						
Josh. 22:8	בנכסים רבים	1						
Is. 11:16	והיתה מסלה	1		4				
Ez. 45:1	ובהפילכם את הארץ	1						
Josh. 20:1	תנו לכם	1			5			

189

	TORAH	SEDER					SOURCES	
Deut.	Heading	1	2	3	4	5	Y	M
* 1:1	אלה הדברים	1	1	1	1			
2:2	רב לכם	2	2	2	2		Y	
2:31	ראה החלתי	3	3	3	3		Y	
* 3:23	ואתחנן	4	4	4	4		Y	
4:25	כי תוליד		5					
4:41	אז יבדיל	5	6	5	5			
6:4	שמע ישראל	6	7	6	6		Y	
* 7:12	והיה עקב	7	8	7	7		Y	
9:1	שמע ישראל אתה	8	9	8	8			

Zech. 8:16	אלה הדברים	1							
Ob. 21	ועלו מושיעים	1							
Josh. 10:12	אז ידבר יהושע	1		3					
Hab. 3:11	שמש ירח			3					
Amos 2:9	ואנכי השמדתי			3					
Is. 33:2	ה׳ חננו לך קוינו	1							
Jer. 31:20	הבן יקיר לי							7	8
Josh. 20:8	ומעבר לירדן	1							
Zech. 14:9	והיה ה׳ למלך	1		3					
Is. 54:10	כי ההרים ימושו	1							
Josh. 1:10	ויצו יהושע							7	

TORAH		SEDER				SOURCES
Deut.	Heading	1	2	3	4	Y
10:1	בעת ההוא אמר	9	10	9	9	
11:10	כי הארץ אשר	10	11	10	10	
12:20	כי ירחיב	11	12	11	11	
13:2	כי יקום בקרבך		13			
14:1	בנים אתם	12	14	12	12	
15:7	כי יהיה בך	13	15	13	13	....
*16:18	שפטים	14	16	14	14	
17:14	אשימה עלי	15	17	15	15	
18:14	כי הגוים האלה		18			
20:10	כי תקרב	16	19	16	16	Y
*21:10	כי תצא למלחמה		20			
22:6	כי יקרא קן	17	21	17	17	Y
23:10	כי תצא מחנה	18	22	18	18	Y
23:22	כי תדר נדר	19	23	19	19	
24:19	כי תקצר	20	24	20	20	
*26:1	והיה כי תבוא	21	25	21	21	Y
28:1	והיה אם שמוע	22	26	22		Y
28:15	והיה אם לא				22	
*29:9	אתם נצבים	23	27	23	23	Y
30:11	כי המצוה	24	28	24	24	
31:14	הן קרבו	25	29	25		Y
*32:1	האזינו	26	30	26	25	
*33:1	וזאת הברכה	27	31	27	26	Y

HAFTAROT				SOURCES					
Prophet	Heading	1	2	3	4	5	6	7	8

Prophet	Heading	1	2	3	4	5	6	7	8
I Kings 8:9	אין בארון							7	8
									8
Is. 54:2	הרחיבי מקום אהלך							7	8
Zech. 13:5	לא נביא אנכי								8
Is. 63:8	אך עמי המה							7	8
Amos 8:4	שמעו זאת							7	8
Is. 35:3	חזק ידים								8
Is. 56:1	שמרו משפט								8
Is. 32:1	הן לצדק	1							
Is. 33:22									8
Mic. 5:11	והכרתי כשפים								8
Is. 66:12	הנני נטה אליה	1							
Is. 2:4	ישפט בין הגוים								8
Is. 31:5	כצפרים עפות			3					
Is. 1:16	רחצו הזכו							7	8
Is. 19:21	ונודע ה׳ למצרים							7	8
Hos. 10:12	זרעו לכם לצדקה							7	8
Ez. 44:30	וראשית כל בכורי							7	8
Is. 55:2	למה תשכלו			3					
Jer. 33:10	עוד ישמע							7	8
									8
Josh. 24:1	ויאסף יהושע							7	8
Is. 48:14	הקבצו כלכם							7	8
I Kings 2:1	ויקרבו ימי דוד	1							
Is. 1:2	שמעו שמים	1							
Josh. 1:1	ויהי אחרי מות			3	4	5	6		

193

APPENDIX II

KARAITE READINGS OF TORAH, PSALMS, AND HAFTAROT

The British Museum Manuscript Or. 2531, Margoliouth (*Catalogue,* II, 460-61) contains a list of Torah, Psalms, and Haftarot read in the Karaite synagogue of Damascus. The Sabbath readings of the Torah and haftarot are almost identical to those of the Annual Cycle. Of special interest, however, are the selections of the psalms which appear to be a unique Karaite innovation. It is possible though that, like the other Karaite Scriptural choices, they are ultimately based on Rabbinite customs. As has been pointed out above, Pesikta Rabbati, Soferim, and Aggadat Bereshit—all authentic rabbinic works—contain allusions to special psalms that accompanied the Torah and haftara readings.

The photographs of the Manuscript are from the remains of Mann's papers for Volumes II and III. I am profoundly grateful to Victor E. Reichart for making them available to me.

For quick reference a summary of the list of psalms has been prefixed. I have also added in brackets a few corrections of obvious scribal slips.

194

KARAITE SABBATH PSALMS

Parashah	Psalm
1. בראשית	8
2. נח	29
3. לך לך	15
4. וירא	11
5. חיי שרה	52
6. תלדות	23
7. ויצא	132
8. וישלח	60
9. וישב	91
10. מקץ	39
11. ויגש	133
12. ויחי	67
1. שמות	94
2. וארא	76
3. בא	114
4. בשלח	66
5. יתרו	96
6. משפטים	[82]
7. תרומה	84
8. תצוה	132
9. כי תשא	130
10. ויקהל	87
11. פקודי	132
1. ויקרא	50
2. צו	20
3. שמיני	67
4. תזריע	139
5. מצורע	39

KARAITE SABBATH PSALMS

קדש לבנים דאגש

וֹתְלֶבְּדְוֹת דְּצְהֶק ־ מַזְמוּר ﬞﬞ דּוּבִי לֹא שַׁחְקֵר עדד כֹֿב
המגדרה הַלְאֹבִי ﬞﬞ מֶעשָׁא דְּצֶד ﬞﬞ אוֹלֹהֹא ואכּדהא
וְהַדְּבֶה לֹֿ מִנֵא יֶהֹתֹ וְדוֹֹבֹ ﬞ וְהַשֹ מַדְמֹוֹנֹוֹת"

וֹיָּשׁא יֵַעְקֹב מַזְמוּר זְכֹוּר שֶׁ לֹֿ וְרֶָאֹתֹ שֶׁ בֹד עדד קֹֿבֹ
המגדרה הוֹשֹׁע ﬞﬞ וְשֶׁמֹתֹ קֹֿבֹוֹאֹיֹס אוֹלֹהֹא ואכּדהא
וּהֹנֹבֹיֹא שֶׁהֹּמֹּ ﬞ וֹ

וֹיִשְׁלַח יַֿעְקֹב מַזְמוּר בְּדַצַֿוֹתֹ אֶת אֲנֹס נֶַדַּי עדד ﬞﬞ
המגדרה עוֹבֹּיֹה ﬞﬞ מַזֹן עֹדוֹבֹדֹנֹה אוֹלֹהֹא ואכּדהא
וְהֹיֹתֶה לֶֿכֹֿ בֹהֹלֹוֹכֹֿרֹ וֹ

וַיֹּשֶׁב יַֿעְקֹב מַזְמוּר וֹנֶשֶׁב בְּמֶֿהֹר יַכֹּוֹן" עדד בֹֿא
המגדרה בוֹלֹוֹיֹהֹלֹֿא בֹֿ אֶמַדֹּ ﬞﬞ דְּנֹבִי שֶׁב" אוֹלֹהֹא ואכּדֹקֹא
וְשֶׁמֹי אֶת טוֹבִי וְשֹׁבֶדֹ נֹאוֹס ﬞﬞ"

וַיֹהִי מְקֵֿץ מַזְמוּר אֶמַרְתִֿי שַׁדְעֶדֹה קֹדֹבֹֿ מֶחֹטוֹֿא עדד לֹֿ
המגדרה כּוֹלֹכֹּיֹס ﬞﬞ יַֿיְצֵק שֶׁלֹמֹֹה וְהֶדֹ" אוֹלֹהֹא ואכּדהא
וַיֹהִי כַֿהֹשֹׁלֶה בֹלֹמֹתֹמֹֿה שֶׁכֹֿבֹ וֹשֶׁצֶֿאֹל"

וַיֹּגֹשֹׁ אֹלִיו מַזְמוּר הֹנֹה מֶה טוֹב וּמֶה נֶַבִֿיס" עדד קֹֿבֹֿ
המגדרה בוֹחֹוֹמֹּשֹׁ לֹֿ וַיֹהִי דְּצֶֿרֹיֶֿ וְאֶמַדֹ בֶן שֶׁחֹמֹהֹלֹֿ אוֹלֹהֹא
ואכּדהא בֹהֹיוֹת מֹֿקֹנֹֿשֹׁי קֹֿרֹוֹכֹֿ בֹדֹוֹכֹֿ וֹ

וַיֹהִי יַַעְקֹב מַזְמוּר אֶלֹהֹיס יֶַמֹבֹי וֹיֶכֹּבֹֿדֹנֹי עדד סֹֿ
המגדרה כּוֹלֹכֹּיֹס ﬞﬞ וַיֹּקֹֿדֹוֹרֹֿמֹי דֶֿוֹד לֶֿמֹדֹוֹת" אוֹלֹהֹא ואכּדהא
וַהֹבֹן עֹֿלֹכֹֿבֹֿוֹתֹן תֹֿאֹוֹד וֹ

וְאֵלֶה שֶׁמֹוֹת מַזְמוּר אֶל בֶֿמֹוֹתֹ נֶַֿ עדד צֹֿ
המגדרה בוֹחֹוֹמֹּשֹׁ ﬞﬞ וַיֹהִי דְּצֶֿרֹיֶֿ וֹ בֹנֹאֶֿבֹֿ הוֹדֹע אֶת וֹדֹֿ
אוֹלֹהֹא ואכּדהא וַיֹצֶֿא כֶֿבֹ שֶׁס בֹד בֶֿבֹֿ לֶֿאֹכֹֿרוֹמֹֿוֹק נֹאֹסֶֿדֹֿ"

ܒܐܠܡܬܗ' ܘܠܐ ܝܓܘܬ ܠܐܚܕܐ' ܬܬܨܕܩ ܥ ܟܠܝ ܒܝܬ ܝܨܐ ܐܢܗ
ܝܓܥܠܬܗ ܚܘܠܒ' ܘܐܢ ܬܗܠܘ ܥܝ ܡܢܬܗ ܝܟܢܓ ܘܐܢ ܟܐܢ ܝܓܘܪ
ܡܢܗ ܢܐܚܕ ܝܥܠܠܐ ܡܢܗ ܐܫܝܐ ܡܢ ܩܕܡ ܠܬܩܠܥ ܠܬܩܠܥ ܘܠܐܨܠܘܬ
ܘܢܢܥܝ ܡܠܐ ܕܟܓܝܠܐ ܕܠܟ ܢܬܬܐܠ ܢܥܒܘ ܟ
ܡܠܐ ܢܬܩܒܘ ܠܬܩܕܘܣܐ ܠܟܠ ܦܘܥܗ ܡܓܐܠܘܕ'
ܘܒܐܩܡܠܥܟܗ' ܡܢ ܝ ܕܒܓܐܝܣ ܝܢܟܟ

''הראשונית <u>מזמור</u> יֵשֵׁא אֱלֹובֵ֫בֶ֫ד־.ן' עֵבֶּד־ ח
המזמור בשעתיה הֵן עַבְדִּי אֶתְמָכְךָ בּוֹ' אולהא' ואכברהא
אֵלֶּה הַדְּבָרִים וַבְּשִׁיתֶה וְאֵלֹא עֵֽבֶתְּתֶּהּוֹ וֵ֫

''תולדות נח מזמור קָדוּ בֶּׁטֶׁא בְּנֵ֫י אֵבֶּסַ'' עֵבֶּד־ כֹּה
המתולדה בטלשוה יֵ֫בֵּן עֶפְרָה לֹא נֶבֵּעֶה'' אולהא' ואכברהא
וַלֹּקְדוֹשׁ ישְׂרָאֵל כִּי פָאֲרָךְ וֵ֫

'' מזמור יֵאָמִינֵיוּר וַֿהֱאַתֵּֿלֶ֫ךָ'' עֵבֶּד־ טֹוֹ
המתולדה בטלעתיה מ' וְאַבְׁגֵּי תַּֿמֵּֿדֵּׁוֵּ֫נֵּֿנֵּֿ' אולהא' ואכברהא
אֵלֹֹקֵי וֵיִּשְׂרָאֵל לֹא אֵֽעֵֽבֶדֵֿכֶה וֵ֫

''וִירָא אֵלֵ֫יוֹ מזמור בַּיָּ֫בֵּא מָחָ֫יִתֵּ אֵ֫ין ק רֵֿאֵֿאֵֿמֶ֫רֵּוֹ עֵבֶּד־ יֹֹא
המתולדה ד' וְאִשָּׁה אַחַת מִנְּשֵׁי מִדְּהַ֫בֵ''אולהא' ואכברהא
וַתִּשָּׂא אֵת בְּנָהּ וַתֵּצֵא וֵ֫

''מיי שְׂ֫לֶ֫עַ֫ה מזמור הֹושִׁיעָה יֵ֫בֵ֫ה כִּי גָּמַ֫ר חָסִ֫יד'' עֵבֶּד־ יֹֹב
המתולדה ח נֵיהֵֿמֵֿלֵֿךֵ דָּוִד זֵֽקֵֿן'' אולהא' ואכברהא
יְחִי אֵֽדֵֽנִי הַמֵּֿלֵֿךֵ דָּוִד לֵֿעֵֿוֹלֵֿם וֵ֫

ܬܘܠܕܘܬ ܝܨܚܩ

ܩܕܫ ܠܒܕܢܡ ܕܡܢܫ

וַיַּקְהֵל | מַזְמוֹר לְדָוִד קֹנַח מִנְעַד שִׁיר וְמַעֲתָן | עַבֵד פֿ

ܗܡܕܘܪܗ | ܡܠܟܒܝܣ ܕ ܙ | וַיּשַׁלַּח הַמֶּלֶךְ שְׁלֹמֹה אוֹלֵא וֿאבּדוהא
וַתֵּתֶן תָּלְאֵבֶת הָעַמּוּדִים ״

אֵלֶּה פְקוּדֵי | מַזְמוֹר זִכְרוֹנֵא לְדָוִד אֵת | עַבֵד קֹלֵב
ܗܡܕܘܪܗ | ܒܡܠܟܒܝܣ ܕ ܙ | וַנַּעַשׂ תִּירוֹסְאֵת אוֹלְהָא וֿאבּדוהא
לְדַבֵּת הַבַּיִת לַהֵיכָל זָהָב ״

וַיִּקְרָא | מַזְמוֹר לֵ אֱלֹהִים הַדָּבָר | עַבֵד ܢ
ܗܡܕܘܪܗ | ܒܘܫܥܝܗ ܕ ܐܒܕ ܥܒ ܙܘ נָצַרְתִּי אוֹלֵא וֿאבּדוהא
וּמִבַּלְעָדַי אֵין אֱלֹהִים ״

ܢܬܐܢ ܢܕܒܪ ܩܕܡܗ ܠܦܪܫܝܘܬ
ܓܕ ܡܢܢ ܠܡܢܘܒܪܘܬ

נܛܗ וַיַּקְהֵל ܐܬܐܢܒ | ܠܡܙܡܘܪ ܡܣܟܘܣ ܕܙ ܠܦܪܫܗ
ܠܗܡܕܘܪܗ ܒܘܫܥܝܗ ܕ ܢܙ ܒܙ ܟܗ אֲמַר וַיּאמֶר אוֹלֵא וֿאבּדוהא
ܐܦ ܬܐܒܝܒ ܘܡܥܒܪܬܘ ܠܝ ܢܢܘ ܒܙ ܒܙ ܒܙ ܕܒܪ ״

נܛܗ פְקוּדֵי ܐܬܐܢܒ | ܠܡܙܡܘܪ ܡܣܟܘܣ ܡ ܠܦܪܫܝܪ
ܠܗܡܕܘܪܗ ܒܡܠܟܒܝܣ ܕ ܗ וַתִּשְׁלֵמֶה כָּל הַמְּלָאכָה אוֹלֵא וֿאבּדוהא
וּבְעָוֹן מִלְּאָ לֵאמֹר ״

נܛܗ וַיִּקְרָא ܐܬܐܢܒ | ܠܡܙܡܘܪ ܡܣܟܘܣ ܡ ܕ ܠܦܪܫܗ
ܠܗܡܕܘܪܗ ܒܘܫܥܝܗ ܕ ܠܐ ܒܙ ܡܢܒܕܘܠܬܗ קָרוֹב אוֹלֵא אܒܢܗܐ
ܒܙ ܡܠܒܕܘ ܗܘܐ וֹנܫܝܒܕܘ ״

וְאִלָּא אֶלְאַבְּקְהַם מִזְמוֹר נוֹעַד בְּהוּוָדָה צָהְיִּס עדר עׁוֹ
הַפטׁורה בַּמְחֹזוֹ מ בֹא וְלֹא יִהְיֶה עוֹד לְבֵּית אֱלֹהֵא וָאבֹרְהַא
פְּתוּן פֶּה וְנַדְ נִדְכֵּי אֶבְּכֵּאֶ ─ וֹד

בָּא אֶל קַרְעִה מִזְמוֹר בְּצֵאת יִשְׂרָאֵל מִמִּצְרָיִם עדר קִיד
הַפטׁורה בֵּשַׁעֹרה מ וֹנ תֵּצֵּא מִצְרַיִם הֲנָהַר אֱלֹהֵא וָאבֹרְהַא
וּמַעֲשֵׂה יְדֵי אִשׁוּר וְנַחַלָתִי יִשְׂרָאֵל

וַיְהִי בְּנַסֹעֲךָ מִזְמוֹר הַיְדֵנוּ לֹאֱלֹהִים לְבָהָאֶרֶךְ עדר כֹּוֹ
הַפטׁורה בְּשׁוֹפֻּתַׁיִם מ ה וַיַּקָּב עַד אֱלֹהִים אֱלֹהֵא וָאבֹרְהַא
וַתִּשְׁאַקְטַ הָאָרֶץ אַרְבָּעִיס שָׁנָה

וַיִּשְׁמַע יִתְרוֹ מִזְמוֹר שִׁירוּ מֶלֶךְ כֹּל הָאָרֶץ עדר צֹן
הַפטׁורה בֵּשַׁעֹרה מ וֹ וַיֹּהְיֶה שַׁבָּתָ בַּיּוֹם אֱלֹהֵא וָאבֹרְהַא
חֲצֹעַת יַּבֵּ צְבָאוֹת מֶבֻּעֵה זָאת

מִשְׁפָּטִיס מִזְמוֹר אֱלֹהִים נִצַּב בַּעֲדַת אֵל עדר מֹבֹ
הַפטׁורה בֹּדֹאוֹ לַהֹנָּבָּר אֲשֶׁר דֹכָהֶ אֶדֹעֵיהוֹ אֱלֹהֵא וָאבֹרְהַא
בֵּן כֶּבֹד עֹדֹועֵ לַכֹּהַד כָּל הַיָּמִיס

תְּרוּמָה מִזְמוֹר מֶה יְדִידוֹת מְאֹזְבְּכֹד וְתֵנֹהֶ עדר פֹּד
הַפטׁורה בֵּמַלְכֹּיִס מ ה וַיַּבֵּ יַדֹן תַּקֹמֵה לֹא אֱלֹהֵא וָאבֹרְהַא
וְלֹא אֲעֲזוֹב אֶת עַמִּי יִשְׂרָאֵל

אַתָּה תְצֵוֶּה מִזְמוֹר זֹכּוֹר יַּבֵּ לְדָוִד אֵת כָּל בְּדֹוֹנַ עדר קֹלֹב
הַפטׁורה בַּמְחֹזוֹ מ לֹב אַתָּה בֶּן אָדָם הַגֵּד וֹד אֱלֹהֵא וָאבֹרְהַא
וְרָאֲצִיתֵ אֶתְכֶה נָאוֹס יַּבֵּ אֱלֹהִיס

כִּי תִשָּׂא מִזְמוֹר מִזְבֻּעֲטֵקְהִיס חֲמָאֵתַכְֻ וֹנָ עדר קֹלֹ
הַפטׁורה בַּמַּלֹבִיס מ וֹה וַיְהִי יַמִיס רַבִּיס לַעֲבַר יַּבֵּ אֱלֹא וָאבֹרְהַא
יַּבֵּ אֱלֹא יַבֵּ הוּא יַּבֵּ הָאֱלֹהִיס יַּבֵּ הוּא הָאֱלֹהִיס

וַיְקֻמֻ

קרס לכנס דמעם

בְּכָל יוֹם בְּרָכִיָ֫ מַזְמוֹר לֵאלֹהִים וַמַגִיד וַיִבְּדָ עדד מֹז
הُقادير ריح בחזקן ס לב וַיְהִי דָּוִד בֶּן אָדָם הָבَא עבد דُ וֹבֶּ
וַיּَבْגَאَيَ וَ אַלَّذِي וَ אלّذَها

וְהَצَלَّתُه מّעד הَ د הَدِيס בָّהِيס ''

שׁَאَيْ בَ מַזְמוֹר לוּבָה וְ אَـُرّادَ הַאَزِيهَ עדד בَ
הُادير ריح בَذُلْعُدَّ ב וَهָיה מֹפّער בَدَ וَבَدَ אַلَّה וَ אَبْדَها
וَاَنَّבَתَّיّْ ל בَ בَاَعَدَّويْ وَيُعَيّر אَתْרَيَّ ''

נَيْسَא אَת מַזְמוֹר לֵאלֹהִים וَמَجِيد וَيُבַّرَّכَنِ עدد מֹז
سَادير ريح سُوفقُديس ס יَـ וַיְהִי אִישׁ מَضَّرَ מِצَّرَ עَ וَ אַלَّها
וَ אَبْדَها وَيَـْשׁَבֶּ הَשׁَعَر וَיِבَرَّכَהُن וَيْ ''

הَدِيبَ וَרَقَّ מַזְמוֹר לَדָוَד פَﺎ אَוّْ وَ وَيَسׁْבַּ עدد בֹَ
وَابْدَها يَـסَ ريح فَبَّدَיّהَ ס בَ בَجَבֶ وَ אَשׁَمْחَىّ בَ צَ بَוֹן אَוْلُؤَ
بِّ يَـَ בَבَّاَ وَתَ שׁَبُّعَת אَכَيَّ ''

נَاَيْס لَقَّ מَזְמוֹר لَבَدَ וَיَـُ עَبَّה يَـَ צَה
هُادير ريح يَـهُوشَعَدَ ס בَ وَيَـَשَّ وَيَهُواَ וَيَشׁَاَوَّ بَرَدَوْ אَولُؤَ وَ אَبْדَها
אَتَّـَ يَـمَلَّ كَ ي بَ وَيَسَّ كَ مَلׁَكَ مَّقَّبَّدَ ''

يَـمَـْ يَـبَّح מَזْمוֹר הַאَزِينَה لَאَلَّהَים وَيَـمَبَّتَ وَ עدد نֹَ
شَـَادير ريح שَؤُؤَول ס فَ וَ אَ وَيَـّمَر شَـْمُوֹ نَـَ بَّעּَ אَلَّلَ وَ אَبْداها
بِّ هُואَיل يَـَ لَ بَـَ عَשَّאَוֹת اَسَّقَّهَ لَـَ بَـَ ''

تَّمَّ اَ לَتُّوבَה מַזְמוֹר مَحَنَّבَ אَلּَهَים كَمَمَّקَّ عدد تֹَ
سَادير ريح שَؤُفقُדيس ס نَـَ وَيَِقَמَ هَנَّبּׁَشَدَّ אَولُؤَ وَ אَبْداها
אَרَّبَّعَת مَتَّيْس بَّاَشَّעَ وَ ''

וَيَـَ بּَلَّق מַזْמוֹר اَنּَהَيْس אَל دَمَي لَ دَ وَ עدד تֹَ

201

צֵאת אַחֲרָן מִזְמוֹר נַצְחֵהֶ יָמָ בְּוֹס צָעֵר' עדֵר כֿ
הַמְּעוֹרֵהּ בּוֹלֵתֵיהּ פֿ ז כֿה צָעֵר יָמָ צְבָאוֹת מֹנֵךֿ וְיוֹצֵם פּֿמֵבִי
יִי עַנֵּר צָהֲדֵנֵה בָּאָמֵו וְבִדֵּרֵךֶ תִעֵנֵהֵם' קוֹל כֿה צָעֵר יָמָ אֶל וְתֵתֵבֹֿֿ לֹֿא לֹֿאֵבֵֿי'

בְּוֹס הַשְּׁמֵינֵיב מִזְמוֹר צֵּהֵים וַמֵבַד וְוַבָדֹֿ צֵבֵֹּ' עדֵר פֿ
הַמּעוֹרֵהּ בְּשֵׁלֹמוֹל פֿ ו נַוֹחָהֹ עֵוֹד כָּוֹד אֵת' אוֹלֹֿה
לֹא אֲשֵׁר נִתֵב בָֿה כֵֿך יֵצֵהֵ הַיָמָ בָּיָמָ בְּשֵׁך'

כִּי מֵקָרָנֵב מִזְמוֹר יָמָ מַקְרָתֵב וַתֵעֵב וַגֿ עדֵר חִלֹכֿנֵוֹ
הַמֵעוֹרֵהּ בְּהֵלֹכֿים פֿ ד וְאִישׁ יָמָ תֵעֵתֵל וַגֿ אוֹנֵהֵא וְאֹכֿדֵהֵא
וֵיֵךֵֿךְ מֵאַתֵל כֿ בֵּעֵת אֵרֵץ''

מֵצֵוֵרֵד מִזְמוֹר צָעֲרֵתֵי אַשֵׁמֵרֵה דֵבְֿבֵּ' עדֵר לֹֿהֵֿי
הַמּעוֹרֵהּ בּ מֵלֹכֿים פֿ ז נֵאֵמֵרֵי אֲבֵי שֵׁעֵד שֵׁאֵמֵנֵוֹ אוֹלֹֿהֵא וְאֹכֿדֵהֵא
וְלֹא הֵשֵׁעֵתֵהֵ מֵעֵד צֵבֵי עֵד שֵׁתֵי''

וְיֵהֵי עֵתֵל מִזְמוֹר אֵשֵׁרֵי בֵּשֵׁוִי צֵנֵעֵד גֵֿ עדֵר לֹֿגֵ
וֵוֵ . . . אֵרֵהּ בַּמֵלֹקֹֿלֹם פֿ ב וֵיֵהֵי דֵבֵרֵהֵוֹד הַתֵנֵצֵמֵנֵוֹ אֹֿלֹֿא אֹורֵהֵא
וְיֵדֵעֵת כִּי אֲנֵיב בֵּיֵ'' ..

קֵדוֹשֵׁים מִזְמוֹר תֵֿפֵהֵ לֹדֵוֹד שֵׁמֵעֵנֵב גֵ עדֵר יֵ
הַמּעוֹרֵהּ בַּמֵלֹקֹֿלֹם פֿ ב וַיֵהֵי בֵּשֵׁבֵי הַשֵׁבֵיעֵ' אֹֿלֹֿהֵא וְאֹכֿדֵהֵא
צְבֵי הֵיא לֹכֿבֵּ בָֿאֵרֵצֵוֹת''

אֵמֵוֹרֵ מִזְמוֹר זֵכֿוֹר יָמָ לֹדֵוֹד אֵתֵרֵעֵ עדֵר תֵֿלֹֿהֵ
הַמּעוֹרֵהּ בֵּתֵהֵלֵים פֿ וֹלֹ וַהֵכֿהֵנֵבֵ הַלֵֿוֵוֹם וַגֿ אֹֿלֹֿא וְאֹֿכֿבֵהֵא
לֹא וְאֹֿכֿבֵ הַהֵתֵנֵבֵם''

תֵם

קדש בגבע דוגש

שׁאֹתָבִיֹס וְשׂאֹנְבוּרֹיֹם   מזמור הָאוּתָבֹם־יֹם צָדֵק   עדו   נֹם
המגורה בֵנשָׁעֹה ה נֹא   אֶנֹבִי אֶנֹבָי הוּא וֹ אוֹלֹהָא ואבֹרהא
וֹבָאוֹכָב אַתָבֵי אֶרֶץ אֶת־וֹשָׁאוֹ־עַתָרָ הֵיכֹו

כִי תֵצֵא   מזמור לְבָוֹד בָּדוֹךְ בֵדוֹךְ בֵבֹי צַבְדֵי וֹ   עדו   קֹמֹד
המגורה וֹשׁעֹי־הַם ־ נֹ ךְ נִ בְּעֶתָ בֹּה לָאוֹ־בֹלֹי   אוֹלֹהָא ואבֹרהא
בֵבֵּ בֹה מֹ וֹעֹבֹּה וֹ אָי עֹגֹו מֹאָתֵי אָוֹ־ם נֹאֹ

וְהָיֹה כִי־תָבֹא   מזמור עֲלֵי־ס וְטָ עֲבֵי־ד וֹ וֹבַבָּ־בֹּדֵ וֹ   עדו מֹ
המגורה הֹ וֹשׁעַ נֹ ־ יֹל שָׁו וֹ־בָה וֹ נֹ אָ וֹ   אָי עֹגֹו   וָ מֹ וְשָׁעֹבֵים
בֹבֵ שֵֹ וֹ־בֹם   וְאָתֹבָ עַתָר מֹ עֹ־בֹבֹ בֹ נֹ וֹ מֹי אֹל בָּ מֹאֹ־־כֵּ   אָי עֹגֹו
אֲשֵׁר נִ בְבֵּ בָּעַתָ בֹ לֵאֹב־וֹתָ נֹ נֹ עֵמֹי־מֹי קֹבֵ־ם

אַתֵֹם נִבָּבֹנֵים   מזמור בֵּוֹה תָזֹ וְ־תֹבֵי נֹ בֹבֹ וֹ וֹ   עֹדֵו   לֹ
המגורה וֹשׁעֹי־הַם מֹ אֹ שָׁאוֹ שֶׁ אֶשָׁבֵי־שֶׁ בֵּ נֹצֵ אֹלֹהָא ואבֹרהא
אֲבֵי עֲבֵר בֹּצֵדֹ־קֹה לֵב לָה וֹשָׁאֵי־נֹ

הַאֲזֵינֹ־וֹ   מזמור לְבָוֹד מֹ־בֹא אוֹדֵי וְ נֹ שֵׁ עֹבֵי וֹ וֹ   עֹדֵו   בֹּמֹ
המגורה שֵׁאֹ־מֹאֹל מֹ בֹבֹ וֹ עֲבֵד בֹבֹוֹדֵ לֵ בֹּ   אוֹלֹהָא ואבֹרהא
לֵבֵ וֹ וֹ בְּתֵר־וֹ עֲד עֹ־וֹלֵם

וְאָתֹ־הֹ בֹ־בֹדֹתֵ בֹּה   מזמור אֵלֹהֵי־ם וֹ מֹ־עֲבֵי־ד וֹ נִ בֵּ בֹבֹ וֹ נֹ   עֹדֵו   מֹ
המגורה הֹ וֹשָׁעַד מֹ אֹ וֹ יֹהֵי אֲמֵרֵי מֹ וֹתֹ־מֹ שֶׁ אֹלֹהָא ואבֹרהא
וַיֹהֵי וֹ־יֹא אֶת יֹהוֹשָׁעַד וַיֹהֵי שֶׁ־מֹ לֹ וֹ בֹּלֵ הָאֹבֵץ

המגורה יֹוֹם תֹזֵ וֹ־עֹבֵ בֹּה בֵ שֵׁ־אֹ־לֹ מֹ אֹ וֹ יֹהֵי אֵישׁ אֹמֵ וֹ מֹי
הֹעֲמֵ־יֹם וֹ אֹבֹרהא כִּ נֹ עַבֵ־בֵן נֹ אֹ עֹ־שֵׁ לֵ־בֹבֹא כֹ־בֹ
המגורה יֹוֹם הַבֹּוֹרֵים בֹּוֹעֹ־ה בֵ אֹ וֹ יֹהֵי־וֹ בֹּ־וֹ יֹאֹ אֵל וֹ לֹה וֹ
וֹ עֹגֹו וֹ הֹ־וֹ־ה וַבֹּה : קֹוֹל מֹי אֹל־בֹּ־וֹךְ לֵאבֹרה

הַמְּסֹרָה עֹלֹבֹ ה ה וְהָיָה שְׁאֵרִית יַעֲקֹב אוּלְהָא וְאכֹרהָא
וְהַצְבִּיעַ לְכֵּתֶּר בֹּם אֲנֹהֵיךְ וּגֹ

מִנְחָם מִזְמוֹר שָׁבִיתִי מִנְשַׁפֹּא וְצֶדֶק עֵדֶר קָיָם
הַמְּסֹרָה עֹלֹבּים סֹ' יֹ' וְעֵד יָשׁ הַיָּמָה זְנֻיְתוֹ אוּלְהָא וְאכֹרהָא
וַיֹּאמֶר אֶזְבְּדו וַיְשָׁרְתֵהו

אֵלֶּה מַסְעֵי מִזְמוֹר קֹלֹ דְּאֹדִיס וְאַצְעַמֵה וּגֹ עֵדֶר נֹן
הַמְּסֹרָה יְשַׁעֹיֹה סֹ' מֹ' נַעֲתוּ נַתֲעוּ עַתֲתוּ אוּלְהָא וְאכֹרהָא
אֲנַחֹ יֹהֹ יְשֹׁכְּבָי לֹא אֲעֹתֲבֶם

אֵלֶּה הַדְּבָרִים מִזְמוֹר הַעֲמָעִיס וְהַפְּלִיס עֵדֶר יֹט
הַמְּסֹרָה יִרְמֹיֹה סֹ' לֹ' וְאֵלֶּה הַדְּבָרִים אֲשֶׁר אוּלְהָא וְאכֹרהָא
וְעַבֹּדִי אֶת דָּוֹד יְשֹׁבֹּגו בְּאוּס בֹּאֹנֹה בֹּכֹ

וְאַתֲעֹיֵם מִזְמוֹר תֲפֹּכֶה לְדָוִד שִׂמְעָה אֵל צֶדֶק וּגֹ עֵדֶר זֹן
הַמְּסֹרָה יִרמֹיֹה סֹ' לֹב וְאֶתֲפֹּכֹד אֶת יֹש אֹלֹ אֲפֹרהָא
לְחֹאוֹב לָהֶם וְלַבֹּנֵיהֶם אֲחֲרֵיהֶם וּגֹ

וְהֹיֹה יַעֲקֹב מִזְמוֹר בַּד לְשֹׁכֹּבֹ דְּבָרֶיךָ וּגֹ עֵדֶר קָיָם
הַמְּסֹרָה יְשַׁעֹיֹה סֹ' מֹ' וַנֹּאמֶר צִיֹּן עֲזָבַ אוּלְהָא וְאכֹרהָא
יְהֹוֹה בְּאֹס יֹא וְיֹש בִּדֹן בֹּאֹלֹהָי

רְאֵה אָנֹכִי מִזְמוֹר לְיָש בֹּאֲרֶץ וּמֹלֹוֹאֵהֹ וּגֹ עֵדֶר בֹֹל
הַמְּסֹרָה יְשַׁעֹיֹה סֹ' גֹל עֲנֹבֹךְ סֹוֹעֲרָה אוּלְהָא וְאכֹרהָא
וְהֵקֹלֹוֹאוֹ יִשְׂרָאֵל כִּי פֹאֲרֹךְ וּגֹ

שׁוֹפְטִים

204

קדיש לבתר דימשׁ

אתקלה מא רחמד / ואתבסא זל קראה הַאֲזִינֵו/ בּולב
ראחד מן לאסבוע כאב אנתא / ותֵּקלה בּעבד לאן
ומא ה ותֵּקלה מנא ה בּדינתבֹ טאנתרלוס תֹאחד
שבוֹיס הַאֲב עבד מֵקוֹס וִיתִּי / בַּתֵּלוּשׁה וּ תא אמן

וַיְדַבֵּר מֹשֶׁה

בְּאָזְנֵי כָּל קְהַל   יִשְׂרָאֵל אֶת דִּבְרֵי
הַשִּׁירָה הַזֹּאת   עַד   תֻּמָּם :

הַאֲזִינוּ הַשָּׁמַיִם וַאֲדַבֵּרָה

וְתִשְׁמַע הָאָרֶץ אִמְרֵי פִי : יַעֲרֹף כַּמָּטָר לִקְחִי
תִּזַּל כַּטַּל אִמְרָתִי כִּשְׂעִירִים עֲלֵי דֶשֶׁא וְכִרְבִיבִים
עֲלֵי עֵשֶׂב : כִּי שֵׁם יְיָ אֶקְרָא הָבוּ גֹדֶל
לֵאלֹהֵינוּ : הַצּוּר תָּמִים פָּעֳלוֹ כִּי כָל דְּרָכָיו
מִשְׁפָּט אֵל אֱמוּנָה וְאֵין עָוֶל צַדִּיק וְיָשָׁר הוּא :
שִׁחֵת לוֹ לֹא בָּנָיו מוּמָם דּוֹר עִקֵּשׁ וּפְתַלְתֹּל :
הֲלַיְיָ תִּגְמְלוּ זֹאת עַם נָבָל וְלֹא חָכָם הֲלוֹא
הוּא אָבִיךָ קָנֶךָ הוּא עָשְׂךָ וַיְכֹנְנֶךָ : זְכֹר
יְמוֹת עוֹלָם בִּינוּ שְׁנוֹת דּוֹר וָדוֹר שְׁאַל אָבִיךָ
וְיַגֵּדְךָ זְקֵנֶיךָ וְיֹאמְרוּ לָךְ : בְּהַנְחֵל עֶלְיוֹן
גּוֹיִם בְּהַפְרִידוֹ בְּנֵי אָדָם יַצֵּב גְּבוּלֹת עַמִּים
לְמִסְפַּר בְּנֵי יִשְׂרָאֵל : כִּי חֵלֶק יְיָ עַמּוֹ יַעֲקֹב

205

הפטרה יום אחד הסוכות   זכריה ס יד וְהָיָה אֶת הַיּוֹם הַהוּא
אולה ואכרהא   צְבָאוֹת בַּיּוֹם הַהוּא ''

הפטרה שבת פורים   שמואל ס טו וַיֹּאמֶר שְׁמוּאֵל
אינהא ואכרהא וְהֵם שָׁמוּעַ וַיָּבֶן הָרְמָתָה ''

הפטרה יום אחד המצות   יהושע ס ג וַיֹּאמֶר יְהוֹשֻׁעַ
אולהא ואכרהא לֵוִי שָׁמַ וּ כָּל הָאָרֶץ וג

הפטרה שבת קֹדֶש ביחזקאל ס לז כֹּה אָמַר אֲדֹנָי עֹוד זֹאת וג
אולהא ואכרהא כָּיָ דָוִד עַבְדִּי וּבָרִיתִי נָאוּם ''

הפטרה יום שבּבּ יְעֶצֶת בֵּית דָּוִד וְהִי תקרֹאת שלֹ
מוּשָׁה הָעֵינָי

הפטרה תֵּם הַשְׁבוּעות ביחזֹקא ס א וַיְהִי בִּשְׁלֹשִׁים שָׁנָה וג
אולהא ואכרהא בָּרוּךְ כְּבוֹד יְיָ מִמְּקוֹמוֹ ''

הפטרה שבת וְהוּא חֹלֵש ישעיה ס סו כֹּה אָמַר יְיָ
הַשָּׁמַיִם כִּסְאִי אולהא ואכרהא יָבוֹא כָל בָּשָׂר
כָּל נִשְׁמַתֹות לְפָנַי אָמַר יְיָ :

אַלֵּה מָא יִכָּתֵב שַׁבַּת אן יכֹ מִתַּחַל מָה רֹוּסָה יקֹרָא מָה
שָׂלֹא אָשֹׁלֹא בֵּינַהֻ וג וְהִי הפטרה אֵתֹם נִצָּבִים
כֻּלֻּהֻם מַ הַאֹ הֹנֹ וֹלֹבֹ

חֵעלֹה

206

חֶדֶשׁ לְבֻדַּם וּעֲשֵׂ

וּבְחוּנֵי הִשְׂגָּה וְחָטְבֵ מְיִדִי וְשֵׁן בְּהֻמוֹת אֲשַׁלַּח בַּם
בְּם חֲמַת זֹחֲלֵי עָפַר : מְיחוּץ תְּשַׁבֶּל מֶרֶב
וּמֵחֲדָרִים אֵימָה גַּם בָּחוּר גַּם בְּתוּלָה וּוּנֵק עַם אִישׁ
שֵׂיבָה : אָמַרְתִּי אַפְאֵיהֶם אַשְׁבִּיתָה מֵאֲנוֹשׁ זִכְרָם :
לוּלֵי כַּעַם אוֹיֵב אָגוּר פֶּן יְנַכְּרוּ צָרֵימוֹ פֶּן יֹאמְרוּ
יָדֵינוּ רָמָה וְלֹא יְהֹוָה פָּעַל כָּל זֹאת : כִּי גוֹי אוֹבֵד
עֵצוֹת הֵמָּה וְאֵין בָּהֶם תְּבוּנָה : לוּ חָכְמוּ יַשְׂכִּילוּ זֹאת
יָבִינוּ לְאַחֲרִיתָם : אֵיכָה יִרְדֹּף אֶחָד אֶלֶף וּשְׁנַיִם
יָנִיסוּ רְבָבָה אִם לֹא כִּי צוּרָם מְכָרָם וַיהֹוָה הִסְגִּירָם :
כִּי לֹא כְצוּרֵנוּ צוּרָם וְאֹיְבֵינוּ פְּלִילִים : כִּי מִגֶּפֶן
סְדֹם גַּפְנָם וּמִשַּׁדְמֹת עֲמֹרָה עֲנָבֵמוֹ עִנְּבֵי רוֹשׁ אַשְׁכְּלֹת
מְרֹרֹת לָמוֹ : חֲמַת תַּנִּינִם
יֵינָם וְרֹאשׁ פְּתָנִים אַכְזָר : הֲלֹא הוּא כָּמֻס עִמָּדִי
חָתוּם בְּאוֹצְרֹתָי : לִי נָקָם וְשִׁלֵּם לְעֵת תָּמוּט
רַגְלָם כִּי קָרוֹב יוֹם אֵידָם וְחָשׁ עֲתִדֹת לָמוֹ :
כִּי יָדִין יְהֹוָה עַמּוֹ וְעַל עֲבָדָיו יִתְנֶחָם כִּי יִרְאֶה כִּי
אָזְלַת יָד וְאֶפֶס עָצוּר וְעָזוּב : וְאָמַר אֵי אֱלֹהֵימוֹ
צוּר חָסָיוּ בוֹ : אֲשֶׁר חֵלֶב זְבָחֵימוֹ יֹאכֵלוּ יִשְׁתּוּ
יֵין נְסִיכָם יָקוּמוּ וְיַעְזְרֻכֶם יְהִי עֲלֵיכֶם סִתְרָה :
רְאוּ עַתָּה כִּי אֲנִי אֲנִי הוּא וְאֵין אֱלֹהִים
עִמָּדִי אֲנִי אָמִית וַאֲחַיֶּה מָחַצְתִּי וַאֲנִי אֶרְפָּא

חֲבֵב יִחֲלֶתוֹ : וַיּוֹצִאֵהוּ בְּאֶרֶץ מִדְבָּר וּבְתֹהוּ יְלֵל
יְשִׁימֹן יְסֹבְבֶנְהוּ יְבוֹנְנֵהוּ יִצְּרֶנְהוּ כְּאִישׁוֹן עֵינוֹ :
כְּנֶשֶׁר נָעִיר קִנּוֹ עַל גּוֹזָלָיו יְרַחֵף יִפְרוֹשׂ כְּנָפָיו
יִקָּחֵהוּ יִשָּׂאֵהוּ עַל אֶבְרָתוֹ : יְיָ בָּדָד יַנְחֶנּוּ וְאֵין
עִמּוֹ אֵל נֵכָר : יַרְכִּבֵהוּ עַל בָּמֳתֵי אֶרֶץ וַיֹּאכַל
תְּנוּבֹת שָׂדָי וַיֵּנִקֵהוּ דְבַשׁ מִסֶּלַע וְשֶׁמֶן מֵחַלְמִישׁ
צוּר : חֶמְאַת בָּקָר וַחֲלֵב צֹאן עִם חֵלֶב כָּרִים וְאֵילִים
בְּנֵי בָשָׁן וְעַתּוּדִים עִם חֵלֶב כִּלְיוֹת חִטָּה וְדַם עֵנָב
תִּשְׁתֶּה חָמֶר : וַיִּשְׁמַן יְשֻׁרוּן וַיִּבְעָט שָׁמַנְתָּ
עָבִיתָ כָּשִׂיתָ וַיִּטֹּשׁ אֱלוֹהַּ עָשָׂהוּ וַיְנַבֵּל צוּר
יְשֻׁעָתוֹ : יַקְנִאֻהוּ בְּזָרִים בְּתוֹעֵבֹת יַכְעִיסֻהוּ
יִזְבְּחוּ לַשֵּׁדִים לֹא אֱלֹהַּ אֱלֹהִים לֹא יְדָעוּם מֵחֲדָשִׁים
מִקָּרֹב בָּאוּ לֹא שְׂעָרוּם אֲבֹתֵיכֶם : צוּר יְלָדְךָ
תֶּשִׁי וַתִּשְׁכַּח אֵל מְחֹלְלֶךָ : וַיַּרְא יְיָ וַיִּנְאָץ
מִכַּעַס בָּנָיו וּבְנֹתָיו : וַיֹּאמֶר אַסְתִּירָה פָנַי
מֵהֶם אֶרְאֶה מָה אַחֲרִיתָם כִּי דוֹר תַּהְפֻּכֹת הֵמָּה
בָּנִים לֹא אֵמֻן בָּם : הֵם קִנְאוּנִי בְלֹא אֵל כִּעֲסוּנִי
בְּהַבְלֵיהֶם וַאֲנִי אַקְנִיאֵם בְּלֹא עָם בְּגוֹי נָבָל
אַכְעִיסֵם : כִּי אֵשׁ קָדְחָה בְאַפִּי וַתִּיקַד עַד שְׁאוֹל
תַּחְתִּית וַתֹּאכַל אֶרֶץ וִיבֻלָהּ וַתְּלַהֵט מוֹסְדֵי הָרִים :
אַסְפֶּה עָלֵימוֹ רָעוֹת חִצַּי אֲכַלֶּה בָּם : מְזֵי רָעָב

המחבר

וְאֵין מִזְּוֹ מַצִּל : כִּי אֶשָּׂא אֶל שָׁמַיִם יָדִי וְאָמַ

כִּי אָנֹכִי לְעֹלָם : אִם שַׁנּוֹתִי בְּרַק חַרְבִּ

וְתֹאחֵז בְּמִשְׁפָּט יָדִי אָשִׁיב נָקָם לְצָרַי וְלִמְשַׂנְאַי

אֲשַׁלֵּם : אַשְׁכִּיר חִצַּי מִדָּם וְחַרְבִּי תֹּאכַל בָּשָׂר

מִדַּם חָלָל וְשִׁבְיָה מֵרֹאשׁ פַּרְעוֹת אוֹיֵב :

הַרְנִינוּ גוֹיִם עַמּוֹ כִּי דַם עֲבָדָיו יִקּוֹם וְנָקָם יָשִׁיב

לְצָרָיו וְכִפֶּר אַדְמָתוֹ עַמּוֹ : וַיָּבֹא

מֹשֶׁה וַיְדַבֵּר אֶת כָּל דִּבְרֵי הַשִּׁירָה הַזֹּאת בְּאָזְנֵי

הָעָם הוּא וְהוֹשֵׁעַ בִּן נוּן : וַיְכַל מֹשֶׁה לְדַבֵּר

אֶת כָּל הַדְּבָרִים הָאֵלֶּה אֶל כָּל יִשְׂרָאֵל :

וַיֹּאמֶר אֲלֵהֶם שִׂימוּ לְבַבְכֶם לְכָל הַדְּבָרִים

אֲשֶׁר אָנֹכִי מֵעִיד בָּכֶם הַיּוֹם אֲשֶׁר תְּצַוֻּם אֶת

בְּנֵיכֶם לִשְׁמֹר לַעֲשׂוֹת אֶת כָּל דִּבְרֵי הַתּוֹרָה

הַזֹּאת : כִּי לֹא דָבָר רֵק הוּא מִכֶּם כִּי הוּא

חַיֵּיכֶם וּבַדָּבָר הַזֶּה תַּאֲרִיכוּ יָמִים עַל הָאֲדָמָה

אֲשֶׁר אַתֶּם עֹבְרִים אֶת הַיַּרְדֵּן שָׁמָּה לְרִשְׁתָּהּ :

אֵין כָּאֵל יְשֻׁרוּן רֹכֵב שָׁמַיִם בְּעֶזְרֶךָ וּבְגַאֲוָתוֹ

שְׁחָקִים : מְעֹנָה אֱלֹהֵי קֶדֶם וּמִתַּחַת

זְרֹעֹת עוֹלָם וַיְגָרֶשׁ מִפָּנֶיךָ אוֹיֵב וַיֹּאמֶר

הַשְׁמֵד : וַיִּשְׁכֹּן יִשְׂרָאֵל בֶּטַח בָּדָד עֵין יַעֲקֹב

אֶל אֶרֶץ דָּגָן וְתִירוֹשׁ אַף שָׁמָיו יַעַרְפוּ טָל :

חזק

בשם יי נעשה ונצליח

נבתדי אולא בתרתיב קראה פרשיות בתורה ואקול יגלי ויא עלי
טול לסנה תבתדי מן תאני יום שמיני עצרת פרשה בראשית
ולו אתפק שמיני עצרת יום לומענה אקראהא פי לשבת עלי
ספר תורה יגלי ויא   ותם עלי לכיאל כל סבת פרשה אלא
ישֶה תָצֶוֶה יתהאג יכון פיהא שבת פרשה פוליס ולו אנך תקבמאהא
יאן פי בעץ אוקאת ירתפן פה כי תשא פיתהאג לקסס ושתא
אשֶר תְצֶוֶה לאגל שבת כי תשא   ותם אלו פָרָשׁה וַיִקְהֵל
פֿוּדֵי אחתכב לֿהסאב אן תכון פרשה צו אֵת אַהֲרֹן פי שַׁבֶּת
שַׁבַּתּוֹן מוֹעֵד חַג הַמַּצּוֹת   ואן כאן לזמאן צייק אֵנַגֵעֵ וַיַּקְהֵל
וְאֵלֶה פְּקוּדֵי סוא   ואן אתפך יום ראשון של חג הַמַצּוֹת
לשבת תחתאג תבתדי פה פרשה צו   ואן אתפך יום ראשון
חג הַמַצּוֹת יום לאחד תתחתאג תנמנע אֵחֲרֵי מוֹת וּקְדֹשִׁים
מענה לאן מבאדך תבתדי ספר וַיִקְרָא פי לשבת לוי יעקבדה
חג הַשָּׁבוּעוֹת   ותם אלו פרשה רָאֵשֵׁי וּמַסְעֵי   אחתב
יכאב מתה נצבים לאן תתחתאג תקראהא והבתעהא פי יום
כמור לאגל כתם לתורה יגלי ויא פי יום שמיני עצרת ואן
ראית לזמאן צייק אנמע ראשי ומסעי סוא ואיצא
פי לפנן לכלאים עלי הדה לקאעדה   למרכורה לא תזיד
ולא תנקץ ושלום

נבתדי בתרתיב קראה לפרשיות ותקאסימהא עלי ספר תורה
מי יְמֵי הַחוֹל וְהַשַׁבָּתוֹת   וְרַאֵשֵׁי חֵדַשִׁים   וִימֵי הַמוֹעַדִים
ומעא יתהאג לאמר ליה עלי טול לסנה

THE DATE OF THE MEKILTA DE-RABBI ISHMAEL

SCHOLARLY papers can derive from any one of a variety of stimuli or a combination of them. The present paper derives from a series of problems which have compelled me to search the material as well as myself. This paper represents a most untraditional approach to a book inordinately precious to me. I found myself resisting the logic of my observations, simply because the conclusion to which I was drawn represents an about-face from my traditional approach to the literature. Nevertheless, the issues are compelling enough to be presented in the arena of notice where my peers can consider my present handling of the array of problems.

The Mekilta de-Rabbi Ishmael contains halakic and aggadic comments on sections of the Book of Exodus. It is the consensus of scholars (to wit, Zunz, Weiss, Friedmann, Hoffmann, Bacher, Lauterbach, Ginzberg, J. N. Epstein, Finkelstein) that the Mekilta of Rabbi Ishmael reflects the second century tannaitic halakah.[1] In his

---

[1] L. Zunz, *Die gottesdienstlichen Vorträge der Juden*[2] (Frankfurt a.M., 1892), pp. 49–53, dates the sources of the halakic midrashim at the latest in the first half of the third century, though he grants that the Mekilta was edited later. I. H. Weiss (ed.), *Mechilta* (Wien, 1865), pp. XVIII f., argues that the anonymous sections of the Mekilta emanated from Ishmael's academy, but that a substantial part was added later, some of it by the amoraim, with Rab (Abba Arikha) as its final editor. M. Friedmann, *Mechilta de-Rabbi Ismael* (Wien, 1870), pp. XVI ff., rejected Weiss' hypothesis that Rab was the Mekilta's editor. Friedmann argues that this book was known to the talmudists as Sifre or Sifra, works which were known as *halakah* and differed in structure from *mishnah*. A. Geiger, *Urschrift*[2] (Frankfurt a.M., 1928), pp. 140 f., regards the Mekilta as a depository of premishnaic halakah. D. Hoffmann, *Zur Einleitung in die halachischen Midraschim* (Berlin, 1886–87), pp. 3 ff., 36 ff., believes that all *baraithot* of the Talmud which present the halakah as it is derived from scriptural verses were originally part of the halakic midrashim, now lost. A substantial part of this tannaitic exegesis, though not preserved in the Talmud, is to be found in works such as the Mekilta. W. Bacher, *Die exegetische Terminologie der Tannaiten* (Leipzig, 1899), tr. into Hebrew (Tel Aviv, 1923), follows Hoffmann's principles. For Lauterbach, see next note. Finkelstein, see note 3. J. N. Epstein (ed. posthumously by E. Z. Melamed), *Introduction to Tannaitic Literature, Mishna, Tosephta, and Halakhic Midrashim* (in Hebrew, Jerusalem, 1957), pp. 501 ff., traces the material of the halakic midrashim, including the Mekilta, to Ezra, LXX, Philo, and to the schools of Akiba and Ishmael, but the anonymous passages of the Mekilta

117

masterly edition of the Mekilta, Lauterbach summed up the prevailing point of view: "Both in its halakic and haggadic portions the *Mekilta* shows itself to be one of the older tannaitic works. It contains very old material and has preserved teachings of the early Tannaim. Its halakic teachings in many instances reflect the point of view of the older Halakah, which was different from that of the later or younger Halakah; hence some of its interpretations of the law are not in agreement with the interpretations accepted in the Talmud."[2] Finkelstein has raised the question whether the haggadic material was not a later interpolation, but he endorses the view that the Mekilta indeed reflects the Ishmaelite school of biblical exegesis which interpreted Scripture more literally than the rival school of Rabbi Akiba.[3]

In this study the question is raised whether the Mekilta de-Rabbi Ishmael should be regarded as an authentically tannaitic midrash or whether this work is instead a posttalmudic compilation or, indeed, concoction, deliberately using the names of tannaim for authority, or even inventing names. For the purpose of this paper, it is assumed that our inherited Mekilta is a unitary work; this assumption will be defended below. Here it suffices to say that both the halakic and haggadic sections of the entire Mekilta cite the same names, use a similar vocabulary, and display the same general characteristics of the book as a whole.[4] This study discusses only the Mekilta of Rabbi

---

emanate only from the latter (pp. 550–568). E. Z. Melamed, *Halachic Midrashim of the Tannaim in the Talmud Babli* (in Hebrew, Jerusalem, 1943), follows the path of his mentor Epstein, but his compilation of the talmudic exegetical comments in effect has created a new halakic midrash.

[2] J. Z. Laut(erbach), ed., *Mekilta de-Rabbi Ishmael* (New York, 1933), p. XIX (cf. below, note 28). See also his "Midrash and Mishnah," *JQR*, N. S. 5–6, (1916), dating the terminology of the halakic midrashim to the pre-Hasmonean period, subsequent to which the Mishnah form was introduced.

[3] L. Finkelstein, "The Sources of the Tannaitic Midrashim," *JQR*, N. S. 31 (1941), pp. 211–243, reacts to Ch. Albeck's (cited below, note 85) finding that the halakic midrashim had made use of our talmudic texts. Finkelstein reiterates Hoffmann's thesis (*Zur Einleitung*, pp. 72 ff.), that in addition to Ishmael's Mekilta on Exodus there existed in the talmudic period an Ishmaelite Mekilta on the remaining three books of the Torah; the extant Sifre on Numbers belongs also to this school. The aggadic material of the Mekilta on Exodus, Finkelstein grants, originated from an independent midrash, subsequently joined with the much older halakic Mekilta. See also below note 17.

[4] Lauterbach, "The Arrangement and the Division of the Mekilta," *HUCA* 1 (1924), p. 434; *Mekilta* 1, pp. XVI–XVIII, defends the integrity of the Mekilta. Epstein, *Introduction to Tannaitic Literature*, pp. 572–588, argues that the nine sections originally were independent treatises, each of which has a different proportion of Akiba's or Ishmael's school; but he grants that the halakic and haggadic material within each treatise emanated from the same editor. Cf. the previous note.

Ishmael. Yet much of what is said here of the Mekilta of Ishmael applies also to the Mekilta of Rabbi Simeon ben Yoḥai, possibly an imitation of the former.[5] Respecting the Sifra, Sifré, and Sifré Zutta the question remains open, though obviously the problems confronting the reader of the Mekilta are interwoven with those of the other halakic midrashim.[6]

The nub of the paper involves the question of the date of the author(s) or editor(s) of the Mekilta.

I

The oldest testimony to the existence of a Mekilta comes from the first half of the ninth century. There was written about this time the first extensive rabbinic code, Simeon Kayyara's *Halakhot Gedolot*; it refers to our book as Mekilta on Exodus.[7] Despite this reference,

[5] The Mekilta de-Rabbi Simeon ben Yoḥai was first published by Hoffmann (Frankfurt a.M., 1905) from quotations of the Midrash Hagadol on Exodus by the fifteenth-century Saadia ben David al-Adani of Yemen (ed. Margulies, Jerusalem, 1955). This Mekilta was edited on the basis of Mss. by E. Z. Melamed (from J. N. Epstein's notes, Jerusalem, 1955). Cf. now Karl Gottfried Eckart, *Untersuchungen zur Traditionsgeschichte der Mechiltha* (Berlin, 1959), though Eckart used Hoffmann's archaic edition. It is clear that for the most part the Mekilta of Simeon reproduces the one of Ishmael, but sometimes modifies the text to bring the tannaitic midrash into greater conformity with the tannaitic exegesis of the Babylonian Talmud.

[6] Stylistically and structurally all of these halakic midrashim appear to be similar, the differences being mainly in the amount of aggadic material and the names of the authorities listed. But the matter requires detailed analysis to determine whether or not the same author wrote all of these works.

[7] *Halakhot Gedolot* ([ed. Warsaw, 1875], 144a; [Berlin, 1888], pp. 633 f.), lists the number of the biblical books, Mishnah, Tosafot (Tosefta). But both texts, though differing, are corrupt:

Warsaw ed.	*Berlin ed.*
ושׁשׁה סדרי תוספות ותשעה דבורים תורת	ששׁה סדרי תוספות ותשעה [דיבורים] שׁל תורת
כוהנים וארבעה מדרש סופרים ספרא וספרי	כהנים וארבעה מדרש סופרים חצונות וקטנות אין
שהם ארבעה ספרי ואלו הן בראשית רבה	מספר ספרא וספרי שהן ד' ספרי ואילו הן
ומכילתא דואלה שׁמות וספר	בראשית רבה ומכלתי דאלה שׁמות
וידבר ואלה הדברים וכולהו פירושם בתורת	וכולהו פירושׁין בתורת כהנים וחיצונות וקטנות
כוהנים וחיצונות וקטנות אין מספר	לעל . . . .

The meaning of this passage (cf. Num. Rabbah XVIII, 21; Tanḥuma, *Koraḥ*, 12) is not clear. Because it is the oldest extant summary of rabbinic literature, a rough paraphrase is offered in English: "And six orders of Tosafot (Tosefta); and nine sections (?) of the Priestly Code (Sifra on Leviticus); and four scriptural midrashim, called Sifre and Sifra, consisting of four books: Genesis Rabbah, Mekilta of Exodus, the Book of Numbers and Deuteronomy. And all of these books are commentaries

the evidence is nevertheless clear that the Mekilta was not used as a source for the *Halakhot Gedolot* (neither in its French nor Spanish version).[8] Saadia Gaon (died in 942) not only refers to the Mekilta on Exodus, but directly cites it, this apparently supplying the first verifiable citation.[9] Samuel Hanagid of Granada (died in 953), in his introduction to the Talmud, appears to be the first who names the book the *Mekilta de-Rabbi Ishmael.*[10] However, Hanagid lists this title among works such as the "Mishnah of Rabbi Eliezer ben Jacob" and the "Alphabet of Rabbi Akiba;" the former is known to us from an obscure talmudic reference to a work lost centuries before Hanagid's time;[11] the latter is a medieval pseudograph parading under Akiba's name.[12] Hence, Hanagid's testimony is necessarily uncertain.

Extensive verifiable references begin to appear in about the year 1000, becoming numerous in the eleventh and twelfth centuries. Hai Gaon (died in 1038) cites the book as the Mekilta of the Land of Israel;[13] the lexicographer Yeḥiel ben Nathan of Rome (died in 1106)[14]

(like?) in the Priestly Code (Sifra?); and (in addition to these books there are) numerous apocryphal and minor books . . . ." (The passage goes on to quote B. Sukkah 28a).

Although the meaning is somewhat obscure, it is nevertheless clear that the *Halakhot Gedolot* believed that the Sifra was the oldest of all midrashic works, and that Genesis Rabbah, Mekilta, and Sifre were modeled after it.

[8] Hildesheimer, in the index (p. 136) to his edition of the *Halakot Gedolot*, cites ten references where the Mekilta was presumably used by the geonic author. But an analysis of these passages shows that they were derived from the Babylonian Talmud, not from the Mekilta, though there is no doubt that the *Halakhot Gedolot* did cite the Sifra and Sifre. Thus for example, Hildesheimer cites Pasḥa, X, p. 34; Laut. I, 77 f., as the source of a passage in *Halakhot Gedolot*, p. 59a (Warsaw ed.); p. 139 (Berlin ed.). But it is likely that the source used here was B. Pesaḥim, 43a, whose wording is closer to that of the *Halakhot Gedolot* than is the text of the Mekilta.

[9] Harkavy in *Hakedem* I (1907), p. 127, citing Mekilta, *Baḥodesh* 10, p. 239; Laut. 2, 276. In citations from the Mekilta, the pagination refers to the editions of Horowitz-Rabin, Berlin, 1930, 2nd ed., Jerusalem, 1960, followed by that of Lauterbach, New York, 1933 (3 volumes).

[10] See Samuel Hanagid, *Introduction to the Talmud*, usually printed at the end of B. Berakhot.

[11] See B. Yevamot 49b; cited also 37a, 60a, etc.: "The Mishnah of R. Eliezer b. Jacob is small but excellent" (משנת ר' אליעזר בן יעקב קב ונקי). This is not to be confused with Mishnat R. Eliezer (or, by its other name, "Midrash Rabbi Eliezer of the Thirty-two Hermeneutic Rules"; also known as Midrash Agur) on Prov. 30, or Pirke de-Rabbi-Eliezer, mentioned below.

[12] See Zunz, *Gott. Vort.*, p. 178 (Hebrew ed., p. 333, n. 67).

[13] A. Harkavy, *Teshuvot Hageonim* (Berlin, 1887), p. 107, Hai Gaon's responsum to Samuel Hanagid.

[14] See A. Kohut's *Index to Arukh Completum* 107b for references to the Mekilta.

and Rashi (died in 1105), refer to the book as Mekilta;[15] and the eleventh-century talmudic scholar of North Africa — Nissim ben Jacob — names it the Mekilta of Rabbi Ishmael.[16]

It remained for Maimonides to give a precise formulation: "The sages of the Mishnah also composed other works which expounded upon the words of the Torah: Rabbi Hosha'ya, the pupil of the saintly Rabbi (Judah Hanasi), wrote a commentary on the Book of Genesis (Rabbah); and *Rabbi Ishmael expounded upon from the beginning of Exodus till the end of the Torah* — and this is called Mekilta. And Rabbi Akiba also was the author of a Mekilta. But other sages authored midrashim as well. All of these works were composed before the Babylonian Talmud."[17] This is not the place to comment upon these enigmatic, and in my judgment, erroneous, words. It would seem, however, that Maimonides already was in possession of the Mekilta de-Rabbi Simeon ben Yoḥai in addition to the Mekilta de-Rabbi Ishmael.[18] Since Maimonides had no inherited tradition by which to explain the authorship of either Genesis Rabbah or of the halakic midrashim, he was the first to infer that the names Rabbi Hosha'ya or Rabbi Ishmael (the first authorities cited in the relevant texts) referred to authorship.[19] He further reasoned that since one Mekilta was authored by Rabbi Ishmael, the other halakic midrash must have been authored by Ishmael's contemporary, Rabbi Akiba. It is evident that the standard assumption of the existence of two tannaitic midrashic works — those by Ishmael and Akiba — rests primarily upon Maimonides.[20]

[15] The Mekilta de-Rabbi Ishmael was Rashi's favorite source on the relevant sections of Exod. 12:1 ff.; Rashi did not use the Mekilta of Simeon ben Yoḥai.

[16] See Nissim's commentary on Shabbath 106b printed in the margins of the Wilno editions of the Talmud.

[17] Maimonides, *Yad*, Introduction. Cf. D. Hoffmann, *Midrasch Tannaim zum Deut.* (Berlin, 1909), pp. IV ff. and Finkelstein, above note 3, who uphold Maimonides' statement that the Mekilta of Ishmael extended from Exodus to Deuteronomy.

[18] For the opinion that Maimonides utilized both midrashim (cf. n. 5), see Finkelstein, "Maimonides and the Tannaitic Midrashim," *JQR*, N. S. 25 (1935), pp. 469–517. Kasher, *Mekore Ha-Rambam* (New York, 1943), claims to have traced 100 passages of Maimonides to the Mekilta of Simeon b. Yoḥai.

[19] Cf. Albeck, Introduction to Genesis Rabbah being part of vol. 3 of *Midrash Bereshit Rabba*² . . . ed. . . . by J. Theodor and Ch. Albeck (Hebrew, Jerusalem, 1965), pp. 93 f., who shows that though the early medieval rabbis dubbed our Genesis Rabbah as Midrash of Rabbi Hosha'ya, it does not necessarily follow that they intended to refer to authorship; they merely wished to identify the introductory words.

[20] Maimonides' position is upheld by Finkelstein, *JQR*, N. S. 31 (1941), pp. 211–213. See also Friedmann, *Mechilta*, pp. LXVII ff.

There remains the possibility, however, that the amoraim of the Babylonian Talmud knew the Mekilta of Rabbi Ishmael but under different names, such as "The School of Rabbi Ishmael," or Sifra, or Sifre.[21] In fact, Maimonides, on the basis of a questionable reference in Berakhot 11b, attributed these latter works to Rab, the founder of the Academy of Sura in the year 219.[22] I do not know the meaning of the much-commented-on passage, in Sanhedrin 86a, by Rabbi Yoḥanan (died 279): "Unless otherwise stated, the Mishnah is by Rabbi Meir; unless otherwise stated, the Tosefta is by Rabbi Nehemiah; . . . Sifra is by Rabbi Judah; . . . Sifre is by Rabbi Simeon: all of them follow (the teachings of) Rabbi Akiba."[23] There seems little likelihood that these works listed in this passage knew of a midrash emanating from the School of Rabbi Ishmael.[24] The frequent references in the Babylonian Talmud to a tanna of the school of Ishmael have nothing to do with either the text or traditions of the Mekilta under consideration.[25]

[21] The "School of Rabbi Ishmael" or "Tanna of the School of Rabbi Ishmael" (תנא דבי רבי ישמעאל) is frequent in the Babylonian Talmud, but not recorded in the Palestinian Talmud or other amoraic midrashim. Sifra is mentioned in B. Berakhot 11b where this work (according to the vulgar editions) is identical with Talmud, in contrast to the halakic midrashim (see Rashi ad loc.). But cf. Dikduke Soferim, ad loc.; Friedmann, Mechilta, pp. XVI f. See also P. Berakhot, 3c. For other references see next note.

[22] Berakhot 18b refers to "Tanna Sifra (or Safra) of the School of Rab," commenting on II Sam. 23:20 and Eccles. 9:5. See Maimonides, Introduction to Yad; Aaron ibn Zeraḥ, Ẓedah Ladderekh, Introduction (Sabbioneta, 1567), 14b; Weiss, Mechilta, p. XIX. See Friedmann, Mechilta, pp. XVI–XXIX, who refutes at length Weiss' view that Rab authored the halakic midrashim. Friedmann neglects to mention that his own edition of the halakic midrash on Num. and Deut. is named Sifre debe Rab (Vienna, 1864).

[23] None of these books are referred to in the Palestinian Talmud. B. Shabbath 137a, Eruvin 96b, Yoma 41a, Kiddushin 53a, Shav'uot 13a, Bekhorot 61a and Keritot 22a, mention the Sifra, alluding to Judah ben Illai as its author. Cf. Alexander Guttmann, "The Problem of the Anonymous Mishna," HUCA 16 (1941), 137–155.

[24] So, for example, Weiss, Mechilta, pp. XVI ff.; Hoffmann, Zur Einleitung, pp. 15 ff. But it should be remembered that nowhere in the talmudic or midrashic texts is there a reference to the halakic midrashim as emanating from Ishmael's school. Because certain parallel passages in the midrashic texts are attributed to Rabbi Ḥiyya, Malbim proposed that Ḥiyya (a pupil of Judah Hanasi) authored these works. See next note.

[25] The relevant passages are cited in Friedmann, Mechilta, pp. LV–LXVII, of which only the first two can be discussed here. Commenting on Exod. 12:2, "This new moon," Pasha I cites Ishmael to the effect that Moses displayed the new moon to Israel; Akiba, however, is quoted as saying that the new moon was one of the three items (the others being leper and lampstand) which Moses had difficulty understanding, so God Himself showed it to him. The Mekilta then quotes: "Some say that Moses had also difficulty with the manner of ritual slaughtering" (p. 6; Laut. I, pp. 15 f.). Friedmann cites a number of rabbinic sources which contain parallel passages

II

Scholars have dated the Mekilta on internal evidence. Consistent with the usual dating has been its classification as a tannaitic midrash on the following presuppositions, which I discuss below: a) some of the halakah preserved in the Mekilta antedates the halakah of the Mishnah or the Talmud; b) the arrangement of the halakah according to scriptural verses (Mekilta, Sifra) preceded the topical arrangement of the halakah (Mishnah); c) the authorities quoted in the Mekilta are

---

to Akiba's statement, all of which differ from the Mekilta: Exod. Rabbah (XV, 28) citing an anonymous authority varies the four items, excluding ritual slaughtering, but lists instead the making of the oil for the anointment of the priest; Num. Rabbah (XV, 4) lists three items, also anonymously (also in Tanḥuma, *Shemini* 8 (11); *Baha'alotkha* 3 (4); in the Pesikta de-Rab Kahana (*Haḥodesh*, ed. Mandelbaum I, 104) and Pesikta Rabbati (78a) the three items are attributed to Simeon ben Yoḥai; Sifre Num. 61 follows the Mekilta in referring the text to Akiba; however, Menaḥot 29a attributes the tradition to the tanna of the school of Ishmael. Friedmann, in desperation, resolves the variants thusly: the Pesikta took the passage from the Sifre (if so, why did they vary it from Akiba, as found in the Sifre, to Simeon ben Yoḥai?), but the Babylonian Talmud borrowed the passages from the Mekilta, which the amoraim attributed to Ishmael; hence, Menaḥot 29a refers to the tanna of the school of Ishmael (if so, why did not the Babylonian Talmud cite Akiba as does the Mekilta?), but the late midrashim finding contradictory sources quoted our passage anonymously. An analysis of all the parallels (even those omitted by Friedmann) shows that a direct relationship exists only between the Mekilta and Menaḥot 29a (the other dozen references are too remote to be relevant). The only problem is which of these two is the original text and which the secondary. Only Menaḥot 29a gives a full discussion of the manufacturing of the lampstand of the desert and of Solomon, quoting first Rabbi Yoḥanan that Gabriel the Archangel showed Moses how to make the lampstand and only thereafter mentions Ishmael's school as a source (the passages found in the Mekilta). It follows that the Mekilta borrowed from Menaḥot 29a. The inverse is inconceivable because the Mekilta records a controversy between Ishmael and Akiba; the former claiming that only the new moon was shown to Moses by God, the latter claiming three items. As the Babylonian Talmud attributes the view of the three items to the tanna of the school of Ishmael, the talmudic editor(s) could not have been aware of the Mekilta text; the talmudic editor(s) moreover are not even aware of any controversy in this matter. Thus it would seem that it was the author of the Mekilta who adapted the passage found in Menaḥot 29a into a dispute between Ishmael and Akiba, a dispute not recorded in any other source. Unlike Friedmann, it must be assumed that *Pasḥa* I (p. 7; Laut. pp. 18 f.) was adapted from B. Sanhedrin 42a rather than vice versa. For here again, the quotation seems to be inserted from Sanhedrin 42a where it belongs, into the Mekilta, where it does not. Friedmann (p. LXIII) himself cites a dozen passages from the Babylonian Talmud where the School of Rabbi Ishmael is quoted dealing with comments on the Book of Exodus, but which are *not* in the Mekilta. The conclusion is inescapable that the editors of the Babylonian Talmud did not necessarily know of any book identical or similar to the Mekilta. See note 85.

as a rule tannaim; d) many of the exegetical technical terms of the
Mekilta were already becoming archaic in mishnaic times; and, e) the
Palestinian and Babylonian Talmuds contain direct quotations from
the Mekilta.

Supposition a) was advanced by Geiger and Lauterbach, who
dated much of the Mekilta in the premishnaic period.[26] But the
question immediately arises: where are these premishnaic materials to
be found? One thinks naturally of Jubilees, the Qumran texts, Philo,
Josephus and the Gospels. In none of these is the occasional halakic
overtone or nuance more than something passing and, with the possible exception of the Scroll of Damascus, never is it couched in pure
rabbinic form. It does not seem just to designate this sparse material
as premishnaic or tannaitic. Yet granting that the halakah of the
Mekilta occasionally coincides with such premishnaic or protomishnaic
halakah, the Mekilta follows the text of the Mishnah and Tosefta
precisely as they have come down to us, and thus could hardly be
authentically premishnaic.[27] The passages of the Mekilta cited by

---

[26] See note 2. A. Geiger, *Urschrift²*, p. 141, note, cites the parallel between the
Mekilta (on 23:7; *Kaspa* II, p. 327; Laut. III, pp. 170 f.), that Simeon ben Shetaḥ
sentenced to death a false witness, whereupon Judah ben Tabbai accused him of
judicial murder, and the more lengthy description of this incident in the other
talmudic texts (B. Makkot 5b; Tosefta VI, 6, p. 424), which reverse the facts of the
incident. Geiger says that because of its very nature ("wie wir unten ihn kennen
lernen, sowohl als die schmucklose und präcise Erzählung") the Mekilta leaves no
doubt that it alone has preserved the original formulation of the anecdote. However,
an analysis of the relevant texts tends to show that the Mekilta took the anecdote
from the Babylonian Talmud. The Mekilta's version reads הרגנוהו "we have killed
him," when what was meant was מי הרגו לזה או אני או אתה "Who killed this man, I or
you?", as reported in B. Sanhedrin 37b; Mekilta: היודע ובעל מחשבות, "He who knows
and Who is the master of thoughts"; B.T: היודע מחשבות, "He Who knows thoughts."
Hence, the citation of the Mekilta appears to be a tampered version of the story found
in the talmudic texts.

[27] The Mekilta frequently quotes the Mishnah directly, using the phrase מכאן
אמרו. This phrase appears in the first edition of the Mekilta sixty-three times, mostly
citing our Mishnah verbatim or, less often, a Baraitha or Tosefta. Examples: *Pasḥa*
V, p. 16; Laut. I, p. 40, quoting M. Arakhin II, 5; Laut. *ibid.*, p. 17, quoting M.
Berakhot V, 5; Laut. I, p. 42, to M. Pesaḥim V, 5. For a partial list of the Mekilta's
references to the Mishnah, Baraitha, or Tosefta, see W. Bacher, *Tradition und
Tradenten* (Leipzig, 1914), pp. 170 ff.; Epstein, *Mavo lenusaḥ ha-mishnah*, pp. 728 ff.
L. Ginzberg, in a Hebrew article, "On the Relationship between the Mishnah
and the Mekilta," which originally appeared in *Studies in Memory of M. Schorr*
(New York, 1944), and reprinted in *'Al Halakhah Ve-'aggadah* (Tel Aviv, 1960),
pp. 66–103, pp. 284–290, especially pp. 80, 89, 90, 103, argues that the phrase מכאן
אמרו does not necessarily mean that the Mekilta was citing the Mishnah, even
though the wording in the two works is identical. But Ginzberg's reasoning is not

scholars as remnants of the early halakah reveal a subjectivity that precludes the dating of the work as a whole.[28] The occasional apparent difference between the halakah of the Talmud and that of the Mekilta may not be that of priority, but may be due to the latter's misunderstanding of the former, or indeed to our ignorance of both.[29] The basic fact which must weigh in the evaluation of the Mekilta is that its

---

convincing. In the passage cited above (M. Berakhot V, 5), the Mekilta quotes: "From here they say: 'One's agent is like himself'." To which Ginzberg remarks (p. 90) that the Mekilta could not have been quoting the Mishnah because this must have been a common saying. Ginzberg misses the point that the purpose of the Mekilta's citations of the Mishnah was not its novelty but its authoritativeness as a source of Jewish law.

In the reference (cited above) to M. Arakhin II, 5, Ginzberg admits (p. 90) that the verbatim coincidence between the Mekilta and Mishnah should presume interdependence. But he proceeds to argue that since the passage of the cited Mishnah betrays an "old" literary source, it is likely that both the Mishnah and Mekilta were dependent on a premishnaic text. Here again Ginzberg ignores the fact that very frequently "From here they say," in the Mekilta, does coincide with our Mishnah or Tosefta. Only by discrediting the bulk of these citations of the Mishnah in the Mekilta could there be an argument about a certain particular quotation. Ginzberg discusses nine passages of the Mekilta (where the phrase מכאן אמרו does not appear), maintaining that they antedated their mishnaic parallels. When there were variants in the two sources, Ginzberg automatically presumes that the Mishnah altered the text of the pre-Mekilta source. Actually, as in example I (pp. 67–69), the text of M. Kerithot VI, 9 (end) relates but little to the introduction of the Mekilta (see below notes 88–89). It is probable that this final paragraph of the tractate, of aggadic nature and not related to the subject matter of the tractate as a whole, is one of the frequent postmishnaic additions (see end of M. Berakhot, Peah, Mo'ed Katan, Sotah, Eduyot, etc.). Even granting that M. Kerithot VI, 9, is an authentic Mishnah, it is clear that it was not taken from our Mekilta since the instances and the text as a whole do not correspond. Ginzberg's example III (pp. 76–78) merely shows that the text of the Mekilta presupposes the existence of the Palestinian or Babylonian Talmud. For the view that the halakic midrashim used our Mishnah and Tosefta, see Melamed in *Papers: IV World Congress of Jewish Studies* (Jerusalem, 1967) I, pp. 163–166 (Hebrew Section); cf. his *The Relationship between the Halakhic Midrashim and the Mishnah and Tosephta* (Jerusalem, 1967), which I have as yet not seen.

[28] See previous note. Lauterbach, *Haẓofeh* IX (1925), pp. 235–241, argues that Mekilta on Exod. 12:46 (*Pasḥa* XV, pp. 55 f.; Laut. I, p. 124) conformed to the older halakah, which prohibited the breaking of the Paschal lamb's bone whether or not it had meat on it, in contrast to the younger halakah (P. Pesaḥim VII, 9, p. 35a; B. Pesaḥim 84b–85a), which presumably prohibited the breaking of the bone only if it contained meat. Actually, the Mekilta's interpretation of 12:46 makes sense only if the existence of the relevant talmudic references are presupposed. As to the different conclusions in the talmudic and Mekilta texts, it seems that the author of the Mekilta follows here Zevaḥim 97b which in fact prohibits the breaking of a bone under any circumstance.

[29] Cf. I. H. Weiss, *Dor Dor Vedorshav²* II (Berlin, 1924), pp. 228 f.

halakah and the Talmud's are virtually identical.[30] It is this over-
whelming identity, rather than the variations, which requires explanation for the simple reason that if the Mekilta were very ancient the
variants would be infinitely more striking.

Our ignorance of the methodology of the halakah and its evolution
during the period of the Second Temple prevents the verification of
argument b). But let us accept Lauterbach's thesis that the older,
pre-Maccabean halakah was arranged according to scriptural verses,
and that the topical arrangement began during the Maccabean period.
This thesis does not, however, necessarily support the accompanying
view that the pre-Maccabean formulation of the halakah corresponded
to that of the later halakic midrashim or of the Mekilta. The texts of
Qumran, for example, suggest alternate conceivable methods of presentation.[31] Linguistically and structurally, the formulation of the halakah
in the Scroll of Damascus, though still remote from that of the Mishnah, is more related to it than to the Mekilta. When they cite a biblical
verse, the authors of the Dead Sea scrolls employ formulas such as
אשר אמר "for it is said" or אשר כתוב "for it is written"; in the Mishnah
the formulas are שנאמר and שכתוב, respectively. The hermeneutic
terminology of the halakic sections of the Scroll of Damascus is primitive compared to that of the Mishnah, and is certainly far removed
from the highly developed exegetical idiom of the Mekilta.[32]

Presupposition c), namely, that the texts of the Mekilta (though
not necessarily its final edition) are tannaitic, is based on the names of
the authorities cited in this book. The following is a list of names,
arranged in descending order of frequency, which are mentioned in the
first edition of the Mekilta ten times or more:[33]

[30] The scholars who believe that the mishnaic halakah reflects the one promul-
gated during the Second Temple may argue that the Mekilta preserves traditions of
the pre-70 period. The writer believes that the tannaitic texts reproduce essentially
the halakah as formulated by the rabbis between 80 and 200, frequently differing
from the Pharisaic traditions of the pre-70 oral law. Except in a few instances the
Pharisaic halakah is not known.

[31] The formulation of halakah in the Scroll of Damascus mainly follows a topical
order, using the negated imperative (one shall not). Its relation to the mishnaic texts
has been studied by Ginzberg (*Eine unbekannte jüdische Sekte* I, New York, 1922),
who exaggerated the relationship between the halakah of the scroll and the rabbinic
tradition. Cf. also Rabin, *Zadokite Documents* (Oxford, 1958), index, pp. 87–90.

[32] Cf. p.Hab. III 2, 13, 14; Damascus Scroll IX, 1–XVI, 15; Manual of Discipline
VIII, 14.

[33] For a full list of the authorities cited in the Mekilta, see Weiss (*Mechilta*,
pp. XXIX–XXXV), Hoffmann (*Zur Einleitung*, pp. 83–90), and B. Kosovsky
(*Concordantiae verborum quae in Mechilta d'Rabbi Ismael reperiuntur*, Jerusalem,
1965).

83–60	54–30	29–20	18–10
Ishmael	Nathan	Judah	Eleazar
Joshua	Rabbi	Isaac	Simeon
Eliezer	Eleazar of Modi'in	Simeon b. Yoḥai	Meir
Akiba	Josiah	Jose	Eleazar b. Azariah
	Jose of Galilee		Judah b. Betherah
	Jonathan		Pappias
			Gamaliel

If the names listed are treated as identical with those preserved in the Mishnah and the Tosefta (Ishmael ben Elisha, Joshua ben Ḥananya, Eliezer ben Hyrcanus, Akiba ben Joseph, etc.),[34] then the Mekilta would be a significant tannaitic text.

The basic question, however, is not that of the names, but rather, whether the citations in the Mekilta are historical or pseudepigraphic.[35] On the premise that the quotations are genuine, the list of names is puzzling. The scholars who maintain that the Mekilta has preserved segments of the older halakah of the Second Temple ought to explain why (except for one mangled paraphrase of the Babylonian Talmud or Tosefta)[36] the pre-70 zugot (pairs) of authorities go unmentioned.[37] Also notable is the role of Rabbi (or Rabban) Yoḥanan ben Zakkai, founder of the academy of Yavneh in the year 70, who is listed in the Mekilta seven times, but only in haggadic texts, some of which are rephrasings from the Babylonian Talmud and postamoraic lore.[38]

[34] The problem whether the author of the Mekilta meant Eleazar to be identical with Eleazar ben Azariah or Eleazar of Modi'in or another person altogether; Jose with Jose ben Ḥalafta or Jose of Galilee; Simeon with Simeon ben Yoḥai, is avoided in this statistical analysis.

[35] The question involves passages which have no talmudic parallels.

[36] See above n. 26.

[37] The zugot are listed in M. Ḥagigah II, 2; Avot I, 4–15. Incidentally, Mekilta, Amalek III, p. 190; Laut. II, 165 f., alludes to Avot I, 7; or rather to Avot de-Rabbi Nathan IX, p. 42, which the author of the Mekilta regards as identical with the Mishnah. Shema'yah and Avtalyon, though, are cited once in Beshallaḥ (p. 99; Laut. I, 220), in an aggadic quotation, where the sequence of authorities is as follows: Rabbi, Eleazar b. Azaryah, Eleazar b. Judah of Bartota (?), Shema'yah, Avtalyon, Simeon of Kitron, a sequence which arouses suspicion as to the authenticity of the traditions. Cf. also the sequence in the Mekilta of Simeon b. Yoḥai (pp. 57–9), note to p. 57, 4.

[38] Mekilta, Nezikin, II, p. 253; Laut. III, 16, depends on B. Kiddushin 22b; not on Tosefta Baba Kamma VII, 5, p. 358, where the passage is cited anonymously. Mekilta, ibid., XV, 299; Laut. III, 115, depends on B. Baba Kamma 79b; rather than on Tos. ibid., VII, 2, p. 357; Mekilta Baḥodesh, I, 203 f.; Laut. II, 193 f., seems to follow Avot de-Rabbi Nathan, XVII, p. 33a (a posttalmudic source), rather than B. Ketubot 66b–67a; or Sifre, Deut. 305; or Tos. ibid., V, 10, p. 267; or P. ibid., V, end,

Not one halakah is cited in his name. The oldest material in the tannaitic literature is that respecting the controversies between the schools of Shammai and Hillel,[39] but the Mekilta knows of only two disputes, both evidently borrowed from the Babylonian or Palestinian Talmuds.[40]

Moreover, an analysis of the second and third generations of tannaim in the list arouses the suspicion that some of the cited authorities are manufactured. Of the second generation, Rabban Gamaliel II was the most influential figure as the founder of the Hillelite dynasty of patriarchs during the last decades of the first century. But he is at the bottom of the list with ten occurrences,[41] all but one in haggadic

p. 30c. For only Avot de-Rabbi Nathan, and after it the Mekilta, attributes the story to Yoḥanan ben Zakkai; the talmudic sources and the Tosefta cite here Simeon ben Eleazar. Mekilta, *ibid.*, XI, p. 245; Laut. II, 290 is related to Sifra, *Kedoshim* 92d, rather than to Tos. Baba Kamma VII, 6, p. 358, which reports this passage anonymously. The passage of Mekilta, *Nezikin* XII, p. 292; Laut. III, 99, is related to Tosefta, *ibid.*, VII, 10, p. 359, but the Mekilta strings together here B. *ibid.*, 67b, resulting that Yoḥanan ben Zakkai follows Meir and precedes Akiba in a controversy. There is no reason to assume that the author of the Mekilta ever used Yoḥanan ben Zakkai's name fictitiously, but there is no doubt that his sources were primarily the Babylonian Talmud or posttalmudic works.

[39] See M. Eduyot I, 1 ff.

[40] P. Eruvin X, 1, p. 26a, records that Rabbi required an annual check of one's phylacteries, but that Simeon ben Gamaliel did not; the text concludes with a quote from Hillel the Elder, who, it is said, displayed his maternal grandfather's phylacteries, indicating seemingly that no checkup is required. Apparently, because the halakah follows Hillel, the author of the Mekilta (*Pasḥa*, 17, p. 69; Laut. I, 157), "corrected" the Palestinian Talmud, reversing the views of Hillel and Shammai, the former requiring an annual check, but the latter not; the Mekilta concludes tautologically with Shammai the Elder displaying his grandfather's phylacteries. The other reference to the two schools is *Nezikin* XV, p. 300; Laut. III, 117, which abstracts B. Baba Meẓi'a 44a.

[41] Five out of the ten times occurring in an anecdote (adopted from B. Kidd., 32b; Sifre Deut., 38) about Gamaliel's remarkable hospitality. Like Abraham and Moses (Exod. 18:12), Gamaliel personally entertained his guests (Amalek III, pp. 195 f.; Laut. II, 177 f.). That Tebi, Gamaliel's slave was permitted to wear phylacteries, the author of the Mekilta (*Pasḥa* XVII, p. 68; Laut. I, 154) found in P. Eruvin X, 1, p. 26a, as becomes clear from the context. The question of Judah of Kefar Acco (not recorded elsewhere, but evidently modeled after Simeon b. Judah of Kefar Akko, B. Sanh. 110b, etc.), addressed to Gamaliel (Amalek IV, p. 196; Laut. II, 180), why does Scripture say that Moses boasted: "For the people come *to me* to inquire of God"? (Exod. 18:15) appears to be a manufactured passage. This inquiry was modeled after the one mentioned in B. Avodah Zarah 54b, which is found also in the Mekilta (*Baḥodesh* VI, 226; Laut. II, 244–246). In abstracting the *sugya* of B. Baba Kamma 42b–43a (cf. P. Baba Kamma 4b), the author of the Mekilta either through carelessness or by design changed the views of the authorities, inserting the name of Gamaliel, which apparently was not in the sources.

material, though the insignificant Eleazar of Modi'in, not mentioned in the Mishnah and only rarely alluded to elsewhere, is named in the Mekilta forty-eight times.[42] Gamaliel's rival Eleazar ben 'Azariah, who became the head of the academy of Yavneh when the former was forced to resign, appears in the Mekilta thirteen times. Joshua, another opponent of Gamaliel, is recorded seventy-two times.[43] It is not only the disproportionate over-representation or under-representation of certain tannaim, but the lack of any discernible pattern respecting the names which raises the great possibility that the names cited in the Mekilta have no historical basis.

This impression that the names cited in the Mekilta are mostly pseudepigraphical is strengthened when one analyzes the third generation of tannaim listed in this book. Ishmael, it is true, heads the list of all the sages mentioned in the Mekilta. But its author appears to be ignorant of the historical Ishmael ben Elishah.[44] In the Mekilta, Ishmael records a tradition in the name of Meir,[45] who lived a generation or two later; he debates with Jonathan or Josiah,[46] who probably lived a century later,[47] and is referred to as a martyr by Akiba.[48]

---

[42] See above note 34. Eleazar of Modi'in is mentioned in Avot III, 2, but this tractate names men otherwise not found in, and should not be considered part of, the Mishnah. There is only one halakic reference to him in the talmudic literature (B. Shavu'ot 35b), though the Babylonian Talmud mentions him about a dozen times, occasionally together with Gamaliel. In the other halakic midrashim he is mentioned only twice (Sifre Numb. 137; 157).

[43] See the sources cited in note 33.

[44] In the Mishnah and talmudic texts, Ishmael often debates with Akiba, Tarfon, Jose of Galilee, and less often with Eleazar ben Azariah. Though cited in almost every chapter of the Mekilta, there is no evidence that the author cared who were Ishmael's contemporaries or pupils. See below, p. 130.

[45] Mekilta, Nezikin XIV, p. 298, 5; Laut. III, 112, 61, app. crit. This reading of the editio princeps and Ms. Vienna is correct. Influenced by B. Baba Kamma 14a, modern editors, including Horowitz-Rabin and Lauterbach, read Simeon ben Eleazar.

[46] Pasḥa III, p. 12; Laut. I, 28 (with Josiah); VI, 22; Laut. 50, (with Jonathan and Isaac); VIII, p. 28; Laut. I, 63 f. (with Jonathan and Jose of Galilee); XI, 37; Laut. I, 84 (with Jonathan and Isaac); Nezikin VII, p. 271; Laut. III, 56 (with Josiah and Nathan or, as Lauterbach reads, Jonathan); VIII, p. 275; Laut. III, 64 (with Josiah and Jonathan); IX, p. 278; Laut. III, 70 (ibid.).

[47] See below note 65.

[48] Mekilta, Nezikin XVIII, p. 313; Laut. III, 141 f., commenting on Exod. 22:22, reports that when Simeon (ben Yoḥai?; Gamaliel?; both lived a generation or two after Ishmael) and Ishmael were to be martyred, the former was wondering what evil deed he had done. To which the latter replied that it must have been because he had let the litigants wait for a judgment while he amused himself. The parallel story is reported in Avot de-Rabbi Nathan XXXVIII, pp. 114 f. and Semaḥot VIII. It is the latter, which also has Akiba's comment and which depicts the ten martyrs, that appears to have been the Mekilta's source. The historicity of

Because neither the Babylonian nor Palestinian amoraic tradition ever refers to Ishmael of the Mekilta, Frankel proposed that the author or editor of the Mekilta was not the famous rival of Akiba, but an obscure amora named occasionally in the Palestinian Talmud as Rabbi Ishmael the father of Judan.[49] Friedmann and Lauterbach are right in rejecting this ingenious identification,[50] but their reasoning that the citations in Ishmael's name record the words of a famous tanna or his school is equally unacceptable. Many of the quotations of Ishmael in the Mekilta are clearly apocryphal.[51]

The same applies to the Mekilta's sixty citations of Akiba. In the Mishnah and the Talmuds, Ishmael and Akiba display differing methods of biblical exegesis. The former adheres more strictly to the plain meaning of Scripture or to formal hermeneutic rules than the latter.[52] But the Akiba of the Mekilta is void of any exegetical personality, except when the Mekilta is clearly dependent upon older mishnaic or talmudic texts.[53] In the latter literature (to cite another

---

Ishmael ben Elishah's martyrdom is, however, defended by some scholars. See the literature cited in G. Alon's *Toledot Hayehudim Bitekufat Hamishnah Vehatalmud*, II (Tel Aviv, 1955), p. 11, n. 85. Although he believed that the Mekilta was tannaitic, Alon rejects the story as a late legend. See also the fictional treatise, the Midrash of the Ten Martyrs.

[49] Z. Frankel, *Einleitung in den Jerusalemischen Talmud*[2] (Berlin, 1923), 108b–109b, remarks that Rabbi Ishmael of the Palestinian Talmud is usually an amora. P. Pesaḥim II, 4, p. 29b, in the name of this Ishmael, according to Frankel, cites the Mekilta, *Pasha* VIII, p. 26; Laut. I, 60; also recorded in B. *ibid.*, 35a, as based on the school of Ishmael. An analysis of the parallel passages makes it clear that the editors of the Babylonian and Palestinian Talmuds had not seen the citation of the Mekilta, but that the latter is based on the Babylonian Talmud. This is necessarily so, as the author of the Mekilta sums up here several sections of the Babylonian Talmud.

[50] Friedmann, *Mechilta*, pp. LXXIV–LXXVII; Lauterbach, *Mekilta* I, p. XXIV, note 19.

[51] Cf. the mystical texts of Hekhalot Rabbati, attributed to Ishmael (A. Jellinek, *Bet ha-midrash* III [Leipzig, 1855', 83–108.).

[52] See M. Sotah V, 1–2; cf. B. Sanhedrin 51a; M. Kerithot II, 5; Yoma VI, 8; Shevu'ot III, 5. See also Frankel, *Introduction to the Mishnah*[2] (Warsaw, 1923), pp. 112–130; H. L. Strack, *Introduction to the Talmud and Mishnah* (Philadelphia, 1931), p. 112; Epstein-Melamed, *Introduction to Tannaitic Literature . . .*, pp. 521 ff. (who should be used cautiously).

[53] Mekilta, *Pasha* III, p. 11; Laut. I, 26, on Exod. 12:4, *And he and his neighbor shall take.* Ishmael takes the verse that one may bring in new members to partake with him from his paschal lamb; Akiba, that one may offer the sacrifice by himself. There is no apparent difference in the exegesis. In fact, however, the Mekilta seems to have attributed to the latter Jose's view (M. Pesaḥim VIII, 7), in contrast to that of Judah, who sanctions the partaking from the lamb only as part of a group. The author of the Mekilta apparently adopts the gaonic ruling that when Judah and

example), Jose of Galilee emerges as a distinct halakist — he sanctioned the boiling of poultry in milk —[54] whereas in the Mekilta he is named thirteen times with no allusion to his individualism.

In contrast to the Mishnah and other related texts, the most important men of the fourth generation of tannaim — Meir, Judah ben Illai, Jose ben Ḥalafta — play a relatively minor role in the Mekilta.[55] The usual explanation is that these authorities belonged to Akiba's school which rivaled that of the Ishmaelite exegetic tradition. The weakness of this argument is that if Akiba is cited sixty times, why then were his pupils not equally presented? The real problem, however, is not that Meir, Judah, or Jose are not frequently mentioned, but that when they are cited their views and exegesis seem similar to those of the tannaim presumably of the Ishmaelite school.[56] The apocryphal nature of the citations may explain why the author of the Mekilta appears to forget sometimes that Judah with or without his patronymic Illai, Jose and Jose ben Ḥalafta, or Simeon and Simeon ben Yoḥai, are the same person.[57] Some reflections of the *Sitz im Leben*, indeed, the tension behind the exegetic debates frequently so clear in the Mishnah and the Talmud, are absent from the Mekilta.

Jose differ, the halakah follows the latter. Incidentally, in B. *ibid.*, 91a, the contrary views are said to be based on the exegesis of Deut. 16:8, indicating that not only did the author of the Mishnah not know of Akiba's position, but that the Talmud did not even know of Akiba's supposed exegesis of Exod. 12:4. *Pasḥa* IV, p. 13; Laut. I, 32 f., cites Akiba as quoting the 13th hermeneutic rule, attributed by the Sifra to Ishmael, but which the Mekilta says Ishmael refuted. On the other hand, the Mekilta (*Nezikin* X, 283; Laut. III, 80) cites a pupil of Ishmael interpreting the particle *et* as an inclusive, supposedly the trademark of Akiba's hermeneutical method (B. Ḥagigah 12a).

[54] See M. Ḥulin VIII, 4; B. *ibid.*, 116a; Shabbath, 130a: cf. *Kaspa* V, p. 336; Laut. III, 190, quoting the Mishnah. One may profit from leavened bread on Pass-over (Pesaḥim 32b). A second son born from a union of a Jew and a converted Gentile woman is considered legally first-born in regard to inheritance and must be offered to a priest because when she gave birth to their first son, she was not yet converted (M. Bekhorot VIII, 1). Most of the citations of Jose of Galilee in the Mekilta deal with haggadic material in contrast with the talmudic tradition which cites him as a halakist.

[55] Meir is mentioned in the Mishnah 330 times, in the Tosefta 452 times; Judah, in the Mishnah more than 600 times, Jose 330 times.

[56] Sometimes, though, the Mekilta merely reproduces the Mishnah (*Nezikin* X, p. 284; Laut. III, 83, citing M. Baba Kamma II, 4; or *ibid.*, X, p. 284; Laut. III, 84, citing M. *ibid.*, IV, 9).

[57] In the Mishnah, Judah, Jose, and Simeon are never cited by their patronymics. The Mekilta follows this method when citing Simeon in the halakah, but in haggadic passages the patronymic is used. See also in regard to Judah, Mekilta, *Vayyassa* I, pp. 153, 14 f.; Laut. II, 87, 41; on Jose, *Amalek* I, 176; Laut. II, 136, 18, indicating that the Mekilta is dependent on the older texts.

The Mekilta features names such as Nathan, Josiah, Jonathan, Isaac, and Papos (or Pappias), which are never mentioned in the Mishnah,[58] and are comparatively rare elsewhere. In fact, it would appear that Papos is one of the names, listed below, which the author of the Mekilta invented.[59] Nathan is known from the talmudic literature where he is sometimes dubbed the Babylonian.[60] This and the mention of a certain amora from Ḥuẓẓal by the name of Josiah prompted Halevy to propose that Nathan, Josiah, and Jonathan were members of the academy of Ḥuẓẓal, a school which supposedly flourished in Babylonia since the days of Ezekiel, Ezra, and Hillel.[61] Halevy, now followed by Neusner, claims that much of the Mekilta was originated in the Babylonian academy of Ḥuẓẓal.[62] There is no doubt, however, that except for paraphrases from the Babylonian Talmud, the Nathan of the Mekilta is a name of convenience as well as a historical personality. Consider the chronological anomalies: he is said to have debated with Akiba and Ishmael, on the one hand, and with Judah Hanasi, on the other; and he is a pupil of Simeon ben Yoḥai and Jose ben Maḥoz, the latter apparently a fictitious name.[63] Jonathan

---

[58] Excepting Avot, a tractate not properly part of the Mishnah, which mentions Jonathan (Avot IV, 9), and the last Mishnah of Berakhot, which cites Nathan.

[59] Laut. follows most Mss. in reading פפייס (Pappias), but ed. pr. reads פפוס (Papos). In rabbinical literature he is a figure representing heretical views. In B. Sabbath 104b (uncensored texts) Papos ben Judah equals Jesus. In B. Berakhot 61b, he is contrasted with Akiba, both were martyred; the former for rather foolish reasons, the latter for the sanctification of God's name. Gen. Rabbah XXI, 5, p. 200, Akiba challenges Pappias' interpretation of Gen. 2:22, that Adam was created an angel. Mekilta, Amalek III, p. 194; Laut. II, 175, citing B. Sanhedrin 94a, quotes Pappias' accusation that it was Jethro (not the Jews) who had first blessed God (alluding to Exod. 18:10).

[60] B. Sabbath 134a. The citations of Nathan in M. Berakhot (end) and Shekalim II, 5, were not in the original text of the Mishnah (see Palestinian Talmud ad loc.). He was a younger contemporary of Rabbi. B. Horayot 13b, reports that Nathan and Meir plotted to remove Simeon ben Gamaliel from his office of patriarch, but this is probably not historical. According to B. Baba Meẓi'a 86a, Nathan and Rabbi were the editors of the Mishnah.

[61] I. Halevy, Dorot Harishonim (Berlin, 1923) II, pp. 181 ff.

[62] J. Neusner, A History of the Jews in Babylonia (Leiden, 1965), I, pp. 179 ff. and passim; see my review in CCAR Journal XIII, 5 (April, 1966), pp. 74–77.

[63] With Ishmael, Pasḥa XVI, p. 61; Laut. I, 137; Nezikin XV, p. 299; Laut. III, 114; with Akiba, Nezikin VII, p. 273; Laut. III, 60; as a pupil of Simeon ben Yoḥai, Beshallaḥ IV, 101; Laut. I, 225 f.; quoting Abba Jose of Maḥoz, ibid., III, p. 99; Laut. I, 220 f. It should be noted that the Mss. frequently confuse Nathan with Jonathan. It is possible that by Nathan the author of the Mekilta referred to the presumed author of Avot de-Rabbi Nathan, a work frequently quoted. For in Amalek IV, p. 200; Laut. II, 186, citing I Chr. 2:55, the Mekilta reports that upon Nathan's death, wisdom disappeared. It is curious that Avot de-Rabbi Nathan

and Josiah were of the generation that bridged the tannaitic and the amoraic periods and may be classified as belonging to either.[64] In the Babylonian Talmud they are occasionally mentioned together, but the author of the Mekilta converted them into leading antagonists:[65] they are said to have debated with Eleazer (80–100), a tanna of the second generation, as well as with Judah Hanasi (circa 200).[66] The well-known debates between Hillel and the sons of Betherah (40–10 B. C. E.?), whether or not the Passover sacrifice may be performed when the fourteenth of Nissan fell on the Sabbath, is rephrased by the author of the Mekilta as a controversy between Josiah and Jonathan.[67]

The name of Rabbi (Judah Hanasi) occasionally appears in the secondary passages of the Mishnah.[68] In the Mekilta, however, Rabbi is one of the most frequently cited names. Sometimes the Mekilta, instead of referring to the Mishnah, refers simply to Rabbi.[69] In some instances where Rabbi is said to have debated with tannaim of different generations, the citations are suspect.[70] Also found in the Mekilta is the epithet Rabbenu Hakadosh, a title of Rabbi of amoraic vintage and in fact recorded elsewhere only in late amoraic or geonic texts.[71]

The following is a partial list of the Mekilta's authorities whose historicity is not attested elsewhere: Abba Ḥanan, Abba Jose of Maḥoz, Jose of Modi'in, Abshalom Hazaken, Issi ben Gurya, Issi ben Shammai, Antoninus, Zerikah, Ḥananya ben Halnisi.[72] It could be argued that

---

XXXV, 53a, also comments in a similar spirit on I Chr. 2:55. The Mekilta seems to say that Nathan's comments on Yabeẓ were applicable to himself.

[64] See Tosafot Yeshanim, to Yoma 57b.

[65] Because of the Mekilta, it is generally assumed that Josiah and Jonathan are tannaim, but it is likely that they were of the first generation of amoraim. Jonathan was a pupil of Ḥiyya (Berakhot 18a).

[66] See *Pasha* IV, p. 13; Laut. I, 30 f.; *Beshallaḥ* I, p. 81; Laut. I, 183.

[67] For Hillel's debate with the sons of Betherah, see P. Pesaḥim VI, 1, p. 33a; B., *ibid.*, 66a; Tosefta, *ibid.*, IV, 13, p. 165 (Lieberman). Mekilta, *Pasha* V, p. 17; Laut. I, 40 f., attributes the controversy to the interpretation of Exod. 12:6. Cf. Sifre, Num. 65, 142; Sifra (ed. Weiss), p. 103b.

[68] See Frankel, *Introduction to the Mishnah* (Hebrew), pp. 226–228.

[69] Mekilta, *Nezikin* VIII, p. 276; Laut. III, 67, evidently citing B. Sanhedrin 79a; *Shabbatha* II, p. 345; Laut. III, 206.

[70] With Akiba, *Pasha* VI, 21; Laut. I, 49.

[71] Mekilta, *Beshallaḥ* II, p. 125; Laut. II, 21; *ibid.*, VI, p. 137; Laut. II, 50. The title Rabbenu Hakadosh was sometimes incorporated from a marginal note. See B. Shabbath 156a; Pesaḥim 37a; P. Megillah III, 2, 74a. Cf. also the medieval treatise, Pirke Rabbenu Hakadosh, ed. Grünhut (Jerusalem, 1898).

[72] The various patronymics of Issi were evidently inspired by B. Pesaḥim 113b; Yoma, 52b: "Joseph of Ḥuẓẓal is identical to Joseph of Babylon, Issi ben Judah, Issi ben Gur Aryeh, Issi ben Gamaliel, Issi ben Mahallel, but what was his real name? Issi ben Akiba." See also Niddah 36b, and Tosafot, *s. v.* "Issi." At least one citation

these and other similar names resulted from scribal corruptions or that the names are historical, but by chance alone are missing from our talmudic records.[73] Yet even the names which are well known in the talmudic literature and which are unquestionably historical appear in ,questionable contexts in the Mekilta.[74]

The conclusion seems inescapable: the authorities cited in the Mekilta cannot be regarded as historical unless they are confirmed in the more reliable texts of the Mishnah, Palestinian or Babylonian Talmud. Certainly, the names of the tannaim cited in the Mekilta do not necessarily prove the time or place of the work any more than the names Akiba, Eleazer, or Elijah relate to the books known as the Alphabet of Rabbi Akiba, Hekhalot de-Rabbi Ishmael, Pirke de-Rabbi Eliezer, or Seder Eliyyahu. All of these instances only show the existence of pseudepigraphical works during the saboraic and geonic periods. Furthermore, as passages citing authorities are of questionable historicity, so too are those passages which appear anonymously.[75]

With respect to point d), Isaac Hirsch Weiss, in his introduction, described the Mekilta's style as loftier and more pleasing than that of the other talmudic and midrashic texts, and from this he concluded that the Mekilta must be older.[76] Weiss's own taste, however, seemed

---

of Issi found in the Mekilta seems to have originated in geonic times. *Kaspa* II, p. 337; Laut. III, 192, records a curious rationalization of the prohibition of milk and meat, not known in the talmudic literature; the passage in Deut. 12:23 which prohibits blood, it is said, means to include also the eating of milk and meat. Proceeding from B. Niddah 9a, Zemaḥ Gaon (*Geonica*, ed. L. Ginzberg [New York, 1909] II, p. 33) explains that milk and blood are of the same substance changing from one to the other, as women do not menstruate during pregnancy. The responsum concludes with proof from Deut. 12:23. Ginzberg (p. 22) missed that this view was abstracted in the Mekilta in the name of Issi. Cf. also *Methivot*, ed. B. Lewin (Jerusalem, 1934), 114, which evidently is older than Zemaḥ's responsum, for it does not have the citation from Deuteronomy.

[73] For attempts to explain the names Issi, see Hoffmann, *Zur Einleitung*, p. 39; Epstein-Melamed, *Introduction*, pp. 571 f.

[74] See above, pp. 129–130.

[75] Frequently, the anonymous suggests the source. See above, note 27 that מכאן אמרו implies as a rule a citation from the Mishnah, occasionally a Baraitha or Tosefta. כיוצא בזה or וכן seems to indicate citations from Gen. Rabba. Cf., for example, Mekilta, introductory section (*Pasha* I, pp. 1 f.; Laut. I, 1–3) with Gen. Rabbah (I, 14, pp. 13 f.); Mekilta (*Pasha* VII, p. 23 f.; Laut. I, 54; *Beshallaḥ* II, p. 85; Laut. I, 192 f.) with Gen. R. (L, 10, pp. 523 f.); Mekilta (*Shiratha* X, p. 151; Laut. II, 82) with Gen. R. (LXXX, 10, pp. 964 f.) where the former appears to render into Hebrew the Aramaic term דכוותה. Albeck's thesis, Introduction to Genesis Rabbah (cf. n. 19), pp. 58 ff., that the Mekilta and Gen. R. independently used a lost source, is inacceptable because the texts certainly show interdependence, and because it unnecessarily creates a new unknown.

[76] Weiss, *Mechilta* pp. XXI f.

to have improved with the passage of time, for in his masterly history of the rabbinic tradition he completely omits his earlier compliments, and instead refers to the Mekilta's style as childish and therefore concludes that the work was drastically revised by its amoraic editor.[77] Style, however, is too vague and too susceptible of subjectivity to permit the dating of a literary work. The Hebrew of the Rabbis, not a literary tongue, seems to have changed little through the centuries from the completion of the Mishnah to the end of the first millennium.[78] Nevertheless, certain usages of the Mekilta suggest that its author was already far removed from the Hebrew of the tannaim and amoraim. Only a few barbarisms of the Mekilta can be cited here: נדבר (speak), adapted evidently from נדברו, Mal. 3:16; הכתיב (writes), הכתבת (you write); אמרת (you interpret); יוכשר (to be ritually fit).[79] More faulty is the author's rabbinic syntax such as the overuse of pronominal suffixes.[80] Certainly, the Hebrew of the tannaim and amoraim is less stilted than that of the Mekilta.

A reliable method of dating rabbinic works can emerge from the exegetical vocabulary. Judged by this alone, the Mekilta is posttalmudic. The ubiquitous formula used by the tannaim to cite Scripture was שנאמר (for it says).[81] While the Mekilta uses the tannaitic formula, it proliferated into a multiplicity of variants:

שכבר נאמר	(it is said once)
לכך נאמר	(hence it says)
שכך נאמר	(for it says thusly)
לכן נאמר	(hence it says)
ומה נאמר	(but what does it say)
למה נאמר	(why does it say)
ועל זה נאמר	(therefore it says)
נאמר ... ונאמר ...	(it says here ... but it says there)
שנאמר בו	(for concerning it, it says)
הוא שנאמר	(this is what it means when it says)

---

[77] Weiss, *Dor Dor* II, pp. 228–231, esp. p. 228 n. 4.

[78] See E. J. Kutscher, *Studies in Galilean Aramaic* (in Hebrew, Jerusalem, 1952; offprint *Tarbiz*, vols. 21–23); "Leshon Ḥazal" in *Sefer I.I. Yalon* (1963), pp. 246–280.

[79] For a full list of citations, see B. Kosovsky, *Otzar Leshon Hatanna'im* (Jerusalem, 1965). For נדבר see Weiss, *Mechilta*, p. XXII. In the Tosefta, this term appears only in Berakhot I, 14 f., p. 5 (Lieberman); cf. Sifra, p. 3d (Weiss).

[80] In general, the Hebrew of the Mekilta is to the Mishnah and Tosefta what Kalir's poetry is to biblical Hebrew, except that much of the Mekilta is made up of quotations from older talmudic texts.

[81] For references, see B. Kosovsky, *ibid.* (n. 79), *a.l.* The English rendition below is only approximate, for the technical meaning of these terms can be understood only in their context.

בכלל שנאמר	(to include in what it says)
מה שנאמר	(that which it says)
כענין שנאמר	(as it says elsewhere)
לפי שנאמר	(because it says)
מפני שנאמר	(because it says)
כל מקום שנאמר	(wherever it says)
ממשמע שנאמר	(it implies to say)

The Mishnah never employs — and other tannaitic texts only rarely — the verb כתב (write) to introduce a Scripture citation. It was standard amoraic to use כתב in its Aramaic form.[82] Not only was כתיב (it is written) or דכתיב (for it is written) borrowed in the Mekilta from amoraic usage,[83] but the term (א)הדה הוא דכתיב (this is what it means when it is written), characteristic of the Palestinian Talmud and early aggadic midrashim,[84] was also taken over by the Mekilta. Aramaic was a living tongue for the tannaim and amoraim, but a foreign language for the author of the Mekilta. Hence, these borrowings must be explained as imitations of amoraic texts.

Moreover the author of the Mekilta shows a genius for borrowing and inventing hermeneutic terms. Here it is only possible to scratch the surface of this problem. But enough has been said to show that the vocabulary incorporates an extension of tannaitic and amoraic technical terms. The fact that the Mekilta attributes the same stereotyped terminology to tannaim of diverse schools or generations shows that the wording is the Mekilta's own rather than that of the authorities to whom it is attributed.

There is no need to deal at length with supposition e), the argument that Mekilta must be regarded as a tannaitic work because it is cited in the Palestinian and Babylonian Talmuds. Chanoch Albeck, in

[82] Proceeding from the assumption that the Mekilta and similar works are tannaitic, W. Bacher (*Exegetische Terminologie*, I, pp. 88 f. II, p. 91) failed to distinguish between basic tannaitic and amoraic terminology. But even he noted the peculiarity that the Aramaic form appears only in some halakic midrashim or so-called amoraic *baraithot*.

[83] כתיב in its many forms appears in the Mekilta more than one hundred times. Because the Mekilta was a rather rarely used text, the contamination from the Babylonian Talmud or midrashim was probably minimal.

[84] See Frankel, *Einl. . . . jer. Talmud*, 9a; 10b; Albeck, Introduction to Gen. Rabbah (n. 19), 26 f. See also Mekilta, *Baḥodesh* IV, 216, 2; Laut. II, 222, 20, for the phrase כמה דאת אמר, a typical formula of Gen. Rabbah (here adopted from Gen. Rabbah XCIX, 1, p. 1272, 2). Note also Albeck, *ibid.*, p. 17, who cites Mekilta, *Amalek*, p. 116; Laut. II, 135, who calls attention to the *petiḥta* in the halakic midrashim. Since the petiḥta is essentially a posttalmudic phenomenon, it attests to the lateness of the Mekilta.

his perceptive study of the halakic midrashim, has shown that the discussions of the amoraim presuppose their ignorance of the Mekilta, but that the author of our Mekilta certainly made extensive use of the amoraic texts of the Palestinian and Babylonian Talmuds.[85] The Mekilta recast amoraic interpretations found in the Babylonian and Palestinian Talmuds into its own style and cites them frequently with tannaitic names.[86] Finkelstein differentiates between the Mekilta's halakic texts, which he regards as tannaitic, and its aggadic material, which he believes to have been inserted. There is no evidence, however, that the Mekilta has been seriously contaminated by extraneous additions.[87] The style of the book is uniform throughout both haggada

[85] Ch. Albeck, *Untersuchungen über die halakischen Midraschim* (Berlin, 1927), pp. 91–120. My own studies have independently corroborated Albeck's conclusion. Thus the Mekilta on Exod. 21:33 (*Nezikin* XI, 287 f.; Laut. III, 90–94), dealing with responsibility for damages in case one opens a pit, reproduces amoraic interpretations of B. Baba Kamma 49b ff., sometimes using the term דבר אחר (another interpretation). In fact the Mekilta can be understood (as in fact traditional scholars always have) in light of the Babylonian Talmud. On the other hand, if such presumably tannaitic comments as found in the Mekilta were in existence, the relevant amoraic exertions to explain the halakah do not make sense. See next note.

[86] Cf. for example Mekilta, *Pasḥa* XV, pp. 56 f.; Laut. I, 127, with B. Yevamot 45b–46a, commenting on Exod. 12:18:

Mekilta	B. Yevamot
רבי נתן אומר	אמר רב חמא בר גוריא אמר רב הלוקח עבד מן
שאין תלמוד לומר המול לו אלא להביא את	העובד כוכבים וקדם וטבל לשם בן חורין קנה
העבד שטבל לפני רבו ויצא לבן חורין מעשה	עצמו בן חורין.... מתיב רב חסדא מעשה
בבלוריא שטבלו מקצת שפחותיה לפניה ומקצתן	בבלוריא הגיורת שקדמו עבדיה וטבלו לפניה ובא
לאחריה ובא מעשה לפני חכמים ואמרו את	מעשה לפני חכמים ואמרו קנו עצמן בני חורין לפניה
שטבלו לפניה בנות חורין לאחריה משועבדות	אין לאחריה לא. אמר רבא לפניה בין בסתם
ואף על פי כן שמשוה עד יום מותה.	בין במפורש לאחריה במפורש אין בסתם לא.

It is obvious that the Mekilta paraphrased the ruling of the sages to conform with Rabba's interpretation of the story. Note also how the Mekilta transformed an amoraic text into a tannaitic one. Cf. also Gerim II, 4.

[87] Contrary to Albeck, *Untersuchungen*, 120: "Ebensowenig wie über die Zeit lässt sich über den Ort der Abfassung unserer hal. Midraschim Bestimmtes behaupten. Einzelne sprachliche Eigentümlichkeiten können in dieser Hinsicht kein Kriterium abgeben, da wir nicht den Urtext, wie er aus der Hand der Redaktoren hervorgegangen ist, besitzen." Weiss, *Dor Dor* II, pp. 228 ff., however, rightly remarks that our text of the Mekilta is substantially the same as it came down from the editor's hand. Certainly the Mekilta is less retouched than, say, the Mishnah, the Babylonian Talmud or Genesis Rabbah. If contamination occurred, it is reflected in the Mekilta de-Rabbi Simeon Ben Yoḥai. The Mekilta of Simeon ben Yoḥai relates to that of Ishmael as Pesikta Rabbati does to Pesikta de-Rab Kahana, Tanḥuma to Tanḥuma Buber, Deut. Rabbah to Deut. Rabbah (ed. Lieberman), or Halakhot Gedolot (ed. Hildesheimer) to standard Halakhot Gedolot. See also note 7.

and halakah. In fact, its legal lore is even more easily traceable to the amoraic halakah than is its legendary or strictly interpretive material. Thus the introductory section of the Mekilta (on Exod. 12:1) attempts to show that though the name of Moses usually precedes in Scripture that of Aaron, the two brothers were in fact of equal status. The text then catalogs other verses where it is claimed that precedence in citation does not necessarily mean precedence in rank. The wording and organization of the passage seems to indicate that the author of the Mekilta copied here the entire section from Genesis Rabbah, which comments on the problem of whether or not Genesis 1:1 implies that the heavens were created before the earth.[88] The text of Genesis Rabbah, however, is in turn traceable in part to the Palestinian Talmud, an expanded form of which is also found in the Tosefta. Because of the multiplicity of possible sources and because the Mekilta's style is distinct from standard rabbinic, the tracing of the source of the passage in the Mekilta to Genesis Rabbah is only probable and not certain. But the next passages of the Mekilta dealing with the calendar are clearly identifiable as adaptations from the Palestinian and Babylonian Talmuds.[89] In general the Mekilta reproduces the halakah of the amoraim, rather than that of the tannaim.

Yet, it should be stressed that the existence of a tannaitic school of biblical exegesis is not questioned in this paper. What is questioned is the claim that the Mekilta of Ishmael and necessarily its variant, that of Simeon ben Yoḥai, are first-hand witnesses of the tannaitic midrash. A compilation of the scattered midrashic passages of the Mishnah could serve as an authentic guide to the tannaitic exegesis of

[88] See above, note 27, for Ginzberg's view that the Mekilta reflects a source older than M. Keritot V, 9. ('Al Halakhah Ve-'aggadah, 67). But it is clear that Gen. Rabbah I, 14, pp. 13 f.; Lev. Rabbah XXXVI, 1, pp. 833–837, Tosefta, Keritot (end), and the Mekilta are interrelated, as Ginzberg says. Hence the relationship of these texts should not be confused with that of M. Keritot (Sifra, beg. Kedoshim). See next note.

[89] See previous note. That Gen. Rabbah is here dependent on P. Ḥagigah II, 77c, is clear because the entire chapter I of Gen. Rabbah is built on P. Ḥagigah II (cf. Gen. R. I, 1–14, pp. 2–14, with P. Ḥagigah 77a–c). If so, the concluding section of Gen. Rabbah I, under discussion, must also come from P. Ḥagigah. Hence Lev. Rabbah and the Mekilta must presumably be here dependent on Gen. Rabbah. The latter still retains the wording of the original, which the author of the Mekilta in the manner of the late midrashim simplified by editing out the authorities.

Ginzberg (ibid. [n. 27], 76–78), by cutting out key parts of the Mekilta passage, misrepresents the text (p. 7; Laut. I, 17 f.). A great scholar, he felt that he could tell intuitively what was original in a text and what was a later addition. This in turn led him to consider his expurgated text as antecedent to the Mishnah (see above note 27). The reader, however, has no choice but to compare the text of the Mekilta with the Palestinian and Babylonian Talmuds.

the Bible. Of lesser degree of authenticity, but still largely tannaitic, are the thousands of midrashic texts cited in the Palestinian and Babylonian Talmuds, as well as in the Tosefta. An analysis of these exegetical passages suggests that there was no essential difference between the midrash of the tannaim and that of the amoraim; both use the identical methodology and technical vocabulary. The Babylonian Talmud, moreover, with its highly developed methods of citation, uses the identical terms (תניא, תנו רבנן, תניא) regardless of whether the reference is to tannaitic midrash or to straightforward halakah. This seems to indicate that the nature of these sources from which the halakic and midrashic passages were drawn was one and the same. Furthermore, of the nearly four hundred tannaitic comments pertaining to the Book of Exodus, compiled from the Babylonian Talmud by E. Z. Melamed, few if any show dependence upon the Mekilta. Even Melamed, who never doubts the tannaitic nature of the Mekilta, grants that there is no reason to believe that the Babylonian Talmud made use of Ishmael's Mekilta.[90] How then is the remarkable kinship between the midrash of the Mekilta and that of the Talmuds to be explained? The conclusion is unescapable that the author of the Mekilta constructed a "tannaitic" midrash from the material he found in the Mishnah, Babylonian and Palestinian Talmuds, and Tosefta.

III

An analysis of both the halakic and aggadic parts of the Mekilta suggests a fourfold division of its sources: 1) texts such as the Mishnah or Tosefta copied by the author, roughly verbatim; 2) passages taken from the talmudic or midrashic literature, but lightly retouched and put into the mouth of tannaitic authorities; 3) material taken from the last-mentioned sources, but completely recast; and 4) passages

[90] See Melamed, *Halachic Midrashim* (n. 1), Introduction, *passim*, esp. p. 36, who notes, however, that there is a linguistic link between the Babylonian Talmud and the Mekilta of Simeon ben Yoḥai. In fact, this is only so because Melamed was then using Hoffmann's edition of this Mekilta, based on the fifteenth century Yemenite Midrash Hagadol, whose author altered the Mekilta's text contaminating it with the wordings of the Babylonian Talmud.

Incidentally, Melamed's *Halachic Midrashim* is a remarkable compilation of the tannaitic midrash, as reported in the Babylonian Talmud. The author's amazing industry, however, was of little avail in describing the nature of this midrash because he proceeded from the premise that the halakic midrashim antedated the Babylonian Talmud. In light of the hypothesis that the midrashic collections based much of their material on the biblical exegesis preserved in the Talmud, Melamed's work assumes added significance.

directly attributable to the author of the Mekilta. It goes without saying that only in regard to 1) and partly 2) may the Mekilta be cited to shed light upon tannaitic and amoraic texts.

There is a basic difference between the composition of the Mekilta and that of the Mishnah, Tosefta, or Palestinian and Babylonian Talmuds. Because of the growth of the latter through accretion, it is not correct to use the terms authors, but only editors. Judah Hanasi retained essentially the form of the Mishnah he had found, using primarily scissors and paste to organize the material. The Tosefta originally consisted of some tannaitic passages omitted from the Mishnah which with the passage of time were labeled *baraithot*. Our inherited Tosefta, however, contains in addition many other tannaitic citations (*baraithot*) taken from the Palestinian and Babylonian Talmuds. The early amoraim (as attested in the Palestinian Talmud) hardly distinguished between a mishnah and a baraitha or, indeed, between tannaitic and amoraic authority. In the later amoraic period, however (as attested in the Babylonian Talmud), a hierarchy was constructed, according to which Judah Hanasi's Mishnah came to be regarded as the most authoritative postpentateuchal text, followed by the less authoritative baraithot, and followed in turn by the amoraic elaborations and comments. In the centuries-long process of making the tannaitic texts intelligible, the amoraim increased the rabbinic literature manifold beyond what it was during the tannaitic period, resulting in the collections known as Palestinian and Babylonian Talmuds. The Mekilta of Ishmael, however, is not a collection of diverse texts, but the work of a real author. And as such it is closer to the eighth century *She'iltot* of Aḥai than to the talmudic texts.[91]

Perhaps an inquiry into the possible date and place of origin of the Mekilta will shed light on why such a pseudograph was concocted. Some clues have already been intimated. The Palestinian Talmud was edited about the year 425; the Genesis Rabbah within a century later.[92] The author of the Mekilta used not only these texts, but also apocryphal tractates such as Gerim (Proselytes),[93] Semaḥot[94] (euphe-

---

[91] Aḥai wrote the *She'iltot* in 747 (*Iggeret Sherira Gaon*, ed. Lewin, 103), sections of which found their way into certain midrashic works (see Tanḥuma, *Bereshit*, 2 — She'ilta I). Though based strictly on the Babylonian Talmud, the *She'iltot* was written in Palestine, where Aḥai migrated. It fuses halakah and aggadah, is arranged according to the pericopes of the Torah, uses an exegetic vocabulary of its own, while mainly reproducing the original passages of the Talmud.

[92] See Albeck, Introduction (n. 19), pp. 93–96.

[93] Cf. Mekilta, *Nezikin* XVIII, pp. 311 f.; Laut. III, 137–141, with Gerim IV, 1–4. For variants in the two texts see commentaries.

[94] Cf. *ibid.*, XVIII, p. 313; Laut. III, 141–143, with Semaḥot VIII.

mistic name for Mournings), and Abot de-Rabbi Nathan, tractates written in the sixth century or later.[95] The Mekilta offers one of the early testimonies to the use of the Babylonian Talmud in the West. Attempts to gather the lore of the academies of Sura and Pumbedita began in the fifth century by Rab Ashi and Rabbina, but the work was abruptly concluded after the Moslem conquest of the Sassanian Empire in 651.[96] Some time must have elapsed before the Babylonian Talmud penetrated into Palestine and North Africa. Since it was utilized by the author of the Mekilta, he could not have lived before the beginning of the eighth century.

Certain passages of the Mekilta give the general impression that we are dealing with a posttalmudic work. The iconoclastic movement which shook the Byzantine empire during the reigns of Leo III (717–741) and Constantine V (741–775) is echoed in a parable of the Mekilta: "A king of flesh and blood who entered a province; the people built icons, formed sculpture, and struck coins for him. After an interval they covered his icons, smashed his sculptures, and defaced his coins."[97] Again, the calendar retrojected to the exodus is that of the posttalmudic period — Nisan has thirty days; Iyyar, twenty-nine — which the Mekilta attributes also to Rabbi Shila, evidently a Palestinian amora.[98]

Commenting on Exod. 20:6, *Baḥodesh*, Chapter Six, alludes to a period of religious persecution. The text extols the righteous men who become martyrs on account of their observance of the commandments, such as circumcision, the recitation of the Torah, the eating of unleavened bread, or the ceremony of lulab. Many, the author suggests, flee the country to save their lives, but God loves the ones who stay in the Holy Land and die sanctifying His name. The persecution alluded to cannot refer to that of Hadrian, which

[95] Substantial sections of the Mekilta have close parallels in Avot de-Rabbi Nathan (e. g., Mekilta, *Beshallaḥ* V, pp. 100 f.; Laut. I, 123 f., with Avot de-R. Nathan XXXIII, 48b–49b. Cf. Zunz-Albeck (n. 12), p. 45; pp. 51 f. Since these tractates drew from the Babylonian and Palestinian Talmuds, they must be later than the sixth century. Even if it be argued that these and similar tractates are younger than the Mekilta, it is clear that the aggada of these treatises is similar to that of the Mekilta. In some instances, it has been shown that our Mekilta is dependent on them (see notes 48, 59, 63, and 100).

[96] Cf. Julius Kaplan, *The Redaction of the Babylonian Talmud* (New York, 1933).

[97] Mekilta, *Baḥodesh* VIII, 233; Laut., II, 262. Cf. P. Shekalim VI, 1, 49d; Cant. Rabbah on 5:14. The latter apparently was the Mekilta's source; the parallels do not have the passage on the icons.

[98] Mekilta, *Beshallaḥ* I, pp. 83 f.; *Vayyassa* I, p. 159; Laut. I, 189; II, 99 f. Cf. B. Shabbath 87b–88a, which evidently forms the basis of this passage, but which is much less definite about the dates of the exodus.

was limited in scope and which was political rather than religious basically. It follows that the Mekilta refers to the attempts of the Christian emperors, commencing with Justinian, to uproot the Jewish religion.

An uncensored text of the Babylonian Talmud relates that before the people of Israel took upon themselves the yoke of the Decalogue, God had offered it to the nations of the world, particularly to the Romans and the Persians (Sassanians).[99] In the Mekilta as well as in another contemporary book — the Pirke de-Rabbi Eliezer — it is said that God singled out the sons of Esau (Christians) and the sons of Ishmael (Moslems). It is clear that the author of this passage lived when the Arabs ruled the Near East.[100]

Some may argue that all these passages are late interpolations into an early work or a late re-editing of an old text. But the case for a posttalmudic dating of the Mekilta does not rest on them alone. Rather, it is based on an array of considerations: The halakah, the sources, the names of the authorities, the technical vocabulary, the tendency towards abstractions, as well as the external evidence, all point in the same direction — that the Mekilta is a posttalmudic work. The references to the calendar instituted during the geonic period or to the Moslem dominance of the Near East must not be treated as marginal glosses or additions. In fact it is unjust to speak of a compiler or editor of the Mekilta. This book had a real author, whose personality is evident in both the formulation of the material and the architecture of the work. Incidentally, the eighth century was a particularly productive period of pseudepigraphs among Christians and Moslems as well. The Mekilta may not be dated much later than the year 800 because, as noted above, Simeon of Kayyara names the book in the first half of the ninth century.[101]

The problem of where the author of the Mekilta lived is more complex, and probably beyond solution. That it was Palestine appears at first sight to be a good guess. The Palestinian Talmud and midrashim seem to permeate the Mekilta. Moreover, in geonic texts it is sometimes

---

[99] B. Avodah Zarah 2b. Cf. B. Shabbath 89a–b; Gen. Rabbah XCIX, 1271 f.

[100] See previous note. Mekilta, *Baḥodesh* V, 221; Laut. II, 234 f. Ammon and Moab are also mentioned to show that all Arab tribes were present at Sinai. In Pirke de-Rabbi Eliezer XLI, however, only the sons of Esau and Ishmael are cited. Cf. also Sifre, Deut., 343, which claims that the Torah was given in four languages: Hebrew, Latin, Arabic and Aramaic. Note the failure to mention Greek, which would have been inconceivable during the Greek or Roman domination of the Near East.

[101] See above, note 7.

dubbed as the "Mekilta of the Land of Israël."[102] But other indications suggest that it was published elsewhere. It is difficult to assume that Babylonian influence reached Palestine in the eighth century. Moreover, the Hebrew of the Mekilta appears to be defective when compared with contemporary Palestinian works. Egypt or some other North African location, where both Palestinian and Babylonian roots were planted, appears a more plausible place of the publication of the Mekilta. This might explain the author's selection of the exodus upon which to build his comments. In fact the Mekilta as a whole seems to be dominated by Egypt, perhaps the native country of the author. But I would leave the question open.

The above considerations flow together to suggest that the basic purpose of the Mekilta may well have been to vindicate the rabbinic tradition. Its author invoked the venerable memory of the tannaim, possibly to strengthen the spread of the amoraic halakah of the Babylonian Talmud, a work which was to become the authoritative guide of Jewish law. Possibly, though, the purpose of the Mekilta was to counterpoise the talmudic dialectics, suggesting instead that, with the aid of tannaitic hermeneutic principles, the halakah could be systematically derived directly from the Torah. Another possibility may be that the Mekilta reflects the rabbinic response to the Karaite assaults on talmudic Judaism. About the year 760 Yehudai Gaon of Sura proclaimed the Babylonian Talmud as the only authoritative source of the halakah.[103] Around this time Anan ben David had made an attack upon the entire rabbinic tradition as a distortion and misinterpretation of Scripture. The author of the Mekilta may have responded to the Karaite tendencies he had encountered by showing that the rabbinic traditions arose from a sound and formal exegetical interpretation of the Torah. The earliest attested citation from the Mekilta is used in a polemics against the Karaites.[104] Unfortunately, the knowledge of the tannaitic period and the history of the halakah of the Mekilta's author was rather limited. "Childish blunders" (as put by Weiss) are evident throughout the book. Nevertheless, as an eighth century work it displays a remarkable acquaintance with the

[102] See *Responsen der Geonim* (*Teshuvot Hageonim*, ed. Harkavy, Berlin, 1887, p. 107; *Ozar Hageonim*, ed. Lewin, Baba Kamma, Haifa, 1953, pp. 6–7), a responsum of Hai Gaon. This should dispose of the claim that the Mekilta was written in Babylonia. See above, notes 61–62. Epstein-Melamed, *Introduction* (n. 1), p. 547, n. 20, interprets enigmatically "Mekilta of the Land of Israel," to mean that it was brought from Palestine, not that it was written there.

[103] See *Ginze Schechter*, ed. Ginzberg (New York, 1929) II, pp. 557 ff.

[104] Harkavy, in *Hakedem* I (1907), p. 127, citing Mekilta, *Baḥodesh* X, p. 239; Laut. II, 276.

sources. He constructed a refreshing commentary on parts of the Book of Exodus, fusing it with early medieval haggadah. The author's capacity to build upon the old and invent a new hermeneutic terminology shows some of the similar imaginative genius displayed later by the author of the Zohar.

The traditional halakists (except perhaps Maimonides)[105] rightly paid little serious attention to the Mekilta. In the scale of halakic authority, the Mekilta's position is generally regarded as lower not only than that of the Palestinian Talmud and Tosefta, but also of nonhalakic works such as Midrash Rabbah or Tanḥuma.[106] We can explain this lower position only as their evaluation of the Mekilta as one more apocryphal treatise. Writing in 986, Sherira Gaon (who never names the Mekilta) seems to have alluded to works such as the Mekilta with these words: "When we now find texts of *Baraithot* we do not rely upon them, for they are not studied, because we do not know whether or not they are authentic, except those of Rabbi Hiyya only, which are read by scholars. There are other *Baraithot*, which they call 'minor,' such as Derekh Ereẓ, but they are not to be used as halakic sources."[107]

Sherira Gaon's testimony in regard to the unauthentic *Baraithot* allegedly produced during the geonic period seems to be applicable to the Mekilta as well. Around the year 600 and onward a remarkable revival of the Hebrew literature took place. This becomes evident in the dramatic shift from Greek and Latin to Hebrew in the epigraphical remnants of the period, in the fervent labors of the Masoretes, in the rise of the *piyyut*, and in the adoption of Hebrew (outside of Babylonia) as the language of both the aggadah and halakah. The Mekilta of Ishmael and its variant, the Mekilta of Simeon ben Yoḥai, may be regarded as works which utilize masterfully the hermeneutics of the tannaim and amoraim to summarize the talmudic halakah and aggadah pertaining to the Book of Exodus.*

---

[105] See note 18.

[106] Cf. Responsa of *Tashbaẓ* (Simeon b. Ẓemaḥ Duran) III, No. 52.

[107] *Iggeret Sherira Gaon*, p. 47. See also Hai Gaon's definition of "Mekilta," as a selection of *halakhot* gleaned from the whole Talmud (Ginzberg, *Geonica* II, p. 39). I am indebted to Professor J. Petuchowski for this note.

* My colleagues Lewis Barth, Eugene Mihaly, Jakob Petuchowski, Samuel Sandmel, and David Weisberg have kindly read this essay. I am profoundly grateful for their helpful comments. Naturally, they do not necessarily subscribe to the views, not to speak of the central thesis, expressed in this paper.

CHRONOMESSIANISM

THE TIMING OF MESSIANIC MOVEMENTS
AND THE CALENDAR OF SABBATICAL CYCLES*

THIS paper presents an outline of the evidence in the biblical, Qumran, New Testament, and rabbinic literature for a hitherto unnoticed but apparently at one time widespread belief, that the inevitable coming of the messiah would take place during the season when Israel celebrated the sabbatical year. Sabbatical messianism, or chronomessianism, are appropriate terms for a phenomenon that inspired a search in the scriptural prophecies for the exact date of the redeemer's coming. Although most powerful in the apocalyptic tradition, chronomessianism appears as well in the mainstream of Judaism. The locus classicus of chronomessianic doctrine is found in Daniel 9, particularly in the mysterious verses 24–27. This study will trace the impact of Daniel 9 on the literature of ensuing centuries. A fascinating question arising from this investigation is whether chronomessianic doctrine was a factor in the timing of the launching of certain movements, such as John the Baptist's ministry or Bar Kochba's rebellion against the Romans.[1]

I

The pre-history of chronomessianism may be traced in several biblical pasages. Isa. 23:15–18 predicts that Tyre will be forgotten for seventy

* Professors John Strugnell, Chanan (Herbert) Brichto and Mr. Hershel Statman have rendered valuable assistance in the editing of this paper, for which I wish to express my profound gratitude.

1 For more extensive bibliographical citations, see "The Calendar of Sabbatical Cycles During the Second Temple and Early Rabbinic Period," *HUCA,* 44 (1973), 153–196. The following items should be added: Zuckermann's "Ueber Sabbatjahrzyclus, etc." (*ibid.* p. 156 note 12) is now available in an English translation by A. Lowy, "A Treatise on the Sabbatical Cycle and the Jubilee (New York: Hermon Press, 1974); Nachum Sarna, "Zedekiah's Emancipation of Slaves and the Sabbatical Year," in *Orient and Occident. Essays Presented to Cyrus H. Gordon* (Neukirchen-Vluyn: Butzon & Bercker Kepelaer, 1973), 143–149. To note 97 p. 180, add: A. A. Akavia, *Sinai* 30 (1951), 118–137.

years, at the end of which time the Lord will again remember the famous city.[2] Jeremiah employs the 70-year period for the length of Judah's coming exile in Babylonia (Jer. 25: 11–12; 29: 10).[3] The use of the number 70 might reflect the Jewish affinity for the numeral seven and its multiples, evidenced in weekly and yearly sabbaths (shemittah) and the jubilee; alternately, it might have been a common Near Eastern convention for the maximum life expectancy or the normal span of two or three generations.[4] Whatever that number's function in Jeremiah, Zech. 1:12 regards the number 70 as the precise length of Judah's exile. By fusing Jeremiah's "70-year prophecy" with the assertion in Lev. 26:34–35, 43, that during the exile the land would atone for the sabbaths that Israel had violated, 2 Chron. 36:21–23 suggests not only that Jeremiah's words came true, but explicitly interprets Cyrus' edict as having reference to them.

Whatever the precise meaning of these passages, the credit for inventing sabbatical messianism belongs to the author of Daniel 9.[5] Zech. 1:2 and 2 Chron. 36:21–23 merely repeated Jeremiah's prophecy to account for the length of the exile; the interpretation in Daniel was future-directed. The author of Daniel openly acknowledges that he uses Jeremiah, specifically, and other "books" where the reference may include Zechariah, without question the Chronicler, from whose views he dissents.[6] Stressing the novelty of the discovery in a lengthy introduction (1–23), the author of Daniel goes on in 9:24–27 to present his own chronological exegesis of Jeremiah's 70-year prophecy. Before proceeding with a review of chronomessianic doctrine and movements, it will be necessary to analyze this passage in some detail, particularly to determine how it was generally understood in antiquity.

The ancient Jewish exegesis of Dan. 9:24–27 differs from modern scholarship in two significant ways. With a few exceptions,[7] all medieval and recent commentators translate the key-word *shavu'a* (supposedly

---

2   For a view that this passage is a postexilic addition, see O. Procksch, *Jesaia* I (KAT, Leipzig, 1930), 305.

3   See W. Rudolph, *Jeremia* (HAT, Tübingen, 1968), 161, 184 f.

4   Cf. Ps. 90:10; Jer. 27:7. For a review of ancient lore in reference to 70 years, see P. Grelot, "Soixante-dix semaines d'années," *Biblica* 50 (1969), 169–186, esp. 173–175.

5   Cf. R. H. Charles, *Critical and Exegetical Commentary on the Book of Daniel* (Oxford, 1929), pp. xxvii f.; D. S. Russel, *The Method and the Message of the Apocalyptic* (London, SGM Press, 1964), 16 f.

6   Dan. 9:2 cites "books." The use of 2 Chron. 36:21 is apparent a) in the word "To fulfill" (לִמְלֹאות), which varies from כִּמְלֹאות in Jer. 25:12 and 29:10. Dan. 9:10–14 also suggests an awareness of the Chronicler's use of Lev. 26 in citing Jeremiah.

7   Grelot, note 4; M. Delcor, *Le livre de Daniel* (SB, Paris, 1971), 194–204.

following the LXX) as heptomad or a "week," seven years.[8] The ancient exegetes, it will be shown, understood *shavu'a* to refer to the seven-year cycle, the last year of which was "the year of the Lord" (Lev. 25:2), the equivalent of the year of shemittah or release (Deut. 15:1–2), when debts were canceled and land lay fallow.[9] The difference between the two interpretations is that, according to the former, any septennial number will do; according to the latter, however, each seven-year period had its fixed place in a series, precise in beginning and end. A second difference stems from the first. Modern exegetes interpret the passage without reference to Jewish chronology current at that time.[10] The ancients, however, took it for granted that the numbers in 9:24–27 had to harmonize with their calendar of sabbatical cycles.[11] No student would undertake to determine the day of the week without reference to the Jewish or Christian calendar; yet none of the nineteenth or twentieth century commentators, I have concluded, tries to harmonize Daniel with the sabbatical cycles as they were uninterruptedly observed during inter-testamental and early rabbinic times. This study attempts to show that such a harmonization is plausible, perhaps even compelling.

That *shavu'a* meant the sabbatical cycle is attested in Qumran, rabbinic and epigraphic documents. In its description of the beginning of rule of Light, the Manual of Discipline mentions the monthly and annual seasons: the period of years "for their weeks" (לשבועיהם); and at the beginning "of their weeks" a period of "freedom (דרור i.e., jubilee)."[12] The so-called Zadokite Document alludes to the Book of Jubilees in these words: "And the exact statement of the epochs of Israel's blindness to all these, behold it can be learnt in the Book of the Divisions of Times into their Jubilees and Weeks" (ספר מחלקות העתים ליובליהם ובשבועותיהם).[13] These and similar passages allude to the sabbatical cycles known to have been observed in Palestine from the post-exilic period to the fifth or sixth Christian century.[14] A recently excavated

8. Cf. Schürer, III, 266 f.; J. A. Montgomery, *Daniel* (ICC, New York, 1927), 373, who notes the possibility of *shavu'a* meaning sabbatical cycle, but ignores it in 390–401; A. Bentzen, *Daniel*[3] (HAT, Tübingen, 1952), 73–77; Russel, *Method* (note 5), 195–202.

9 Seder Olam, 28; 30; Yer. Ta'anit IV, 5, 68d; Naḥmanides' *Commentary* on Exod. 12:2 and 20:8.

10 Cf. references cited in notes 5, 7–8.

11 Seder Olam, 28 (p. 65, Ratner ed.); Yalkut Shim'oni on Amos 7:17, no. 547; Dan. 9:24, No. 1066; B. Yoma 54a. Although Saadia, Rashi, and Ibn Ezra diverge widely in the hermeneutics of Dan. 9:24–27, they agree that these verses referred to the traditional calendar of sabbatical cycles.

12 IQS 10:8–9. See also below notes 26–29.

13 CD 16:3–4.

14 Cf. B. Zuckermann (note 1), 5–45; Wacholder, *HUCA,* 44 (1973), 156–

synagogue at Khirbet Susiya contains fragments of a mosaic dated in the "second year of the Week (שלשבוע) .... four thousand years ... after the world was created."[15] This inscription comes from a synagogue probably built not before the fifth Christian century, yet the basic meaning of *shavu'a* had hardly changed through the centuries.[16]

In contrast to the Chronicler, who had understood Jeremiah's 70-year prophecy literally, Dan. 9:24 interpreted it as 70 sabbatical cycles (שָׁבֻעִים שִׁבְעִים) equal to ten jubilees or 490 years; each of Jeremiah's years being equal to a shemittah cycle, seven of which made up a jubilee, at the end of which the Hebrews in bondage gained their freedom. But Jerusalem's sins have been so grave, in the author's opinion, that ten jubilees "are decreed concerning your people and your holy city, to finish the transgression, to put an end to sin, and to atone for iniquity, to bring in everlasting righteousness, to seal both vision and prophet, and to anoint a most holy place" (v. 24). Daniel never uses the term jubilee directly, but his numbers can be only understood in light of Lev. 25:1–23, which gives seven sabbaticals as the maximum time of sanctioned bondage. Lev. 25:10, to be sure, may be plausibly interpreted to mean that a jubilee cycle consisted of 50 years, not of 49. But a 49-year jubilee is taken for granted by the author of the Book of Jubilees. Even the rabbinic tradition which generally supposes a 50-year jubilee for the period of the First Temple argues a 49-year jubilee for the Second. Moreover, as has been stated above, the observance of shemittah cycles is attested, while the assumption of an extra year for the jubilee year is totally unwarranted by the evidence. This is not to say, however, that during the intertestamental period the Mosaic injunction regarding the jubilee was entirely ignored. The author of Daniel 9 not only assumed the reality of a jubilee period, but without mentioning it directly made it the most significant unit of the divine divisions of time. What appears to have happened is that the seventh shemittah (i.e., the 49th year) was legally considered both a sabbatical and jubilee year.[17]

The Book of Daniel reflects an interest in chronography that is unique in the biblical tradition. This interest, however, reflects not an antiquarian's passion for accurate dating of events, but a purpose to strengthen the author's prophetic vision. The names of the Babylonian

---

196, Cf. J. Jeremias, "Sabbathjahr und neutestamentliche Chronologie." *ZNW*, 27 (1928), 103.

15 S. Gutman et al., "Excavations in the Synagogue at Khirbet Susiya," *Qadmoniot*, 5 No. 2 (1972), 47–52, esp. 51a.

16 M. Nedarim, 8:1, rules that a vow "this *shavu'a*," limits its validity to the remainder of the current cycle, inclusive of the shemittah year.

17 In accordance with the opinion of Judah, who argued, however, that the 50th year counted also as the first year of the next shemittah cycle; the sages differ (Arakhin, 12b; cf. Seder Olam, 15, and passim).

and Persian kings and the fictional dates which are interspersed throughout the Book of Daniel were inserted there to give an appearance of historicity to the prophetic material.[18] In some passages, indeed, the author weaves chronological lore into the very essence of the prophecy. This is the case in chapters 7–8, which relate the sequence of the four kingdoms that was to conclude at "the end of days;" it is particularly evident in 9:24–27, which uses Jeremiah's 70-year prophecy to structure a "chronology" of the future. An analysis of these verses suggests that the author proposed a threefold division of history:

A.   The rebuilding of the temple

B.   The prophetic epoch, described in our passage;

C.   The postprophetic epoch, presumably identical with the messianic age. Thus Daniel's interpretation of Jeremiah's 70-year prophecy transcended the antiquarian interest in chronology and chronography, claiming as it did, to reveal the schedule of the future. Unfortunately, the author tells nothing of A and C; but we should be grateful that he chose to detail Epoch B which is likewise divided into three periods:

1.   The rebuilding of the temple

2.   Persecution

3.   The bridge between the prophetic and postprophetic epochs.

1.   "Know then and understand: from the time that the word went forth that Jerusalem should be restored and rebuilt, seven weeks shall pass till the appearance of one anointed, a prince; then for sixty-two weeks it shall remain restored, rebuilt with streets and conduits" (25: NEB). Daniel defines the first stage of the prophetic epoch (when "the word went forth") as an unmistakable reference to Leviticus' admonition and to Jeremiah's oracle, cited in Dan. 9:2. Our passage points out that from the time of the prophecy, presumably uttered just prior to the exile, until the restoration of Jerusalem and the appearance of the "anointed prince" (evidently a reference to Zerubbabel), there elapsed seven sabbatical cycles (one jubilee or 49 years). But Daniel seems to insist that the time of the exile was to be counted as part of the sixty-two cycles, the period of Jerusalem's rebuilding. A possible justification for regarding the two as segments of a single time-unit is that since the exile was integral to the fulfillment of Jeremiah's prophecy of redemption it became a part of the period of restoration. Therefore, the subtraction of seven sabbatical cycles (one Jubilee) reduces the period of the 62 sabbatical cycles (8 and 6/7 jubilees) to 55 sabbatical cycles or 7 and 6/7 jubilees = 385 years.

---

18   The fictional nature of Daniel's chronological lore has not prevented scholars of many generations from transforming it into historical chronology. Cf. H. H. Rowley, *Darius the Mede and the Four World Kingdoms in the Book of Daniel* (Cardiff, University of the Wales Press Board, 1959).

2. "At the critical time, after the sixty-two weeks, one who is anointed shall be removed with no one to take his part; and the horde of an invading prince shall work havoc on city and sanctuary. The end of it shall be a deluge, inevitable war with all its horrors. He shall make a firm league with the mighty for one week; and, the week half spent, he shall put a stop to sacrifice and offering ... then, in the end, what has been decreed concerning the desolation will be poured out" (26–27: NEB). The period of crisis, according to our passage, would occur during the final sabbatical cycle of the ninth jubilee, which verse 27 splits into two equal segments, the second more horrible than the first.

3. Daniel makes no explicit mention of the third period of the post-prophetic epoch, but its existence is apparent, as verse 24 listed 70 sabbatical cycles, while verses 25–27 accounted for only 63, leaving 7 cycles as a remainder. It may thus be assumed that the third period of this epoch lasting seven sabbatical cycles = one jubilee, was intended to serve as a bridge between the prophetic epoch and the coming of the messianic kingdom.

Table 1 sums up the chronology implicit in the three periods:

TABLE ONE
DANIEL'S PROPHETIC EPOCH

Dan. 9	Period	No. of Jubilees	No. of Sabbatical Cycles	No. of Years	Remarks
24	1–3	10	49	490	entire epoch
25	1	8 6/7	62	434	exile plus restoration
25a	1a	1	7	49	exile
25b	1b	7 6/7	55	385	restoration minus exile
27	2	1/7	1	7	persecution
27a	2a	1/14	1/2	3 1/2	stage I of persecution
27b	2b	1/14	1/2	3 1/2	stage II of persecution
24–27	3	1	7	49	bridge to messianic age

We are now faced with the question which has confronted every student of Dan. 9:24–27. How are we to identify the chronology underlying this passage? We must further address an additional question: In what respect does our study presume to offer a more satisfactory answer to Daniel's messianic numerology than do the numerous scholarly proposals made hitherto?[19]

---

19 Consult the bibliographies assembled in the works cited in notes 5, 7–8. As to the dates of the sabbatical cycles, see the tables in *HUCA* 44 (1973), 185–196, cited in note 1. Zuckermann's tables of sabbatical cycles (note 1), presently the consensus, assume a chronology described in note 21.

To address the second question first, the explanations proposed hitherto fail to take account of the obvious link between Daniel's chronology and the then current calendar of sabbatical cycles. As has been stated above, *shavu'a* in the sense of seven years always referred, in ancient texts, to the computing of the shemittah cycle. The chronology proposed here is the first attempt, to our knowledge, to interpret Dan. 9:24–27 in light of the then current sabbatical calendar.

As is now almost universally accepted, any approach that attempts to solve the numerology of Dan. 9:25–27 must presume that our passage refers to the onslaught on Judaism by Antiochus IV Epiphanes. Since verse 27 predicts that this persecution will last a sabbatical cycle, split into two stages, the problem is how to synchronize this sabbatical cycle with the then current calendar. Now since Antiochus IV ascended the throne of Syria (according to cuneiform tablets) between Ululu 11 and the end of the month of 137 (September 4 and 22 of 175) and was murdered in Kislimu 148 s.e. (November 20–December 18 of 164 B.C.E.), the single sabbatical cycle of the Jewish calendar alluded to in verse 27 could only be either 176/75–170/69 B.C.E. or 169/68–163/62 B.C.E.[20]

Which of these two sabbatical cycles does the evidence better fit? Arguments in favor of the first: a) Antiochus IV in fact became king at the end of the first year of the cycle; b) Hellenization of Judaea commenced soon thereafter; and c) Dan. 9:26, "the anointed shall be removed" (וכרת משיח) apparently refers to Antiochus' replacement of the rightful high priest, an event which seems to have taken place in 172 or 171 B.C.E.

Daniel's words, however, become unquestionably more pointed in light of the second alternative: a) "the horde of the invading prince shall work havoc with the city and sanctuary," is a perfect fit for Antiochus' pillage of the Temple in the autumn of 169 B.C.E., at the beginning of the sabbatical cycle; b) the division of the sabbatical into two segments, during the second of which "sacrifice and offering will cease" would not fit into the first but does accord with the second alternative; and c) the same may be said of "the desolations" (שקוצים משומם). As to the reference to the removal of Onias, the date of this event is obscure and cannot be cited to refute the evidence which so strongly supports the cycle of 169/68–163/62 B.C.E. Now if the sabbatical cycle recorded in verses 26–27 alludes to the Julian years 169/68–163/62 B.C.E., which corresponded to the 63rd sabbatical cycle, as well as to the last cycle of the 9th jubilee, Daniel's underlying sabbatical chronology can be reconstructed

---

20 A. J. Sachs, and D. J. Wiseman, "A Babylonian King List of the Hellenistic Period," *Iraq,* 16 (1954), 202–212, esp. 209. R. A. Parker and W. H. Dubberstein, *Babylonian Chronology 626 B.C.–A.D. 75* (Providence, R. I., Brown University Press, 1956), 23; Wacholder, *HUCA* 44 (1973), 160–163.

as shown in Table 2. (Suppose, however, that the first alternative, or some other exegesis of Dan. 9:24–27, is to be preferred, then deduct from Table 2, seven Julian years, or adjust dates otherwise as needed.)[21]

TABLE TWO
DANIEL'S SABBATICAL CHRONOLOGY

Dan. 9	Epoch	Period	No. of Jub.	No. of Sabb.	No. of Years	B.C.E.	Remarks
24	I					Until 604/03	preprophetic epoch
24	II	1–3	10	49	490	603/02–114/13	prophetic epoch
25		1	8 6/7	62	434	603/02–170/69	restoration, including exile
25a		1a	1	7	49	603/02–555/54	exile
25b		1b	7 6/7	55	385	554/53–170/69	restoration minus exile
27		2	1/7	1	7	169/68–163/62	persecution
27a		2a	1/14	1/2	3 1/2	169/68–166/65	stage I
27b		2b	1/14	1/2	3 1/2	165/64–163/62	stage II
24–27		3	1	7	49	162/61–114/13	end of prophetic epoch
24	III					After 113/12	messianic age

A recurring discrepancy between the proposed reconstruction of Daniel's dates and the chronology based on reliable sources presents a problem. Daniel apparently dated the exile in 604/03 B.C.E. but it occurred either in Nisan of 597 B.C.E., if the writer referred to the first Babylonian exile, or in Av of 587, if the second was meant. Cyrus issued his edict in 538/37; not in 554/53, as is suggested in our interpretation of the passage. The answer to these objections is that Daniel's dates, as they related to the remote past, were often approximate or artificial, made to fit into a more or less arbitrary chronomessianic structure, exemplified by the book's chapter headings which date by a fictive Darius the Mede.

More problematical, however, is the inconsistency of the date of the placement of the "abomination" in the Temple. According to I Macc. 1:54, it occurred in Kislev of 145 S.E. = December of 167 B.C.E.; Table 2 seems to date the event in the spring of 165. Although the difference between the two datings is only about fifteen or sixteen months, it does represent a serious objection to the calculation, as it is too large an

21 See note 19. By deducting 1 Julian year from the dates, Table 2 would conform to the sabbatical chronology of the consensus. See Maimonides, Shemittah X, 1–8.

error for contemporaneous chronology. In fact, however, the difference may be reduced by six months, as in Jewish tradtion, half a week is not 3½ days or years, but 3, since the sabbath day or year is not normally part of the computation. If so, Daniel may have dated the second stage of Antiochus' persecution in the fall of 166 B.C.E.; I Macc. 1:54, some ten months earlier. This method of computation would reduce Daniel's departure from the historical date to ten months, perhaps a permissible deviation in a chronomessianic book.

Daniel appears nearest to the historical date in his evident timing of the end of the persecution, presumably in Tishri of 163. For most purposes, however, in the ancient Jewish calendar, the year commenced in Nisan. And if Daniel intended to time, using the customary postdating, the cleansing of the Temple on Nisan 1 149 S.E. = April 163 B.C.E., this timing departs from that of I Macc. 1:54 by only three or four months.

Because Dan. 9:24–27 offers the classical locus of sabbatical chronomessianism, a relatively large section of this study dealt with this passage, permitting now a more abbreviated treatment of the evidence for this belief in subsequent Jewish writings. No matter how divergent their opinions might have been among men such as the author of the First Book of Maccabees, the members of Essene groups, Josephus, or the talmudic sages, they regarded Daniel's numbers as a guide to the date of the redemption. Even Christian chronography, which ultimately developed into a science, had had its foundation in Daniel.[22] To be sure, the ancient Jewish exegetes frequently misapplied or abused our passage; but their understanding, in contrast to that of modern scholarship, that Daniel referred to sabbatical messianism is right. Only with the gradual disappearance of the agricultural laws of shemittah from Jewish life did the link between the calendar and the expectations of redemption finally disappear.

II

Qumran Writings

If Daniel 9 pointed out the messianic implication of the sabbatical cycles, the author of Jubilees elaborated the same divisions of time for the creation of the world and Israel's history until the entry into Canaan. By its very formal title, "The Book of the Divisions of Times into their Jubilees and Sabbatical Cycles," the author shows his indebtedness to Daniel 9, as both *'ittim* and *shavu'ot(im)* were probably inspired by

---

22 H. Gelzer, *Sextus Julius Africanus* (Leipzig, 1880), I, 24–26.

Dan. 9:25.[23] Although the Book of Daniel never mentions the term directly, the jubilee forms the essence of Dan. 9:24–27. Daniel, we are told, became aware of the meaning of the sabbatical division by studying Jeremiah and Chronicles, with the aid of Gabriel (Dan. 9:2, 21–27). Jubilees' introductory sentence attributes the division of time into sabbaticals and jubilees to the Lord, as he had spoken to Moses on Mount Sinai. The angel of the Presence, according to Jub. 1:29, informed Israel that these periods would prevail from the creation "until the sanctuary of the Lord shall be made in Jerusalem in Mount Zion," i.e., probably to messianic rather than Solomonic times.

During the sabbatical year, according to the War between the Children of the Light and the Children of the Darkness, special sacrifices were ordained. Warfare was prohibited.[24] Thse nature of these sacrifices is obscure; the prohibition of warfare may have reflected a strictly sectarian view. But it seems clear that there existed, confirmed in writings so diverse as Josephus and Tacitus,[25] a tendency to equate the laws of the yearly sabbaths with those of the weekly sabbaths.

The recently published fragments from a partially preserved *pesher* offer a fascinating presentation of sabbatical chronomessianism.[26] Although written in the familiar Qumran style, the *pesher* applied Daniel's insight into what evidently was an anthology of biblical passages related to the sabbatical and jubilee themes, but which also included allusions to the reigns of the Righteous (Melchizedek) and Wicked (Melchiresha^c). After commenting on Lev. 25:13 in regard to the Israelites' return to their patrimony in the year of דרור (jubilee), the remission of debts in Deut. 15:2, and freedom (דרור) to the captives, proclaimed in Isa. 61:1, 11QMelch 3 II continues: "Its interpretation is: that He will proclaim them to be among the children of Heaven and of the inheritance of Melchizedek ... For He will restore (their patrimonies?) to them and proclaim freedom to them and make them abandon all of their sins. This shall take place during the sabbatical cycle (*shabu'a*) of the first jubilee following the ni[ne] jubilees, and on the D[ay of Atone]ment f[alling]

---

23   The term *'eth* is used 13 times in the Book of Daniel. CD 16:3–4.

24   IQM 2:6–10.

25   *A.J.* XIII, 234; Tacitus, *Hist.*, V, 4, 3.

26   A. S. van der Woude, "Melchisedek als himmlische Erlösungsgestalt in den neugefundenen eschatologischen Midraschim aus Qumran Höhle XI," *OTS* 14 (1965). 354–373; M. de Jonge and A. S. van der Woude, "11Qmelchizedeq and the New Testament," *NTS* 12 (1965–1966), 301–326; J. T. Milik, "Milkî-şedeq at Milkî-rešac dans les anciens écrits juifs et chrétiens," *JJS* 23 (1972), 95–144; "4Q visions de 'Amram et une citation d'Origène," *RB*, 79 (1972), 77–97. The citations below follow Milik's transcription of what is labeled as 11QMelch in *JJS*.

at the en[d of the ju]bilee, the tenth;[27] To forgive on it (the day of atonement) for all of (the sins) of all the children of [God and] the men of the lot of Melchizedek."[28] Although its main thought is quite clear, the precise chronology of the *pesher* remains obscure. There is no doubt, however, that the tenth jubilee alludes to the chronology of Dan. 9:24's 70 sabbatical cycles, which equals 10 jubilees, when Melchizedek will overcome Me(a)lchiresha[c]. Any lingering doubt that this is so disappears when one reads in line 18 of our fragment: "And the herald of good tidings (Isa. 52:7a) refers to the messiah, the Spirit concerning whom it was said by Dan[iel (9:25): 'Until the coming of the messiah, the prince, 7 sabbatical cycles...'"[29] Despite the fact that the *pesher* utilizes a long list of biblical passages, Dan. 9:24–27 remained the key to the author's chronology of sabbatical messianism.

Rabbinic Traditions

The Seder Olam, attributed to Rabbi Jose ben Ḥalafta (second century C.E.), but clearly a chronographic anthology of material stemming from several generations of scholars preceding and following Rabbi Jose, represents the rabbinic chronomessianic school. In chronicling the biblical events this treatise often adds the alleged current sabbatical and jubilee dates. The author does this particularly when he deals with momentous occasions, such as the building of Solomon's Temple or the disaster to Sennacherib's army.[30] Chapters 29–30 of Seder Olam, which may be regarded as a kind of midrash on Dan. 9:24–27, tailor the chronology of the burnings of the First and the Second Temples to make them conform to the author's view of Daniel's sabbatical numbers: 10 Jubilees = 70 Sabbatical cycles = 490 years elapsed from Nebuchadnezzar's to Titus' conquests of Jerusalem. To be sure, the Seder Olam, like the Book of Jubilees, formally merely furnished a chronicle of the past, but its deterministic chronology clearly points to a didactic lesson in the divine design of time.

We have place here for only a few of the numerous talmudic allusions to chronomessianic expectations. Of the paragraphs that make up the Eighteen Blessings, a fourth century Palestinian amora, Rabbi Aḥai,

27   This reading differs from that of Milik's rendition of 11QMelch 3 II lines 6–7 (*JJS* 23 [1972], 99): "Et cet événement [*aura li*]eu dans la première semaine (d'années) du jubilé suivant des neu[f] jubilés. El 'le j[our des Expa]tions' (*Lev.* 25:9) est a f[in du] dixième [jub]ilé...."

28   11QMelch 3 II, 4–8.

29   11QMelch 3 II, 18.

30   Seder Olam Rabbah (ed. Ratner), 11, 15, 23, 24, 25, 26, 27. Sennacherib's disaster, for example, is said on the basis of Isa. 37:30 to have occurred in a shemittah year (ch. 23, p. 53a–b).

noted that the seventh blessing (גאולת ישראל) dealt with the redemption of Israel, which he took to show that "Israel would not be redeemed except during the year of the sabbath."[31] An identical motif was ascribed to Ps. 126, relating the return of Zion, to its being the *seventh* of the fourteen psalms of Ascent.[32] A frequently cited Baraita describes the apocalyptic events of the seven years prior to the messiah's coming (all of which would be disastrous, except the years of shemittah) with the redeemer making his appearance during the postsabbatical year.[33] Mishnah Avot (5:8) expresses the link between redemption and the sabbatical year thus: "Exile came to the world because of idolatry, incest, the shedding of blood, and the (non-observance of) shemittah." For just as the observance of shemittah hastens redemption so its violation causes exile.[34]

Furthermore, talmudic computations of the messiah's expected appearance figure dates that coincided with Sabbatical chronology. "Just as the seventh offers a release to the Jew, so the world will be released during the seventh millennium," the epoch of the universal sabbath.[35] Sanhedrin 97b promises that the messiah would appear "after the year 4291 of the creation of the world"; its being in the Jewish calendar a shemittah year evidently played a role in the choosing of this specific date.[36]

Not only did the chronomessianic school claim to date the year when the redemption would come, but it presumed also to predetermine the season of the year. Rabbinic chronographers, including the authors of Seder Olam, dated events such as the angelic announcement of Sarah's impending pregnancy, Isaac's birth and God's covenant with Abraham as having occurred on the night of the 15th of Nisan.[37] The early *payyetan*, Yannai, who apparently flourished in the seventh century, using one line for each biblical incident, filled a twenty-four-line alphabetic acrostic poem, with incidents all of which allegedly occurred on the night of the 15th of Nisan; Abraham's victory over the four kings, Jacob's wrestling with the angel, Gideon's dream, the angel's striking the Assyrian army,

31   Yer. Berakhot, II, 4, 4d–5a; cf. B. Megillah 17b.

32   Yer. *ibid.*

33   B. Megillah 17b; Sanhedrin, 97a; Pesiqta d'Rab Kahana, *Bahodesh* I, 97 f. (Mandelbaum ed.), Songs Rabbah on 2:11.

34   Cf. B. Shabbat, Targumim and Rashi, Lev. 26:34–35, 44. Rabbi Elijah of Vilna's biblical calendar, appended to the Seder Olam (Waxman ed.; New York, 1952), identifies the ten shemittah years neglected by Israel during the preexilic period.

35   B. Sanhedrin 97a; cf. Av. Zarah 9a. See also Gelzer (note 22); Seder Eliyyahu Rabbah 2.

36   Av. Zarah 9b, which gives year 4231 A.M. is apparently a corruption.

37   Seder Olam, 5; B. Rosh Hashanah, 11a.

Daniel in the lions' den, concluding with the expected coming of the redeemer.[38] These Midrashic datings were of course based on nothing except the parallel with the timing of the Exodus. Their purpose was not so much to time the miraculous incidents as to emphasize the point that, in the words of the Mekilta and Tanḥuma, בניסן נגאלו ובניסן עתידין להגאל, "During the month of Nisan they (Israel) were redeemed; they will be redeemed again in Nisan."[39]

III

So far I have outlined the chronomessianic lore from Jeremiah to the late talmudic tradition. In this section I propose to show that the sabbatical calendar was probably a factor in the timing of the following messianic movements:

1. the commencement of John the Baptist's ministry; 2. the ascribed date of Jesus' birth; 3. Ababus; 4. the prophet of Egypt; and 5. Bar Kochba's uprising against Rome.

1. John the Baptist's Sabbatical Date

What is the evidence for the likelihood that John the Baptist commenced his ministry during or near the period when the Jews celebrated the year of release? Luke 3:1–2 offers a sixfold synchronism for John's date:

"In the 15th year of Emperor Tiberius, when Pontius Pilatus was procurator of Jerusalem, when Herod was prince of Galilee, his brother prince of Ituraea and Trachonitis, and Lysanias prince of Abilene, during the high priesthood of Annas and Caiaphas." It should be noted that this passage makes no mention of a sabbatical date, which might lead to a negative conclusion, that the sabbatical cycle played no or only a minor role in John's timing. Such a deduction is unwarranted because: a) even Graeco-Jewish historians, such as Josephus, customarily did not mention the year of the sabbatical cycle, perhaps since the Jews of the Diaspora did not observe shemittah; b) Luke addressed himself primarily to Gentile Christians; and c) conversely, Luke perhaps had no need to mention the chronomessianic link as it was taken for granted. The question whether John the Baptist's preaching coincided with the period of shemittah can be decided only on the basis of the contemporary calendar.

At first sight it should be a simple matter to convert Luke's "15th year of Emperor Tiberius" into a Julian date since Roman chronology

---

38 M. Zulay (ed.) *Piyyute Yannai* (Berlin, Schocken, 1938), 92 f.
39 B. Rosh Hashanah, 12b; Mekhilta, *Pisḥa*, 14, p. 52 (Harowitz and Rabbin); Tanḥuma, *Wayyera'*, 17.

during this period is well attested. But the matter is complicated because it is not known which of the divergent calendars or regnal calculations Luke had in mind. Finegan and Hoehner have summarized the extensive scholarship on this point: [40] a) assuming that the reference is to Tiberius' dynastic reign, which commenced on August 19 of 14 C.E., Luke meant the year running from August 19 of 28 to August 18 of 29; b) if Luke's dating was the one customary in Antioch, presumably Luke's home town, the 15th year ran from Tishri 1 of year 27 to the end of Elul of year 28; c) by Babylonian and Jewish convention, the beginning of the regnal year fell in the spring, the 15th year of Tiberius ran from Nisan 1 of the Julian year 28 to the end of Adar of year 29 and d) if Luke followed the usage of Roman historians, such as Livy and Tacitus, Tiberius' 15th year commenced on January 1 and ended on December 31 of the year 28. Whichever of these methods of dating was intended by Luke, the whole or a part of Tiberius' 15th year coincided with the current sabbatical year that ran from Tishri 1 of year 27 to Elul 29 of year 28.[41]

If this synchronism of John's ministry is, or at least was assumed by Luke to have been historical, and if the synchronism was not a sheer accident, only under possibility b) could John have commenced his mission anytime during the year and still coincide with the sabbatical year. Under possibilities a), c), or d), however, his first public appearance could have taken place only during a fraction of the year. The largest fraction would have occurred under possibility d), from January 1 of 28 C.E. to Elul 29 by Jewish reckoning; from Nisan 1 to Elul 29 of 28 C.E., assuming possibility c); but only about a month, i.e. Elul of 28 C.E. under a). Whatever the fraction, if Luke's report of John's ministry in the 15th of Tiberius is historical, it coincided with the "sabbath of the land" in the Jewish calendar. But even if Luke or his sources invented the date, a problem which I do not here attempt to evaluate, the sabbatical calendar probably was a factor in John's timing. The fact that John began his ministry in 27/28, a year that happened to have been a shemittah, does not prove that he had deliberately planned the synchronism. For all we know, since John had to begin preaching sometime, if he was going to do it at all, the coincidence might reflect an accident. But the tradition of chronomessianism since Daniel suggests strongly that John planned the timing of his appearance in a season when preachers customarily called on the people to repent, for the "day of the Lord" was approaching.

If this timing was both deliberate and consistent with popular Jewish

40 J. Finegan, *Handbook of Biblical Chronology* (Princeton, N. J., Princeton University Press, 1964), 259–280; H. W. Hoehner, *Herod Antipas* (Cambridge, University Press, 1972), 307–312.
41 Wacholder, *HUCA,* 44 (1973), 190.

chronomessianism, John will have begun his ministry before or during the Passover season. "On Passover they were redeemed and on Passover they will be redeemed again." (It is of course more than a coincidence that Christ rose in the Passover season.) A major festival date for John, assuming Luke's dating was intended to be precise, rather than approximate, would exclude possibility a) from the above mentioned listings. Thus Passover of 28 C.E. during the period of shemittah appears to be the most reasonable date, from a chronomessianic point of view, for the beginning of John the Baptist's ministry.

2. *The Sabbatical Date of Jesus' Birth*

Chronomessianic beliefs may also help explain why early Christian writers assigned the birth of Jesus to certain dates. We need not stop here to review the diverse traditions of the ancients and the immense scholarship of the moderns on this point. What ought to be remembered, however, is that the determination of the exact dates of birth, except in royal families or in circles among whom horoscopes were popular, was in antiquity rarely possible even for contemporaries. The date of Jesus' birth became a problem only after he had been proclaimed Christ by his followers. In other words, the question of Jesus' birth became enmeshed in chronographic and historical factors. Hence, it may be assumed that, presented with the problem of assigning the year of birth to Jesus, the early Christian writers, having absorbed the doctrine of sabbatical messianism, would tend to pick a timing in consonance with this belief.

Three sabbatical dates were available to Christian historians while remaining faithful to the Gospels: Tishri of year 9 to Elul of 8 B.C.E., 2/1 B.C.E., or 6/7 C.E. Luke (2:1–2) evidently chose the shemittah of 6/7, since he mentions Quirinius' census. That Sulpicius Quirinius became the procurator of Syria in C.E. 6 is attested by Josephus and possibly by an inscription.[42] A number of scholars posit, however, mainly on the basis of Luke, that Quirinius served in some kind of official post in the Near East also in 4-2 B.C.E.[43] If so, it might still fit with the chronomessianic tradition which would have expected the messiah during the shemittah of Tishri of year 2 to Elul of 1 B.C.E. In fact the earliest Christian chronographers from Clement to Eusebius offer the equivalent of 3/2 or 2 B.C.E.,[44] which tends to support the view that the ancient writers tended to favor a date that fell on the very eve of or during a shemittah.

---

42 Schürer, I, 516 f.
43 *A. J. XVIII*, 1–2. *Cf. the literature cited by H. L. Feldman*, in the LCL edition of Josephus, ad locum; cf. S. Sandmel, "Quirinius," in *IDB*, III, 975–977.
44 Finegan, *Handbook of Biblical Chronology*, 215–249.

3. *Agabus*

A certain Agabus, who together with other prophets came from Jerusalem to Antioch, according to Acts 11:27–30; 12:25, predicted a worldwide famine which in·fact occurred during Claudius' reign. Joachim Jeremias took it for granted that whenever a famine is mentioned in Palestinian sources, it necessarily referred to deprivations caused by sabbatical years,[45] as if famines in Palestine other than during shemittah years or outside Palestine were, in antiquity, rare occurrences. Josephus (*A. J.* XX, 101) reports a famine in Judaea about that time, but divergent readings in the text, epitome and the Latin translation make it doubtful whether the famine occurred under Fadus (C.E. 44–45?) or under both Fadus and Tiberius Alexander (C.E. 45), or only during Tiberius Alexander's sole procuratorship (46–48). Contextually, the last date is the only plausible one under the circumstances.

4. *The Egyptian Prophet*

Little is known of the Jew of Egypt, labeled the prophet, except that Josephus brands him as one of the impostors who had promised to show to his followers "unmistakable marvels and signs...in harmony with God's design."[46] In Jerusalem and elsewhere he collected, according to Acts (21:38) 4,000 men, according to Josephus 30,000; but he was finally defeated by Felix, the Roman procurator, who with a large army slew some 400 of the prophet's followers and captured 200. The prophet himself, however, escaped unhurt, and his scattered believers continued to plague the land for a while.

The timing of this prophet is likewise poorly attested. We know that the procuratorship of Felix lasted from 52 to 60 C.E. Since Josephus records the story of this movement after having mentioned first Nero's accession, which took place in September of 54, and Felix's murder of the high priest, Jonathan, which apparently had occurred in early 55, the timing of this messianic movement coincided with the sabbatical year of 55/56.[47] In light of what has been said so far Nisan of 56 appears to be the likely date of the Egyptian prophet, a date that may have been regarded as "in harmony with God's design."

45 Jeremias (note 14) conveniently cites the ancient evidence on contemporary famines.

46 *A.J.* XX, 167 f.; cf. *B.J.* II, 61–63; Acts 32:38.

47 *A.J.* XX, 158 f. dates Nero's gift to Agrippa in the first year of Nero's reign, i.e. 54/55; 20:160–168 relates the rise of the Sicarii and the murder of Jonathan. Cf. *B.J.* II, 250–270.

5. *Bar Kochba*

Bar Kochba is the popular name (the rabbis called him Bar Koziba; he himself used Shimeon bar or ben Kosebah) of the leader of the second revolt against the Romans in 132–135. His official title was *nasi'*, denoting chief, prince, or king.[48] That his followers regarded Bar Kochba as the messiah of the Jews is almost certain. The very choice of the popular name of Kochba, denoting star (cf. Num. 24:17), instead of Bar Koziba (Liar) suggests a claim of messianism. His coins and documents are dated according to a new era, that of "the Redemption of Israel" or "Freedom of Israel." Rabbi Akiba called him king, messiah. Ancient Jewish, Christian, pagan, now reinforced by numismatic and papyrological documents, combine to round out for us a picture of a messiah in action.[49]

As with regard to John the Baptist's ministry and the date of Jesus' birth, the timing of the beginning of Bar Kochba's revolt appears to synchronize with the season of shemittah.[50] Eusebius dated the revolt in 132–135 C.E. and the rabbinic tradition maintains that it lasted three and a half years. A number of scholars have dated the beginning of the revolt during Tishri of 132, but recently found numismatic and papyrological evidence has shown that spring of 132 is the correct date.[51] The nearest shemittah season lasted from Tishri 132 to Elul of 133. In other words, the timing of the uprising evidently coincided with the Passover season, on the eve of the Sabbatical year, in accordance with chronomessianic divine design.

Another point needs to be noted. The Julian date of 132/33, when the Bar Kochba rebellion commenced, happened to have been both a sabbatical and a jubilee year; which may have been an additional factor in the rise of the pitch of messianic fervor. As has been noted above (Dan. 9:24–27), the Qumran, and rabbinic writings, strongly suggest that the celebration of the jubilee year continued to be observed during inter-testamental times, as every 7th shemittah, or 49th year, was proclaimed a jubilee.[52] Unfortunately, unlike the dates of shemittah, none of those of the jubilee has survived. According to the reconstruction proposed

48   J. T. Milik, in *Discoveries in the Judean Desert II* (Oxford, Clarendon Press, 1961), 118–171.

49   Yer. Ta'anit, IV, 7 p. 68d; Aristo of Pella in *FGrH*, 201; Eusebius, *Eccl. Hist.* IV, 6.

50   For the scrupulous observance of the customs of shemittah during Bar Kochba's rule, see *Discoveries in the Judean Desert* II, 125 ff., suggesting perhaps that Hillel's *perozbol* (M. Shevi'it, 10:3–8) had not been operative at the time.

51   B. Kanael, "Notes on the Dates Used During the Bar Kokhba Revolt," *EJ* 21 (1971), 39–46; Wacholder, *HUCA*, 44 (1973), 155, and passim, 153–184.

52.   S. Safrai, "Yovel," in *Encyc. Hebraica* (in Hebrew), says that there is no shred of evidence for the existence of jubilee since the postexilic period. That

above, however, 603/02–555/54 B.C.E. constituted a jubilee cycle in Daniel's calendar, which Table 3 extends to the Bar Kochba period, showing that 132/33 C.E. was a jubilee year.

TABLE THREE

JUBILEE CYCLES

No. of Jub.	B.C.E.	No. of Jub.	B.C.E.	No. of Jub.	B.C.E., C.E.
1	603/02–555/54	6	358/57–310/09	11	113/12–65/64
2	554/53–506/05	7	309/08–261/60	12	64/63–16/15
3	505/04–457/56	8	260/59–212/11	13	15/14–32/35 C.E.
4	456/55–408/07	9	211/10–163/62	14	35/36–83/84
5	407/06–359/58	10	162/61–114/13	15	84/85–132/33

It is evident that the observance of the sabbatical years and jubilees during the intertestamental times played a far larger role in the consciousness of Israel than has been hitherto recognized. Immense as were the effects of the calendar of sabbatical cycles on the agricultural and social life of the people, its influence was no less on the formulation of Jewish religious beliefs. Concepts such as creation, history, apocalypse, and eschatology all became enmeshed with the calendar of sabbatical cycles. In the 7th year debts were cancelled, hard labor in the fields stopped; the voice of freedom was heard throughout the land as the steps of the messiah were believed to have become more and more audible.

---

a specific Pentateuchal commandment was altogethr ignored, however, seems unlikely, especially in view of the observance of shemittah. Aside from Dan. 9:24–27 and the literature cited in notes 26–29, see also Yer. Sanhedrin V, 1, 22c; B. Sanhedrin, 40b. In fact, supposedly, the Book of Jubilees is rather inconceivable without the assumed existence of some aspects of the institution of the jubilee.